Place Branding

Place Branding

Glocal, Virtual and Physical Identities, Constructed, Imagined and Experienced

Robert Govers and Frank Go

First published 2009 by
PALGRAVE MACMILLAN

Palgrave Macmillan in the UK is an imprint of Macmillan Publishers Limited, registered in England, company number 785998, of Houndmills, Basingstoke, Hampshire RG21 6XS.

Palgrave Macmillan in the US is a division of St Martin's Press LLC, 175 Fifth Avenue, New York, NY 10010.

Palgrave Macmillan is the global academic imprint of the above companies and has companies and representatives throughout the world.

Palgrave® and Macmillan® are registered trademarks in the United States, the United Kingdom, Europe and other countries.

ISBN 978–0–230–23073–6

This book is printed on paper suitable for recycling and made from fully managed and sustained forest sources. Logging, pulping and manufacturing processes are expected to conform to the environmental regulations of the country of origin.

A catalogue record for this book is available from the British Library.

A catalog record for this book is available from the Library of Congress.

10 9 8 7 6 5 4 3 2 1
18 17 16 15 14 13 12 11 10 09

Printed and bound in Great Britain by
CPI Antony Rowe, Chippenham and Eastbourne

Contents

List of Figures, Tables and Exhibits   viii

Preface   x

Acknowledgements   xiii

Chapter 1   Introduction   1
                   Background   3
                   Relevance   5
                   The Need to Deconstruct the Place Branding Model   9
                   Branding as a Solution   12
                   Place Branding   13
                   Definitions   16
                   How to Read this Book   21

Part 1   **Towards Place Branding**   **23**

Chapter 2   The Origins of Place Branding   25
                   The Philosophy of Place Branding (1641–1950)   25
                   The Psychology of Place Branding (1890–1990)   29

Chapter 3   Immediate Discipline   34
                   Marketing under Pressure (1980–2000)   34
                   New Marketing Emerges (2000–5)   36
                   Current Perspectives and the Need for a Place Branding Model   40

Summary of Part 1   43

Part 2   **Place Brand Strategy**   **45**

Chapter 4   Strategic Place Branding Elements   49
                   Place Identity as Sustainable Competitive Advantage   49
                   Projected Place Image   59
                   Product Offering Based on Identity   67
                   Conclusion: Brand Strategy Gap   71

Chapter 5   Signature Case Dubai: Brand Strategy   73
                   Introduction   74
                   Historical Constructions of Dubai   76
                   Dubai in the New Globalized Economy Today   81
                   Diversified Product Offering   88
                   Creating Brand Dubai   95

	Success Factors	98
	Brand Dubai and Its Cultural Identity	103
	Conclusion	105

Chapter 6   **Case Zeeland (The Netherlands): Place Identity Research**   **108**

	Research Background: Dutch Zeeland	110
	Survey Method	111
	Results	112
	Conclusion	116

Chapter 7   **Case Flanders (Belgium): Place Identity Research**   **117**

	The Existence of a Flemish Identity	118
	Bottom-up Flemish Place Identity Survey	123
	Conclusion	128

Summary of Part 2   **130**

Part 3   **Place Brand Performance**   **133**

Chapter 8   **Place Brand Performance Elements**   **135**

	Place Experience as Hedonic Consumption	136
	A Product Offering that Delivers the Place Experience	139
	Experiencing Place in Alternative Ways	142
	Projecting Place Experiences: Pictures and Text	144
	Conclusion: The Place Brand Performance Gap	148

Chapter 9   **Signature Case Dubai: Projected Image Research**   **151**

	Data Collection	152
	Content Analysis of Pictures	155
	Content Analysis of Text	156
	Results	157
	Conclusion	165

Chapter 10   **Mini Case Zeeland (The Netherlands): Place Experience**   **168**

	Experience Branding Zeeland	169
	Encounters of Host and Guest	173
	Conclusion	174

Summary of Part 3   **175**

Part 4   **Place Brand Satisfaction**   **177**

Chapter 11   **Place Brand Satisfaction Elements**   **179**

	Perceived Place Image	180
	Visitor Identity as Image Self-focus	184
	Temporal Environmental or Situational Influences	187

| | | Shared Meaning through Narratives | 189 |
| | | Conclusion: Place Brand Satisfaction Gap | 191 |

Chapter 12	Case The Netherlands: Perceived Image Research	194
	Research Background	194
	Survey Method	195
	Data Collection	200
	Results	202
	Conclusion	205

Chapter 13	Signature Case Dubai: Perceived Image Research	208
	Survey Method	208
	Questionnaire	210
	Comparative Cases	215
	Sample	218
	Results	222
	Conclusion	237

Summary of Part 4	241

Part 5	**Conclusion**	**243**
Chapter 14	The 3-Gap Place Branding Model	245
Chapter 15	Signature Case Dubai: Research Conclusions	250
Chapter 16	How to Build Strong Place Brands that Bridge Gaps	254
	Place Brand Analysis	256
	Designing the Place Brand Essence	257
	Place Brand Implementation	260
	Final Thoughts	268

Appendix I: Suggested Reading	270
Appendix II: Survey Content Analysis Procedure	271
Dubai	273
Canary Islands	276
Flanders	278
Florida	280
Morocco	282
Singapore	285
Wales	288

Bibliography	290
Name Index	309
Subject Index	315

LIST OF FIGURES, TABLES AND EXHIBITS

Figures

1.1	Polyinclusive levels of hedonic consumption experiences	6
3.1	The 3-gap place branding model	41
5.1	Map of the United Arab Emirates, including Dubai	75
5.2	Population breakdown of Dubai, by country of origin	82
5.3	Dubai's growth in supply of rooms in hotels and serviced apartments	86
5.4	Dubai's hotel performance statistics, 2000–7	86
5.5	Hotel establishment guests, by nationality	88
5.6	Dubai visitors' trip purposes	89
5.7	Map of Dubai including major ongoing development projects	91
5.8	Jumeirah properties: Madinat Jumeirah and Burj Al Arab	93
5.9	Dubai's heritage in the Bastaqya and Shindagha area (H.H. Sheikh Saeed's house)	103
6.1	Map of the Netherlands, including Zeeland	109
7.1	Current map of Flanders	119
7.2	Map of the County of Flanders (16th century)	120
7.3	Level of regional attachment of the Flemish	126
7.4	Residents' perception of Flemish identity	127
8.1	A model of network navigation for virtual experiences	145
9.1	Dubai website focal themes of images through clustering of motifs	160
10.1	Culinary festival 'De Smaek van Zeàland' held in Middelburg	170
10.2	Imaginative branding of folklore	171
10.3	New Zealand Edge	172
11.1	Components of place image and an example of four of these for Nepal	181
11.2	Choice set model	186
12.1	Survey sample designs and travel behaviour, awareness and patronage	199
12.2	Place image among four different awareness and patronage groups	203
13.1	Sample across destinations	219
13.2	Sample according to age of respondent	219
13.3	Number of countries visited	222
13.4	Sample according to income, family life cycle and occupation	222
13.5	Perceptual map of destinations and their image components	230
16.1	Gap-bridging place branding guide	255

Tables

2.1	Three approaches to the concept of image	31
2.2	Fields of study within environmental psychology in five travel phases	32
5.1	Opening of a typical instant messaging conversation in Dubai	83
6.1	The three most-selected images and the top-5 emotional adjectives connected with them	115
6.2	Multisensory elements of Zeeland, according to residents	116
7.1	Respondents' geographical attachment	122

7.2	Flemish identity according to self-reflective literature	124
9.1	Sample distribution	154
9.2	Dubai website images content analysis results	159
9.3	Website focal themes and differences between sectors in Dubai	161
9.4	Frequency list of unique words in all Dubai website text	163
9.5	Central concepts of website content for sectors	164
11.1	A taxonomy of procedures for measuring place image	182
12.1	Place image attributes	197
12.2	The most common attributes used in place image studies	198
12.3	Sampling frames for first measurement	200
12.4	Results of factor analysis on thirty-two items measuring place image	201
13.1	Countries of residence of respondents	220
13.2	Sample across continents	221
13.3	Image descriptions for seven sample destinations	225
13.4	Information sources	232
13.5	Information sources for each of seven sample destinations	233
13.6	Perceived image of Dubai according to cultural background	234
13.7	Perceived image of Dubai according to gender	235
16.1	Constructive elements of identity	256

Exhibits

13.1	First page of the image survey questionnaire	210
13.2	Initial wording of central image survey question as proposed in the Delphi discussion	212
13.3	Final wording of page two of the image survey questionnaire resulting from the Delphi discussion	214

PREFACE

The topic of place branding is moving from its infant stage into adolescence. In application it is receiving widespread attention: many regions, cities and nations have established their place brand, are working on it, or have at least already given it some thought. However, there is a dearth of publications that deal with the topic in a comprehensive manner. That is to say, most titles emphasize one aspect, such as principles, case studies or specific areas of research, as opposed to treating the subject in its full breadth. While these, and practical guides on place branding, can offer highly valuable contributions, what seems to be missing is a textbook that brings the fundamentals, design and methods together in a systematic format that is academically grounded, but at the same time useful for practice. This is the void that the present volume is trying to fill.

Simon Anholt, in his 2007 book *Competitive Identity*, puts it well: 'although the usual context of brand theory may be buying and selling and promoting consumer goods, this is a thin layer that covers some of the hardest philosophical questions one can tackle: the nature of perception and reality, the relationship between objects and their representation, the phenomena of mass psychology, the mysteries of national identity, leadership, culture and social cohesion, and much more besides'. Many of these questions will be addressed in this book. It departs from the assumption that a principles-based approach to place branding should help readers to achieve a balance between the conceptual and the practical, private and public interest, the potential conflict between continuity as captured in the heritage of place and change in the culture of any society. Therefore the present text on place branding, while dealing among other things with topics such as the importance of creating a logo and slogan, it does not offer quick solutions. Instead, it follows principles that we believe can, if applied diligently, help the reader to develop an understanding that place branding encompasses a process unfolding in phases, each with its own challenges and opportunities. Accordingly, the present text embraces the following principles. It is:

- *Systematic*. One can read in the existing literature on the topic that it is linked to concepts such as place identity, image and consumption experience of place. Authors have acknowledged the relevance of processes of globalization versus localization, and the tension or parallels between virtual and physical worlds, but what do all these concepts really mean?

What are their impacts on place brands? How can they be studied? On all of these topics there is a significant body of knowledge, once in a while referred to or expanded upon by place branding experts, but most often, unfortunately (but understandably so) outside of their span of control. The present volume attempts to place the many sources of knowledge within the place branding literature in a systematic framework so that readers can understand the antecedents of the subject, the state-of-the-art of place branding, and where the study of place branding appears to be heading.

- *Applied scientifically.* This book is useful for researchers and students who want to acquire a broader and in-depth understanding of the domain; but at the same time, it is also a book for those practitioners who are looking for a little more profundity and support to underpin their existing knowledge and skills. The main body of the book builds on an accessible 3-gap model that brings all aspects of place branding together. Theoretical chapters provide insight into the relevant concepts, and case studies provide examples of application and, particularly, relevant areas of research that are of interest to academics as well as practitioners as they provide input into the place branding process. A second model, presented in the concluding section, provides an overview of this branding process and the important elements it encompasses; again, a useful frame of reference for practitioners.

- *Practical.* One of the aims of this book is to explore the subject with the hope that the resulting dialogue will help to develop strategies and policies that can aid both the regeneration of local economies and the preservation and enrichment of local cultures and natural environments. With the term 'culture', we include all those elements, material and immaterial, that comprise people's distinct character, expressed through a blend of monuments, relics, contemporary society and business. Every part of the book features a chapter of what we refer to as the volume's signature case, Dubai. This rapidly developing city state in the Middle East has done a tremendous job, many would argue, in creating for itself an impressive global brand presence through the bold actions of building attractive product offerings – mega-projects, investment opportunities and tourism experience icons – while, riding the waves of attention that these projects receive, building themselves a strong projected image. This success, its historical background, the results, the actors, the future perspective, the success factors and implications for the Dubai brand are all described in detail in one of the early chapters. The first author's residency in Dubai between 1999 and 2003, his frequent visits afterwards and the research he conducted there, provide a unique insight. It is the research that also questions the sustainability of the Dubai brand as risks of an identity crisis, inconsistent projected images and erratic perceived images in Western markets in particular seem to be a threat, as will be illustrated in later chapters on research into case Dubai. Besides Dubai, other cases such as Flanders (Belgium), the Netherlands and its province Zeeland, but also perceived image research on Morocco, Florida, Singapore, Wales and the Canary Islands will be presented. These are not descriptive case studies of what happened when and where, but are analytical, providing an insight into research methods that are useful for place branding; hence, again, useful for both academics and practitioners.

In summary, in writing this book, the authors have tried to present place branding in a systematic, applied scientific and practical way from a design and methods perspective. Readers will find this book helpful because of the following features:

- First, it explains in detail what place branding is, why it has become increasingly important in our globalized world, and how it is rooted in long-established world views.

- Second, it provides a thorough overview of concepts and issues that are central or closely related to place branding, and how they can be exploited to build strong place brands.

- Third, it provides an insight into relevant bodies of knowledge for transfer to practical application.

Whether the authors have succeeded or not depends on you, the readers, and how you interpret and are able to make use of its concepts and techniques. The authors look forward to your feedback.

ROBERT GOVERS
rgovers@rgovers.com

FRANK GO
fgo@rsm.nl

ACKNOWLEDGEMENTS

First and foremost, we are indebted to Gerard van Keken and Stéphane Léonard for the major contributions they made to some of the case studies presented in this book. We would also like to thank Simon Anholt, Nicholas Ind, Roger Pride and Sicco van Gelder for their early reviews of the final text. Many other people have been involved in one way or another in earlier versions or the research activities linked to this volume. We name them in alphabetical order: Ward Bonduel, Dimitrios Buhalis, Manuela De Carlo, Peter Dieke, Karin Elgin Nijhuis, Alun Epps, Anil Fatingan, Daniel Fesenmaier, Matthias Fuchs, William Gartner, Ulrike Gretzel, Tim Heath, Jafar Jafari, Rob Jansen, Myriam Jansen Verbeke, Kuldeep Kumar, Slawek Magala, Reinoud Magosse, Peter Matla, Cor Molenaar, Jamie Murphy, Zoreisha Niamat, Aashna Pancham, Jan Peeters, Paolo Russo, Giovanna Segre, Ronald van den Hoff, Jos van Hillegersberg, Corné van Mechelen, Johan van Rekom, Jeroen van Wijk, Erik van 't Klooster, Philip Vanstraelen, Costas Verginis, Koen Vermunt, Hannes Werthner and Karl Wöber.

We are also very much indebted to Samuel and Peter Daams of Travellerspoint.com; Leon Weerts at KLM Royal Dutch Airlines; and Gerhard Hardick and David Thomson at Jebel Ali Internationals Hotels, for being such visionary tourism industry professionals, for believing in our research and for their support. Similar words of thanks need to be addressed to Jeff Mitchell of MeetURplanet.com; Dan Parlow at MyTripJournal.com; Joseph Kultgen and Jeremy Ahrens of Trekshare.com; James Clark of iTravelnet.com; Anne Bleeker at Jumeirah, Dubai; Anita Mehra at the Dubai government's Department of Civil Aviation; and various people at the Dubai government's Department of Tourism and Commerce Marketing, and the Dubai Tourism Development Company of the Dubai Development and Investment Authority. We are also grateful to Eleanor Davey Corrigan and Stephen Rutt of Palgrave Macmillan for their help, Keith Povey and Elaine Towns (of Keith Povey Editorial Services) for copy-editing and query-raising, and of course to colleagues and management of our past and present institutions: Erasmus University's Rotterdam School of Management; Katholieke Universiteit Leuven; Hotel School The Hague and the Emirates Academy of Hospitality Management.

We would like to thank the following parties or individuals for allowing us to use some of their material: Kit Jenkins; Elsevier (*Journal of Economic*

Psychology and *Annals of Tourism Research*); David Palfreyman and Mohammed Al Khalil (*Journal of Computer Mediated Communication* of the International Communication Association); Editor Philip Pearce of the *Journal of Tourism Studies*; Government of Dubai – Department of Tourism and Commerce Marketing; Anita Belhane of belhane.com, Brian Sweeney and Kevin Roberts of New Zealand Edge; Tourism Flanders and the American Marketing Association (*Journal of Marketing*). Photo credits (Chapters 6 and 10) are to Ruden Riemens, Gerard van Keken, Anda van Riet and Karina Leijnse.

Every effort has been made to contact all the copyright-holders, but if any have been inadvertently omitted the publishers will be pleased to make the necessary arrangement as soon as possible.

CHAPTER 1

Introduction

We are ruled by extravagant expectations:

(1) Of what the world holds. Of how much news there is, how many heroes there are, how often masterpieces are made. Of the closeness of places and the far-ness of places.

(2) Of our power to shape the world. Of our ability to create events when there are none, to make heroes when they don't exist, to be somewhere else when we haven't left home. Of our ability to make art forms suit our convenience, to transform a novel into a movie and vice versa, to turn a symphony into mood-conditioning. To fabricate national purposes when we lack them, to pur-sue these purposes after we have fabricated them. To invent our standards and then to respect them as if they had been revealed or discovered.

...We have become so accustomed to our illusions that we mistake them for real-ity. We demand them. And we demand that there be always more of them, bigger and better and more vivid. They are the world of our making: the world of the image. (Boorstin 1962, pp. 3, 4)

In this present-day world of parallel virtual and 'real' experiences, our extravagant expectations seem only to escalate. The common saying, 'It's a small world' is increasingly true. In contrast to Boorstin's query about how exotic the nearby can be, we now ask ourselves how nearby the exotic can be; and not how familiar the exotic can become, but how to preserve the exotic of the unfamiliar. But Boorstin was prophetic when he observed that 'Now [in the 21st century more then ever] all of us frustrate ourselves by the expectation that we can make the exotic an everyday experience (with-out it ceasing to be exotic); and can somehow make commonplaceness itself disappear' (Boorstin 1962, p. 77).

With technology, we have in fact succeeded in doing so. As Harvey (1989, p. 293) puts it: 'The image of places and spaces becomes as open to production and ephemeral use as any other.' We have 24/7 access to the exotic world of National Geographic and Discovery Channel, true-to-life movie experiences, interactive 'edutainment' museums, themed attraction parks, simulators, up-to-the-minute live news from around the globe, and, of course, the internet with which we can visit any place on earth virtually via our computer screens, or even exist in the virtual worlds such a Second Life. We can build social networks and interest groups across time and space through Web 2.0; global virtual communities of practice (Wenger *et al.* 2002) without leaving our house or cave; the most successful virtual community to date perhaps being Al-Qaeda (built on 'resistance identity' (Castells 1997)).

The way we brand places has changed profoundly, both from a supply (projecting of identity) as well as demand (perceiving of images) perspective. In contrast to mass media projection and standardised tour package consumption, place identity is now being produced, imagined and consumed through dynamic interactive processes, in physical as well as virtual environments (Molenaar 1996, 2002). How to respond to these 'unfamiliar' new environments where information and communication technologies (ICTs) invade and collide with everyday life, and hence how to deal with multiple discourses and processes of, for example, the 'authenticity', of identities, images or experiences, while trying to achieve and manage singular meaning of brand, is the key perspective of this book, focusing on design and methods.

Criticasters, such as the activist and author of *No Logo: Taking Aim at the Brand Bullies*, Naomi Klein (2000), claims that 'Our intellectual lives and our public spaces are being taken over by marketing ... It's important for any healthy culture to have public space – a place where people are treated as citizens instead of as consumers.' However well-intended, it is unlikely that the human race can live without commercial space, or the internet for that matter. The question is therefore whether conventional thinking about brands can be transformed to respond to the emerging new environments. Cyberspace presents new opportunities for markets, organizations, consumers and citizens. Such opportunities seem to go far beyond our current capabilities to respond effectively. Indeed, the reconfiguration of 'glocal', virtual and physical identities forces a reflection on the need for greater balance between commercial space and public space. In this context we believe that there is an urgent need to re-think traditional assumptions on brand making, imagining and experiencing, particularly in the exciting field of place branding. Instead of employing a one-way push process of supply-driven mass communication, borrowed from manufacturing, place identity affords interactive dynamics and shifts in power to networks of consumers, citizens and corporations – both large and small – whose role, presence in markets, but particularly their perspective on applying place branding methods and designs, as described in this book, can make a difference in order to deal with the complex potential conflict between continuity and change; a familiar problem that most countries and corporations are facing.

BACKGROUND

As the online population topped 1 billion in 2005, there were close to 177 million hostnames (over 70 million active websites) serving the internet in August 2008 (up by 24 per cent compared to December 2003) (Netcraft 2008). Many of these websites project images of places and it is highly unlikely that they are all consistent and true representations, as in the information age, place projections are increasingly controlled by a network economy (Werthner and Klein 1999, p. 3) and not in local communities. The network society constitutes the new social morphology for a capitalist economy based on innovation, globalization and decentralization. Dominant functions in society (such as financial markets, transnational production networks and media systems) are organized around the spaces of flows of capital, information, technology and images, which link them around the world. However, subordinate functions and people, in the multiple spaces of places, are being fragmented. Different locales become increasingly segregated and disconnected from each other (Castells 1996, pp. 470, 1, 6).

Thus the emerging network society raises questions about the expanding digital divide and increasing social exclusion. Rifkin (2001b) has warned us that the migration of human commerce and social life to the realm of cyberspace isolates part of the human population from the rest in ways never before imagined. Some have argued that our society should safeguard the 'human moment', the 'high-touch', face-to-face contact between people (Hallowell 1999, p. 64) and to design for infrastructure that integrates the physical and the virtual, as 'people enjoy and need social and sensual contact; they do not want to be disembodied' (Huang 2001, pp. 149–50). Under conditions of intense competition in rapidly expanding time-focused service industries and the increased connectivity of society, Pruyn (2002) also raises the issue of client relationships, which he refers to as the *relationscape* (analogous with the focus on the *servicescape*). He emphasizes the importance of interaction processes on the internet; that is, questions, answers and follow-up questions (supported by Molenaar 1996, 2002).

'A dynamic communication process, therefore, whereby the consumer is the "sender" and "receiver" of information and who moreover is free to define the time and the pace of the interaction (*self pacing*)' (Pruyn 2002, p. 27). Some have even argued for a 'third rationality for information systems in which trust, social capital, and collaborative relationships become the key concepts of interpretation' (Kumar and Dissel 1998, p. 199), because it seems that many indeed feel disembodied as we move from industrial to cultural production (Rifkin 2001b):

> Commerce in the future will involve the marketing of a vast array of [extravagant] cultural experiences rather than of traditional industrial-based goods and services. Global travel and tourism, theme cities and parks, destination entertainment centers, wellness, fashion and cuisine, professional sports and games, gambling, music, film, television, the virtual worlds of cyberspace and electronically mediated entertainment of every kind are fast becoming the centre of a new hyper-capitalism that trades in access to cultural experiences. The metamorphosis from industrial production to cultural capitalism is being accompanied by an equally significant shift from the work ethic to the play ethic. The Age of Access is about the commodification of play – namely the marketing of cultural resources including rituals, the arts, festivals, social movements, spiritual and fraternal activity, and more. Transnational media companies ... are mining local cultural resources in every part of the world and repackaging them as cultural commodities and entertainment. (Rifkin 2001a, paras 7, 8, 11)

As the online elite produce ephemeral images of places, spaces and cultures, the have-nots become increasingly disconnected. It even seems that the extravagant expectations of those that 'have access' lead to even more extravagant terrorist actions as we become increasingly inoculated to the daily catastrophes that our world endures. What does it take these days for those on either side of the divide to feel connected and to be awe-inspired? In promoting place image in a globalized yet divided world should we not return to a renewed focus on identity and human interaction? Because of its geographical location, being at the crossroads of civilizations, our signature case of Dubai – which we look at repeatedly in various parts in this book – is an interesting one. It is a modern melting pot of global cultures, with an 80 per cent expatriate community and an aspiration to become a global hub for tourism, entertainment, technology and trade in the new economy. Past and present place image research seems to have focused on measuring place-performance against attributes that define our extravagant expectations with regard to travel. These include the perfect climate; the most friendly, multilingual and culturally rich local population; the lowest possible cost; the most accessible yet most exotic location; the most interesting and adventurous or entertaining activities on offer; and the best-organized tourist infrastructure and highest quality facilities, yet with unspoilt and most attractive natural beauty. Discourse contends that satisfying all these conditions will result in a strong place brand and subsequent preferred ranking in peoples' consideration sets when deciding on their next travel destination, place to invest in, trade with or migrate to. But is not there more to this (see Chapters 11 and 13)? In this postmodern era, should one not be looking for differences, subjectivity, social contact and otherness (Harvey 1989)?

This is relevant when places compete for tourism, trade (export), talent (attracting a skilled workforce and foreign students) and treasury (or attracting investment). In our perspective, potential investors, temporary migrant workers (or expatriates/expats), or professionals travelling to identify trade opportunities are also tourists. Nevertheless, we shall generally use the word 'visitor' to emphasize the wider perspective that we apply. At the same time, we need to state that while it is commonly agreed that place branding aims at attracting tourism, investment, talent and trade (Kotler and Gertner 2002; Kotler *et al.* 1993), we feel that though these seem to be separate categories, tourism reaches across them all, as leisure travellers, expats, business travellers and investors often use many of the same facilities such as transport, hospitality and travel services; and are sometimes even drawn to the same attractions. While these different markets might be looking for different aspects of place (such as expats for housing, health care and schooling systems; investors for government policy and economic potential; and traders for strong local brands and factor cost benefits) we shall often refer to tourists or visitors as including the different types of travellers (leisure, as well as business travellers, including students, temporary workers, potential investors and traders) and tourism industry examples and research, as they have a particular significance for place branding. In the end it is all about attracting people – visitors. People who want to experience a place in order to be inspired through being relaxed and absorbed in its culture, or to determine whether they would want to live there, invest there or trade products from there.

RELEVANCE

Technological advancement and increased international competition thus affect the way in which places are imagined, perceived and consumed. Creating place image is no longer a one-way 'push' process of mass communication, but a dynamic one of selecting, reflecting, sharing and experiencing (Molenaar 1996, 2002). Tourism (for holidaymakers, business travellers, investors and expats) is indeed often referred to as a hedonic consumption experience (Vogt and Fesenmaier 1998), which 'designates those

FIGURE 1.1 | Polyinclusive levels of hedonic consumption experiences

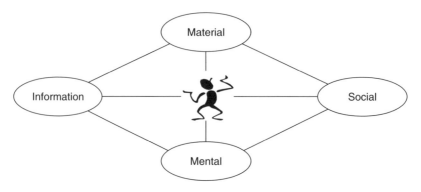

Source: Go and Van Fenema (2006).

facets of consumer behaviour that relate to the multisensory, fantasy and emotive aspects of one's experience of products' (Hirschman and Holbrook 1982, p. 92). With experiential products such as travel and tourism, the consumption experience is an end in itself, and the planning of a trip is an ongoing enjoyable and interactive social process, where fantasy and emotions also play an important role, and consumers are involved in ongoing information search (Decrop and Snelders 2004). By going through this process and collecting all this information, the consumer creates an 'image' or 'mental portrayal or prototype' (Alhemoud and Armstrong 1996; Crompton 1979; Kotler *et al.* 1993; Tapachai and Waryszak 2000, p. 37) of what the travel experience might look like. Such an image is generally accepted (Echtner and Ritchie 1991, 1993, 2003; Padgett and Allen 1997, p. 50; Tapachai and Waryszak 2000, p. 38) to be based on attributes, functional consequences (or expected benefits) and the symbolic meanings or psychological characteristics that consumers associate with a specific place (or service), and therefore the image influences place brand positioning.

In trying to operationalize the various dimensions of hedonic consumption experiences and related image formation at different levels, it is useful to refer to a polyinclusive approach (Go and Van Fenema 2006). The polyinclusive model, as depicted in Figure 1.1, helps to explain the need to deconstruct the place brand concept, from both a demand and supply perspective.

First, on the demand side, a new lifestyle is emerging characterized by mobility, fast-pacedness, polyscriptedness, and parallelization of experiences (such as walking while listening to an iPod, or 'floating in multiple blind dates in virtual chat-rooms' (Magala 2002, p. 2) while at work), plus 'the blocking out of sensory stimuli, denial, and cultivation of a blasé attitude, myopic specialization, reversion to images of a lost past ... and excessive simplification (either in the presentation of self or in the interpretation of events)'(Harvey 1989, p. 286). People enter, occupy and exit multiple spaces at different times and in an unsynchronized manner. These multiple spaces are categorized in Figure 1.1 as material space (place), information space (such as online representations), mental space (such as perceived place image) and social space (sharing place experiences with and through social relations). Interaction in these spaces or worlds leads to complex, if not chaotic, patterns but also to novel opportunities (Go and Van Fenema 2006, p. 1). For example, their participation in increasing numbers of and different social networks (on- or offline) implies that consumers are confronted, on a daily basis, with contrasting world views, many of which can be characterized as emotional, leaving a mental imprint, with which consumers are forced to cope. Werthner and Klein (1999, p. x) even argue that, for some, it is becoming ever more difficult to distinguish 'virtual' from 'real'.

Second, from a supply perspective, the argument is 'that global technology has deconstructed both nation-states and the old-metaphysics of (social) presence' (Featherstone and Lash 1995, p. 13) (see also Castells 1997; Hall 1996; Ohmae 1995). 'An essential issue is the emergence of transnational mediascapes, ethnoscapes and technoscapes: international social, political and cultural institutions are superseding national ones. The global increasingly informs the local, so deconstructing ideas like the "nation state"' (Featherstone and Lash 1995, jacket blurb) and in its wake the traditional theoretical concept of place image is unavoidable. It also raises questions about decision-making processes and power struggles at the local level, as it needs to be determined where and how place identity should be positioned in the global flows of images dominated by the media, and who should be responsible. As Castells (1996, p. 476) argues, in the network society 'image-making is power-making'. Therefore this book presents an alternative model dealing with emerging issues regarding the way that place identities are constructed, imagined and experienced, under conditions of seemingly pertinent discontinuity and interactivity. Already it seems apparent that this requires an approach positioned at the interface of strategic marketing, and information and communication technology (ICT) from a marketing channel and consumer focus (Van Bruggen 2001; see also Chapter 3), because the question that many in this increasingly virtual and globalized world are asking is, 'Where is the sense of place'?

Place consumption experiences share the characteristics of other services, in the way that production and consumption take place simultaneously. Therefore, consumers, as well as other visitors and residents, participate actively in the service operation and create meaning for the event. It implies that consumers are also actively engaged in the process of creating and attaching meaning to place image, which by definition is a consumer-orientated concept (Padgett and Allen 1997, p. 50). Therefore, one could assume that the media and the interactive nature of the internet add whole new dimensions to place branding. The effects of developments in ICT are therefore profound, changing consumers' extravagant expectations and shifting power structures in the distribution channel. Information (available anywhere, at any time) 'is the key to the omnipresence of global brands, computer reservation systems, transnational benchmarking and the need to view competition both from [chaotic] international and at the same time local perspectives' (Go and Haywood 2003, p. 87).

From a supply perspective, therefore, the sense of urgency should be acknowledged at the decision-making level of local, regional and national government bodies; that is, by tourism promotion boards, convention bureaus, chambers of commerce, investment and export agencies (in general place marketers). Until now, these actors have concentrated on imaging 'spaces of places'; that is, 'the locale whose form, function and meaning are self-contained within the boundaries of physical contiguity' (Castells 1996, p. 423). Unfortunately, the importance of spaces of flows, where capital, information, technology, organizational interaction (people) and images, sounds and symbols are moved (Castells 1996, p. 412), has as yet received limited acknowledgement in many places. These spaces of flows have been termed ethnoscapes, mediascapes, technoscapes, financescapes and ideoscapes by Appadurai (1996, p. 33), where 'the suffix – *scape* allows us to point to the fluid, irregular shapes of these landscapes' (emphasis in original). The importance of 'the relationship between the space of flows and the space of places, between simultaneous globalization and localization' (Castells 1996, p. 425), can be observed in regions and 'city states', including Silicon Valley, Singapore, Kuala Lumpur and vicinity, Dubai or Hong Kong, to name but a few (Ohmae 1995).

In the network society, place marketers are under renewed pressure to decide whether and how to project local identity of place in the expanding global flows of images. The time that destination marketing organizations were able to do this single-handedly, with only those 'insiders' at boardroom level, is over. In the network society, 'outsider' local agents of change need to be included in the decision-making process as well. Participatory relations need to be instigated between those initiating and involved in the conversion of resources, including heritage, hospitality and manpower, into resources supporting modern functions of place; and those involved in the shaping and projection of the place marketing images. As a consequence of this pressure on place marketing decision-making processes, several contradictions and conflicts have emerged.

As Morgan and Pritchard (1998; Pritchard and Morgan 2001) explain, place identities are constructed through historical, political and cultural discourses, and are influenced by power struggles. The flows of organizational interaction, and their related legislative framework, involve a distinctive hierarchical structure composed of relationships among national, regional and local governments. The latter tend to be dominated by political processes. As identity and image are often linked to ideology, the risk that the decision-making process might be hijacked by power struggles is all too real. 'What is depicted or not depicted in destination image advertising, and on whose authority it is selected, involves a more complex question of what comprises the destination and who has the power to define its identity' (Fesenmaier and MacKay 1996, p. 37). And Ateljevic and Doorne (2002, p. 648) 'reveal imagery as a political process that encodes and reinforces the dominant ideology of tourism culture, essentially a global process which manifests locally and explicitly involves the construction of place'.

At the same time, an overlapping framework is that of the flow of capital, involving multinational enterprises, including hotel chains and tour operators, major credit card companies and banks; and global decision-makers that influence processes at the local level (Go and Pine 1995). A good example is the case of Morocco's branding campaign as discussed by Polunin (2002, p. 4). The Moroccan tourist board thought it had a winning strapline – 'A Feast for the Senses' – which was supported by stunning visuals of the Moroccan countryside and culture. Initially widely accepted, the branding campaign was later sabotaged by German tour operators who sought a sun and sea product for their clients.

This book examines, among other aspects, this tension between cultural identity and commercial interest. In particular, there is a desire within the cultural community and public sector to project imagery that represents an authentic identity of place, whereas commercial actors are keen to stage authenticity (Cohen 1988, p. 371; MacCannell 1973) to represent desirable activities, or convenient commodities for consumption. Yet, at the same time, the expanding flows of technology and information empower local people and responsible consumer and trade groups to take up their own co-ordination and control role as communities of practice (Harvey 1989, p. 303). Hence the confrontation of supply and demand perspectives when dealing with the consequences of a changing society on the way that places are constructed, seems to require repeated attention, and will be given it in this book.

THE NEED TO DECONSTRUCT THE PLACE BRANDING MODEL

As part of these changes on both the demand and supply sides (host versus guest perspective), where consumers create confused subjective place images based on an onslaught of information from a wide variety of online as well as offline sources of varying quality, the online environment presents whole new challenges. Information systems that connect the economic actors and in which trust, social capital and collaborative relationships become the key concepts of interpretation (Kumar and Dissel 1998, p. 199), are essential. To build the networks needed for consistent imaging of place across sectors and pressure groups, and to create a strong identity in a versatile online environment, place branding might just hold one of the keys (Govers and Go 2003; Van Ham 2001). Anholt (2002) supports this idea when he states: 'As brands gradually become the dominant channel of communication for national identity, it becomes ever more vital to push other channels – by encouraging first-hand experience via tourism; by the careful management of international perceptions of a nation's foreign policy decisions; and by the representation of national culture' (pp. 233–4).

But in order to achieve this, a deconstruction of the place branding paradigm seems unavoidable. 'Deconstruction, as a poststructuralist interpretive method, has been used to comment on post-modern culture and to question commonly held truths and values. It has been termed a "criticism of received ideas"' (Fesenmaier and MacKay 1996; Norris 2002, p. 134) (see also Harvey 1989, ch. 3). However, deconstruction can be applied to various scholarly activities as a method for questioning established models and practices. It refers to the necessity to deconstruct traditional ways of thinking and behaviour. In other words, first one destroys and then one constructs. That process of deconstructing is not only an approach of postmodernist philosophy but is also known as 'creative destruction' within innovation theory (Schumpeter 1975, p. 82). This research on innovation confirms that business organizations that are able to apply innovation to improve their processes or to differentiate their products or services, outperform their rivals. However, the challenge of innovation is inherently risky; most new technologies and new products are not commercial successes. In short, innovation can enhance competitiveness, but means 'breaking the rules'; that is, a different set of knowledge and skills is required from those of everyday practice in the place marketing context. This book hopes to facilitate that.

The deconstruction approach applied here has several antecedents and implications, from both a theoretical and a practical perspective. First, from a theory building perspective, the unique selling point of this book is that it will, probably for the first time ever, analyse the concept of place branding from a design and methods perspective, at an integrative level, as we disassemble the place branding model into its constituent parts. This decomposition is traced back to the first philosophers of the modern era, such as René Descartes and John Locke, who laid the foundation for the research into aspects of identity, image and experience. Based on a further review of parent and immediate disciplines, the need to deconstruct place branding, and the way this should be done, is argued in detail from a theoretical perspective. It provides close-up insights into the many components of the place branding model. While emphasizing the dynamics of the model and its constituent parts, traditions in literature are confronted and innovations suggested, particularly through the review of the impact and application of ICT. Empirically, the need to deconstruct the place branding model and its measurement, will be illustrated in various cases. The research reported there provides evidence for the assertion that traditional place brand image measurement methodologies are incapable of explaining consumer perceptions, preferences and choice. Hence, again through a process of creative destruction, the use of innovative methodologies is suggested in order to reconstruct the place brand measurement paradigm from the ground up.

From an applied perspective, the research context of the signature case of Dubai, which is presented in Chapters 5, 9 and 13, illustrates the need to deconstruct place branding vividly. The different ways in which national brands (such as, for example, Dubai – and by extension its place brand) are perceived in a different country (the Netherlands, say) and how this diversity of perceptions can be managed in international branding campaigns is central to the existing research into place image. Concentrating on satisfying extravagant expectations, Dubai is trying to lure visitors to a fantasy Middle East with 7-star hotels, underwater and in the sky; man-made islands in the shape of palm trees and the world map; and an Arabian Florida. Dubai not only creates place brand images, but even transforms 'those images into material simulacra in the form of built environment, events and spectacle' (Harvey 1989, p. 290). This is illustrated by project developments such as The Lost City, The Venetian Village Resort, The Brazilian Tree House Resort, The Old Town, Dragon Mart, The Forbidden City, or the Dubai Shopping Festival. But what about the Arabian cultural identity and Bedouin heritage and the long-established (mis)perceptions of the East, in relation to the West? To what extent does the 'new fulfilment' of extravagant expectation overshadow such latent perceptions of a looming 'clash of civilisations' (Huntington 1993) and the misperception of the Middle East region as a bunch of oil-obsessed despotic states populated by white-robed men (Said 1981)?

When evaluating place branding in a region such as the Middle East, we have to conclude that traditional place image theory is inadequate, as there seems to be a need to link image to issues of identity and communication within a time-spatial context (as opposed to '"disembedding", and the hollowing out of meaning in everyday life' (Featherstone and Lash 1995, p. 2)). This leads to the need for places to build brand equity (Aaker 2001; Aaker and Joachimsthaler 2000; Riezebos 1994) and sustain their competitive advantage, as opposed to competing on global standardized attributes based on extravagant Western media-generated expectations. One of the goals of this book is therefore to understand how people construct their perceptions of places, and how place marketers could manipulate image projections in order to influence tourist, trade and investment behaviour and build brand equity in a competitive market. To facilitate this, the model developed in this book attempts to provide a better insight into the way in which place identities are constructed, imagined and experienced.

BRANDING AS A SOLUTION

From a polyinclusive perspective, it is the stories we construct from trip-related expectations and experiences that create meaning in mind space, but also in social space, shared with others in information space. As Go and Van Fenema (2006) correctly observe, organizations facilitate this process by 'developing brand stories, concepts and visions that drive organisational operations and culture'. These brand stories often include emotional aspects and real or fantastic imagery that includes visual and auditory sensations, and sometimes even gustatory (Coca-Cola), olfactory (scented pages in fashion magazines) or tactile (soft teddy bear premium with quantity fabric softener purchase) experiences. A brand itself is the good name of a product, an organization or a place; ideally linked to its identity (Kapferer 2004). It is a short-cut to an informed buying decision, but, most important, a brand is a 'promise of value' (Kotler and Gertner 2002; Van Gelder 2003). According to Van Gelder (2003) 'Brands are created, stimulated and applied by people working in organisations seeking to create worthwhile experiences for their customers that will induce behaviour beneficial to the organization' (p. 1).

The multiplexed interactions between customers and the products and services in a country, region or city provide temporary opportunities to connect and add value at both the individual and the group level. In a global arena, interdependencies are created that require the mapping of the factors relevant within the value creation cycle to enable, exploit and leverage seamlessly integrated, semi-customized, knowledge-intensive service experiences. The theoretical models of the tourism network, service experience, intra- and inter-organizational collaboration, country-of-origin effects and brands are operationalized to enable interacting actors to maximize customer value and place image projections at minimal cost.

The usefulness of place branding in this respect is contended by Gnoth (2002) and Kriekaard (1993) – using city names. Van Raaij (1995, p. 16) refers to the term 'brand' as being closely related to aspects of identity, image, quality and visitor satisfaction. In fact, Riezebos (1994, p. 264) compares a number of constructs – such as perceived brand quality, brand attitude, brand image, brand loyalty and brand equity – with the construct being studied in his book on brand added value. Wolf (2003) stresses the urgent need for place marketers to take branding seriously, particularly with the growth of the online market. But, of course, in the context of bridging the brand image gaps as presented in this book, we wish to refer to branding as being much more than merely creating a logo and a slogan. This is well supported by Fesenmaier and MacKay (1996):

> As something more than just a pretty picture, image is purported to represent and convey a culture as it is expressed by a selective authoritative voice. Processes such as branding, which use names, designs and symbols to build image, can leave much out. As a result, image is a simplified impression of a place for which cues are used to trigger inferences and influence attitudes. Sometimes these cues have unintended as well as intended symbolic value. (Fesenmaier and MacKay 1996, p. 39)

Kotler (2000, p. 404) lists the various levels of meaning a brand could possess: Attributes; Benefits; Values; Culture; Personality; and the User (consumer). The overlap with many of the components discussed as part of the place branding model in this book is evident.

PLACE BRANDING

The above definitions immediately highlight some of the differences between corporate or product branding and place branding; the latter being well-defined by Blain *et al.* as:

> the marketing activities (1) that support the creation of a name, symbol, logo, word mark or other graphic that both *identifies* and *differentiates* a destination; (2) that convey the *promise* of a memorable travel *experience* that is uniquely associated with the destination; and (3) that serve to *consolidate* and *reinforce* the recollection of pleasurable *memories* of the destination experience, all with the intent

purpose of creating an *image* that influences consumers' *decisions* to visit the destination in question, as opposed to an *alternative* one. [Emphasis as in original].
(Blain *et al.* 2005, pp. 331–2)

Pike (2005) summarizes six issues that make the application of branding
theory to places a complex undertaking, such as the multidimensionality;
heterogeneous interests of stakeholders; the politics involved; the need for
consensus; difficulty in applying the concept of brand loyalty; and the
availability of limited funding.

The people who create place brands (or at least those who decide on what
should or should not be created, stimulated and applied) are often working
in government or semi-governmental organizations. Typically, destination
marketing organizations (DMOs) are involved. However, the 'promise of
value' and 'worthwhile experiences' are created on location, by all actors,
public or private, making their small or large contributions to the process of
hosting visitors, in all their variety, in order to induce behaviour beneficial
to their own organization, but also, they hope, to the country, region or city
as a whole and to all stakeholders involved. Where branding using the term
'destination' implies a tourism perspective, place branding provides an
even wider perspective that would include all interactions of a place with its
environment, including political, outside investment, trade, immigration
and media issues. Both destination branding and place branding could
include country, region or city branding.

To add to the complexity, product or corporate brands may often be
designed using a clean sheet of paper on which to create their 'identities',
but this cannot happen with places:

They have personalities already moulded and constrained by history and preconceptions. They consist of a broad heterogeneous range of personalities that will
cause confusion and are likely to resist being shoehorned into a homogeneous
mould. But if branding is to work, there must be a common cause and consensus
among stakeholders. The long process of consulting, co-opting, and involving stakeholders, followed by distilling from their input the essence of a place's personality,
is probably the toughest part of the place branding exercise. (Polunin 2002, p. 3)

According to Anholt (2003) 'A national brand strategy determines the
most realistic, most competitive and most compelling strategic vision for
the country, and ensures that this vision is supported, reinforced and
enriched by every act of communication between the country and the rest of
the world' (p. 11). The importance of place branding is also illustrated by
Olins (1999), who states that 'when countries change, it can take quite a
long time for damaging, left-over stereotypes to disappear. Branding works

when it projects and reinforces a changing reality – but it can be counter-productive if it isn't rooted in fact' (p. 15). This reality is also crucial for Anholt (2003, p. 34) when he refers to place branding as building a competitive identity, using two mottoes: *'actions speak louder than words'* and *'don't talk unless you have something to say'* [emphasis in original]. In other words, place branding is not just about communicating, but also about stimulating and executing creative and innovative 'on-brand' ideas; that is, actual investment in local products, tourism services, infrastructure, education, sports, health care and cultural heritage.

At the same time, following Hall (1996) (see Chapter 4) places are composed not only of cultural heritage, but also of symbols and representations. A place is a discourse – a way of constructing meaning –, which influences and organizes both the actions of visitors and the conceptions of the local residents themselves. Visitors perceive images by producing meanings about a particular place with which they can identify. These are contained in the stories that are told about it; memories, which connect its present with its past; and images that are constructed of it. As Anholt (2002, p. 230) explains, it is important to study 'the different ways in which national brands are perceived in different countries and regions ... and how this diversity of perception can be managed in international branding campaigns'. Places use narratives, consciously or unconsciously, to influence peoples' decision-making processes and to develop place brand equity.

Aaker and Joachimsthaler (2000, p. 17) define brand equity as a set of 'brand assets (or liabilities) linked to a brand's name and symbol, that add to (or subtract from) ... (the value provided by) ... a product or service'. The assets and liabilities on which the brand equity is based will differ from context to context. However, they can be grouped into five categories: brand loyalty; name awareness; perceived quality; brand associations in addition to perceived quality; and other proprietary brand assets – for example, trademarks or channel relationships. The brand equity model (Aaker and Joachimsthaler 2000) provides the basis for the detailed deconstruction of the place branding paradigm, as discussed above, from a gap perspective. That is, what specific gaps should places bridge in order to influence tourist, trade and investment decision-making, so that loyalty, positive brand awareness, perceived quality and other positive brand associations and assets ensue?

The importance of this question contradicts the dearth of research in this area, because place branding has really only received the attention it deserves since the early 2000s. Morgan and Pritchard edited the first edition of their book *Destination Branding* in 2002. The *Journal of Brand Management* published a special issue of country branding in 2002, and the *Journal of Place Branding* (now the *Journal of Place Branding and Public*

Diplomacy) published its first volume in 2005. The first destination brand-ing conference in Macau was also held in 2005. So why this increasing interest in recent years? As we have already illustrated above, there might be several explanations. Intensified globalization has made people foot-loose and led to increased competition between countries, regions and cities (Van Ham 2008), requiring an answer to the question: 'Where is the sense of place?' Countries, regions and cities increasingly compete for attention and influence in order to attract investments, talent, events and visitors on a global scale. At the same time, famous countries, regions and cities have built a strong 'promise of value', but also, an attractive place image is a source of pride for the population, businesses, institutions and investors already present, hence creating additional competitive strength. As Simon Anholt puts it: 'in today's global marketplace, where brands and products can come from almost literally anywhere, their *"rootedness"* will surely become more and more important to consumers in their constant search for brands with trustworthiness, character and distinctiveness' (Anholt 2003). However, this dynamic link between place identity, image and experience from a branding perspective is not clear in the literature, where there is ambiguity in the use of concepts. One of the purposes of this book is there-fore to build a place branding model that links the various concepts. Building on this, it is clear that the application of ICT, global new media and the internet hold opportunities for the future of place branding. Hence, particular attention is given to this issue throughout the book.

DEFINITIONS

Brand

A brand is the good name of a product, an organization or a place; ideally linked to its identity (Kapferer 2004). It is a short-cut to an informed buy-ing decision, but most important, a brand is a 'promise of value' (Kotler and Gertner 2002; Van Gelder 2003). According to Van Gelder (2003) 'Brands are created, stimulated and applied by people working in organisations seeking to create worthwhile experiences for their customers that will induce behaviour beneficial to the organization' (p. 1).

Place Branding

Place branding refers to branding and building brand equity (Aaker 2001; Aaker and Joachimsthaler 2000; Riezebos 1994) in relation to national, regional and/or local (or city) identity. Brand equity is built through: brand loyalty; name awareness; perceived quality; brand associations in addition to perceived quality; and other proprietary brand assets – trademarks, channel relationships. Place branding can be used to mobilize value-adding partnerships and networks among public and private actors in order to build a coherent product offering (which includes tourism, trade, temporary employment and investment opportunities), communicated in the right way in order to guarantee the emotion-laden place experience that consumers are seeking (bridging the identity, image and experience gaps). In other words, a place brand is a representation of identity, building a favourable internal (with those who deliver the experience) and external (with visitors) image (leading to brand satisfaction and loyalty; name awareness; perceived quality; and other favourable brand associations as listed above).

Place Experience

In hedonic consumption, the experience is an end in itself (Hirschman and Holbrook 1982; Leemans 1994; Vogt and Fesenmaier 1998). Hirschman and Holbrook (1982, p. 92) emphasize the importance of multisensory, fantasy and emotive aspects of experiential or hedonic products (the 'three Fs': fantasies, feelings and fun: Holbrook 2000, p. 178; Holbrook and Hirschman 1982). Urry (2002) clarifies and extends the argument that place experiences have a fundamental visual character, drawing an analogy with Michel Foucault's concept of the gaze. He develops the notion that there are diverse gazes. Others prefer the alternative metaphor of 'performance', or the way that Fairweather and Swaffield (2002, p. 294) describe it as 'the graded experience of the Elizabethan theatre ... in which some of the audience become active participants, some choose to remain detached spectators, and others move between the two. Furthermore, watching others in the audience perform becomes part of the experience'. So experiences seem to involve the senses; the mind (cognitive processes linking perceptual observations to existing concepts, including processes of imagination creating fantasies); emotions (affect); active participation or passive gazing; and social interaction.

Place Identity

Place identities are constructed through historical, political, religious and cultural discourses; through local knowledge, and influenced by power struggles. National, cultural, natural, social and religious assets become important identifiers (Morgan and Pritchard 1998). We shall often refer to the 'true identity of place', by which we mean the full set of unique characteristics or set of meanings that exist in a place and its culture at a given point in time, nevertheless realizing that this identity is subject to change and might include various fragmented identities. In any case, it is argued that, if the right expectations are to be created in the minds of potential visitors, and to avoid unpleasant surprises, the 'true identity of place' should be the foundation on which to build the place brand propositions. Some practical moorings are provided by Noordman (2004) in his listing of structural (location and history), semi-static (size, physical appearance and inner mentality) and colouring (symbolism, communication and behaviour) elements of place identity.

Place Image

Place image was first defined by Hunt (1971) as the total set of impressions of a place, or an individual's overall perception (Bigné *et al.* 2001; Fakeye and Crompton 1991; Hunt 1971; Hunt 1975). It has also been referred to as a 'mental portrayal or prototype' (Alhemoud and Armstrong 1996; Crompton 1979; Kotler *et al.* 1993; Tapachai and Waryszak 2000, p. 37) of what the travel experience might look like. 'The image of a destination consists, therefore, of the subjective interpretation of reality made by the tourist' (Bigné *et al.* 2001, p. 607). Such an image is generally accepted (Echtner and Ritchie 1991, 1993, 2003; Padgett and Allen 1997, p. 50; Tapachai and Waryszak 2000, p. 38) to be based on attributes, functional consequences (or expected benefits), and the symbolic meanings or psychological characteristics consumers associate with a specific place (or service), and therefore the image influences positioning and ultimately our behaviour towards other places (Anholt 2007). Also, place image is a clear antecedent of quality, satisfaction, decision-making and post-purchase behaviour (Bigné *et al.* 2001; Kotler *et al.* 2003).

It is apparent that, similar to the discussion above about the 'true' identity of place, 'the' place image does not really exist either. Different projections and perceptions are individual or community constructions, and different individuals and communities might have different or fragmented insights. Arguably, it would be better to refer to the 'dominant view', which would normally correspond more or less to a place's identity, in line with Hall's (1996) narrative of the nation. Therefore, when we refer to 'the' place image, what is really meant is the 'dominant image' or the tendency towards stereotyping place. Nevertheless, for the sake of readability, we refer generally to 'the' image, as if it were a single concept, keeping in mind that it is in fact an individualized construct that incorporates many variations and interpretations.

Place Marketing

Place marketing, for us, is the traditional segmentation, targeting and positioning approach to the promotion of place, sometimes including channel network decisions as well as product development. Many parties can be involved in this, such as tourism promotion boards or destination marketing organizations; export, trade and investment agencies; convention bureaux; ministries of foreign affairs; chambers of commerce; financial institutions; and larger corporations and/or trade associations. Such place marketers often look at place promotion from only one or a few perspectives, utilizing, as mentioned earlier, a target market approach. In the place branding context they would have to co-operate extensively with each other, as well as with other public and private actors.

Product Offering

Globally, places are being marketed as attractive locations for tourism, trade, talent (education and employment opportunities) and treasury (investment opportunities). Each of these four categories include product or factor offerings that enhance market potential. For example, the components that build the tourism product are commonly referred to as the four As: Attractions; Amenities (or hospitality industry, that is, accommodation, food and beverage (F&B)/catering services and retailing); Access (or transport); and Ancillary Services (or visitor centres, insurance and financial services) (Cooper *et al*. 2000; Page 2003). Talent is being attracted through some of the same offerings, including a rich and dynamic supply of cultural activities, but also by offering income tax benefits, good health care and international schooling systems, and attractive housing. Additional offerings for investors and traders include tax relief and factor cost benefits (such as cost, productivity or quality benefits on land, raw materials and/or labour). All these elements should make places appear more attractive from the outside.

Projected Narratives

Projected place image includes all marketing communication originating from place marketers. However, what we are particularly interested in is how this creates meaning through the narration of identity. The real question about identity is: what comprises place, and how do we define its identity and project it accordingly, using narratives and visuals? In general terms, how would place marketers delineate these narratives? Several authors, such as Anderson (1991) Hall (1996) and McLean and Cooke (2003) provide help. There is the narrative of place as it is told and retold in history books, literature, the media and popular culture, with often corresponding heroes, great leaders and great events. Second, there is the emphasis on origins, continuity, tradition and timelessness, often also embodied in language. A third discursive strategy is the invention of tradition, formalized through the creation of museums and other attractions, and perhaps in educational systems. A fourth example is that of the foundational myth, supported by maps and emblems; and finally, projected identity is also often symbolically grounded in the idea of a pure, original people or 'folk' (Hall 1996, p. 613) with their music and food. Note that all these overlap with Noordman's (2004) colouring elements of identity.

Tourism

In order to understand the frame of reference of this book, we need to specify what we consider to be 'tourism'. We tend to adhere to the widest definition, such as that formulated by the World Tourism Organization.

Tourism is defined as the activities of persons travelling to and staying in places outside their usual environment for not more than one consecutive year for leisure, business and other purposes not related to the exercise of an activity remunerated from within the place visited.

The use of this broad concept makes it possible to identify tourism between countries as well as tourism within a country. 'Tourism' refers to all activities of visitors, including both 'tourists (overnight visitors)' and 'same-day visitors' (WTO 2000).

Hence, we do not tend to exclude any type of tourism, neither business travel, nor domestic travel, nor same-day trips. Place identities, projected and perceived images are of relevance in all cases, whatever the person's travel purpose is likely to be, or whatever the distance between place of residence and destination. So it includes those individuals travelling for business – identifying investment or trade opportunities – or those who are planning to relocate temporarily for employment purposes. Of course, as a trip turns out to be a business trip or a holiday, the relevance of different aspects of the place brand will either increase or diminish in importance. However, the perceived image is still the same, only the way in which it impacts the formulation of expectations is different. At the same time, examples and arguments throughout this book are often drawn from and formulated within the context of international leisure travel as it facilitates clarity. None the less, this does not imply that the findings and conclusions do not apply to other forms of international exchange.

HOW TO READ THIS BOOK

The book is structured according to the 3-gap place branding model as depicted in Figure 3.1. Part 1 will discuss the foundation of the 3-gap place branding model, elaborating on the parent and immediate disciplines that influence the formulation of the model. Those readers who wish to get into the model immediately can 'jump' to Part 2. There, the place brand strategy gap will be elaborated on by finding the link between place identity, projected image and product offering. Part 3 examines the consumption experience and how this impacts on the place brand performance gap; followed by Part 4, in which we look more closely at perceived place image and how it is influenced by experience, personal background, other consumers and temporary and situational influences. Each part will be accompanied by several research-based case studies, with case Dubai repeatedly reappearing. Finally, in Part 5 we shall draw some conclusions based on our theoretical 3-gap model and the research work we have conducted on the cases, in order to end this book with a 3-gap bridging place branding guide that will help practitioners and researchers alike to improve or enhance their place branding activities.

PART I

Towards Place Branding

The Third Wave thus begins a truly new era – the age of the de-massified media. A new info-sphere is emerging alongside the new techno-sphere. And this will have a far-reaching impact on the most important sphere of all, the one inside our skulls. Taken together, these changes revolutionize our images of the world and our ability to make sense of it. (Toffler 1980, p. 165)

This section will discuss the antecedents of the 3-gap place branding model, elaborating on the parent and immediate disciplines that influence the formulation of the model. It examines where we have been and where we are today. An historical journey into parent concepts of modern philosophy and early psychology will be the focus of Chapter 2, followed by a look at current developments in the relevant area of strategic marketing at the interface of information and communication technology (ICT) in Chapter 3. Readers who wish to go straight to the 3-gap place branding model can 'jump' to Part 2.

What we want you to take away from this Part 1 is to:

- Appreciate that the link between identity, experience and image, which is so essential in place branding, is not something new, but has been discussed for many years in modern philosophy.

- Understand that we can only experience reality through our senses and through what others tell us, so perceptions are essential.

- Describe how perceptions or images are filed in memory through inferences, schemata and stereotypes; and how these create holistic impressions that are essential in place branding as it tries to build positive place images by (re)constructing and projecting identities, building expectations around worthwhile place experiences.

- Understand that, increasingly, images are created through global media, which are influenced by the progressive convergence of ICT developments.

- Appreciate that globalization and ICT developments possibly lead to dis-intermediation, but on the other hand also foment the need for trust, social interaction and co-creation in virtual and physical encounters, thus laying the foundations for the social web.

- Recognize that what emerges is a move away from the one-way 'push' process of mass communication and fixed channels, to a situation where image creation is a dynamic, interactive process of sharing, reflecting, selecting, debating and experiencing.

- Comprehend that this dynamic image creation or place branding process needs to bridge the three gaps between identity, experience, and projected and perceived images, that will be addressed in this book.

CHAPTER 2

The Origins of Place Branding

Place branding links place identity with projected and perceived images through communication and experience. This, in terms of place marketing contexts, is perhaps a rather novel perspective, but it is in fact nothing new and can be rooted in the teachings of early modern philosophy starting in the seventeenth century. This developed further in the twentieth century with the input from early psychology.

THE PHILOSOPHY OF PLACE BRANDING (1641–1950)

The philosophical foundation for this book can be dated as far back as 1641, when Descartes published his *Meditationes de Prima Philosophia* (Meditations on First Philosophy). While Descartes' reasoning is best known for the Latin translation of his expression in the discourse, 'Cogito, ergo sum' ('I think, therefore I am'), it is his theory of 'ideas' that is of particular interest here. Descartes, as the founder of modern philosophy, was the first to approach epistemology from a rationalist (knowledge based on reason) but individualistic perspective, which would make him the progenitor of the ideas presented in this book.

Descartes held that there are only three sources from which we derive ideas: all our ideas are either 'adventitious' (entering the mind from the outside world, through sensory information); 'factitious' (manufactured by the mind itself); or 'innate' (inscribed on the mind by God) (*Meditations III*). 'But I don't yet know that there is an outside world, and I can imagine almost anything, so everything depends on whether god exists and deceives me' (Kemerling 2001, Section: Descartes: God and Human Nature, Clear and Distinct Ideas). Descartes will then go on to prove that God does exist and is not a deceiver, which means that ideas are either a reflection of reality or created by the mind itself. So ideas may also be considered objectively, as the mental representatives of things that really exist. According to a representative realist such as Descartes, then, our ideas are valid or relevant only when they correspond to the reality of the world around us; and therefore a foundation is laid for the concept of 'image' connected to 'identity'. The mind's (image) interaction with the body or reality (identity) through 'experience' was left by Descartes for others to discover.

Locke, one of the first philosophers to comment on experience, as another representative realist and great philosopher in the British tradition as opposed to the continental European tradition, but nevertheless clearly influenced by Descartes in this same era of the seventeenth century, had similar ideas as he spoke of primary and secondary qualities of objects in his 1690 *An Essay Concerning Human Understanding*: 'The primary qualities of an object are its intrinsic features, those it really has, including the "Bulk, Figure, Texture, and Motion" of its parts. The secondary qualities of an object, on the other hand, are nothing in the thing itself but the power to produce in us the ideas of "Colours, Sounds, Smells, Tastes, etc."' (Kemerling 2001, Section: Locke: The Origin of Ideas, A Special Problem). But Locke also linked these ideas of identity/character and image/perception, to experience. By experiencing objects, the secondary qualities are determined by our sensory organs. For Locke experience was the only source of knowledge, so he was clearly a product of his time, when empiricism emerged as the dominant epistemological foundation. About fifty years later, David Hume, in Book I of *A Treatise of Human Nature* (1739) and *An Enquiry Concerning Human Understanding* (1748), would carry this work even further.

But returning to the end of the seventeenth century, Locke also makes the interesting point that to observe identity we may have to rely on others to acknowledge and ascribe identity to us. Hence the idea of projected image is conceived, and for this Locke believes that language is an all-important vehicle. All this, however, leads to a worrying conclusion by Locke: 'Any effort to achieve genuine knowledge of the natural world must founder on our ignorance of substances. We have "sensitive knowledge" [knowledge based on sensation; produced by the senses] of the existence of something that causes our present sensory ideas. But we do not have adequate ideas of the real essence of any substance' (Kemerling 2001, Section: Locke: Knowledge and its Limits, The Extent of Knowledge). And even if we did think that we knew the real essence of substances, we would be unable to demonstrate any link between that reality and the sensory ideas it produced in us. So, one will never really know what the real identity of things is; it is all based on projected and perceived images, and projected images of the perceived images of others, and so on; a perpetuating system of illusion.

Often, perceptual illusions can be explained by acknowledging that secondary qualities are dependent on our senses, but, in theory, the possibility is preserved that truthful information about the primary qualities can be ascertained. However, the historian may be able to collect detailed information and expertise about (what he or she perceives to be) the identity of place, but that knowledge does not necessarily help others to enhance their appreciation of that place.

Pierre Bayle, in *Historical and Critical Dictionary* (1697), drives us even further into scepticism as he claims that instances of perceptual illusion also apply to the primary qualities of substances, because who is to say that the historian is right and not deceived by his or her own senses? George Berkeley, in *A Treatise Concerning the Principles of Human Knowledge* (1710) offered a solution to this problem by contending that the only thing one can do is to acknowledge that there are no material objects: 'Esse est percipi' – 'To be is to be perceived'. For Berkeley, only the ideas we perceive directly are real. Immaterialism is the only way to protect ourselves against the perils of scepticism. It seems that the latter perspective forms the foundation for a virtual world, and the Wachowski brothers' movie, *The Matrix*. Indeed it seems that, with technology these days, as illustrated by Go and Van Fenema's (2006) polyinclusive model of hedonic consumption experiences in Chapter 1, anyone with an internet connection today can experience places and objects without entering material space. It begs the question of whether a real physical world remains for the purposes of marketing and consumption? Without answering this question here, it appears that Berkeley laid the foundation for phenomenal idealism: 'what we usually describe as physical objects have no reality apart from our individual, private perceptual experiences of them' (Kemerling 2001, Section: A Dictionary of Philosophical Terms and Names, Phenomenalism).

The ontological discussion of whether or not there is a material world continued for quite some time, and even goes on today, but during the enlightenment of the eighteenth century, Immanuel Kant provided a new perspective on our problem. Very much influenced by the sceptical arguments of David Hume, 'Kant supposed that the only adequate response would be a "Copernican Revolution" in philosophy, a recognition that the appearance of the external world depends in some measure upon the position and movement of its observers' (Kemerling 2001, Section: Kant: Synthetic A Priori Judgments, The Critical Philosophy). Kant's constructivism brought rationalism and empiricism together in his *Critique of Pure Reason* (1781, 1787). He defended knowledge as being created by individuals through their sensory perceptions of experiences over time and space, together with a reasoned interpretation of those 'perceived images' and their connections, in order to create inferences for future occurrences. In other words, knowledge and perceived images are personal constructs of 'the knower', dependent on a person's cognitive capacities and personal experiences of 'the known' from certain locations at certain points in time (later, this will be referred to as self-focus). But in the end, Kant, an idealist, also failed to find any satisfying answer to the question of whether the known exists out there in a material world. Many of his contemporary idealists believed that only mental entities are real, so physical things exist only in the sense that they are perceived.

Søren Kierkegaard added another interesting insight in his *Afsluttende Uvidenskabelig Efterskrift* (Concluding Unscientific Postscript) (1846) as he emphasized the importance of the subjective truth of the individual, the 'appropriate relation between object and knower'. 'At one level, this amounts to acceptance of something like the slogan, "It doesn't matter what you believe, so long as you're sincere"' (Kemerling 2001, Section: Kierkegaard: The Passionate Individual, Subjective Truth). This existentialist view was also shared by Martin Heidegger and John-Paul Sartre.

In the late nineteenth century, some philosophers grew dissatisfied with the excessive subjectivity fostered by the philosophy of the later German idealists, including Kant. Borrowing their methods from the emerging sciences of psychology and sociology, these phenomenologists wanted to return to the objectivity of experiential content. The basic approach of phenomenology, under the influence of Hume's empiricism, was first developed by Franz Brentano in his *Psychologie vom empirischen Standpunkt* (Psychology from an Empirical Standpoint) (1874). Later, Edmund Husserl, a student of Brentano, influenced Heidegger's phenomenology as his teacher. Heidegger, in *The Way Back into the Ground of Metaphysics* (1949), reaches the culmination of this progression of existentialist thought by stating that 'there is no abstract essence of human nature; there are only individual human beings unfolding themselves historically'. This led him to a conception of human existence as active participation in the world, 'being-there' (*Dasein*) (Kemerling 2001, Section: Heidegger: Being There (or Nothing), The Ground of Metaphysics). Phenomenological psychologists in turn also focus on subjective experience: 'This approach seeks to understand events, or phenomena, as they are perceived by the individual and to do so without imposing any preconceptions or theoretical ideas' (Atkinson *et al.* 1987, p. 10).

G. E. Moore, in *The Refutation of Idealism* (1903), also developed his own approach, in which he argued that we must always make a clear distinction between the object of any experience and the experience itself. The latter should be analysed as the absolute link between the object and the perceiver's conscious awareness of that object. Moore emphasized the common-sense beliefs that each of us holds about, for example, our own body, other human bodies, our own experiences, and the experiences of other human beings. Again, the triangle of identity–image–experience seems to re-emerge, though Moore had difficulty in dealing with the 'mental facts' about conscious experiences. He relied heavily, as did Bertrand Russell and Ludwig Wittgenstein later, on the analysis of language. Russell's lectures on *Our Knowledge of the External World* (1914) and *Logical Atomism* (1918) took this even further. Russell believed that all human knowledge begins with sensory experiences, and for him these sense-data are not merely mental events, but rather the physical effects caused in us by external objects. Various other British and American realists also worked on this issue of perceptual sense-data versus physical objects. Wittgenstein, in his posthumous *Philosophical Investigations* (1953), started a movement of philosophy which believed that the analysis of the ordinary language of people would eliminate traditional philosophical problems. This analysis of ordinary language is also the foundation of the methodology used in some of the research case studies presented in this book.

THE PSYCHOLOGY OF PLACE BRANDING (1890–1990)

In the late nineteenth century, at the time of William James' *The Principles of Psychology* (1890), in the USA, psychology began to emerge as an academic discipline independent of philosophy. Some of the body of knowledge that was developed over the following century is also relevant for this book as part of the parent disciplines. In particular, the area of cognitive psychology – which studies the processes of perception, memory and information processing by which individuals acquire knowledge regarding the physical world around them – is of interest. Much of the research on perceived image is grounded in this vast body of knowledge. Linked back to the philosophy of Kant, constructivism is a particular area of inquiry within the domain of cognitive psychology that is of particular significance. Constructive memory theory argues that, when we perceive something, we use our general knowledge of the world around us to *construct* a more complete description of the event. Our total memory therefore goes beyond the original information given. Human beings do this in several ways (Atkinson *et al.* 1987, pp. 272–6): simple inferences; stereotypes (a group of inferences about the personality traits or physical attributes of a whole class of people) ; and schemata (a mental representation of a class of people, objects, events or situations). Stereotypes are thus a kind of schema because they represent classes of people. However, schemata can be used to describe not only our knowledge about particular objects and events, but also our knowledge about how to act in certain situations, such as eating in a restaurant or checking in at an airport. By linking schemata to each other in complex networks of inferences, we simplify our cognitive processes. However, the price we pay is that an object or event can be distorted if the schema used to encode it does not quite fit.

Within the discipline of psychology, the domains of social psychology and environmental psychology are of particular relevance. Environmental psychology deals with 'the study of the interaction between people and their environment. Environment within the context of environmental psychology includes the physical environment and well as the social situation' (Fridgen 1984, p. 21). At the same time, other commentators would argue that social psychology is a separate field of study, where 'the job of the social psychologist is probably best seen as explaining how people operate as social psychologists [themselves]; that is, how they make sense of their social world, of the relations between themselves, others, society and its institutions' (Stringer and Pearce 1984). Whether there are two separate fields of study or the one subsumes the other seems to be a fruitless discussion because, of course, against the backdrop of places, both social and environmental variables are clearly integrated within the same setting. John Crotts, Fred van Raaij and several others argue that economic psychology is a specific branch of social psychology, dealing with consumer preferences, buying behaviour and customer satisfaction (Van Raaij and Crotts 1994, p. 2).

Whereas microeconomics and behavioural psychology assume a direct relationship between stimuli and responses, economic psychology introduces the intervening factor of the subject (person) with its perceptions and preferences. The following passage also seems to indicate a triangle: stimulus (identity of place)–perception (image)–response (experience), as was observed above through the learning of earlier philosophy. 'Stimuli must be perceived and evaluated, before they elicit responses or have an effect on responses. Individuals differ in their perception and evaluation of reality and act according to their perceived/evaluated reality and not to the stimuli as such ... Perception, evaluation and expectation can each become an intervening variable between stimulus and response' (Van Raaij and Crotts 1994, p. 7).

Based on the work by Poiesz (1989) in the *Journal of Economic Psychology* and later by Pruyn (1990, [2nd edn 1999]), Van Riel (1996, p. 111) examines image as part of the corporate communication domain. There, image is also contrasted with identity. In particular, Van

TABLE 2.1 Three approaches to the concept of image

Level of elaboration	Conceptualization	Typology	Measurement implications	Measurement methodology
High	Image is stored in memory as a network of meanings	Image is a complex structure	Qualitative research: a deeper assessment of associations	Free format methods Structured methods: ■ Laddering ■ Kelly Grid
Middle	Image is the weighted sum of beliefs about an object: perceptions about salient attributes X the importance of these attributes	Image is an attitude	Explicit methods: identify the salient attributes and present them in the form of statements	Attitude questionnaires: ■ Considerations ■ Appreciations
Low	Image is a general, holistic impression of the place that the object occupies relative to competitors	Image is a broad impression	Implicit methods: relative localization of the object using multidimensional scaling	Multidimensional scaling of: ■ Resemblances ■ Preferences

Source: Translated from Van Riel (1996, p. 112), which was reproduced from Poiesz (1989, pp. 457–72). Reprinted with the kind permission of Elsevier.

Riel classifies images into three groups, based on the level of consumer elaboration, which is determined by the extent to which a subject is involved with an object. Table 2.1 provides an overview of the three levels of consumer elaboration of image, and the corresponding conceptualization, typology and measurement methodologies. Later in this book, many of these methodologies will resurface when discussing the measurement of place image in the research case studies.

Within the broader field of social psychology, the term 'image' has had a number of uses (Stringer 1984). Influential accounts have been produced by Boulding (1956) and Boorstin (1962), who indicate that it refers to a reflection or representation of sensory or conceptual information. According to Stringer (1984, p. 149): 'In Boulding's sense, the image is built on past experience and governs one's own action. It is not static, nor "objective" – there is an essential value component. Furthermore, it has social aspects'. Boulding stated that 'Part of our image of the world is the belief that this image is shared by other people like ourselves who are also part of our image of the world' (Boulding 1956, p. 14). Fridgen (1984, p. 20) also stated that travel and the environment are inseparable. The relationship

TABLE 2.2 Fields of study within environmental psychology
in five travel phases

Travel phase	Field of study
1. Anticipation	*Imagery.* Image is a central concept in environmental preference studies and tourism research. Tourists probably use perceived images of people and settings that go beyond the promotional brochure ... For potential travellers in this anticipation stage, the image of vacation sites and social situations is a powerful factor within the decision process. Images influence spending patterns, planned length of stay, and planned activity patterns (Fridgen 1984, pp. 25–6).
2. Travel to the destination	*Environmental perception en route.* The trip to the destination site takes the traveller through a number of environments each of which is viewed only briefly, often from the capsule of a car or train ... How are images and impressions generated by design, and how can this process give a more effective impact on the tourist passing through? (Fridgen 1984, pp. 27–8).
3. On-site behaviour	*Authenticity.* Authentic settings are successful and provide satisfaction to the tourist when there is environment–behaviour congruence, a fit between what happens in the setting and what is expected of the setting (Fridgen 1984, p. 30).
4. Return travel	*Environmental perception en route.* As Phase 2.
5. Recollection	*Perceptions at home.* During the recollection phase of travel, the tourist consolidates impressions and perceptions into memories, emotions, and evaluations. Expectations that initiated the trip are now merged with actual experiences. Shortfalls and achievements are reflected upon and integrated into new images. After travelling, people's attitudes and perceptions of the vacation, the host community, and environment should have changed (Fridgen 1984, p. 32).

Source: Fridgen (1984).

between traveller and place is a person–environment relationship: 'Travelling is an act of exploration.' Fridgen provided an overview of the research areas that are of interest within the domain of environmental psychology (including the social) by applying the conceptual framework of Clawson and Knetsch (1966), who offered a five-phase experiential conceptualization of recreation. In every phase, Fridgen mentions specific areas of research that will also be examined in greater detail in this book.

Kunkel and Berry (1968) were some of the first to study image in a service industry setting in the 1960s, in the context of retail store image, from a behavioural psychology and learning perspective. Later, however, commentators realized that image was more than learned expected reinforcements (stimuli) associated with prior experience. Imagery was described as a distinct way of processing and storing multisensory information in working memory. In essence, it is now believed that 'imagery processing' depends on more holistic, or *Gestalt*, methods of representing information. Imagery processing is often described as mental picturing, though sight is not the only sensory dimension that can be incorporated into it. Imagery can include any or all of the senses – sight, sound, smell, taste and touch (though the latter three are considered inferior by far (Atkinson *et al.* 1987, p. 172)). Imagery processing contrasts with 'discursive processing' which is characterized by pieces of information on individual features or attributes of the stimuli rather than more holistic impressions (Echtner and Ritchie 2003, p. 39; MacInnes and Price 1987). Such holistic impressions are essential in place branding as an attempt is made to build positive place images by (re)constructing and projecting identities, building expectations around worthwhile place experiences.

CHAPTER 3

Immediate Discipline

This book on place branding draws first and foremost on the discipline of strategic marketing at the interface of information and communication technology (ICT) with a marketing channel and consumer focus (Van Bruggen 2001). As illustrated earlier, an important supporting discipline is economic psychology, particularly as it applies to the fundamentals of cognitive, social and environmental psychology. These areas of inquiry will often be applied specifically in the place marketing domain but also frequently beyond it. They relate to the way in which places are positioned in the global flows (Castells 1996) – ethnoscapes, technoscapes, mediascapes and ideoscapes (Appadurai 1996). These spaces of globalized experience that influence the image and its relationship to the sense of place, need to be understood in order to create effective marketing strategies.

MARKETING UNDER PRESSURE (1980–2000)

The interdisciplinary field of marketing and ICT probably first emerged when Alvin Toffler introduced the concept of the 'Third Wave' in 1980. The Third Wave, after the agricultural and industrial revolutions, represented the dawn of the information age. Its emergence had major consequences for the evolution of the marketing discipline; for example, in the application of the concept of mass-individualization. In Toffler's words: 'demands for participation in management, for shared decision-making, for worker, consumer, and citizen control, and for anticipatory democracy are welling up in nation after nation. New ways of organising along less hierarchical and more ad-hocratic lines are springing up in the most advanced industries' (Toffler 1980, p. 67).

Mass-individualization resulted in consumers becoming increasingly demanding and versatile (Werthner and Klein 1999, p. 13). It seemed ever more difficult to 'retain consumers in the straightjackets [*sic*] of segmentations based on sex, age or social class' (Go *et al.* 1999, p. 13). As Bloch *et al.* (1996, p. 114) stated: 'Consumers wish more frequent, but shorter travel, last minute reservations, global advice, service quality, market transparency, and a certain self-service mentality – e.g. "modern" travellers begin to gather recreational micro-services on their own and form their customised travel package. These developments lead to an elimination of non value-adding stages (... but particularly non value-adding players ...) in the service systems' and the rise of what Toffler referred to as the 'prosumer'. Characterized by a self-service mentality, the prosumer has caused the 'do-it-yourself industry' and the self-help movement to explode. New industries were spawn based on collapsed prices and packaging (flat-packs) optimized for 'easy assembly' at home. In addition, the production of own goods and services in leisure, or rather 'unpaid work' time gained in popularity.

In turn, the mass-customization movement triggered the need to satisfy these mass-individualized customers through 'flexibilisation' (Werthner and Klein 1999, p. 157); that is, the capacity of organizations to respond to the needs of customers in a flexible manner. This concept, with Pine (1993) as the spiritual father, recognized that in mass-individualized markets, mass production no longer worked. Organizations aiming for mass-customization utilize a wide variety of specific value chains tailored to the individual product or customer, through the use of loosely linked dynamic networks of players involved in the production and assembly of the product or service on offer. Normann and Ramírez (1993) termed this the 'value constellation', in which the consumer is given a more prominent and central role than in the traditional value chain. All this, of course, was only made possible through technology, as one of the characteristics of dynamic networks is the broad availability of open information systems. Network theory explains this co-evolution logically, as there are only two ways of dealing with complexity in extended multi-player networks (as in tourism, for example, where there are many suppliers and many consumers who have to 'cross the information cloud', as Werthner and Klein (1999, p. 6) put it). Reducing complexity in such networks can be achieved through intermediaries, which in the past created the basis for the traditional rigid and extended value chains. Alternatively, ICT can drastically increase the information-handling capacity of a network and hence reduce the need for intermediaries and fixed value chains. An explanation of these principles is provided by Van der Heijden (1995) and Werthner and Klein (1999, p. 181).

With the consumer firmly a part of the value constellation, Pine and Gilmore (1998a, 1998b, 1999) heralded the start of a new era: the 'experience economy'. In the experience economy, business is perceived as a stage and companies must design memorable events, for which they even charge admission. However, we tend to agree with Wolff Olins' director, Robert Jones, who criticized Pine and Gilmore's work as follows: 'to posit the arrival of a fourth economic era based on the existence of Chuck E. Cheese's seems to be tendentious. The truth, surely, is that we're still firmly in the service era, that all service companies deliver experiences; and that they always have' (Pine II and Gilmore 1998b, p. 173). We would indeed argue that, for most businesses, goods are not just props and services that are placed on the stage in order to sell experiences. Rather, it would seem to be a matter of the hedonic aspects of the consumption of many goods, and the experiential aspects of most services, becoming more important as areas where businesses can achieve competitive advantage when commoditization of goods and services proliferates. It is interesting to note that marketing researchers (Hirschman and Holbrook 1982; Holbrook 2000; Holbrook and Hirschman 1982) realized the significance of the hedonic and experiential aspects of consumption long before Pine and Gilmore wrote their book. Nevertheless, Pine and Gilmore should be praised for bringing these issues into the spotlight and raising the level of attention that marketers attach to the emotional aspects of consumption, though perhaps with some delay, even in non-Anglo-Saxon markets (Piët 2004). In place marketing in particular, this is essential.

NEW MARKETING EMERGES (2000–5)

The World Wide Web offers entertainment, games, social play activities and information free of charge, in order to sell goods and services on the side. It attracts over a billion users, its growth is exponential, and it is therefore the obvious medium to observe in an attempt to understand how the experience economy operates and unfolds. Since travel is experiential in nature, and the largest and fastest growing online industry, we focus our research on this. However, one thing we have to keep in mind is that, considering the opportunities provided by technology, but at the same time taking into account the digital divide, 'access' is a major issue (McKenna 2002; Rifkin 2001a, 2001b). As Rifkin (2001a, Sections 12 and 13) explains:

> The young people of the new 'protean' generation are comfortable conducting business and engaging in social activity in the worlds of electronic commerce and cyberspace and they adapt easily to the many simulated worlds that make up the cultural economy. Theirs is a world that is more theatrical than ideological and more oriented towards a play ethos than towards a work ethos. For them, access is already a way of life. People of the twenty-first century are as likely to perceive

themselves as nodes embedded in networks of shared interests as they are to perceive themselves as autonomous agents in a Darwinian world of competitive survival. For them, personal freedom will be about the right to be included in webs of mutual relationships.

'Simultaneously, the lines of communication between people are owned and controlled by information and communication technology transnational corporations, making access not a privilege but a pre-requisite for participating in culture and community' (Matrix 2002, Section 2). In the information age, being disconnected is equivalent to being outside the system, invisible, and disempowered. But the same applies to businesses, 'for in the new economy access to consumers ... is becoming more important to a company's bottom line than selling actual products' (Straus 2000, Section16). Therefore, Shapiro and Varian's book *Information Rules*, published in 1999, was timely. Shapiro and Varian (1999) discussed how to deal with the network economy in the information age, while maintaining that the fundamental economic principles of competition and business success had not changed dramatically. We tend to agree with Shapiro and Varian when they argue that the most important question to be answered is how to 'lock-in' your customers.

Slowly but surely management decision-makers are beginning to realize that collecting mountains of information about customers may contribute little towards gaining their loyalty. Instead, a recent school of thought holds that there is a need for renewed social interaction between organizations, companies, places and their customers, as well as customers with other customers. Prahalad and Ramaswamy (2000) argue that businesses need to co-opt customer competence (supported by Molenaar 1996): 'Thanks largely to the Internet ... individual consumers can now address and learn about businesses either on their own or through the collective knowledge of other customers. Consumers can now initiate the dialogue; they have moved out of the audience and onto the stage' (Prahalad and Ramaswamy 2000, p. 80). Consumers have become co-creators, who 'are not prepared to accept experiences fabricated by companies. Increasingly, they want to shape those experiences themselves, both individually and with experts or other customers' (Prahalad and Ramaswamy 2000, p. 83; Prahalad and Ramaswamy 2004a, 2004b, 2004c, 2004d). Thomke and Von Hippel (2002) argue that organizations should involve customers in their research and development processes. A direct dialogue with customers seems the only way to find out what customers really think. Zaltman (2002, p. 26) argues that many customers 'don't know what they think', so surveys, focus groups and data-mining only scratch the surface. Organizations also need to probe the subconscious mind, which has a large impact on consumer decision-making. The best way to do this seems to be to incorporate 'customers as innovators' into companies' extended enterprise value constellations (Normann and Ramírez 1993; Thomke and Von Hippel 2002). This holds true particularly for industries where the following characteristics apply: where market segments are shrinking and customers are increasingly asking for customized products; where customers and suppliers require an intense dialogue to find a solution, and where some customers complain that products do not match requirements and response is too slow; and finally, where competitors use high-quality, computer-based simulation and rapid-prototyping tools internally to develop new products (Thomke and Von Hippel 2002, p. 77).

We would argue that most of these characteristics apply to place marketing as well. So how can such places co-opt customers? Again, it appears to be evident that technology plays a central role. Provide consumers with the full functionality of user-friendly global distribution system (GDS) access, fully linked to property and revenue management systems of all suppliers, and travellers will create their own trips. Trends towards this ideal situation can already be observed online with any of the major cybermediaries (which they refer to as 'dynamic packaging' – Davies 2004). An important core competency on which to compete in future will be an organization's ability to utilize customers as a source of competence, and encourage active dialogue with customers and between customers. Web 2.0 virtual communities, collaborative filtering leveraging the online community to make personalized recommendations and viral marketing (Sweet 2005) are some of the tools in use in order to co-opt customer competence and 'embrace the market as a forum' (Prahalad and Ramaswamy 2000, p. 83).

The logical final consideration in this progression of technology at the interface of marketing is the concern for 'the human moment' (Hallowell 1999); that is, the physical social interaction between people, and the integration of 'the physical and the virtual' (Huang 2001, p. 150), and an emphasis on the 'relationscape' (Pruyn 2002, p. 27). 'People enjoy and need social and sensual contact, they don't want to be disembodied' (Huang 2001, p. 149) and 'for businesses to do well, you can't have high tech, without high touch' (Hallowell 1999, p. 64). This is supported in the information management literature, where there is a call for 'a third rationale of information systems in which trust, social capital, and collaborative relationships become the key concepts of interpretation' (Kumar and Dissel 1998, p. 199). Relationships are 'the accumulation of past experiences and consequences of future expectations [that is image]' (Kumar and Dissel 1998, p. 214). In collaborative relationships, 'bonds, or the "tying" between partners' (Kumar and Dissel 1998, p. 214), become important elements. 'The informational elements of the bond are highly dependent upon the "meaning" attached to information, which itself is also culturally dependent. Meaning is not something that is transmitted, but arises and changes in the use of words. Finally, since meaning is inherently social (i.e. intersubjective) ... the social aspects of bonds may be a significant factor' (Kumar and Dissel 1998, pp. 214–15). In addition, mutual trust is an important element in building social communities, but 'trust does not reside in IT/IS' (Kumar and Dissel 1998, p. 215).

Earlier, Van der Heijden (1995), who based his analysis on transaction cost theory, argued that information technology can reduce transaction costs in dynamic networks and hence reduce the need for stable, long-term relationships with a limited number of intermediaries. As a result of increased information-processing power, flexible relationships with an increasing number of actors are possible, and have led to disintermediation. However, it raises the issue of whether a focus solely on transaction cost reduction within particular business contexts results in a sustainable competitive position, when aspects of social bonds and trust are disregarded. Kelly (1999, quoted in Werthner and Klein 1999) argues that, in the new economy, 'wealth is not gained by perfecting the known, but by imperfectly seizing the unknown'. Or Nooteboom (2000, p. 104), more specifically: 'A fundamental shortcoming of transaction cost economics is its static nature and exclusion of innovation'. Within a network context it is important to recognize that 'people and firms, require outside sources of complementary cognition to complement their own biased and myopic cognition' (Nooteboom 2000, p. 104). A corollary of the interdependence within networks is the need for and significance of including trust in the theory formation in order to facilitate interaction and the social aspects of bonding culminating in relationships (Kumar and Dissel 1998, pp. 214–15). For this, computer mediated communication is not a panacea (Van Fenema 2002, p. 543).

Is it mere coincidence that the applications on the internet which have become most popular in recent years are the ones facilitating social interaction (also referred to as Web 2.0)? 'Click-to-talk', online forums, virtual communities, Wikis, instant messaging, free webmail, and, of course, blogging and online video have gained ground rapidly. 'Roughly 11 million UK Internet users visited online social network sites regularly in 2007. And the market is booming – 60% of respondents to an early-2008 survey said they had created a social network profile, up from 27% in 2007' (Williamson 2008, Summary section). 'Social networking is an activity that 37% of US adult Internet users and 70% of online teens engage in every month, and the numbers continue to grow. eMarketer projects that by 2011, one-half of

online adults and 84% of online teens in the US will use social networking'
(Williamson 2007, Summary section). According to Technorati, in June
2008 close to a million blog posts were created daily and the number of new
blogs is still growing rapidly, with 1.5 million blogs posted online over the
last seven days of the measurement, 7.4 million new blogs posted in the
previous 120 days, and 133 million blog records indexed by Technorati
since 2002 (Technorati 2008). The year 2004 'saw the establishment of the
Word of Mouth Marketing Association (WOMMA), and a New York Times
Magazine cover story on buzz marketing' (Blackshaw 2004; Sweet 2005).
Among travellers, a similar trend is emerging, with online travel blogs also
gaining in popularity (Saranow 2004). Apart form the blogs themselves,
virtual travel communities have become popular, providing a rich source of
information for travellers, with the added benefit of being able to share
experiences, post reviews, ask questions in richly populated forums and
communicate one-to-one with other members (Wang and Fesenmaier 2002,
2003, 2004a, 2004b; Wang *et al.* 2002).

CURRENT PERSPECTIVES AND THE NEED FOR A PLACE
BRANDING MODEL

What emerges is a move away from the one-way 'push' process of mass
communication and fixed channels, to a situation where image creation is a
dynamic, interactive process of sharing, reflecting, selecting, debating and
experiencing (Molenaar 1996, 2002). This is done at the individual level
and in micro-segments. All this was prophesied by Toffler in 1980, when he
stated that:

> The Third Wave thus begins a truly new era – the age of the de-massified media.
> A new info-sphere is emerging alongside the new techno-sphere. And this will
> have a far-reaching impact on the most important sphere of all, the one inside our
> skulls. For taken together, these changes revolutionize our images of the world and
> our ability to make sense of it. (p. 165)

This evolution has relevant implications for places. ICT is a natural partner for worldwide networked information-intensive industries that facilitate
tourism, trade, migrant work and outside investment (Sheldon 1997;
Werthner and Klein 1999). Go and Haywood (2003, p. 88) also argue that
'as a result of advances in information and communication technology,
tourism, hospitality and recreation are becoming increasingly integrated
within the experience-economy context'. In this new networked economy
with de-massified media, branding, identity and image take centre stage

FIGURE 3.1 | The 3-gap place branding model

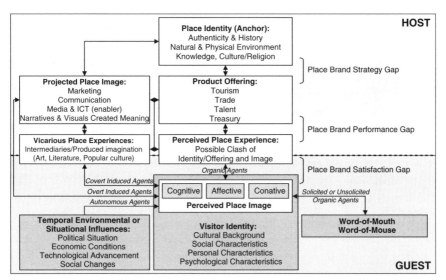

Sources: Based on the idea of the 5-gap service quality analysis model by Parasuraman *et al.* (1985, p. 44) and major contributions from Baloglu and McCleary (1999), Fesenmaier and MacKay (1996) and Gartner (1993).

(Piët 2004; Pine II and Gilmore 1998a, 1998b, 1999; Rifkin 2001b; Shapiro and Varian 1999).

Over the years, the body of literature on place image has grown to a respectable size (a synoptic overview has been provided by Gallarza *et al.* (2002) as well as Pike (2002), who reviewed 142 papers). However, as Baloglu and McCleary (1999, p. 869) suggest 'most studies have largely focused on its static structure by examining the relationship between image and behaviour', from a construct measurement perspective. Studies have concentrated on the relationship between place image and destination preference and visitation intention; destination familiarity and the impact of previous visitation; visitors' geographical locations; trip purpose; situational or temporal influences; the image as projected by the destination; and visitors' socio-demographical variables. 'Little empirical research has focused on how image is actually formed ... analysing its dynamic nature by investigating the influences on its structure and for-mation ... especially in the absence of previous experience with a destina-tion' (Baloglu and McCleary 1999). What we would like to take away from the above discussion is that, in the networked information society and the experience economy, it is exactly this dynamic nature of place image that is of key importance. Because, as Toffler (1980, p. 301) argues: 'in our modern world we cannot see the future in the same way we solve problems – by dismantling problems into their component parts. We must practice, instead, synthesis.'

Figure 3.1 therefore tries to deconstruct place branding and image formation in order to identify those elements that have a dynamic influence on how place brands are formulated in the mind of the consumer. This model provides the basis for the detailed synthesis of the place branding paradigm, as addressed throughout this book from a strategic place marketing point of view. This is done from a 3-gap perspective, confronting host–guest (supply and demand) perspectives, based on the idea of the 5-gap service quality analysis model by Parasuraman *et al.* (1985, p. 44). The model will be the source of reference for a detailed discussion in the rest of this book.

Summary of Part I

Place branding aims to link place identity and perceived images through memorable place experiences and projected images. This idea of bridging the gap between reality and perception, and how it can be influenced by experience and communication, is, however, not new. It has long been a major topic of discussion among philosophers. Descartes, as the founder of modern philosophy, could be perceived as the progenitor of the ideas presented in this book, as he laid the foundation for representative realism, which contends that our ideas are valid or relevant only when they correspond to the reality of the world around us. Sceptics such as Locke, Hume, Bayle or Berkeley, however, argue that there is no proof of an existence of an outside material world; we only have perceptual knowledge through our senses, and hence 'to be is to be perceived'. Similarly, idealists such as Kant believe that physical things exist only in the sense that they are perceived. This leads to constructivism, in which knowledge and perceived images are personal constructs, and hence perceptions, and as a result realities are subjective. This is further emphasized by existentialists such as Kierkegaard, Husserl, Brentano or Heidegger, who believe that all that matters is that humans participate actively in the world; 'being there' (*Dasein*). Finally, realists such as Moore, Russell or Wittgenstein worked on the issue of experiential sense-data versus physical objects. This started a movement in philosophy which believed that the analysis of the ordinary language of people would eliminate traditional philosophical problems. This analysis of ordinary languages is also the foundation of the methodology used in some of the research case studies presented in this book.

Later, in twentieth century psychology, particularly in the area of cognitive psychology, which studies the processes of perception, memory and information processing, by which individuals acquire knowledge regarding the physical world around them, is of interest. Linked to Kant's constructivism, constructive memory theory argues that when we perceive something, we use our general knowledge of the world around us to construct a more complete description of the event. Our total memory therefore goes beyond the original information given. Human beings do this through simple inferences, stereotypes and schemata (a mental representation of a class of people, objects, events or situations). Related relevant disciplines are social psychology, environmental psychology and economic psychology. In these areas, 'image' has had a number of uses, but is often related to a reflection or representation of sensory or perceptual information or a distinct way of processing and storing multisensory information, possibly resulting in holistic impressions. Such holistic impressions are essential in place branding as it tries to build positive place images by (re)constructing and projecting identities, building expectations around worthwhile place experiences.

A closely relevant discipline for this book on place branding is strategic marketing at the ICT interface. It relates to the way in which places are positioned in the global flows – ethnoscapes, technoscapes, mediascapes and ideoscapes. These spaces of globalized experience, which influence the image and its relationship to the sense of place, need to be understood in order to create effective marketing strategies. This interdisciplinary field probably first emerged with Toffler's 'Third Wave' or 'information age', in which mass individualization, a self-service mentality (the prosumer) and customization led to flexibilization in value chains, and the consumer later becoming part of the production processes – acting as co-creator. This heralded the 'experience economy', in which consumption is more about co-creating experiences than the exchange of goods and services. But with the consumer moving increasingly on to online platforms, the question of how to create access (for consumers to businesses and vice versa) and 'lock-in' customers, has become more pertinent. While individualization and technology, from the perspective of transaction cost theory, were expected to lead to disintermediation, the renewed need for trust, social bonds, the 'human moment', and integration of the physical and the virtual, has now led to a renewed intermediation and, for example, the strong growth in Web 2.0 applications.

What emerges is a move away from the one-way 'push' process of mass communication and fixed channels, to a situation where image creation is a dynamic, interactive process of sharing, reflecting, selecting, debating and experiencing. In this new networked global experience economy with de-massified media, branding, identity and image take centre stage. The 3-gap place branding model therefore tries to deconstruct place branding and image formation in order to identify those elements that have a dynamic influence on how place brands are formulated in the mind of the consumer. This model provides the basis for the detailed synthesis of the place branding paradigm, as addressed throughout this book. This is done from a 3-gap perspective, confronting host–guest (supply and demand) perspectives through place identities, product offerings, projected and perceived images and experience.

PART 2

Place Brand Strategy

The assertion of any place-bound identity has to rest at some point on the motivational power of tradition. It is difficult, however, to maintain any sense of historical continuity in the flux and ephemerality of flexible accumulation. The irony is that tradition is now often preserved by being commodified and marketed as such. The search for roots ends up at worst being produced and marketed as an image, a simulacrum or pastiche. (Harvey 1989, p. 303)

Part 2, the first part of three perspectives on the 3-gap place branding model, focuses on place identity, product offering and projected image. In Part 3, reflecting the second perspective from which we approach the place branding model, place brand performance, experience will take centre stage, while in Part 4, we shall focus on perceived image.

In Part 2, Chapter 4 will elaborate on the strategic place branding elements that, if not aligned correctly, could result in a strategic place branding gap. It links place identity to product offering and the creation of meaning through projected images. The success, so far, of case Dubai and how it has built a strong brand for itself as a global hub with attractive product offerings, is illustrated in Chapter 5. At the same time, this signature case Dubai also illustrates the importance of linking the place brand to cultural identities. How this can be done and researched is illustrated in Chapters 6 and 7, which focus on resident perception research with regard to the self-image of local identities in Flanders, Belgium, and Zeeland in the Netherlands.

What we would like readers to take away from this part of the book is to:

- Appreciate that place identity can be a competitive advantage for place branding in a globalized world, something that is perhaps insufficiently appreciated in rapidly developing emerging global hubs such as, for example, our signature case, Dubai.

- Be able to categorize elements of place identity as structural elements (location and history); semi-static elements (size, physical appearance and inner mentality); and colouring elements (symbolism, behaviour and communication).

- Be conscious of the fact that place identity is not static, but politically constructed and contested; nevertheless, it can be useful in loading place brand identities, as illustrated in the cases of Zeeland and Flanders.

- Analyse the authenticity of identity, which is often questioned, but in itself is not static and uncontested. There is the objective authenticity, but also the constructed and existential experiential authenticity. We believe that authenticity is about people co-creating things that matter to them.

- Argue that identities, on the one hand, seem to be under pressure from globalization, but at the same time they have the potential to flourish as people look for secure moorings in a shifting world; that is, the glocalization argument, as again illustrated in the cases of Flanders and Zeeland.

- Demonstrate that the place branding strategy results in a projected place image, through the use of planned marketing and communication and the use of narratives and visuals; and that media and ICT, as they converge, are important enablers for projecting place brand images.

- Appreciate that, among this noise of global mediascapes, meaning is created through local narratives, traditions/rituals, myths, events, heroes, local culture (gastronomy, art, literature, popular culture), emblems, religions and languages.

- Be aware, however, that these meanings, as they are created in projected images, are again politically constructed and contested.

- Argue that the product offering of place – tourism, trade, talent (migration) and treasury (investment) – should be part of the place brand strategy and linked to its identity, because, in the end, places sell experiences, and fake brands will be exposed.

- Characterize place experiences, and the services on which they are built, by their intangibility, inseparability (production and consumption take place simultaneously); heterogeneity (varying levels of quality) and perishability.

- Hypothesize, therefore, that socialization and co-creation of personalized experiences will become more important.

■ Evaluate the potential threat of a place brand strategy gap when place identity, product offering and projected image are not aligned, as might be perceived to be one of the issues in our signature case, Dubai, which, even though it has clearly been successful in creating a global place brand – literally from the sand – through concerted actions in terms of product offerings and communication, it is at risk of facing an identity crisis.

CHAPTER 4

Strategic Place Branding Elements

National, regional or local governments, in partnership with the private sector, create the place brand strategy. This involves the evaluation, (re)assembling, (re)positioning and (re)formulation of the identity of place, its product offering, and its communication strategies. The first step in this process is the identification of sustainable competitive advantages. One of these competitive advantages could well be one of the elements of identity of place, particularly when visitors are from diverse cultural backgrounds. The uniqueness of a local culture, as well as the place's physical resources, can create unique advantages that are difficult to copy by rivals (Anholt 2002; Gnoth 2002, p. 266; Ritchie and Crouch 2003, p. 115). This is paramount in a globalizing world of harmonization and 'more of the same', as brands can create the emotional link between host and guest (Van Ham 2004).

PLACE IDENTITY AS SUSTAINABLE COMPETITIVE ADVANTAGE

Sustainable competitive advantage is generally based on either core competencies or unique resources that are superior to those possessed by competitors and difficult to imitate (Aaker 2001, p. 141; Johnson and Scholes 1999, p. 153). For localities, superior resources, which might be difficult for competing places to imitate, are generally to be found in both the unique natural environment (climate, wildlife or landscape) and cultural heritage: and the physical assets, sites reflecting place roots in terms of a rich history, religious or other cultural expressions such as the arts, architecture and design. Competitive advantage might, however, also be created through core competencies – for example, the host community's existing unique capabilities in attracting potential visitors and hosting them during their stay; service values; the organization of civil life; education; or its work ethic. Co-creation of knowledge is a key element in this respect, be it expressed or tacit. Knowledge contained within the host community can play a vital role – for example, in the form of a place's ability to stage world-class events or festivals, exhibitions and conferences; the ability to exploit its intangible heritage and prevailing traditions (perhaps a long-standing tradition of hospitality or a service culture), but also its modern functions in culture, art and architecture, and education, health, work and other cultural values. This set of competitive advantages is what could be referred to as place identity or the product offering's anchor. For some, the essence of branding is the projection of this identity (Melissen 2004).

Identity and Culture

A field of study within strategic marketing, which should be of interest here, is the corporate identity domain. Van Riel (1996, p. 34; translated from Dutch) based on Birkigt and Stadler (1986) defined corporate identity as: 'the self presentation of an organisation: the implicit and explicit offering of cues, with which an organisation reveals its own unique characteristics through its behaviour, communication and symbolism'. Noordman (2004, ch. 8) attempted to translate the corporate communications literature into place marketing, but immediately identified a significant problem. As the lexicographic trace of the word 'corpus' in corporation suggests, these involve single bodies that can easily define their purpose in society from a centrally controlled vision and clear objectives, which can often be reduced down to dominating goals such as profit maximization. Municipalities, regions or countries consist of a plurality of players and interest groups serving many different purposes in society. Even if governing bodies were able to reduce their central objectives to only three – creating employment and a comfortable environment for residents to live in and for visitors to enjoy – even then, visions and missions, and ways in which to achieve them, would often change because of political shifts or power struggles, as illustrated nicely by Paul (2004). On top of that, many private parties also influence this process and interpolate their own ideas about place identity and how to project it. Nevertheless, Noordman was able to identify several elements that define place identity, such as structural elements (including location and history); semi-static elements (including size, physical appearance and inner mentality); and colouring elements (including symbolism, behaviour, and communication).

Structural elements that are pretty well unchanging – the DNA of place if you like – are location (geography and climate) and history (roots). Semi-static elements that can be changed, but that take time to transform, include size and physical appearance, such as superstructures, infrastructure, land-use planning and landscape. Also included as a semi-static element of place identity is the inner mentality of the population, as in the cultural and religious values, often embodied in language, as suggested by Anderson (1991). Colouring elements include symbols (names, logos or emblems such as flags, costumes, folk dances or maps), behaviour and communication. As behaviour and communication are listed by Noordman as colouring elements, it seems that these are less relevant as elements of place identity, but rather fit into the categories of projected image and place experience. This is not in contradiction with the corporate identity literature, where symbols, behaviour and communication are defined as the forms of expression of the corporate *personality* that lies beneath the surface (Birkigt and Stadler 1986). Later, we shall address the way in which in behaviour and communication meaning is created through the link with identity. Several signifying elements that seem to float between identity and colouring elements of projected image and experience will be identified – symbols such as past events and heroes; behavioural elements, such local food, architecture, arts, literature, popular culture and traditions; and communication elements, such as local or national languages.

We tend to share Noordman's critique concerning the many towns, cities and regions that seem to think they can change their identity by simply changing colour; a new logo, a new marketing campaign and perhaps new management. Unfortunately, it is not that simple. As Van Riel's (1996) definition of identity, noted above, makes particular reference only to the colouring elements, it seems to suggest that it is easier for corporations to adjust their identity, together with its structural and semi-static elements, than it is for a city, town or geographical region to do so. It is relatively easy for a corporation to change its location, size, structure, physical appearance (architecture) and even its history (through mergers or acquisitions). The inner mentality is probably hardest to influence – as with other semi-static elements that take years to alter when it comes to place identity (Noordman 2004, ch. 8).

Van Rekom (1994a, 1994b) elaborated on the concept of identity in the area of tourism, and emphasizes the role of employees as they contribute largely to an organization's or a place's identity in their interaction with customers. So, besides known aspects of identity, such as communication and signs and symbols, behaviour by the people involved in the expression of the identity of a given object is also important. As place interactions are high-touch, as we shall see later, it seems fair to emphasize the role of employees as well as local residents. For place branding, this could be translated into the involvement of a host culture, such as that contended by Keillor and Hult (1999): 'National identity is the extent to which a given culture recognizes and identifies with its unique characteristics ... Thus, national identity becomes the "set of meanings" owned by a given culture which sets it apart from other cultures' (p. 67). This emphasizes the importance of local knowledge and the narrative of the people.

As Pritchard and Morgan (Pritchard and Morgan 1998, 2001) explain, place identities are constructed through historical, political and cultural discourses, and are influenced by decision-making processes and power struggles. National, cultural, natural, social and religious assets become important identifiers. Jeong and Almeida Santos (2004) emphasize the role of festivals as a means of reconstructing, reframing and promoting regional identities. They see festivals as a means of providing a link between culture and politics: 'A vehicle through which people can advocate or contest certain notions of identity and ideology ... They occur in specific localities and offer representations of certain elements of those localities, resulting in the creation of a powerful sense of place' (Jeong and Almeida Santos 2004, p. 642). They argue that festivals provide political power, a means of social control, including and excluding certain groups, and thus affecting the contested meaning of place. At the same time, Jeong and Almeida Santos (2004) assert that it provides the opportunity to commoditize local culture for tourism in a globalized economy. This is supported by Ashworth (1991, p. 10), who states that 'the closest analogy is to regard the relics and events of the past as a raw material which is selectively quarried and used in accordance with contemporary requirements. The past is therefore commodified in a modern industry for modern consumption'. These considerations will be discussed in more detail in the next few sections, but first the issue of place identity needs further elaboration.

Pritchard and Morgan (2001, p. 177), in their study of Welsh identity, argue that 'the meaning and representation of Wales as a tourism space is shifting and its identity is contested as a consequence of changing socio-cultural discourses and of struggles among and between its marketers (the mediators) and its consumers'. In other words, identity is constructed, negotiated and renegotiated according to socio-cultural dynamics. Jeong and Almeida Santos (2004, p. 653) agree with this, as they found that cultural politics play an important role in defining the local identity of place through festivals. They illustrate 'the essentially political nature of place identity, not only in the sense that traditional place identity benefits some groups more than others, but also in that it involves a variety of conflicting ideologies'; festivals can function 'as a mechanism for particular groups to consolidate their privileged social status by controlling who participates in the construction of regional identity'. As Castells (1996, p. 476) argues: because of the central role of the media in the network society, 'image making is power-making'. Nevertheless, this book will often refer to the 'true identity of place', by which we mean to include the full set of unique characteristics or set of meanings that exist in a place and its culture at a given point in time, nevertheless realizing that this identity is subject to change and might include various fragmented identities. In any case, it is argued that if the right expectations are to be created in the minds of potential visitors, and to avoid unpleasant surprises, the 'true identity of place' should be the foundation on which to build the place branding proposition.

Nevertheless, this true identity of place can be built on a plurality of different cultural identities, as 'identity is not a zero-sum game'. This was the main message in the UNDP's 2004 *Human Development Report* (Fukuda-Parr 2004), issued in Belgium on 15 July 2004. It states that managing cultural diversity is a challenge for almost any country, as 5,000 ethnic groups are crammed into fewer than 200 countries: 'Two thirds have at least one substantial minority – an ethnic or religious group that makes up at least 10% of the population' (Fukuda-Parr 2004, p. 2). This can be a great asset for some places. The examples of Belgium, Canada, India, Spain and South Africa, among many others, demonstrate that not only is it possible to have unity with diversity, and stability with cultural freedom, but multicultural societies in themselves offer positive opportunities to build culturally richer, more vibrant communities (Muqbil 2004a). Identifying this, the report therefore 'provides a powerful argument for finding ways to "delight in our differences", as Archbishop Desmond Tutu has put it' (Fukuda-Parr 2004, p.v).

The actual product offering of place should be anchored on these unique identities. Without such an anchor, the sustainability and quality of the brand development might come into question, as any success in attracting international visits would result in other places copying the success formula and any competitive advantage being leveraged, or otherwise be perceived by visitors as artificial or fake. This product offering and the way it is based on the identity of place, is referred to by Go and Van Fenema (2006) as the 'material space': 'Material space can be considered as the ... main environment for experiences.' Tourists, investors and expats visit places for a limited time period and move to other sites sequentially, as a human being can be physically present in only one place at a time. Therefore the 'real' place experiences are limited and the place branding strategy needs to be planned carefully if the product offering is to provide the visitor with an experience that provides an opportunity to absorb the true meaning of place. 'This is why identities are so important, and ultimately, so powerful in this ever-changing power structure – because they build interests, values and projects, around experience, and refuse to dissolve by establishing specific connections between nature, history, geography and culture' (Castells 1997, p. 360).

Authenticity and Tourism

The extent to which this identity of place can be experienced in 'reality' (Dietvorst and Ashworth 1995, p. 7), or to what degree places are authentic, has been discussed thoroughly in the literature. As already indicated above, it is often contended that tourism leads to commoditization. One of the first commentators to assert this observation was Greenwood (1977). 'The critical issue is that commoditization allegedly changes the meaning of cultural products and of human relations, making them eventually meaningless' (Cohen 1988, p. 372). 'We already know from world-wide experience that local culture ... is altered and often destroyed by the treatment of it as a touristic attraction. It is made meaningless to the people who once believed in it' (Greenwood 1977, p. 131). Commoditization is said to destroy the authenticity of local cultural products and human relations; instead, a surrogate, covert 'staged authenticity' (MacCannell 1973) emerges. More recently, Jansen-Verbeke stated that 'the trend of cultural consumption is seen by many as a threat in terms of its erosive effect on cultural values and identity. In fact, tourism can mutate culture and heritage in an irreversible way. This means that authenticity has become a lost paradise and is being replaced by virtual experiences' (Jansen-Verbeke 2004, p. 6). This process of moving from authentic to inauthentic has been illustrated by Ashworth and Dietvorst (1995) as they link the concept to Butler's (1980) tourism product life-cycle.

In the later stages, the identity of place is likely to become less authentic. But Boorstin (1962) contended that tourists in general do not even wish to experience reality but rather thrive on pseudo-events that are inauthentic, contrived attractions that disregard the real world. When one accepts these implications, authentic places are doomed to extinction. As Duncan (1978, p. 277, cited in Urry 2003, p. 10) states: 'Over time the images generated within tourism come to constitute a self-perpetuating system of illusions, which may appear as quaint to the local inhabitants as they do to the tourists themselves.' MacCannell introduced the concept of 'staged authenticity' when he argued that the tourist is deceived in his or her quest for authentic place identity: 'It is always possible that what is taken to be entry into a back region is really entry into a front region that has been totally set up in advance for tourist visitation' (MacCannell 1999, p. 101).

'To the degree that this packaging alters the nature of the product, the authenticity sought by the visitor becomes "'staged authenticity'" provided by the touree' (MacCannell 1973, p. 596). But, as Urry (2003, p. 11) indicates, 'the search for authenticity is too simple a foundation for explaining contemporary tourism. There are multiple discourses and processes of the "authentic"', that are likely to expand further in future as a result of the continuous contest between the virtual revolution and the evolution of the cultural identity of place. As Cohen-Hattab and Kerber (2004, p. 59) argue: 'For the tourist seeking identification with a particular religious, historical or nationalist representation, concerns about authenticity and inauthenticity are often superseded by the ability of a site to condense the complexities of region and history into a cohesive, captivating narrative.' Instead of arguing around the dichotomy of whether places are authentic or not, or moving in an inevitably destructive direction, we think that it might be more fruitful to consider authenticity as a moving target that can possibly be reconstructed. Kitchin (2003, p. 7) supports this notion as he states that 'authenticity is not about conceptual simplicity, it's about people co-creating things that matter to them'. Cohen (1988, p. 383) eventually arrives at a similar observation as he concludes that hosts and guests or 'performers and audience [in his words] ... willingly, even if often unconsciously, participate playfully in a game of "as if", pretending that a contrived product is authentic, even if deep down they are not convinced of its authenticity'. What might result is a process of 'emergent authenticity ... as tourist-oriented products frequently acquire new meanings for the locals, as they become a diacritical mark of their ethnic or cultural identity, a vehicle of self- representation before an external public' (Cohen 1988, pp. 380, 3) as a manifestation of the 'invention of tradition' (Featherstone and Lash 1995, p. 12).

Many claim that only experiences can be authentic (Ashworth 2007; Gilmore and Pine II 2007). From the point of view of philosophical scepticism, this makes sense, as we cannot prove that there is a real world out there; all we have are our sensory cues (personal experiences). Hence, by definition, authenticity is individual, and judgements will be based on the person's self-image (Gilmore and Pine II 2007). But we shall never find authenticity in the physical and historical elements of identity, as they are always being manipulated and interpreted by human intervention. We can only experience the physical environments as being authentic, and Gilmore and Pine II (2007) provide some ideas on how to facilitate this. However, what is forgotten is that there is a third dimension – the social. People together, matching self-images of inner mentalities, can co-create authentic experiences of identity; such as, for example, in local food, arts, literature, popular culture and traditions. These elements of created meanings of projected images and experiences will make their appearance throughout this book.

Globalization versus Localization

Place identity is, of course, subject to the pressures of globalization. Prevailing traditions become history, and local modern art and architecture lose their significance in the face of globalization. Issues of global standards versus local uniqueness, McDonaldization or grobalization ('the imperialistic ambitions of nations, corporations, organizations, and other entities ... in seeing their power, influence, and (in some cases) profits *grow* throughout the world' [emphasis in original]) versus glocalization ('the interpenetration of the global and the local, resulting in unique outcomes in different geographical areas') (Ritzer 1998, 2003), become increasingly important, particularly as ICT and improved access and efficiency of international travel make the world appear a smaller place. As McCabe and Stokoe (2004, p. 602) stated: 'The impact of globalization on contemporary societies in the production and consumption of place has profound implications for understanding identity.' As stated in the UNDP's 2004 *Human Development Report*, what is also important in this era of globalization is that 'a new class of political claims and demands has emerged from individuals, communities and countries feeling that their local cultures are being swept away' (Fukuda-Parr 2004, p. 1)

Considering the influence of mass media on place image, as will be illustrated throughout this book, the UNDP report addresses many of the aspects of globalization that are of relevance to the issue of place branding. For example:

In the film industry US productions regularly account for about 85% of film audiences worldwide. In the audiovisual trade with just the European Union, the United States had an $8.1 billion surplus in 2000, divided equally between films and television rights ... Of global production of more than 3,000 films a year Hollywood accounted for more than 35% of total industry revenues. Furthermore, in 1994–98, in 66 of 73 countries with data, the United States was the first or second major country of origin of imported films. (Fukuda-Parr 2004, p. 86)

However, Appadurai (1996) argues that globalization leads to a tension between cultural homogenization and cultural heterogenization: 'Most often, the homogenization argument subspeciates into either an argument about Americanization or an argument about commoditization ... What these arguments fail to consider is that at least as rapidly as forces from various metropolises are brought into new societies they tend to become indigenized in one or another way' (p. 32). This is what Ritzer (2003) referred to as glocalization. This would relate closely to the 'emergent authenticity' arguments presented earlier, and hence lead to heterogenization.

Harvey (1989) also comments on globalization and post-modernity, in which, in economic terms, flexible accumulation, 'marked by a direct confrontation with the rigidities of Fordism, resting on flexibility with respect to labour processes, labour markets, products and patterns of consumption' (Harvey 1989, p. 147), is the standard. Harvey's view involves a time–space perspective:

As spatial barriers diminish so we become much more sensitized to what the world's spaces contain ... Then it is possible for the peoples and powers that command those spaces to alter them in such a way as to be more rather than less attractive to highly mobile capital. Local ruling elites can, for example, implement strategies for local labour control, of skill enhancement, of infrastructural provision, of tax policy, state regulation, and so on, in order to attract development within their particular space ... Corporatist forms of governance can flourish in such spaces, and themselves take on entrepreneurial roles in the production of favourable business climates and other special qualities. (Harvey 1989, p. 294)

As we shall see in the signature case description in Chapter 5, Dubai is a prime example of this.

At the same time, Harvey (1989, p. 302) argues that we 'encounter the opposite reaction that can best be summed up as the search for personal or collective identity, the search for secure moorings in a shifting world. Place-identity, in this collage of superimposed spatial images that implode in upon us, becomes an important issue'. Therefore, 'the relationship between the space of flows and the space of places, between simultaneous globalization and localization' (Castells 1996, p. 425), the sense of local landscapes versus global ethnoscapes, mediascapes, technoscapes, financescapes, and ideoscapes (Appadurai 1996, p. 33) is of prime interest in this context of place image. There is growing awareness that places can build on their cultural heritage through tourism and develop modern urban functions that are linked to the demands of the global knowledge based economy (Go *et al.* 2004). For example, as will be illustrated with our signature case in Chapter 5, through information technology, free-zone projects such as those developed by Dubai's Internet City. Also in Dubai, the 'Knowledge Village' has been designed to become an instrumental and integral part of fostering renewal and innovation in the region, through franchised (Western) education and e-learning. It signals that Dubai has geared up to accommodate the international flow of goods, information and people. In short, in many respects it has become both mobile and global.

However, as suggested by Harvey (1989, p. 303) at the beginning of this chapter: 'the assertion of any place-bound identity has to rest at some point on the motivational power of tradition' [see Hall (1996) in the following section]. 'It is difficult however, to maintain any sense of historical continuity in the flux and ephemerality of flexible accumulation. The irony is that tradition is now often preserved by being commodified and marketed as such' (Harvey 1989, p. 303). As Appadurai (1996, p. 85) suggests: 'the aesthetic of the ephemerality becomes the civilizing counterpart of flexible accumulation, and the work of the imagination is to link the ephemerality of goods with the pleasures of the senses'. At the same time 'there are abundant signs that localism and nationalism have become stronger precisely because of the quest for the security that place always offers in the midst of all the shifting that flexible accumulation implies. The resurgence of geopolitics ... [with the second Gulf War] fits only too well with a world that is increasingly nourished intellectually and politically by a vast flux of ephemeral images' (Harvey 1989, p. 306) – ephemeral images that surely have their impact on places as brands.

Flows of tourism and talent and globalization are closely linked, particularly as the travel and tourism industry is subjected to a process of increased internationalization. For example, the globalization strategies in the hospitality industry (Go and Pine 1995), and the international expansion and mergers and acquisitions of tour operators and airlines, are driving this forward. Multinational companies in the tourism industry are increasingly standardizing products and services, ignorant of the local environment within which they are placed, opposing local social conditions as illustrated above by Harvey. In contemporary society, it matters little where you are in the world, hotels 'look alike', from one place to the next, even if they are continents apart. It is not surprising that this is the case in the hospitality and transport industry, where employment is highly internationalized. Most hotel chains attract management-level recruits from the same well-known hotel schools in Switzerland, the UK, the USA and the Netherlands. Cheaper labour is increasingly attracted from hotel schools in India, China and the Philippines. Once employed, staff members are often relocated from one part of the world to another, every few years. Working many hours at, or staying extensively in, hotels tends to lock both guests and workers into their own narrow professional community and industry environment, which may lead to a sense of social exclusion. Hence, it is evident that contextualizing the globally standardized products and services within the local environment seems an almost impossible task, and many hotels and resorts seem to be small simulacra islands on their own. Jakle terms this the production of 'commonplaceness'(quoted in Urry 2002, p. 55). In his Chapter 4, Urry (2002) himself elaborates on this tension between, on the one hand, the provision of standardized services by the often relatively poorly paid (foreign) service workers who have no bond with the local environment and, on the other hand, the almost sacred quality of the visitors' gaze on some longed-for and remarkable site, which by definition is embedded within a local context. The results of our research on case Dubai, presented in Chapter 9, show some striking examples of this.

So, the advances in mass media and transportation, increased movement of people, ideas and capital, and the spread of new technology seem to thrust us towards a new 'world culture' (Dredge and Jenkins 2003; Reiser 2003). But, as Reiser (2003, p. 311) puts it: 'tourism needs local culture, or at least the image of it (e.g. differentiation between destinations)'. It is the cultural identity of place that represents the attractiveness of the experience of place. But at the same time, as a result of globalization, the assets of cultural and religious heritage that attract inward flows can 'become liabilities if they become a source of conflict' (Muqbil 2004b). Huntington (1993, p. 22) stated:

> It is my hypothesis that the fundamental source of conflict in this new world will not be primarily ideological or primarily economic. The great divisions among humankind and the dominating source of conflict will be cultural. Nation states will remain the most powerful actors in world affairs, but the principal conflicts of global politics will occur between nations and groups of different civilizations. The clash of civilizations will dominate global politics. The fault lines between civilizations will be the battle lines of the future.

The question remains as to whether, and to what extent, postmodern cities in the orient, such as, for example, Dubai, or the multicultural metropolitan areas in the West for that matter, will be affected by such conflicting movements of globalization, localization, clashes of civilization (as according to Magala (2002) modern globalized 'detraditionalization' can lead to fundamentalism), and the competing power struggles and political processes that attempt to define identities of place. The logical question that follows from that is how this will be reflected in the projected images of place. Despite the criticism of place branding specialists such as Anholt (2007), many places still make the sad choice of emphasizing their *dynamic diversity*. These allusions to the importance of such places as hubs in the global flows often seem hardly credible – for example, when we compare the case of Flanders (the Dutch-speaking northern part of Belgium, as presented in Chapter 7) with places such as Dubai. At the same time, such claims represent 'neither fish nor fowl'. This urges us to have a closer look at projected place image.

PROJECTED PLACE IMAGE

The place branding strategy results in a projected place image through the use of planned marketing and communication. Narratives and visuals are used to create meaning in the market, deploying media and ICT as enablers (Magala 2001). Indirectly, places can influence image formation through secondary place interactions with consumers, 'vicarious experiences' (Kim and Richardson 2003; Pan and Ryan 2007) facilitated by intermediaries and produced imagination, such as, for example. in some of the media, literature, arts and popular culture (such as motion pictures, TV shows or music) (Cohen-Hattab and Kerber 2004). Gartner (1993, pp. 197–201) calls these 'induced destination image formation agents' ('overt' and 'covert'). Identity has no meaning without narrative, and created meaning should be a reflection of local knowledge.

Beerli and Martín (2004a, p. 667), based on the work of Gartner, tried to measure the impact on place image of nine secondary information sources: induced sources (brochures issued by the public authorities; tour operator brochures; mass-media advertising campaigns; travel agency staff; and the internet); organic sources (friends and family members who were either requested to, or who volunteered to, give information about the place); and autonomous sources (guidebooks; news/articles/reports/documentaries; and programmes about the place in the media). Organic and autonomous sources will be discussed later, but Beerli and Martín found that, as far as the induced sources is concerned, there was little impact on perceived image. However, a major drawback of their study is that they measured post-visit, as opposed to pre-visit, image. Of course, it is not surprising that, if visitors have just spent one or two weeks in a locality, their perceived image of the place has by then been constructed primarily from experiential and organic data. Lacking these prior to the visit, secondary sources of information will logically have a much higher impact. Beerli and Martín (2004a, p. 678) fortunately acknowledge this limitation in their research, when, at the end of their paper, they state that their study 'made it impossible to measure the pre-visit image of the destination, which would have made it feasible to measure the extent to which secondary information sources influence the formation of the pre-visit image and the way in which primary information sources could alter this image'. Such primary sources of information will be discussed in more detail in Chapter 8, but already here, it might be opportune to state that in some of our research, such as that presented in Chapter 13 on signature case Dubai, it was our particular intention to measure the influence of induced agents prior to the visit and to identify the relative importance of advertising. This is something that has not been done before in place image research.

ICT-enabled Projections

Information technology has been the key enabler of business process reengineering (BPR), creating the radical changes (Hammer 1990), that have taken place in many industries. Hammer prescribes the use of ICT to challenge the assumptions inherent in the work processes that have existed since long before the advent of modern computer and communication technology. While this has happened visibly in sectors such as aviation (Sheldon 1997), other sectors have been condemned to reengineering because of market forces. Innovative players from outside the industry seized the moment when they realized that the internet would hold much promise for information-intensive industries such as travel and tourism (Werthner and Klein 1999, p. 8), where product trial can be only virtual.

'Technology captures and transmits meanings in audio-visual format (voice mail, phone) and textual and graphical expressions (emails, documents). Information or representation space glues people together wherever they are. It provides a real-time and asynchronous layer that connects people through electronic media' (Go and Van Fenema 2006). This information space captures, represents and transmits (parts of) the identity of places and their product offering. This is referred to in Figure 3.1 as the projected place image. The media and ICT are essential enablers in this respect. As media and ICT converge (Werthner and Klein 1999, p. 69), future opportunities become even better. People's perceptions of places, without prior visits, will be co-created in their connection with others or based on what they have seen on television; in virtual representations online; read in magazines, brochures or travel guides; seen in museums, through the arts, read in literature or experienced in the movies. Again, the projected place image as influenced by local public and private actors should be anchored to some extent on a true place identity (Go *et al.* 2004; Onians 1998; Van Rekom and Go 2003).

However, one could argue that with globalization, through the information technology facilitated global flows of information, images, voice and data, national identities are torn down and result in 'the hollowing out of meaning in everyday life' (Featherstone and Lash 1995, p. 2).

Others argue instead that a number of positive possibilities can be opened up. They contend that the seemingly empty and universalist signs circulating in the world informational system can be recast into different configurations of meaning. That these transformed social semantics can — in the context of traditional and self-reflexive social practices — instead inform the (re)constitution and/or creation of individual and communal identities (Featherstone and Lash 1995, pp. 2–3).

What emerges are imagined communities (Anderson 1991): 'These are like traditional and concrete *Gemeinschaften* that people are willing to die for them [*sic*]. However, unlike "immediate communities" which were rendered in qualitative time, full space and immediate forms of socialization, imagined communities are "imagined" in the sense of their very abstraction — of abstract time, space and the social' (Featherstone and Lash 1995, p. 7). Also called virtual communities, these can now be the postmodern "*bestowers* of identity" through the invention of tradition' (Featherstone and Lash 1995, p. 12) (see also (Magala 2001)).

Taken literally, sites such as lonelyplanet.com, virtualtourist.com, expatexchange.com or fita.org could be the places where new place identities are created, defying time, which destroys history; space, which destroys reality; and image/information flows, which destroy the social (Featherstone and Lash 1995, p. 7). This is supported by Kitchin's (2003, p. 7) notion of authenticity being about people co-creating things that matter to them. In popular internet terminology this is referred to as Web 2.0. Apart from developing the place product, including its branding, based on place identity, another essential part of the place branding strategy is therefore to formulate a plan for projecting the 'right' image in this dynamic and versatile online environment. Whenever possible, this should exploit existing on- or offline media or other sources of produced imagination, such as in arts and literature, popular culture or in modern-day virtual communities (Magala 2001). It is not always clear in this respect if one is observing 'overt' or 'covert' induced agents. The lines between advertising and independent information provision and sharing are increasingly blurred, as consumers get involved in the production and assemblage processes where many consumers share information with each other (Dellaert 1999). For example, some communities (virtual or physical) are linked directly to and facilitated by commercial products, such as, for example, in the case of Harley-Davidson HOCs (Harley Owners Clubs) (Oliver 1999, pp. 39–40). Others are facilitated by intermediaries (Lonely Planet), still others are grass-roots, such as Usenet Newsgroups. The importance of covert induced agents, and the sometimes astute way in which they are used to influence consumer choice behaviour, will be discussed later, but the idea that good place marketing needs much more than commercial advertising alone is getting more and more attention (Anholt 2003; Gnoth 2002; Olins 1999).

However, this section intends to focus particularly on the projected place image, using marketing and communication as strategic tools for place brand development. Covert induced agents will be discussed later, as they are particularly useful as a means of providing consumers with alternative place interactions, facilitating secondary experiential sources of place image. Autonomous agents will be discussed in Chapter 11. ICT is significant in all these environments, but particularly needs to be emphasized as a strategic tool for place marketers as well as the way they project image.

Place experiences share the characteristics of other services, similar to the way that production and consumption take place simultaneously when visitors consume the product. Therefore visitors participate actively in the service operation and create meaning within the experience. This implies that consumers are also actively engaged in the process of creating and attaching meaning to the place image (Padgett and Allen 1997). As a consequence, one could assume that the interactive nature of the internet adds whole new dimensions to place marketing. Indeed, Cho and Fesenmaier (2000, p. 314) point out that it is hard to imagine what a place is like without having experienced it. But with the internet, people gain access to interactive multimedia easily, enabling them to enter virtual environments and immerse themselves in virtual experiences, thus enabling them to form more vivid and clearer place images.

Cho and Fesenmaier developed a conceptual framework for evaluating the effects of virtual tours as a means of improving place image by creating virtual experiences in information space. However, before one can evaluate the marketing effectiveness of such virtual tours, it would have to be decided what exactly the image is that the place marketer wants to project, on what identity this should be based, and to what extent all those involved in the creation of identity participate in the formulation of such images (including local, regional, national, multinational, public, private and grass-roots organizations, as well as organized groups of local residents, tourists and other organizations). In other words, what does the place have to offer? And, as a result of such investigation, what is the story that the place marketer wants to narrate in order to create meaning of place and have a positive influence on its perceived image? Hence the need to revisit the concept of place image, in particular the way it is projected by destinations.

Created Meaning

In the abstract of their paper on deconstructing place image construction, Fesenmaier and MacKay provide us with an account of projected image and created meaning. 'The actuality of tourism has been suggested as less important than its expressive representations. What is depicted or not depicted in place image advertising, and on whose authority it is selected, involves a more complex question of what comprises the destination and who has the power to define its identity' (Fesenmaier and MacKay 1996, p. 37). So created meaning defines place identity and projects it accordingly, using narratives and visuals. In general terms we should raise the question as to how place marketers would delineate these narratives. When places are defined at the level of countries, some help in answering this question is provided by Hall (1996). He phrases the question as follows: 'But how is the modern nation imagined? What representational strategies are deployed to construct our common-sense views of national belonging or identity? ... How is the narrative of the national culture told?' Of the many aspects, which a comprehensive answer to that question would include, Hall selected five main elements: first, there is the narrative of the nation, as it is told and retold in national histories, literature, the media and popular culture; second, there is the emphasis on origins, continuity, tradition and timelessness; a third discursive strategy is the invention of tradition; a fourth example is that of the foundational myth (also elaborated on by McLean and Cooke 2003, p. 155); and finally the national identity is also often symbolically grounded in the idea of a pure, original people or 'folk' (Hall 1996, p. 613).

Anderson (1991) refers to nations as being 'imagined communities'. The nation is '*imagined* [emphasis in original] because the members of even the smallest nation will never know most of their fellow-members, meet them, or even hear of them, yet in the minds of each lives the image of the communion' (Anderson 1991, p. 6). Second, it 'is imagined as a *community* [emphasis in original], because, regardless of the actual inequality and exploitation that may prevail in each, the nation is always conceived as a deep, horizontal comradeship' (Anderson 1991, p. 7). Also, Anderson's 'point of departure is that nationality, or, as one might prefer to put it in view of the world's multiple significations, nation-ness, as well as nationalism, are cultural artefacts of a particular kind' (Anderson 1991, p. 4). 'Nationalism has to be understood by aligning it ... with the large cultural systems that preceded it, out of which – as well as against which – it came into being' (Anderson 1991, p. 12). These are the '*religious community* and the *dynastic realm* [emphasis in original]. For both of these, in their heydays, were taken-for-granted frames of reference, very much as nationality is today' (Anderson 1991, p. 12). Religious communities 'were imaginable largely through the medium of a sacred language and written script' (Anderson 1991, p. 12). For example, in Islam, believers from the most distant countries, when they met in Mecca, were able to communicate, because the sacred texts they shared existed only in classical Arabic. 'In this sense, written Arabic functioned like Chinese characters to create community out of signs, not sounds' (Anderson 1991, p. 13).

Of course, Latin was the sacred language of Christendom, but it waned steadily after the late Middle Ages, for two reasons: the explorations of the non-European world and the gradual demotion of the sacred language itself (Anderson 1991, pp. 16–18). As far as the dynastic realm is concerned: 'during the seventeenth century ... the automatic legitimacy of sacral monarchy began its slow decline in Western Europe' (Anderson 1991, p. 21). Gradually, in its place came 'the nation', which was facilitated primarily by 'print-capitalism, which made it possible for rapidly growing numbers of people to think about themselves, and to relate themselves to others, in profoundly new ways' in a new age of mechanical reproduction (Anderson 1991, p. 36). 'If manuscript knowledge was scarce and arcane lore, print knowledge lived by reproducibility and dissemination' (Anderson 1991, p. 37). Hence, to understand what came to represent national culture 'one has to look at the ways in which administrative organisations create meaning' (Anderson 1991, p. 53). These are signs and symbols, with language at the base.

Anderson's significations largely correlate with those of Hall; for example, the narrative of the nation: 'In an age in which history itself was still widely conceived in terms of "great events" and "great leaders" [late nineteenth/early twentieth century], pearls strung along a thread of narrative, it was obviously tempting to decipher the community's past in antique dynasties' (Anderson 1991, p. 109). According to Anderson, traditional people or 'folk' began to be identified through the colonial census, which started during the second half of the nineteenth century. For the emphasis on origins, continuity, tradition and timelessness, according to Anderson, the 'primordialness of language' is again of major importance: 'No one can give the date of birth of any language' (Anderson 1991, p. 144), but 'it is always a mistake to treat languages in the way that certain nationalist ideologues treat them – as *emblems* [emphasis in original] of nation-ness, like flags, costumes, folk-dances, and the rest. Much the most important thing about language is its capacity for generating imagined communities, building in effect particular *solidarities* [emphasis in original]' (Anderson 1991, p. 133). 'Through that language, encountered on mother's knee and parted with only at the grave, pasts are restored, fellowships are imagined, and futures dreamed' (Anderson 1991, p. 154). Furthermore, one could argue that, according to Anderson, the foundational myth was laid down in the 'historical map, designed to demonstrate, in the new cartographic discourse, the antiquity of specific, tightly bounded territorial units' (Anderson 1991, pp. 174–5), ultimately, being immortalized in the map-as-logo. Finally, the invention of tradition is often formalized by the state through the creation of museums and the education system. All this, eventually, is what constitutes identity (Anderson 1991, pp. 204–5).

In the discussion above, the importance of the adjective 'cultural' in cultural identity was emphasized only implicitly. Fortunately, the Dutch sociologist Hofstede's (2001a) definition of culture provides some additional support. According to Hofstede, culture is a mental programme, the 'software of the mind' (Hofstede 2001a, p. 15). Hofstede distinguishes four elements of a culture that could also be related to Hall's and Anderson's definitions: heroes (as part of the narrative of the nation); rituals (which maintain the origins, continuity, traditions and emphasize timelessness); symbols (which often provide a reference to foundational myths); and values (instilled in the people of 'folk'). Symbols are the more superficial elements of a culture. Heroes are models of behaviour; people who have a high symbolic value, high esteem and can function as an example. Rituals are codes of behaviour, ways in which we deal with everyday or annual events, to celebrate something or to express mourning. Values are the collective inclination to choose one course above another; values are feelings with a direction ((Hofstede 2001a, p. 20).

Competing in the global market, place marketers are forced to decide whether and which elements of national, local and regional identity would contribute best to the attraction system of place. And then, which elements of the attraction system would represent place most appropriately through its projected images. But again, according to Fesenmaier and MacKay:

> The images presented in advertisements and brochures are, by definition, out of context and recontextualized to suggest an interpretation. The authoritative voices of the display and destination promotion provide this interpretation and authentication since objects have no voice. However, the authoritative voice cannot singularly represent a destination image. The viewers of the image are also involved in conceiving meaning. (Fesenmaier and MacKay 1996, p. 37)

Also, Ateljevic and Doorne (2002, p. 648) 'reveal imagery as a political process that encodes and reinforces the dominant ideology of tourism culture, essentially a global process which manifests locally and explicitly involves the construction of place'. The way this meaning is conceived by the viewers of the image, will be discussed at length in Part 4. However, in our signature case presented in Chapter 9 we shall study to what extent these identities and images are reflected in the online narratives and pictures that are used to market the fast-growing destination of Dubai. The findings will confirm some of the points made here.

For a brief return to structure, from all projected images we distinguish three groups. First, we have identified and discussed above the overt induced agents, most importantly marketing and promotion. We focused on the fact that places need to identify the elements of identity that they want to use to create meaning through projected images. Another group of projected images involves vicarious experiences, which include covert induced agents. These consist of images as projected by intermediaries and produced imagination through the arts, literature and popular culture (Cohen-Hattab and Kerber 2004). The impact of motion pictures has recently received increased attention here (see Kim and Richardson (2003) and the Inaugural International Tourism and Media Conference held on 24–26 November 2004 in Melbourne, Australia). Vicarious place experiences will be discussed in more detail in Chapter 8, as part of the brand performance gap. The reason for this structuring is that vicarious experiences are not in the first instance under the control of the place marketer and therefore not primarily related to the place branding strategy, at least not a priori. Third, we distinguish autonomous agents that are a result of temporal, environmental and situational influences. Of particular influence here is news reporting, as will be illustrated in Chapter 11. In all the above cases, the media play an important role, but in different capacities, either paid for, as in overt induced agents, or as an autonomous news reporting organizations. A grey area is created by the covert induced agents where the place marketer is not in control, but able to influence the impact of the media on the projected image. It is particularly important to identify the level of influence that these various types of projected images have on the dynamics in the place branding model. Also, their particular impact, in the first instance, generally relates to different gaps in the model. Therefore it seemed sensible to discuss these different types of projected images in different sections, even though they are closely related.

PRODUCT OFFERING BASED ON IDENTITY

Globally, places are being marketed as attractive locations for tourism, trade, talent (employment opportunities) and treasury (investment opportunities). Each of these four categories include product or factor offerings that enhance market potential. For example, the components that build the tourism product are commonly referred to as the '4 As': Attractions; Amenities (or hospitality industry – comprising accommodation and F&B/catering services – and retailing); Access (or transport); and Ancillary services (or visitor centres, insurance and financial services) (Cooper *et al.* 2000; Page 2003). Talent is being attracted through some of the same offerings, including a rich and dynamic supply of cultural activities, but also by offering income tax benefits, good health care and international schooling systems, and attractive housing. Additional offerings for investors and traders include tax reliefs and factor cost benefits (such as cost, productivity or quality benefits on land, raw materials and/or labour). All these elements should make places look more attractive from the outside. Hence, place experiences are often mediated, 'staged' by various public and private actors (MacCannell 1973). Tour packages, chamber of commerce trade missions, hospitality resort ghettos, guided sightseeing tours, shopping malls, international schools' open days, fake airport souvenir art, even the taxi drivers who receive introductory and advanced training on 'how to deal with visitors'. Often several institutions are involved in marketing these products, such as tourism promotion boards or destination marketing organizations; export, trade and investment agencies; convention bureaux; ministries of foreign affairs; chambers of commerce; financial institutions, larger corporations and/or trade associations. Such place marketers often look at place promotion from just one or a few perspectives, utilizing, as mentioned earlier, a target market approach. This is very different from the place branding approach advocated in this book.

But the role of place marketers has shifted in recent years from pure marketing organizations to public–private bodies that are also involved in product development and industry relations. This provides the opportunity for such institutions not just to project the identity of place, but also to change it physically and enhance the product offering: 'This role extension enables a matching of authoritative voice and reconstructed reality in order to verify official imaging' (Fesenmaier and MacKay 1996, p. 38). In other words, place branding involves heavy investment in real place development. Public, private or partnered investment in culture, sports, heritage, neighbourhoods and districts, education, public facilities and entertainment and tourism infrastructure with respect for the local identity of both people and environment, can send powerful messages to the outside world.

Nevertheless, regardless of the physical investment, most elements of the product offering of place involve services such as hospitality, transport, retail, health care, education, financial, business, entertainment and cultural services. But, more than just an assemblage of products, when people visit a place, it is above all a hedonic product, in which various services are offered by a myriad of industries and supporting industries, which, within loosely-coupled networks, create the conditions that enable visitors to experience place. The experiential nature of place consumption is discussed in more detail in Chapter 8. Here, we need to focus on some of the characteristics of services that represent potential barriers to building a coherent product offering and providing a consistent experience of place based on a 'true' place identity.

In general terms, the characteristics that distinguish services from goods are: intangibility, inseparability, variability, and perishability (Hoffman and Bateson 2002, p. 27; Kotler *et al.* 2003, p. 42; Lovelock and Wright 2002, p. 10; Weaver and Lawton 2002, p. 206). First of all, intangibility, which also lies at the heart of the other unique differences between goods and services (Hoffman and Bateson 2002, p. 27), implies that services cannot be tested or sampled prior to purchase. This is one of the reasons why ICT provides such tremendous novel opportunities for promoting place brands through virtual projections (Cho and Fesenmaier 2000). The use of tangible clues is particularly important; for example, through the use of multimedia, artefacts, architecture, design and physical presence in source markets (for example, the design of the foreign destination marketing offices and booths at travel exhibitions, or through travelling museum exhibitions). But, as well as these tangible clues, the way in which physical investments in place development are made should appeal to the imagination in order to facilitate communicability.

Second, in services, production and consumption often take place simultaneously, which is referred to as inseparability. If one wants to experience a visitor attraction – for example, a zoo – one will have to go there and enjoy the experience while it is produced (while the animals and their keepers are going about their normal daily routines of cleaning, feeding and so on). As long as internet, multimedia and virtual reality provide substitute products that are far from experiencing the 'real thing', these types of attractions cannot be copied, stored and shipped to one's home address. This means that passenger transport automatically becomes an integral part of the product, as will hospitality services whenever an overnight stay is required. This is what adds to the complexity of the tourism product. What is more important, though, is the social aspect of services. Inseparability causes the consumer to be part of the production process. Hence the social encounter between the customer and service personnel, as well as other customers, becomes an integral part of the service experience. As a result, different types of customers generate different place interactions. From a place marketing perspective, it is therefore vital to have a detailed understanding of these dynamic processes in order to maximize customer experiences: 'But the concern which is of utmost importance is the service encounter' (Go and Haywood 2003, p. 97)

A third aspect that causes services to be different from goods is variability or heterogeneity. For service organizations, it is very hard to control service quality. Services take place in real time, and the customer is involved in the process. Therefore, not only does the level of service differ from one organization to the next, from one employee within an organization to another, and from one customer to another, but also from one day to the next. To deal with this heterogeneity, two strategies are often proposed: either standardization at a reduced price or customization at a premium price (Hoffman and Bateson 2002, p. 40). However, as was argued in Chapter 3, this appears to be an outdated proposition. Today, co-opting the customer through the flexible use of technology in personalized service encounters (Mittal and Lassar 1996) seems to be the only way forward. Indeed, Bitner *et al.* (2000, pp. 141–2) propose that technology infusion in the service encounter should facilitate 'customisation and flexibility, effective service recovery and spontaneous delight', taking into account the importance of the interaction between customers and employees.

Finally, a major issue with services is their extreme perishability. Services cannot be stored, or unused capacity put on reserve. Without the benefit of carrying an inventory, one of the greatest challenges in the marketing of services is to compensate for perishability by matching demand effectively with supply (Hoffman and Bateson 2002, p. 42; Weaver and Lawton 2002, p. 208). There are various strategies that can be deployed in an effort to try to adjust supply and demand in order to achieve a balance. These strategies include demand strategies such as creative pricing, reservation systems, the development of complementary services, and the development of non-peak demand; but also supply strategies such as utilization of part-time employees, capacity sharing, advance preparation for expansion, utilization of third-party services, and an increase in customer participation (Hoffman and Bateson 2002).

These measures, both those on the demand strategy as well as the supply strategy side, can have their own, sometimes positive, but often negative, effects on place image formation. It follows that within a field involving a myriad of service providers, each representing their own interests and attempting to maximize their own yield, as opposed to the interests and long-term competitiveness and economic sustainability of the place as a whole, decision-making is a daunting task. Therefore, to build a coherent and consistent place experience based on identity is a tremendous challenge, and co-ordinating and orchestrating the maintenance of a positive place image even more so. As a result of this discussion, it is expected that the part of the research on case Dubai in Chapter 9, in which the projected image is evaluated, will generate a mixture of results, where different players are not aligned in their communication.

But already, several issues emerge. If the infusion of technology in service operations as well as the virtual promotion of place brands is the way forward, how will it facilitate the projection of place identity? The paradox is that the solution lies in the personalization of the service encounter – the social interaction between host and guest. Hoffman and Novak (1996, p. 53) and Shih (1998, p. 658) discuss the crucial aspect of 'telepresence' in virtual service encounters (that is, 'the extent to which consumers feel their existence in the virtual space'). If telepresence really occurs, which seems to become ever more likely with the advance of technology, the issue of social presence, reflection of identity and trust will become even more important. The danger lies in public and private actors approaching the technology purely from rationalized perspectives, such as those based on the transaction cost reduction arguments provided by Van der Heijden

(1995). From a marketing perspective, the internet is used all too often purely as a distribution channel, with suppliers providing listings of functional attributes and facilities and bookable options (Gretzel and Fesenmaier 2003). Also, the technology infusion in service operations is generally grounded in cost-reduction and efficiency claims, instead of focusing on enriching customer experiences. What also should be accounted for are the affective elements of customer experience and perception. In addition to rationalization, the technology could be used to facilitate social encounters and to incorporate identity.

The question those actors involved in place marketing should ask themselves is: how do we reflect our cultural narrative, traditions, artefacts, language and 'who we are', and how do we invite (co-opt) the customer to appreciate that identity with us? As mentioned above, physical evidence, through architecture and design, photography and symbols, is of crucial importance. This applies to the physical environment, incorporating references to local identity, but as Huang (2001) argues, this can also be linked to an online environment. As well as collecting information about consumer preferences and buying behaviour, which indeed allows for better customization, a true involvement of the customer in the service delivery process is an area that needs attention and will provide novel opportunities for innovation. Facilitating a more intense social interaction with service delivery personnel and other customers, while the operations are facilitated through technology, would enhance customers' feelings of 'being connected'. Even in an online environment this can be achieved, as can be seen in, for example, Amazon.com or many of the virtual travel communities.

It is interesting to note the reinforcing circle that emerges here. We argue that sustainable place branding can only be achieved if place projections and product offerings are embedded in locality, even when incorporated in the global flows of information, images, technology and organizations. This promotes uniqueness and builds competitive advantage. At the same time, place experiences embedded in locality facilitate cultural understanding between people in their physical social encounters, which again in itself facilitates an appreciation and promotion of local identities, and so on. If this does not happen, it is likely that a place brand strategy gap occurs.

CONCLUSION: BRAND STRATEGY GAP

If the product offering and the way it is communicated fails to match up with the true identity of place, it can create a place brand strategy gap. Such a gap occurs as the fundamental prerequisites for a rewarding host–guest encounter are not present when the images generated within the product offering and the way they are projected come to constitute a self-perpetuating system of illusions, which may appear as quaint to the local inhabitants as they do to the visitors. Both hosts as well as guests will become alienated. From a tourism perspective, Britton (1979, p. 318) formulates this as follows:

> The disparity between advertised image and reality has long been of interest to geographers concerned with settlers to or travellers in a new land. The new persistence of distortion is clearly manifest in the surprise and dismay that international tourists frequently experience when travelling in developing countries. The tourism industry continues to portray these places as 'paradise', 'unspoiled', 'sensuous', or other distortions, presumably to compensate for the obvious poverty beyond the hotel or sightseeing bus ... [and] the inability of the tourism industry to represent destinations as real places. Themes and biases in advertisements, travel journalism, and the travel trade press ... [and] the use of [other] distorted imagery has an adverse impact on the quality of the visitor's experience and on the receiving society.

This is particularly true in places with culturally diverse hosts and guests (often in developing countries, as suggested by Britton). The product and communication strategy might be formulated in ways intended to attract and satisfy visitors based on *their* values and preferences, while ignoring those of the host. However, the local population has to be employed in the industry and deal with visitor encounters on a daily basis. In situations where the local cultural values have not been communicated and the product offering does not incorporate any reference to these local values, it will have a negative effect on visitor satisfaction because of unexpected tensions between host and guest. In such a case, neither visitor nor host community is to blame, but the place brand strategy is, because it had failed to make a genuine effort to represent the host destination in a less glamorous manner in order to raise the 'right' expectations and construct appropriate perceived images in source markets. This will be the topic of Part 4 of this book.

CHAPTER 5

Signature Case Dubai: Brand Strategy

> With the ending of the frigid Fifty Years' War between Soviet-style communism and the West's liberal democracy, some observers ... announced that we had reached the 'end of history'. Nothing could be further from the truth. In fact now that the bitter ideological confrontation sparked by this [last] century's collision of 'isms' has ended, larger numbers of people from more points on the globe than ever before have aggressively come forward to participate in history. They have left behind centuries, even millennia, of obscurity in forest and desert and rural isolation to request from the world community – and from the global economy that links it together – a decent life for themselves and a better life for their children. (Ohmae 1995, p. 1)

This chapter provides a detailed case study analysis of the Emirate of Dubai, the fast-growing global hub of the Middle East. In other chapters, other case studies will be presented, but throughout the book Dubai will repeatedly receive attention. That is why we have called it our 'signature case'. This first chapter on our signature case Dubai will therefore discuss the context of Dubai in depth, after which we shall present our empirical studies of the projected image of Dubai in Chapter 9, and the perceived image in Chapter 13. Of interest in these chapters is the extent to which global facts take a local form. In this sense, we would encourage the reader not to interpret the signature case as being about the specific context of Dubai alone. Rather, it is about a typical example of a rapidly developing region or city-state, riding the waves of globalization, having firmly established itself, in less than fifteen years, as an important node in the network of global flows. It is not just the case study of Dubai that is of central interest, but also the results of the phenomenographical analysis of the way in which this newly established hub is projecting itself and being imagined by an international audience, and the way in which these results have been obtained. The following case study description provides an assessment of the sense of place, and facilitates a comparison of the empirical content analysis and survey results, as presented in later chapters, with the actual product offering and local identity. While Dubai, at the time of writing, in 2008, had not yet developed an orchestrated brand strategy in terms of the use of symbols (logos, slogans), the behaviour and communication of the Emirate has nevertheless built a very powerful international brand. It is particularly this building of brand equity through action that interests us. Hence we provide a detailed analysis of this here and in the following chapters. The findings resulting from this analysis of case Dubai throughout this book are likely to be of interest to many developing countries, regions or cities in the emerging network of global hubs.

A large part of the contribution lies in the innovative research methodologies applied in Chapters 9 and 13, and the way in which they establish the relationships hypothesized in the place branding model. Therefore, for many, as well as the content of the findings on signature case Dubai, the way in which these results have been generated will also be of interest. In this chapter we shall first focus on the fixed and semi-fixed elements of place identity and the product offering of Dubai.

INTRODUCTION

Dubai is one of the seven Emirates comprising the United Arab Emirates (UAE), strategically positioned on the north-eastern tip of the Arabian Peninsula, South of the Arabian Gulf (see Figure 5.1). As a Gulf state, like so many other nations in the Middle East, the UAE has faced many challenges in trying to maintain its impressive economic prosperity following recent events, which had a dramatic impact on its geopolitical environment. In particular, the second Gulf War has shown the tremendous impact that the spread of global media has on projecting place image. Everyone will recall the rivalry between regional and international (read American/European) news broadcasters and their differences in the way in which events were reported. Huntington's (1993) 'The Clash of Civilizations' seemed to have become a reality.

Two Gulf Wars, the events of September 11 2001 in the USA, and the ongoing destabilization of the Middle East have probably not improved the Gulf region's image in the West. But Dubai and its leadership have tried to take advantage of this raised level of attention, illustrating to the world the rapid development of the Emirate, its the high level of modernization, but at the same time not shying away from its identity and heritage. In fact, Sheikh Mohammed bin Rashid Al Maktoum, ruler of Dubai (even as crown prince, before the death of his brother, the previous ruler, Sheikh Maktoum bin Rashid Al Maktoum in January 2006, he was the most visible leader), actively promotes entrepreneurship, curtailment of

FIGURE 5.1 | **Map of the United Arab Emirates, including Dubai**

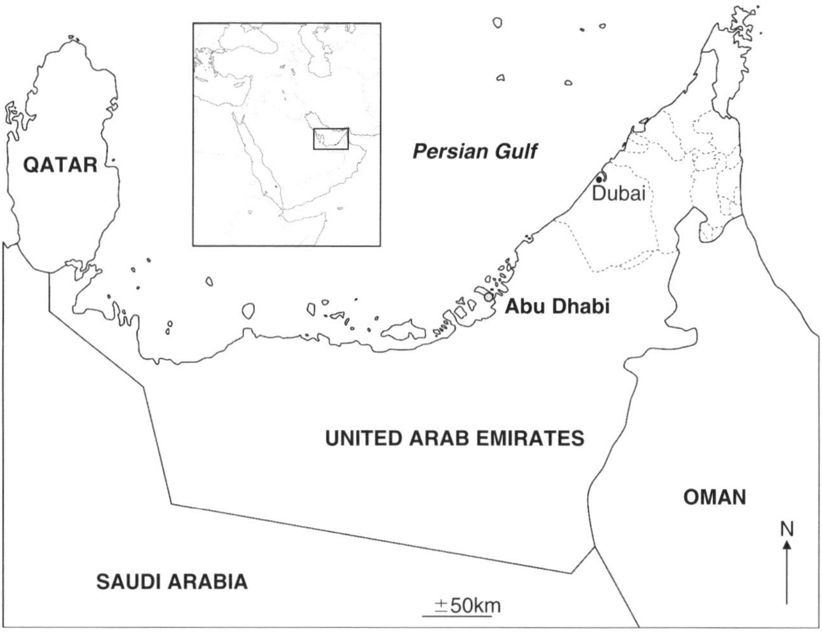

Source: CIA World Fact Book.

bureaucracy and corruption, and modernization, but with respect for heritage, culture and roots. This is illustrated in the UAE's position during the
second Gulf War:

> Sheik Mohammed [who is currently the vice-president] also serves as defence
> minister of the UAE. In this capacity, he oversaw the deployment of 4,000 troops
> to Kuwait in February 2003. Though the UAE opposed the war and advocated giv-
> ing U.N. inspectors more time to find Iraq's famously elusive weapons of mass
> destruction, the sheik made clear that UAE forces would help protect Kuwait.
> Exemplifying a rare instance of Arab unity – the emirates act as a single entity in
> conducting foreign affairs, although each emir remains sovereign within his own
> principality – the UAE serves as a voice of moderation in the often fractious poli-
> tics of the region. (Ringle 2003: p. 3)

In fact, Dubai is using the focus of attention on the region, the renewed
global interest in Islam and Arabic culture, and the attention that Dubai
gets as a rapidly modernizing global hub in the Middle East, as a means of
maintaining and publicizing its identity and heritage. And this raises a key
issue, namely how Dubai might be able to maintain its Islamic identity and

heritage while at the same time globalizing its economy? In fact, development in Dubai is not a matter of tourism dollars supporting the rest of the economy at the cost of losing the identity and authenticity of place, as in many developing nations. Quite the contrary, in fact: the oil dollars and, more importantly, income from trade and foreign investment that are reinvested in infrastructural projects in order to diversify the economy, have created the opportunity to preserve some of the local heritage in a state that was rapidly globalizing in any case. International visits to Dubai have increased only recently, but have rapidly gained significance since the late 1990s, as the oil to non-oil ratio of the gross domestic product (GDP) decreased from almost 36 per cent in 1990 to less than 5 per cent in 2006 (DTCM 2002; Dubai Chamber 2007). In other words, it is not just a matter of – what many people think – local oil wealth being squandered in silly prestigious projects, as we shall show in the rest of this chapter.

HISTORICAL CONSTRUCTIONS OF DUBAI

There are several theories as to how Dubai got its name. One theory is that the word Dubai is a combination of the Farsi words for 'two' and 'brothers', the latter referring to Deira and Bur Dubai, the two parts of Dubai located on either side of the creek that splits the city in half. Others believe that 'Dubai' was so named by people who considered its souk to be a smaller version of a thriving market named 'Daba'. Another possibility is that the name came from a word meaning money – people from Dubai were commonly believed to have money because it was a prosperous trading centre. It is worth mentioning that there is another town named Dubai in the Al Dahna' region of Saudi Arabia, between Riyadh and Ad Dammam.

Dubai was established by people who were originally Bedouin. In the eighteenth century, the most numerous and significant tribe of the UAE was the Bani Yas, made up of around twenty sub-tribes. Originally centred on the Liwa oasis, the Al Bu Falah sub-tribe resettled in 1793 in Abu Dhabi; and from them come the Al Nahyan family, who are the present-day rulers of Abu Dhabi. Traditionally, the members of the Al Bu Falah tribe spent the winter with their camels in the desert, and many of them went pearl fishing during the summer on the boats of other Bani Yas. The Al Bu Falah were the first to acquire property in the Buraimi oasis, and the members of the ruling family have continued this policy systematically up to the present time. In 1833, a large, influential group of the Bani Yas moved to Dubai under the leadership of Maktoum bin Buti Al Maktoum. The Al Maktoum family, a part of the Al Bu Falasah section of the Bani Yas, continues to rule Dubai to this day (Heard-Bey 2001).

In 1952, Sheikh Maktoum bin Buti was succeeded by his brother Sheikh Saeed bin Buti Al Maktoum, who followed his brother's example of making Dubai a safe haven and trading post. He also formed alliances with the sheikhs of Abu Dhabi and Umm Al Qaiwain (an emirate north of the current federalized emirates of Sharjah and Ajman). On the death of Sheikh Saeed, in 1859, Sheikh Hasher bin Maktoum Al Maktoum expanded the policy aimed at regional stability by signing a truce with the British and other sheikhdoms, as a collective to be called, the 'Trucial States'. After Sheikh Hasher's death in 1886, there was a period up to 1912 of several short reigns. In this period the influence of Sheikh Maktoum bin Hasher (the ruler between 1894 and 1906) is notable, as he abolished commercial taxes and facilitated the rapid development of Dubai's port, which became a regular stopping point for steamers. His economic policy is described in British government papers as 'liberal and enlightened' (Burdett 2000, p. 16).

In 1912, a new era began with Sheikh Saeed bin Maktoum Al Maktoum, taking the throne at the age of 34 and ruling for forty-six years until his death in 1958. Sheikh Saeed laid the foundations for diversifying Dubai through the port and souk, pushed by a sharp decline in the pearl fishing industry in the 1930s, because of the arrival of cultured pearls from Japan, and the American and European recession. But true progress only came with Sheikh Rashid bin Saeed Al Maktoum, father of the current ruler, who occupied the throne from 1958 to 1990. It was during his reign that oil was discovered. Being as farsighted as his father, he allowed the oil wealth to be invested in economic diversification through the dredging of the creek to allow access for larger ships and bridging it (with Al Maktoum bridge) to link the two sides (Bur Dubai and Deira), opening the Dubai international airport, and constructing Port Rashid and the Jebel Ali Port, to the south of city. At the same time, investments were made in public health care, schooling and housing, to improve living standards and make Dubai more attractive for potential new residents.

After the British announced in 1968 that they would withdraw from the Gulf completely by 1971, it was Sheikh Rashid who first joined Sheikh Zayed of Abu Dhabi, in 1968, to create a union accord that formed the nucleus of the federation of the United Arab Emirates that was established in 1971. Sheikh Maktoum, the eldest son of Sheikh Rashid, was, in his late twenties, heavily involved in the negotiations. This led him immediately to become the first prime minister of the new UAE under the presidency of Sheikh Zayed and vice-presidency of Sheikh Rashid. When in the 1980s Sheikh Rashid became ill, Sheikh Maktoum and his brothers, Mohammed and Hamdan, formed an effective leadership team that continued with

Sheikh Maktoum as ruler after Sheikh Rashid died in 1990. They together continued the legacy of their father and transformed Dubai into a modern hub, and there was a smooth transition of power when Sheikh Maktoum died in 2006 and Sheikh Mohammed took over as ruler of Dubai and vice-president and prime minister of the UAE. With the way in which the city state of Dubai is now managed and being transformed on an unprecedented scale, Sheikh Mohammed is often referred to internationally as the CEO of Dubai Inc. (Fonda 2006).

The method of consultation of the sheikhs and one of the foundations of the social and management culture of the UAE is the concept of the *majlis* (council). The *majlis* is the publicly accessible part of any household where men congregate: 'In the *majlis* of the sheikh as well as of the business man or of the fisherman on the coast, matters of state and matters of general interest are discussed, while the tiny cups of unsweetened light coffee with cardamom make the round' (Heard-Bey 2001, p. 114). Even today, many influential people still hold open *majlises*, which may be attended by both citizens and expatriates. Rather than in official offices or public agencies, many issues are discussed and decisions taken in the *majlis* of the ruler, which is perceived to uphold its own democratic system (UAE Ministry of Information and Culture 2004, p. 66). The same applies to other Gulf states, and mutual consultation exists with the Gulf Cooperation Council. It is not surprising that several states in the Gulf, such as Bahrain, Qatar and Oman, have followed similar strategies of modernization, though perhaps not on the same scale as Dubai.

But this picture of a rapidly developing region and the modern global hub of Dubai is often not what is perceived internationally, particularly in the West. Since the Second World War, the Middle East has been a region of constant turmoil, which has dramatically influenced the international public perception of this region, as will be illustrated later in this section by Said (1981). It would be hard for anyone in 2009 to be ignorant of the instability in the region, but this state of affairs has not been without historical antecedents. Since the 1950s, colonial withdrawal, Arab–Israeli conflict, the issue of Palestinian refugees, Cold War polemics, US–UK competition for political and economic power and access to the region and, of course, its rich oil resources, have all left their mark. For a brief historical overview of this 'Middle Eastern Muddle' as it evolved in the 1950s–1970s, and its historical relevance to the later geo-political scene, see Graham (1980).

Said (1978, 1991, p. 5) – in discussing how, during earlier times, and still today, the West constructs the Orient – pointed out that 'ideas, cultures and histories cannot seriously be understood or studied without ... their config-urations of power also being studied'. Pritchard and Morgan argue that 'whilst colonialism may have been rejected economically, it continues to exert cultural power in terms of how [for example] tourism imagery constructs peoples and places' (Britton 1979, together with others, cited in Pritchard and Morgan 2001). As Ateljevic and Doorne (2002, p. 650) contend: 'this shift reflects a progressive perpetuation of Western ideology embedded in the power structures of global production and consumption. The so-called crisis of representation and (re)construction of the Other'. With reference to the Arabian Gulf, there are still political movements and scholars who contend that the best approach to deal with the 'situation in the Middle East' (as if there was only a single issue involved) is re-colonization for the sake of securing the world energy supply. As illustrated at length in Said's (1981) *Covering Islam*, political discourse, reporting in the press and the opinion of 'experts' has a tremendous impact on the way in which the West thinks about the East.

As a starting point, it is said that, in a world that has become far too complex and varied, the media, politicians and 'experts' oversimplify reality, for 'ease and instant generalizations' (Said 1981, p. xii). The Orient, and particularly Islamic societies, have suffered from this for a long time, and in recent years it has taken centre stage in world politics:

At present, 'Islam' and 'the West' have taken on a powerful new urgency everywhere [now perhaps more so than in the 1970s, when Said wrote his book]. And we must note immediately that it is always the West, and not Christianity, that seems pitted against Islam. Why? Because the assumption is that whereas 'the West' is greater than and has surpassed the stage of Christianity, its principle religion, the world of Islam – its varied societies, histories, and languages notwithstanding – is still mired in religion, primitivity and backwardness. Therefore, the West is modern, greater than the sum of its parts, full of enriching contradictions and yet always 'Western' in its cultural identity; the world of Islam, on the other hand, is no more than 'Islam', reducible to a small number of unchanging characteristics despite the appearance of contradictions and experiences of variety that seem on the surface to be as plentiful as those in the West. (Said 1981, p. 10)

What Said addressed in 1981 as '*covering* and *covering up*' (p. xii), can still be observed today, and perhaps even more bluntly; one just needs to refer to Michael Moore's *Fahrenheit 9/11*. The horrifying events of the 11 September 2001 (9/11) has polarized the situation. As Said had already stated in 1981: 'Of no other religion or cultural grouping can it be said so assertively as it is now said of Islam that it represents a threat to Western civilization' (p. xii). The question is to what extent this historical, political and cultural discourse has influenced the image that people have of Dubai – arguably one of the most Westernized and liberal parts of the Middle East. It is hoped that many agree with Said's suggestion that 'respect for the concrete detail of human experience, understanding that arises from viewing the Other compassionately, knowledge gained and diffused through moral and intellectual honesty: surely are better, if not easier, goals at present than confrontation and reductive hostility' (Said 1981, p. xxxi).

Indeed, with the increase in trade, travel and tourism, global connectedness and the spread of international media, Said's alternative approach opposing polemics, seems to have gained ground since the mid-1970s. CNN or the National Geographic Channel covering the Hajj pilgrimage in Mecca, or insightful articles such as 'Kingdom on Edge: Saudi Arabia' in *National Geographic* (Viviano 2003), one hopes would help in refining public opinion. In fact, after 9/11, Middle East news websites experienced a surge in popularity in the UK as readers searched for alternative angles on the terrorist crisis (Gibson 2001) and in the USA a renewed interest in the Middle East and Islam was observed (Moore 2001).

Nevertheless, 'no writing [or teaching] is, or can be, so new as to be completely original, for in writing about human society ... no interpretation is without precedents ... and is situational ... Knowledge of other cultures, then, is especially subject to "unscientific" imprecision and to the circumstances of interpretation' (Said 1981, p. 155). One such example merits a last quote from Said:

> In order to make a point about alternative energy sources for Americans, Consolidated Edison of New York (Con Ed) ran a striking television advertisement in the summer of 1980. Film clips of various immediately recognizable OPEC personalities – Yamani, Qaddafi, lesser-known robed Arab figures – alternated with stills as well as clips of other people associated with oil and Islam: Khomeini, Arafat, Hafez al-Assad. None of these figures was mentioned by name, but we were told ominously that 'these men' control America's sources of oil. The solemn voice-over in the background made no reference to who 'these men' actually are or where they come from, leaving it to be felt that this all-male cast of villains has placed Americans in the grip of an unrestrained sadism. It was enough for 'these men' to appear as they have appeared in the newspapers and on television for American viewers to feel a combination of anger, resentment, and fear. And it is this combination of feelings that Con Ed instantly aroused and exploited for domestic commercial reasons, just as a year earlier Stuart Eizenstat, President Carter's domestic policy adviser, had urged the president that 'with strong steps we [should, in original text] mobilize the nation around a real crisis and with a clear enemy – OPEC'. There are two things about the Con Ed commercial that, taken together, form the subject of [Said's] book. One, of course, is Islam, or rather the image of Islam in the West generally and in the Unites States in particular. The other is the use of the image in the West and especially in the United States. (Said 1981, p. 3)

It is of interest here to identify to what extent this image influences consumer perceptions today, particularly with reference to Dubai. While differentiation seems to be taking place, the same imagery still often dominates, because, to be fair, even Michael Moore, while attempting to provide a profound analysis of the Bush administration's actions after 9/11, uses the same imagery to conclude hastily that Bush is sleeping with the enemy. More specifically, we are implicitly told that, in the past, Bush had meetings with white-robed Arab figures and had his businesses financed by Saudi capital, while many Al Qaeda terrorists come from Saudi Arabia, therefore this must be wrong. Has Timothy McVeigh, responsible for the Oklahoma City bombing, had a similar effect on image building with regard to the USA as Osama bin Laden has had on the Middle-East?

DUBAI IN THE NEW GLOBALIZED ECONOMY TODAY

The unprecedented rate of change we observe today is creating a new reality, one that affects each and every one of us politically, economically, socially and culturally. Therefore, we realize that the challenges we face are difficult. (Al Maktoum, H. H. Sheikh Mohammed bin Rashid 2001)

Regardless of the continuous and possibly increasing geopolitical tensions in the region, Dubai is developing fast under Sheikh Mohammed. Not only economically, but also in terms of its socio-cultural and technological environment. With prosperity and development, Dubai has had to import vast numbers of foreign workers. The population of Dubai was estimated to be 1.53 million in 2007 (an increase of 35 per cent over 2005) (Statistics Center of Dubai 2007). Over 80 per cent of this population comprises expatriates, with Asians accounting for approximately two-thirds of these. Only 17 per cent are UAE nationals, and 9 per cent are other Arabs (see Figure 5.2). Approximately 76 per cent of the population is male (Statistics Center of Dubai 2006), because of the large imported male workforce.

At the same time, of the total population in the Gulf Cooperation Council countries, more than half was still below working age in 2001 (HSBC 2001). With such a young population, it is not surprising that Dubai, the 'city of merchants', is a hotspot of innovation. Not only because, considering the age structure and disposable income, this young population is IT-savvy, but also because investments in an information technology infrastructure and globalizing industry and trade are seen as being preconditions for employing this young population in the near future in challenging jobs. They will be looking for white-collar jobs, while demands for labour will remain dependent on imports. The social fabric of the local population and their prosperity has not as at the time of writing created the conditions that encourage

FIGURE 5.2 | **Population breakdown of Dubai, by country of origin**

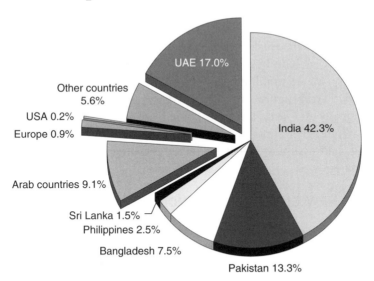

Source: Authors' own visualization of data from 'Dubai Statistics' (Statistics Center of Dubai 2006), Dubai Municipality. Available at http://www.dm.gov.ae/DMEGOV/OSI/dm-osi-mainpage.jsp; accessed 10 October 2007.

young Emirati to seek skilled employment. Emiratization (localization of jobs) initiatives are well under way in the financial and tourism sectors, as appropriate jobs are available there in addition to the public sector, which has traditionally been the main employer of local Emirati. For example, through the initiatives of the Dubai Department of Tourism and Commerce Marketing, the UAE National Human Resource Development and Employment Authority (TANMIA), hotel companies in Dubai and our former colleague of the Emirates Academy of Hospitality Management, John Mowatt, 700 Emirati were working in the hospitality industry in 2008 (DTCM 2008). This is an impressive number considering the fact that, in 2003, a survey among thirty-three UAE hotels showed that out of the 7,362 jobs in these hotels, only fifteen (or roughly 1 in 500) jobs were held by Emirati, with two-thirds of them in managerial positions (Yang 2004).

This shows the cosmopolitan character of the global hub that is Dubai, facilitated by ICT. The UAE has the highest internet penetration rate in the region, with 37 per cent of its residents having online access (CIA 2008), compared with a world average of 21 per cent (Internet World Stats 2008). Mobile phone penetration in Dubai is 163 per cent, with 2.5 million mobile telephone lines (Statistics Center of Dubai 2007), and some segments in the market change phones every seven months, compared to 18–24 months in Europe (AME Info 2003). Nevertheless, Piecowye (2003, Section: Introduction) found that the young female population of UAE National students demonstrated that they, as 'users of CMC [computer mediated communication] technologies in diverse cultural contexts are not simply the hapless victims of globalization via CMC; rather, they are able to determine for themselves what elements of the local and the global they will accept, preserve, or reject in an active process of self-development in dialogue with the multiple cultures surrounding them ... More broadly, [Piecowye's] students stand as examples of users who can consciously choose what elements of global cultures they wish to appropriate while they simultaneously insist on preserving their own cultural values and practices'. Piecowye's study involved a group of twenty-two female university students, of which 94 per cent indicated that they were comfortable using computers and the internet: 'When asked if their [mostly unilingual Arabic speaking and uneducated] mothers used computers the unanimous answer was "never"' (Piecowye 2003, Section: An Application with Students).

In another interesting study, Palfreyman and Al Khalil (2003) looked at the ASCII-ization of Arabic in instant messaging (IM such as MSN or Yahoo Messenger) by female UAE National university students: 'Analyzing ASCII-ized Arabic (AA) can give insights into ways in which CMC is shaped by linguistic, technological and social factors'(Palfreyman and Al Khalil 2003, Section: Abstract). The short extract shown in Table 5.1 shows a sample of the type of discourse studied. The left-hand column is the opening of an online conversation in the corpus used for Palfreyman and Al Khalil's study, while the right-hand column shows an approximate translation in English.

TABLE 5.1 | **Opening of a typical instant messaging conversation in Dubai**

D: السلام عليكم ورحمة الله وبركاته	D: Hello there.
D: مرحبا حمده،، شحالج؟	D: Hi Hamda, how are you doing?
F: w 3laikom essalaaam asoomah ^__^	F: Hi there Asooma ^__^
F: b'7air allah eysallemch .. sh7aalech enty?? [pause]	F: Fine, God bless you. How about you? [pause]
D: el7emdellah b'7eer w ne3meh	D: Fine, great thanks.
D: sorry kent adawwer scripts 7ag project eljava script w rasi dayer fee elcodes	D: Sorry, I was looking for scripts for the java script project and my head is swarming with code.
F: lol	F: lol

Source: Palfreyman and Al Khalil (2003). Reprinted with kind permission of the authors and journal editors.

Although some features of this extract are familiar from other types of CMC in other contexts (turns are typically short, for example, and emoticons such as ^__^ are used to represent emotive content), even a reader with no knowledge of Arabic will notice some linguistic complexity here. The first two turns of the conversation are in Arabic script, then both participants start to use the Latin alphabet instead. The latter part of this extract, although using a different alphabet, still represents Arabic, but letters are interspersed with numerals, and Arabic with English words.... ASCII (American Standard Code for Information Interchange) symbols are used to represent Arabic in IM and other electronic written communication. (Palfreyman and Al Khalil 2003, Section: Introduction)

This could be perceived as a typical example of glocalization, as Palfreyman and Al Khalil found that even other Arabs, more specifically 'non-UAE Arab teachers aged over 40 ... indeed find it almost impossible to read, apparently owing to unfamiliarity both with the orthographic conventions, and with the vernacular used' (Palfreyman and Al Khalil 2003, last para. before Conclusion). In addition, respondents believed that this ASCII-ized Arabic in Dubai originated from UAE National friends and family members studying abroad, where Arabic language support is not provided on computers. This mix of local identity, tradition and globalization is well described by Ringle (2003, p. 1) – though journalistic in style, it merits reference here, as it provides a good third-party account of the situation:

At the Sheikh Rashid terminal of Dubai International Airport – a glittering temple of Ali Baba eclecticism and gateway to this 1,500-square-mile [less than 4,000 square kilometres] principality on the Persian Gulf – a visitor steps onto a carpet patterned after wind-ruffled desert sand, passes goldtone replicas of palm trees and continues past a shop-till-you-drop duty-free store where one can buy a bar of gold or a raffle ticket for a Maserati. A few steps away stands the special departure gate for Hajj pilgrims en route to Mecca. They have their own Starbucks counter. Beyond the terminal lies a startling skyline: high-rise hotels and office buildings of stainless steel and blue glass springing straight out of the desert, the backdrop to a waterfront where wooden dhows laden with Indian teak and spices from Zanzibar sail out of antiquity. Only ten minutes away, in the mind-numbing vastness of Deira City Centre, Dubai's largest suburban-style shopping mall [at the time], children in traditional Arab robes lose themselves in American video games. Veiled women, swathed in billowing black and sporting gold bracelets and diamonds, shop designer boutiques.

So, while the process of globalization in Dubai seems to move faster in some areas than in others, it also needs to be mentioned again, of course, that Dubai has experienced tremendous growth in various economic sectors. Coinciding with the massive change in the socio-cultural fabric, the enlightened political approach and intense technological advancement as described above, alongside the economic development of the Emirate of Dubai, is impressive. Its GDP has been growing at a compounded annual rate of 13 per cent since the year 2000 (Government of Dubai 2007), and reached US$46 billion in 2006 (Dubai Chamber 2007).

As illustrated earlier, this growth is not, as many believe, generated by increased oil revenues, but rather through Dubai's success in building an international place brand for foreign investment, trade and tourism. As the GDP share of oil constantly decreased, trade, for long an important source of income for Dubai, has increased its GDP share by an average of 6.7 per cent per year since the year 2000. A slightly lower, but still significant growth in GDP contribution has been seen in the construction and real estate sectors (Government of Dubai 2007); the latter, probably largely as a result of increased foreign direct investments (FDI). In this regard, the UAE (with US$16 billion, in ninth position) was just behind India (with US$17.5 billion) in the top-10 emerging markets when it came to receiving FDI in 2006 (Economist Intelligence Unit 2007, p. 24). When this is calculated per capita, the UAE is ranked eighth in the world (among all nations, not just emerging markets), just behind countries like Switzerland or Sweden (Economist Intelligence Unit 2007, p. 35).

Much of this FDI is believed to be attracted not only by the growing trade sector, but in particular by the real estate boom (Economist Intelligence Unit 2007). The Statistics Center of Dubai (2007) reports 2007 land deals worth over US$30 billion, and 2,159 buildings completed at US$4 billion. In the same year, Dubai alone had 2.6 million square metres of commercial space under development and was ranked third in terms of global office real estate construction activity. Moscow (2.9 million square metres) and Shanghai (2.8 million square metres) took the top two spots (Colliers International 2007). But again, Dubai's hub function is illustrated by the real estate ownership: 60 per cent of real estate buyers are not from the region, but from Europe or Asia (Plapler and Chan 2007, p. 12).

This influx of talent, second-home owners, investors, traders and tourists has resulted in the number of internationals visitors (those staying in hotel establishments) more than tripling in a decade – from 1.9 million in 1996 to 7 million in 2007 (DTCM 2007d). Not only has demand soared, but so has supply. Figure 5.3 shows the growth in number of hotel rooms between the years 2000 and 2009 (including planned projects under construction or licensed and scheduled to open in 2008–9). That this was and is a healthy growth is supported by the observation that the average price

FIGURE 5.3 | **Dubai's growth in supply of rooms in hotels and serviced apartments**

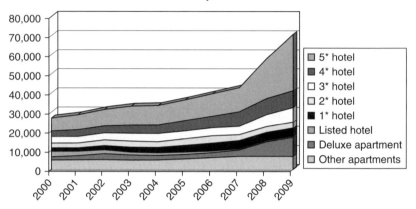

Source: DTCM (2007d) hotel statistics data, including listing of 'on-books' planned projects by UniGlobe Dubai.

FIGURE 5.4 | **Dubai's hotel performance statistics, 2000–7**

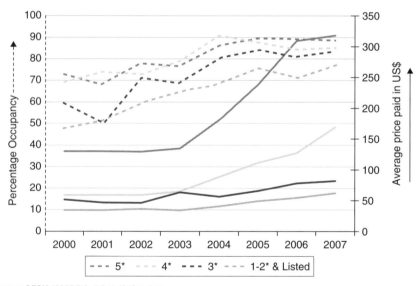

Source: DTCM (2007d) hotel statistics data.

paid per occupied room has soared in recent years, as depicted in Figure 5.4. This price explosion occurred after occupancy levels increased rapidly between 2001 and 2004. Since then, annual average occupancy levels for 3, 4 and 5-star hotels have always been over 80 per cent, and close to 90 per cent for 5-star hotels. This means that, regardless of the increase in accommodation supply and the continuous announcement of new projects, hotels remained virtually full, outpaced by demand, resulting in rapid price inflation. According to HRG's 2007 hotel survey, Dubai was the fourth most expensive destination in the world, with a RevPAR (revenue per available room in their database) of £164.52, after Moscow with £248, New York and Paris; and just ahead of Milan. Dubai had the highest growth rate, however, with a 21 per cent increase in local currency value (HRG 2008) (confirmed by www.hotelbenchmark.com).

This process of growth started in the early 1980s, when Dubai became a popular refuelling station on airline routes between Europe and Asia. The Dubai government then made a conscious decision to build a large-scale resort hotel, outside Dubai, beyond Jebel Ali port, in the empty desert along the coast (Jebel Ali resort). Now in front of Palm Jebel Ali and soon at the heart of the new Waterfront development, the resort, which was refurbished in 2003, attempted to draw a stop-over market into Dubai, by offering a one-stop sun-drenched holiday destination including a 9-hole golf course, riding stables, a shooting club and marina. This proved to be a lucrative decision and soon more resorts were built in the city's southern Jumeirah district, and the destination's attractiveness was enhanced by large, luxurious shopping malls and tours and safaris into the desert. Of course, with economic growth and expanded trade links there also came increased business travel to Dubai, creating the second pillar for a thriving tourism industry (F. Bardin, General Manager of Arabian Adventures and long-standing member of the Emirates Group management team, personal communication, 10 May 2003).

The fact that Dubai is attracting visitors from afar, functioning as a global hub as opposed to just a sea–sun–sand tourist destination, as perceived by many, is illustrated in Figure 5.5. 'Only' 32 per cent of visitors are Europeans, 22 per cent are from Asia and 30 percent are Arabs; and 32 per cent of all these visitors travel to Dubai for business purposes (DTCM 2007b). Figure 5.6 shows that Dubai is serving in particular the long-haul leisure tourism market, but also a balanced business/leisure travel market closer to home. Figure 5.6 further illustrates Dubai's hub function, where 'general holiday' and 'beach' represent only 27 per cent and 10 per cent of leisure trips, respectively, but, for example, 'visiting friends and relatives' and 'shopping' represent another 21 per cent and 16 per cent of leisure trips, respectively. For business travellers, the meetings industry (meetings both informal and organized, incentives, conferences and exhibitions) is highly relevant, but free independent travellers (FIT) also represent 22 per cent of business travellers.

FIGURE 5.5 | **Hotel establishment guests, by nationality**

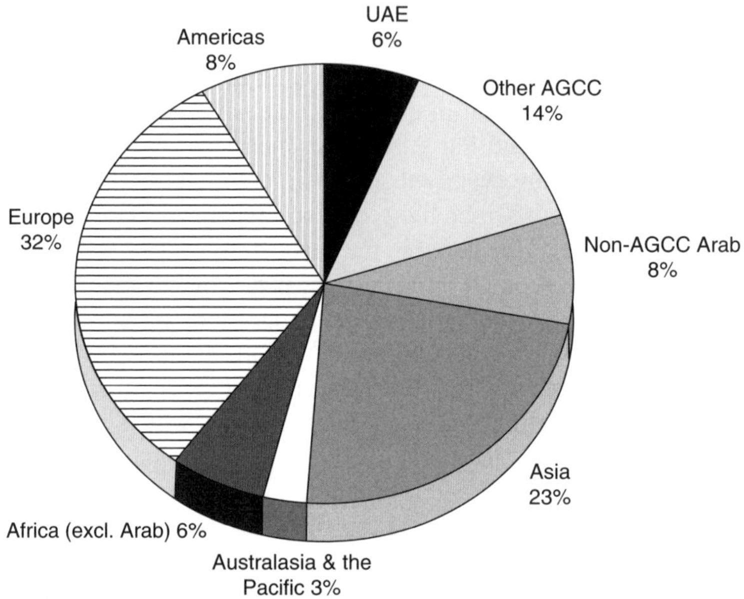

Source: DTCM (2007d). Reprinted with kind permission of the Government of Dubai: Department of Tourism and Commerce Marketing.

So where has all this international attention come from? What does Dubai have to offer?

DIVERSIFIED PRODUCT OFFERING

The success of Dubai as a global brand, to date, has not been built on fancy brand communication strategies, but rather through bold actions with impact. Mega-projects such as islands in the shape of palm trees and the world map have attracted international media attention, but the Dubai Strategic Plan (Government of Dubai 2007) links these landmark developments to policies, and what have been called 'strategic thrusts' across all aspects of civil society as they are needed to sustain Dubai as a global hub. The strategic plan includes a focused economic development plan based on sector prioritizations, aligned with business portfolio management, but with attention being paid to productivity, human capital, innovation and quality of life. This is linked to social development, which includes the preservation of national identity; the increased localization of jobs; improved schooling, health care and social services; raised awareness of equality and acceptable working conditions for Dubai's workforce, and the attraction

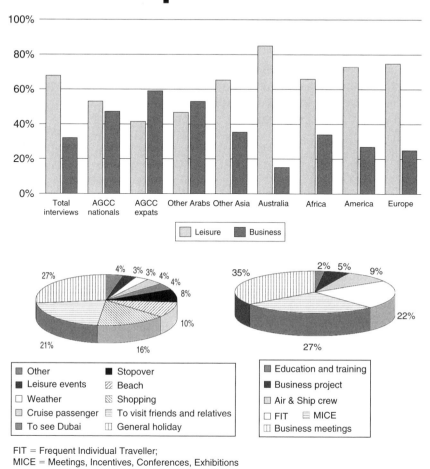

FIT = Frequent Individual Traveller;
MICE = Meetings, Incentives, Conferences, Exhibitions

Source: DTCM (2007b) Reprinted with kind permission of the Government of Dubai: Department of Tourism and Commerce Marketing.

and retention of required expertise; plus an enriched cultural environment. In the areas of infrastructure, land and environment, the strategic plan aims for optimized land use and distribution while preserving natural resources; the provision of efficient energy, electricity and water supplies; an integrated road and transportation system; and a safe, clean, attractive and sustainable environment. Strategic thrusts in the area of security, justice and safety focus on law and order; the protection of rights and freedoms; the management of crises and disasters; access to justice and accuracy, clarity and efficiency in investigations and judgments; plus the protection of general safety, public health and quality of life. Finally, the government itself is aiming for excellence through a strategic and forward-looking focus; enhanced organizational structures and accountability; increased efficiency; enhanced responsiveness and customer service; and empowered and motivated public service employees.

The economic strategy focuses on sectors such as travel and tourism, financial services, professional services, transport and logistics services, construction and trade. The latter is supported by the free-trade zone policy. After the long-established Jebel Ali Free Zone, which focuses on trade, manufacturing, assembly and regional re-export from Jebel Ali Port, the government has created several non-industrial free zones in recent years, such as the Dubai International Financial Centre, Dubai Media City, Dubai Internet City, Dubai Silicon Oasis, Dubai Healthcare City, Dubai Multi Commodities Centre, and the Dubai Biotechnology and Research Park (Dubiotech). Free zones create a tax-free environment where companies are allowed to operate under 100 per cent foreign ownership. Outside of the free zones, taxation still does not apply, but at least 50 per cent local ownership is mandatory.

The vision of the Dubai International Financial Centre is to position Dubai as a universally recognized hub for institutional finance, and as the gateway to the region for capital and investment. Dubai's government hopes that the DIFC will eventually stand on a par with international financial centres in New York, London, Hong Kong and Tokyo. Dubai Media City, in close proximity to Dubai Internet City, is the media community for the region. Inaugurated in January 2001, Dubai Media City has become a global media hub by creating an infrastructure, environment and attitude that has enabled media-focused enterprises to operate locally, regionally and globally out of Dubai. Some of the most widely recognized names in the global media industry, including CNN, Reuters, CNBC, MBC, BBC, EMI and Lintas Middle East North Africa, have established operations in Dubai Media City, where the promise is one of having the 'Freedom to Create'. Dubai Internet City has played a key role in transforming Dubai into a hub for the new economy, and is the regional centre for technology companies wishing to service the region. Dubai Internet City is home to 350 companies, including Microsoft, Hewlett Packard, Oracle, IBM, Cisco, Compaq and MSN Arabia. In the same area, Knowledge Village provides a free zone for international higher education institutes to offer their bachelors and masters programmes (www.tecom.ae).

In order to attract foreign direct investment, second-home ownership and tourism, several remarkable mixed-use projects have received international attention. One of the most impressive projects, which involves the creation of three of the world's largest man-made islands, is Palm Jumeirah (5 km diameter), Palm Jebel Ali (7 km diameter) and Palm Deira (12.45 × 7.5 km). Together with The World, a cluster of 300 islands in the shape of the world

FIGURE 5.7 | Map of Dubai including major ongoing development projects

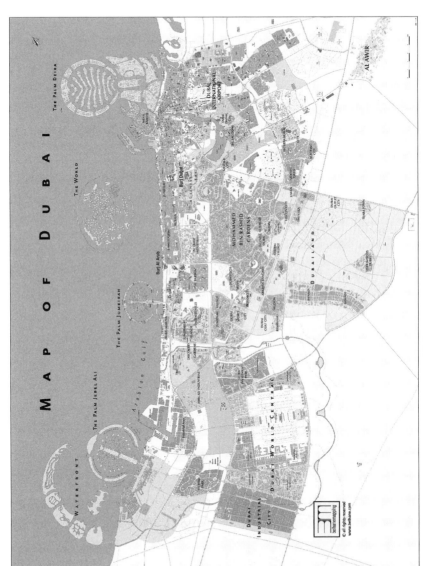

Source: Map reproduced with the kind permission of Belhane.com.

map and the Waterfront development, these projects will add 1,500 kilome-
tres of coastline to the existing 70-kilometre coastline of Dubai. The success of the projects, in addition to the statistics presented above, is
illustrated by the fact that the 4,000 villa apartments on Palm Jumeirah
were sold in 72 hours (Nakheel 2008).

Palm Jumeirah, Palm Jebel Ali and Palm Deira will offer five-star hotels
and resorts including Atlantis, marina berths, a permanent Cirque du Soleil
show, water theme parks, restaurants, shopping malls, sports facilities, luxury spas, schools and mosques, as well as a permanent home for the retired
QE2 ocean liner. In particular, Palm Jebel Ali, as part of the Waterfront
development, will be a tourist destination in itself. The significance of the
concept of designing the major islands in the shape of palm trees is that it
was inspired by Dubai's own heritage, with the date palm and water long
considered to be the most important sources of life, providing the UAE
people with food, shelter and simple boats, thus laying the foundations for
trade, which has been the major source of Dubai's prosperity. Also, Arab
Eclectic will be the signature architectural style on Palm Jumeirah (Dubai
Palm Developers LLC 2003).

Dubai has several attractions that have drawn visitors, second-home
owners and talent to Dubai. First, of course, the warm waters of the Arabian
Gulf combined with year-round sunshine are major natural assets in high
demand. Hence, the strategy of creating investment opportunities through
the creation of waterfront properties does not come as a surprise to many.
Annually, the Dubai Shopping Festival also attracts millions of visitors.
The Global Village funfair, as part of the Shopping Festival, attracted 4.2
million visitors from 160 countries in 2006–7 (Tatweer 2008). Other major
annual events attracting many travellers from around the world are the
Dubai World Cup – the richest horse race in the world; the Dubai Desert
Classic golf tournament; the Dubai Duty Free Tennis Open; and numerous
international exhibitions and conferences.

The focus on sports as one of the place building elements links in with
the huge Dubailand project. When completed, the US$60-billion-plus
Dubailand project will include more than forty-five leisure, entertainment
and tourist facilities. Perhaps one of the most innovative components of the
development is the US$2.5-billion Dubai Sports City. In will be home to
four sports stadiums (a 60,000-seat multi-purpose outdoor stadium; a
25,000-capacity cricket stadium; a 10,000-seat multi-purpose indoor arena;
and a field hockey venue for 5,000 spectators); an Ernie Els golf course; the
International Cricket Council's Cricket Academy and global head office
(relocated from London); the Butch Harmon School of Golf; the
Manchester United Soccer Schools; and a David Lloyd Tennis Academy in
addition to residential, commercial and retail developments. Rein and

FIGURE 5.8 | **Jumeirah properties: Madinat Jumeirah (front) and Burj Al Arab (left, back)**

Source: Photograph by Robert Govers.

Shields (2007) have used this project as an example of how places can use sport as a branding platform. However, we think that this is exaggerating the importance of Dubai Sport City for brand Dubai when seen in the full context of the entire Dubailand project and the economic development and diversification of Dubai as a whole. For example, the main feature of the shopping provision of Dubailand will be the proposed Mall of Arabia (Dubai Tourism Development Company 2003). Together with the adjacent Burj Dubai, the tallest tower in the world, which incorporates the US$1-billion Dubai Mall by Emaar Properties, both malls will be bigger than the Edmonton Mall in Canada or the Mall of America in Minnesota (Jenkins 2004, p. 8). Hence, retail could be seen as another vital element in the diversification strategy of Dubai. Nevertheless, sports and star power have played a major role in building the image of modern Dubai. Think, for example, of stunts like Tiger Woods teeing off from the helipad of the Burj Al Arab, or Roger Federer and Andre Agassi playing tennis there ahead of the Dubai Duty Free Tennis Open. Jumeirah (the Dubai-based company that manages the Burj Al Arab hotel) has estimated that the latter public relations stunt generated US$8.5 million in press coverage.

The common thread in the above description of Dubai's current and future product offering is that, often, in projects, an attempt is made to link new developments to the history and heritage of the region. Islands in the shape of palm trees, the Burj Dubai tallest building in the world inspired by the desert rose, and an emphasis on sports embedded in the culture are just some examples. The same holds true for some of the internationally renowned hotel properties, such as the Madinat Jumeirah, one of the latest additions to Jumeirah's portfolio of flagship properties in Dubai, which also includes the Burj al Arab (or Arab Tower, built on a man-made island 200 metres into the sea, in the shape of a billowing sail of the local traditional wooden vessel called the dhow – see Figure 5.8). Madinat Jumeirah focuses on sustainable tourism growth by taking advantage of Dubai's unique heritage and cultural identity in building a 900-bedroom Arabian resort. The resort includes three hotels, over forty restaurants and cafés, a conference centre, outdoor amphitheatre, health spa, and souk, and 3 km of waterways winding through the resort with villas scattered around them, all designed using local UAE architecture and interior design (Jumeirah International 2003).

Another initiative, focusing on sustainability and the preservation of Dubai's natural heritage is the Desert Conservation Reserve, which will be centred on the Al Maha Desert Resort, the Emirates Airline Group's hotel outside the city. The resort will be expanded almost tenfold to form the heart of a new 225 sq. km Conservation Reserve, safeguarding nearly 5 per cent of Dubai's land and unique desert habitat (Stensgaard 2003a).

Under pressure from the increasing travel demands, intermodal transport systems have been expanded in recent years. As well as a rapidly growing road network infrastructure (including new toll roads), a luxury cruise terminal, promptly developing public bus services and a metro system, of which the first two lines with a combined length of 35 km will open in 2009, the Dubai Department of Civil Aviation opened the US$540-million Sheikh Rashid Terminal in April 2000. It was the world's fastest growing airport in 2007 in terms of international passenger throughput, with a growth rate of 19.3 per cent. The airport handled a total of 34.3 million passengers, well over the projected 33 million for the year, according to Airports Council International. In addition, anticipating this growth, the government of Dubai committed to an expansion plan of US$4.1 billion for Dubai International Airport and its affiliated divisions in 2002 (Rahman 2003). Even as Dubai International's expansion nears completion, work is already in progress on a project to build the world's largest airport barely 40 km away. On completion, the Al Maktoum International at Dubai World Central airport city will be capable of catering for 120 million passengers annually and handling 12 million tonnes of cargo at its sixteen air cargo terminals. One of the total of six runways at Al Maktoum International opened for cargo operations in 2008.

In line with this projected growth of the Dubai travel hub, Emirates Airlines flew in the face of the struggling airline industry by announcing the largest-ever aircraft order at the 2003 Paris Air Show, on top of the orders already registered in 2001 at the Dubai Air Show (Stensgaard 2003b). In November 2007, Emirates signed another historic civil aviation aircraft order for 120 Airbus A350s, eleven A380s and twelve Boeing 777-300ERs worth an estimated US$34.9bn based on list prices. Emirates' total order book in 2007 stood at 246 aircraft, all wide-body, and worth over US$60 billion (Zawya 2007).

CREATING BRAND DUBAI

The imaginative projects that receive considerable international attention create a de facto strong place brand. This is the result of the vision and deter-mination of just a small group of people in Dubai. While the UAE federal government focuses on foreign policy, development aid, defence, education, social welfare, justice and safety, health care and rural development, the international competitiveness of brand Dubai is really sustained through local initiatives and policies in the Emirate of Dubai. The royal family, with Sheikh Mohammed at the helm, is the driving force and visionary inspira-tion. Sheikh Mohammed's son, Sheikh Hamdan bin Mohammed bin Rashid Al Maktoum and Crown Prince of Dubai, is also chairman of the Dubai Executive Council (also called The Corporate Office) that oversees the implementation of the Dubai Strategic Plan as formulated by Sheikh Mohammed, as well as overseeing the operations of the various government departments. The Executive Office also supervises Dubai World, a holding company with executive council member Sultan Ahmed bin Sulayem as chairman (his brother, Khalid bin Sulayem, is director-general of the Department of Tourism and Commerce Marketing). One of Dubai World's companies, Nakheel, is responsible for developing the coastal mega-projects such as Palm Jumeirah, Palm Jebel Ali, Palm Deira, The World and Waterfront. The same company manages various free zones, including the well-established Jebel Ali Port, with Dubai Ports World (DP World) as oper-ator. The latter company received international news media attention with the acquisition of the P&O Steam Navigation Company (UK) for US$6.8 billion, with assets in the USA, which was only approved in 2006 once Dubai Ports World agreed to divest itself of its US assets after a political dis-agreement between President Bush and the US Congress (Economist Intelligence Unit 2007) over national security concerns. Also in the Dubai Executive Council is Sheikh Mohammed's uncle, Sheikh Ahmed bin Saeed Al Maktoum, as vice-chairman. Sheikh Ahmed is president of the Department of Civil Aviation, which manages Dubai International Airport and the future Al Maktoum International Airport, and the new Dubai World

Central airport city. However, Sheikh Ahmed is also chairman and CEO of the Emirates Group, which includes the airline, but also Emirates Holidays tour operators, airport handlers, Dnata travel agents, Emirates Hotels and Resorts, Arabian Adventures incoming operator, and Congress Solutions International. Former chairman of The Executive Office, Mohammed Al Gergawi is now the executive chairman and CEO of Dubai Holding, a holding company belonging to the Government of Dubai (Sheikh Mohammed owns 99.67 per cent of the company) (Zawya 2008). Dubai Holding's member companies include the Jumeirah Group (which manages Dubai's flagship hotel properties such as Burj Al Arab, Jumeirah Beach Hotel, Madinat Jumeirah and Emirates Towers Hotel, but also properties in New York and London, and many others are planned); Tatweer, which is responsible for the Dubailand development; and TECOM Investments, which manages several free zones. Finally, the person in charge of the important Dubai government Department of Economic Development is Mohammed Ali Alabbar, who is also on the Executive Council and is chairman of Emaar, one of the world's largest real estate companies. Emaar is responsible for projects such as Dubai Marina and Burj Dubai and is publicly listed on the Dubai Financial Market, but majority owned by the government of Dubai. It is not surprising, then, that *Forbes* magazine has compared Dubai to a corporation, with Sheikh Mohammed as its chief executive (Swibel 2004)

As mentioned above, there are several government departments which provide the institutional framework for the diversification of the economy. In general, the government acts very much in an enabling capacity, providing the vision, initial infrastructure and investment to attract private sector investors: 'With business-friendly policies in a tax free environment, there appears to be no shortage of private sector companies and individual investors wanting to participate in these projects. To assist this process, the government has set up a number of specialist departments' (Jenkins 2004, p. 9).

The Economic Department was established in Dubai on 18 March 1992. In 1996 the name was changed to the Department of Economic Development. The Department is responsible for the economic planning and reporting for the Dubai economy. It also has responsibility for business licensing, the protection of industrial and trade property rights, business regulation and registration; strategic business planning for Dubai; identification of opportunities for investors; and it offers assistance with project planning and execution (www.dubaided.gov.ae).

The Dubai Chamber (of Commerce and Industry) was established in 1965 in order to defend and protect the general economic interests of its 108,000 members (as at 2008), promote business development and investment opportunities in Dubai, and facilitate network opportunities and the interaction of members with the local, regional and international community. The Dubai

Chamber has sector groups and committees representing economic sectors, such as the Dubai Exhibition Conventions Organizers, Dubai Property Group (Dubai Property Society), Dubai Shipping Agents Association, Supply Chain and Logistics Business Group, Travel and Tour Agent group, and the Land Transport group (www.dubaichamber.ae).

Established in January 1997, the Department of Tourism and Commerce Marketing (DTCM) has two main areas of responsibility. The first of these includes all the functions of the former Dubai Commerce and Tourism Promotion Board (DCTPB), which had been in existence since 1989 and concentrated on the international promotion of Dubai's commerce and tourism interests. The DTCM's second main area of responsibility is as the principal authority for the planning, supervision and development of the tourism sector in the Emirate. As part of its marketing role, the DTCM plans and implements an integrated programme of international promotions and publicity activities. This programme includes exhibition participation, marketing visits, presentations and road shows, familiarization and assisted visits, advertising brochure production and distribution, media relations and enquiry information services. In addition to its head office in Dubai, the DTCM has eighteen overseas offices. The DTCM has been very successful in establishing and promoting brand Dubai, considering the numerous awards it has received for best exhibition stand or promotion campaign. In assuming its administrative responsibilities within Dubai, the DTCM takes care of the licensing of hotels, hotel apartments, tour operators, tourist transport companies and travel agents. Its supervisory role also covers all touristic, archaeological and heritage sites, tourism conferences and exhibitions, the operation of tourist information services, and the organization and licensing of tour guides (www.dubaitourism.ae).

The Dubai Shopping Festival (DSF) Committee co-ordinates the festival, which takes place each year in the mild winter months. Held for the first time in 1996, the Dubai Shopping Festival has been a milestone in the development of the nation's travel industry, as it brought together the private and public sectors. Until 2002, covering the month of March, the DSF was conceived purely as a retail event, the primary aim of which was to revitalize the retail trade in Dubai. It was later developed into a comprehensive tourism product, in line with Dubai's far-sighted ambition to set global standards in every field. Attractions include the Global Village funfair and expo, several firework displays every night, theatre and music performances in public parks, street artists, fashion shows, sporting events, a night souk, desert camp, and, of course, daily raffle draws with a value of over US$1 million, and including prizes of cars, cash and gold. The DSF committee is also responsible for organizing the Dubai Summer Surprises (DSS), a smaller version of the shopping festival, but taking place over the summer months, primarily aiming to entertain resident families to discourage people from travelling abroad for long periods to escape the summer heat. So, apart from entertaining the children, the DSS is needed to keep retail afloat during this quiet period of the year between the beginning of June and the end of August (www.mydsf.ae; see also Gabr 2004).

The Department of Civil Aviation is responsible for managing Dubai's International Airports, the first of which was established in 1959, when the late Ruler of Dubai, Sheikh Rashid bin Saeed Al Maktoum, ordered the construction of the first airfield, located only 4 km from the city centre. Dubai Duty Free celebrated twenty years of operation on 20 December 2003. In 2007, sales reached US$880 million, representing a 24 per cent increase over the previous year, ranking as the third-largest travel retailer in the world after high-traffic airports such as London Heathrow and Seoul Incheon. Raffles of cars, cash and gold are also a major attraction at the airport duty free (www.dca.gov.ae and www.dubaidutyfree.com).

Dubai Municipality, established in the 1940s, designs, builds and manages the municipal infrastructure and other related facilities. Responsibilities that are relevant to brand Dubai include the maintenance of several public parks, three of which include beach facilities. Other relevant activities include coastal zone monitoring and public transportation services. Of significance also is the landscaping of all major public roads, intersections and other public areas, the maintenance of which needs to be done through irrigation. The city's waste water is collected and purified so that desalinated water can be used twice, first for households, then for irrigation. The municipality's Historical Buildings Section takes care of architectural conservation and the maintenance of historical sites (www.dm.gov.ae).

However, even though these government departments create the enabling environment, it is obvious that the major contributor to the success of brand Dubai is the private sector, as will be illustrated in the next section.

SUCCESS FACTORS

In *Sand to Silicon*, Sampler and Eigner (2003) outline a model of how the large-scale rapid growth of Dubai has been achieved, and they pinpoint the reasons for Dubai's success:

- Leadership that is visionary, inspirational and embraces risks; that is demanding but supportive; and that builds confidence.

- A leanness of organizational structure and bureaucracy, which helps to speed things up.

- Openness to outside influence and competition, and to the views of all stakeholders.

- Good communication channels and access to decision-makers.

- A business culture founded on trust – but not without regulation where it is necessary to reinforce trust and confidence in the system.

Jenkins (2004, pp. 12–14) elaborates on a few similar points, plus additional observations about some of the underlying factors of the success of development in Dubai:

First, the ruling family, and particularly the ruler, His Highness Sheikh Mohammed bin Rashid Al Maktoum, have been the main source of entrepreneurial vision. By any comparison, Dubai's transformation from a desert sheikhdom relying almost exclusively on entrepôt trade to a cosmopolitan, urban centre with high standards of living and amenities has been remarkable. Equally noteworthy has been the choice of tourism as a major input to the development and diversification strategy. Despite the Arab tradition of offering hospitality to travellers, commercial hospitality reflected in meeting the needs and demands of international travellers is a different dimension. It reflects well on the tolerance of the ruling family and the Emirati that this development has taken place without upsetting the cultural norms that prevail in Dubai, the country and the region. There are two other aspects of the ruling family's intervention in the development and diversification process. The family is known to be a substantial investor in projects and therefore family members are risk-takers themselves, which provides other investors with a greater degree of confidence in projects. Another feature is the short chain of decision-taking retained in the ruler's corporate office until projects are officially announced and responsibility for implementation is allocated to an individual or organization. Implementation strategy is related to very tight contractual deadlines, which are monitored. The ruling family is effectively the government and is an example of government providing an enabling environment to attract private-sector partners (also supported by Ringle 2003).

Second, what is noticeable in the Dubai experience is the integrated nature of development. Each sector with development potential has been activated. Infrastructural investment is not only project specific but also general. Massive investment in roads, utilities, transportation and the airport, for example, benefit all sectors, including tourism, real estate and industry. In particular there has been a very heavy investment in information technology; for example, Internet

City. In many ways, what has happened and is currently happening in Dubai very much reflects the past experience of Singapore (also supported by Henderson 2006).

Third, the development philosophy is based on the public–private partnership (PPP) model. The importance of the ruling family, its participative involvement in projects, and its continuing entrepreneurial vision and energy, has attracted national and international investors. The Dubai International Financial Centre initiative is not only another way to diversify the economy but will also provide a means of gathering local financial resources and channelling them to projects within the region rather than seeing them flow outwards, which was the situation in the past.

Fourth, all new projects aspire to match, if not surpass, the best international standards. This is noticeable in the field of tourism and leisure, where projects have been aimed at the high end of the market. With increasing investment in this sector, land prices are rising fast and this in turn affects the types of projects that are commissioned. This trend in part explains the mega-project approach and the emphasis given to building 'the biggest and best'. The national airline Emirates reflects this trend, with the purchase or lease of an ultra-modern fleet, achieving award-winning service, and in extending its network. It is one of the few airlines to be consistently profitable since the 9/11 terrorist incident.

Fifth, another aspect of development has been the preference for what can be called iconic projects. There is a case for suggesting that, in building the Burj Al Arab hotel, Dubai has created its own international icon, which, like the pyramids in Egypt and the Taj Mahal in India, is readily identified with the country. Following from this, publicity about Dubailand, the first under-sea hotel, Palm Jumeirah, Palm Jebel Ali, Palm Deira, The World and the current construction of 'the world's highest building' to be named Burj Dubai, all seek to anchor Dubai on the international tourism map. It is noticeable that the Burj Al Arab is able to charge strictly limited groups of tourists US$40 per person for a guided tour of the property!

Sixth, is the ready stream of investors in the new projects. No data is available for the capital investment in development or in the tourism sector. What can be said is that many of the mega projects are, and will be, private-sector financed. The development of a real estate market, even without a finalized legislative framework, has seen many of the local and international banks create a mortgage market. It is very unusual for financial institutions to create such a market without a legal framework, but such is the reputation of Dubai's rulers that this does not seem to have been a hindrance.

Seventh, it is also noticeable that the rapid development and transformation of Dubai seems to have taken place without any social and cultural upsets. Local people seem to be tolerant of visitors, perhaps because there has been a very large expatriate community in the Emirate for some time. It may also be that visitors have been informed of the cultural and social norms prevailing and respect them. This is an area that requires specific research. But regular reading of the local newspapers and the letters columns has shown no evidence of any articles or comments on tourism affecting local social and cultural norms. This does not mean that changes have not occurred, but it does suggest that these have not been particularly negative. Another factor might be the preponderance of visitors from Arab countries [approximately 30 per cent of the market; see Figure 5.5] who are mainly Muslims and are therefore well aware of cultural parameters.

But, of course, there are downsides to this rosy picture. Questions are being raised about over-supply of assets, particularly in the hotel and shopping sectors, and speculative bubbles. The former is not of immediate concern, as long as the tourist board is able to continue to attract yearly increases in visitor arrivals as projected in the strategic plan, which has been successful considering the price hikes and urgent call for expansion heard in the tourism industry, as illustrated above. However, the latter issue in terms of the proliferation of shopping malls is of concern. As the Director of Leasing and Marketing for Dubai Festival City said in an address to the Middle East Council of Shopping Centers: 'Overbuilding is prevalent, the captive radius is shrinking, and with it, customer numbers. This situation is compounded by the fact that in some malls landlords and retailers are facing a situation where the same shopping experience is available in several locations, driving down footfall rates' (Shopping Developments in Dubai 2003, p. 40). At the same time, inflation is high, as is debt financing and money laundering, while competition from neighbouring countries is increasing (Fonda 2006). These are all factors that question the economic sustainability of Dubai Inc., but at the time of writing there is no indication of any weakening.

Also, although positive in economic terms, the globalization through tourism and trade has created its own socio-cultural issues, such as prostitution, access to alcohol and imbalances in cultural norms between hosts and guests. However, none of this has been studied or substantiated, though

2008 saw a police clampdown on 'indecent behaviour' on public beaches after two people were caught allegedly having sex on a beach (CNN 2008). Nevertheless, while one would expect public opinion to raise social issues, particularly in the Gulf region, they seem to be more pressing in other Islamic societies in the Orient, where one would least expect them. The *Washington Post* (Cooper 1997), for example, reported on tourism in the Maldives. The government there bans tourists from bringing alcoholic drinks into the country. It gives vacationers lists of Islamic rules aboard their flights to the Maldives, and actively discourages the local population from seeking employment in the hospitality industry in positions where they have to serve alcohol. These are all policies that the UAE and Dubai governments do not apply. Quite the reverse, in fact: the government runs programmes that are successful in bringing local nationals into hospitality jobs. Only time will tell what the ambitious plans for Dubai's future will bring when it comes to the changing social fabric of the Emirati society. In any case, it is of interest to note that, among others, Magala (2002) has argued that the above-described processes of globalization, modernization and 'detraditionalization' could easily lead to a fundamentalist revival, which 'contrary to appearances, is not a traditionalist come-back, but a post-modern sociotechnical invention, a politicized and rejuvenated, reconstructed religious ideology employed by social movements of alternative modernization' (Magala 2002, p. 8). In any case, in 2007, Dubai police stormed twenty-two brothels in a synchronized raid (DTCM 2007c). The move came after the UAE passed a law to combat human trafficking after receiving international criticism.

Another recurring criticism with respect to Dubai's rapid development is the environmental cost. The effects on marine ecology of the coastal developments are as yet rather unclear. Nakheel has appointed a marine biologist to monitor the effects of the island projects. He acknowledges that existing habitats are being replaced, but also argues that the new habitats increase the biodiversity of the area with new structures, probably without any adverse effect on the broader marine environment of the Gulf as the previous habitat type is abundantly present there (Butler 2005). However, at the same time, a study by Dubai-based Farnek Avireal Total Facilities Management Company in 2007 revealed that five-star hotels in Dubai use up to 225 per cent more energy than their counterparts in Europe. Along with North America and Australia, the Arabian Gulf has one of the world's highest CO_2 emissions on a per capita basis (DTCM 2007a). The World Travel and Tourism Council meeting that took place in Dubai in 2008 fortunately raised the level of attention that these issues receive. This is needed, because many of the concerns discussed above are such that they

FIGURE 5.9 | Dubai's heritage in the Bastaqya and Shindagha area
(H.H. Sheikh Saeed's house)

Source: Photograph reproduced with the kind permission of the Government of Dubai, Department of Tourism and Commerce Marketing.

could receive considerable international media attention if left unattended, taking brand Dubai down as fast as it has come up.

BRAND DUBAI AND ITS CULTURAL IDENTITY

As Cooper (2003) puts it: 'This vision of modern Arabia [as presented above] is somewhat different from the view often presented by the Western media which understandably focuses on regional tensions rather than regional success stories.' Others would argue that Dubai has lost its identity and is building an artificial world. In an effort to change this situation, the Dubai Department of Civil Aviation in 2003 embarked on a campaign reflecting the contrast between modern Dubai as an attractive global business hub and the continuing respect for tradition, heritage and local culture. In eleven roughly one-minute Cultural Voyage Vignettes that preceded the Dubai Duty Free and International Airport advertisements on CNN International, the government attempted to create a global awareness of the rich cultural identity of UAE people. Short interviews with ordinary local Emirati reflected traditions such as: henna body painting by an Emirati woman wearing her *abaya* (full-length black dress), and the *shaila* covering her hair; the use of perfume and incense-burning by a local woman wearing the *burqa* (a face mask covering the nose and mouth, worn only by traditional Emirati Bedouin women); pearl diving from a dhow; falconry in the sand dunes by Emirati men dressed in their traditional *dishdash* and *gutra* (the white full-length shirt and headscarf still used today, the latter held in place by the *agal*, the black cord wrapped around the head); the building of dhows; calligraphy; the traditional *liwa* band consisting of local Emirati men dancing to live music (drums (*tabl*), flute(*mizmar*), goatskin back pipes (*mizwid*) or a lute (*oudh*)); Arabic poetry and songwriting; existing traditional Bedouin herding camels in the desert; and finally a small item about the Bastaqya – the restored historical buildings along the Dubai creek – which was where the country's trade originally began (Mansson 2003).

In particular with respect to the 'conservation of local architecture' and the 'harmonious urban development that combines authenticity and synchronism' (*Gulf News* 2003), the Government of Dubai and the Department of Tourism and Commerce Marketing, and Dubai Municipality in particular, have made considerable efforts to restore many of the typical *barasti* houses. These houses are characterized by the square wind tower or *baadgeer*, open on four sides to catch gusts of wind and funnel them inside as a form of air conditioning, with the highest of these located above the bedroom. Many of these have been restored in the Bastaqya area, as has been the Dubai Museum, housed in the old Al Fahidi Fort and H.H. Sheikh Saeed's House, the official residence of the late Sheikh Saeed Al Maktoum, Ruler of Dubai (1912–58) and grandfather of the present ruler. Finally, a traditional heritage village, located near the mouth of the creek, has been created where potters and weavers display their crafts. 'Here the visitor can look back in time and experience some of Dubai's heritage. The Diving Village forms part of an ambitious plan to turn the entire Shindagha area into a cultural microcosm, recreating life in Dubai as it was in days gone by' (DTCM 2003).

Registration of the historical buildings as world heritage sites with ICO-MOS Unesco, is also being 'followed up with urgency ... as it will raise the importance of these buildings to the international level and help boost tourism' even further (*Gulf News* 2001).

During festive seasons such as the religious *Eid* holidays, national day or festivals and events, these locations, in particular the heritage village and H.H. Sheikh Saeed's House, are used to host festivities and fairs (Gabr 2004). Traditional *liwa* bands perform, together with dance groups; there are plays and other stage performances; wedding rituals; local arts, antiques and handicraft markets; and traditional food stalls. All these are examples of place brand development where heritage builds the 'sense of place' and constructs the identity of a nation (Go *et al.* 2004; Jansen-Verbeke 2004;

McLean and Cooke 2003), both in terms of building the infrastructure and product development as well as marketing, and a good example of tourism being a means of preserving heritage (Go *et al.* 2004). It also encourages some level of appreciation for the local culture among tourists whose primary reason for visiting a location is not for the local culture (it is often the sun, sea, sand and shopping in the case of Dubai). Gabr (2004) supports this notion (though through a dubious survey of residents and domestic tourists in Dubai) by concluding that residents and visitors alike have a positive attitude towards the restoration of historical buildings and their utilization as a way of building respect for the past as well as creating attractions for visitors. The use of historic buildings during festivals and events for museum-like and cultural purposes is also perceived to be positive.

As Van Rekom and Go (2003) argue, this form of 'staged authenticity' (McCannell 1973), 'is a strategy that can work, both in publicity campaigns designed to foster identification with (and of) a distinct local community and campaigns to promote active citizenship' (supported by Onians1998). So much so, in fact, that during the festive seasons these facilities are flooded with Emirati men and women and other Gulf nationals, many of them only in their twenties, to join in the festivities. The very few non-Arabs who visit these places during these periods (Ramadan, for example, is normally not a busy season for Western tourism) blend in with the crowds, and one has the impression of witnessing a 'genuine event', which Cohen (1988) would refer to as an event of 'emergent authenticity' in contrast to 'staged authenticity'. As Van Rekom and Go (2003) indicate, the staged or emergent authenticity therefore seems to 'fit with the way in which the local identity is constructed, imagined and experienced by the local community members' and is at the same time used as a way to react to recent geopolitical events in a positive way to promote Dubai's rapid development as a global hub, but at the same time not denying its roots. Chapter 9 will analyse to what extent these efforts are also reflected in the projected imagery of Dubai online.

CONCLUSION

Based on the analysis of signature case study Dubai as provided in this chapter, we can draw some preliminary conclusions on what are some of the elements of the place identity of Dubai. First, the narrative of the nation seems to revolve around the history of the Bani Yas tribe of the UAE, and the part of the Al Bu Falasah subsection that has been ruling Dubai since 1833 – the Al Maktoum family. The foundational myth seems to incorporate two elements: Bedouin life in the desert, on the one hand; and pearling, the building of dhows and trading that centred around the creek on the other. The latter has been an element with a dominant influence on the character of Dubai, as it splits the city in half. Some even suggest that the creek is responsible for giving Dubai its name. An important socio-cultural tradition is found in Arab hospitality in general, and in particular in the role of the *majlis*, as a place where men meet and discuss politics and decide on future directions, even today. Other traditions often referred to and still practised today are falconry, calligraphy, poetry, songwriting (language) and dancing by the men to the traditional *liwa* bands, and henna body painting and the use of perfume and incense-burning by women. One of the most important artefacts that gave Dubai its historical architectural character is the *baadgeer*, the wind tower that dominates rooftop views over historic parts of the city. Invented traditions include the public celebrations now held during *Eid* holidays, national days and festivals and events in the restored historical quarters of the heritage village around H.H. Sheikh Saeed's House and the Bastaqya. These point towards an emergent authenticity of people co-creating things that matter to them, as many among the local population participate in such events. As far as this original population of Dubai – the Emirati people – is concerned, their identity is largely determined by their religion, their position in the Middle East and their traditional dress that is still worn today. But at the same time it is these elements that also determine the myopic view that the West holds of the region, according to Said (1981). It would be of interest to identify to what extent this assumed stereotyping does indeed dominate, or if more nuanced images exist. The analysis of projected and perceived images that follows in Chapters 9 and 13 should generate some interesting insights.

A priori, other invented traditions such as belly dancing and the tremendous investments in iconic projects, appear to fill a void left by colonialism, exerting cultural power and thereby reconstructing the people of Dubai and their locality. The growth in foreign direct investment, trade and tourism has led to a tremendous import of foreign labour, as well as technology. In a very short period of time, the local population has been forced to deal rapidly with elements of modernity while maintaining traditions. The adoption of mobile technology and instant messaging proves to be an interesting case in point. Other issues that economic growth, internationalization and tourism have brought with them are concerned with the economic and employment positions of the local Emirati as well as environmental concerns. Also, more specifically related to tourism, prostitution, the availability of alcohol, and imbalances in cultural norms between hosts and guests, might become issues in the future. Up to now, as far as the social fabric of the Emirati society is concerned, there do not seem to be any significant tensions, but, of course, if there were, it would be hard to identify them through the secondary sources we used for our analysis. The success factors that have led to the tremendous progress of Dubai, according to the literature, include: the entrepreneurial vision of the ruling family as risk-takers themselves; easy access to decision-makers through a short chain of command, limiting bureaucracy; the integrated nature of development; the use of public–private partnerships; the application of the highest international standards; a focus on iconic projects; the availability of a steady stream of investors; and allowing for progress without social and cultural upsets, where the business culture is still founded on trust as opposed to contractual agreements. However, though these are recurring arguments, both in the literature as well as in our communications with senior officials in Dubai, they appear to be particularly relevant within the context of global flows. The question is how these success factors and current developments are perceived within the local context by disempowered local groups among the resident population. Unfortunately, this perspective was not included as part of our research on Dubai, though it is an interesting focal area within the place branding model, and it will be addressed in the next chapter. Nevertheless, while accepting these limitations, combining all the above observations, it seems that the obvious success of brand Dubai could be summarized as being a global business and tourism hub with a respect for tradition, heritage and local culture, where the place brand is being built through bold action and mega-projects that are very often based on a vision anchored in this local identity. However, whether this concerted effort can be sustained at the level of development and import of investment, talent, tourism and trade that is currently taking place, is questionable. There are signs that the link with the identity of place is weakening. Finally, we need to emphasize that, regardless of the success factors of case Dubai, it is not our intention to suggest that place branding can only work under a 'benign dictatorship' or through iconic projects. The following chapters, with case studies on Zeeland in the Netherlands, and Flanders in Belgium, will illustrate this.

Chapter 6

Case Zeeland (The Netherlands): Place Identity Research

The authors wish to thank Gerard van Keken for his major contributions to this chapter, based on Van Keken (2004) and Van Keken *et al.* (2005).

The case study research presented in this chapter examines whether, and to what extent, residents' perceptions of the cultural identity of a region can be used as the cornerstone for the construction of a region's identity, its projected image and the marketing of the region through a place brand. The area under study here is Zeeland, a province in the south-west of the Netherlands (or Holland colloquially; see Figure 6.1). The study used a combination of qualitative and quantitative research designs. A sample of 5,162 respondents underscores the massive desire of Zeeland's residents to reclaim a measure of control over the process of development and marketing that affect their everyday life. Their knowledge of the culture, their feelings and their sensory experiences provide a good opportunity to gain an insight into the construction of their perceived and experienced identity. The survey results were used in Zeeland's brand identity construction, which will be discussed in Chapter 10.

In this chapter, residents' perceptions are used as a foundation for the construction and experience of a regional identity. The chapter explores the relationship between culture and identity, because it is the cultural differences that imbue most places with their sense of distinctiveness. A resident perception approach is likely to raise potential biases and stereotypes, but has advantages at the same time. For example, it offers a unique opportunity to represent a place's common history and surroundings as experienced by local 'insiders'. In contrast to visitors' perceptions, this is more likely to yield a 'true' sense of identity. Also, residents are more likely to be supportive of a brand identity they have participated actively in creating. On implementation, this sense of participation in contributing to a region's brand identity may increase residents' support.

Figure 6.1 ▌ **Map of the Netherlands, including Zeeland**

This is essential in creating a unique competitive positioning, which is what branding is about. Anholt (2004, pp. 36–7) raises an important issue in this regard, when he states that 'Another good starting point [for place branding] is to look at the resource which, for most places, is their most valuable asset: the people who live there. Building a place brand strategy around the skills, aspirations and culture of the local population is far more likely to result in credible, sustainable and effective results than something cooked up by a team of ministers or PR consultants in closed meeting rooms.' Gilmore (2002, p. 284) also confirms that a country or region's positioning can never be artificially created, imposed from the outside. She emphasizes that a country's brand should be rooted in reality and in fundamental truths about the place, and it needs to connect people. Individuals' very clear sense of place and its values, in almost a spiritual and certainly an emotional sense, would indicate that, if the right nerve was touched, the connection could be powerful.

Morgan *et al.* (2004, pp. 14–15) remark that, while there is a growing body of literature on the process of place branding, there is a dearth of studies investigating the extent to which these brands have an impact on the resident populations of such localities. We have little understanding of whether, and to what extent, residents and smaller business operators embrace the idea of a collective decision-making process with regard to place branding. Therefore research needs to explore the relationship between culture and branding, because it is the cultural differences that imbue most places with a sense of distinctiveness. Gnoth (2002, p. 277) proposes that a brand development process that is being managed 'bottom up', involving visitors and the local industries and community residents, is more likely to succeed than a 'top-down' place brand strategy.

RESEARCH BACKGROUND: DUTCH ZEELAND

As one of the twelve Dutch provinces, Zeeland is situated geographically in the south-west of the Netherlands, south of Rotterdam and north of Antwerp in Belgium. It is famous for the Deltaworks, comprising a system of dikes, bridges and tunnels connecting its various islands and protecting them and their reclaimed land from the sea. The entire province of Zeeland has a population of 370,000. The provincial capital, Middelburg, is home to a mere 45,000 inhabitants, and may be characterized as peripheral, rural and coastal in nature. From the 1960s to the 1990s, Zeeland was a destination that attracted many visitors and was known to its visitors as a place offering 'sun, sea and sand'. However, at the end of the 1990s, Zeeland's tourism growth halted and even went into decline.

Yet the potential for growth in its tourism sector remains. Geographically, it is surrounded by densely populated areas, including the Dutch 'Randstad' (The highly urbanized mid-western part of the Netherlands, which includes Amsterdam, Rotterdam, The Hague and Utrecht); the German Ruhr area; Île de France; and the London area. Scenically, Zeeland is home to extensive areas of water and green pastures, which have given it the title of the 'blue-green oasis'. However, Zeeland is much more than just a coast with an agricultural hinterland. It is a province with a rich history. At the end of the Middle Ages, in the seventeenth century, known as the Golden Age of the Dutch, Zeeland, together with Amsterdam, was one of the centres of worldwide trade. The Dutch East India Company, founded in 1602, was the first multinational company in the world. Zeeland is home to many relics from the past and many stories that remind us of that Golden Age.

This has led to the formulation of a challenging research question; namely, how to position and profile Zeeland as a regional brand identity, so that it can generate added value for its stakeholders – business, trade and industry, inhabitants and visitors. The study reported on in this chapter attempted to provide the input for such a regional brand identity, based on residents' perceptions. The main research questions included:

(i) To what extent do the residents of Zeeland feel connected with the province and its regions?

(ii) Does Zeeland have a regional culture and, if so, how can it be described?

(iii) How do residents experience Zeeland in terms of imagery and affective and multisensory characteristics?

SURVEY METHOD

These issues were addressed in a questionnaire containing 39 questions. The survey was mailed in May 2004 to 1,943 inhabitants of Zeeland and a reminder was sent within ten days. The response rate was 34 per cent (652 responses). The questionnaire was also available online, through which a significant number of 4,510 surveys were completed and returned within two months. These respondents were collected through several means. In many locations, business cards were handed out referring people to the survey. In addition, there were small online advertisements with the slogan 'Test your Zeeuw-ness'. And finally, the twenty-eight organizations that sponsored the study, provided direct links from their websites to the survey. The use of the internet was considered legitimate for research purposes, because both the ownership of computers and access to the internet is very high in Zeeland. Although the province is rural, 81 per cent of residents have a computer and 91 per cent of them have access to the internet (Scoop 2004).

In order to attain a sense of identity, we based our questions on the sensory and experiential emotions that the material or physical attributes of Zeeland, contained in a series of photo images, would trigger in respondents. We used a series of twelve photo images and asked respondents to select the three images they felt were most representative of Zeeland. The twelve images the respondents were offered were selected from an earlier project in which twelve experts – well-known photographers in Zeeland – were asked to look for three photographs of their province. They were to be photographs from their collection which, in their opinion, rendered Zeeland in its distinctive uniqueness. Zeeland is a region made up of peninsulas, as opposed to a continuous landmass, each with its own characteristic identity. The professional (landscape) photographers from six different islands/areas were asked to identify two

distinctive photographs that best represented their home area and one
photograph that best captured the distinctiveness of the Province of
Zeeland as a whole. In total, thirty-six photographs were collected.
These photographs were presented to ninety inhabitants of Zeeland:
thirty tourist entrepreneurs; thirty entrepreneurs from other industries;
and thirty 'ordinary' citizens. These ninety respondents were asked to
choose the twelve photographs that they thought were the most distinctive for Zeeland, and the twelve photographs that were the least distinctive. The resulting pictures were presented to the respondents in the
survey discussed here.

Accompanying the choice of three photographs out of the twelve presented in the resident survey, respondents were asked to indicate which primary affective response each image generated. They had a choice of 25
types of feelings. Respondents were also asked about typical colours,
sounds, smells and tastes they associate with Zeeland. Finally, there were
questions about symbols, heroes, rituals and values aimed at identifying
Zeeland's cultural identity.

Of the responses we received, 363 were rejected as respondents had either
provided incorrect postal codes (therefore could not be identified as residents
of the province of Zeeland) or were not adults (or unidentified). A sample of
4,799 respondents remained for analysis. To enhance the sample and make it
more representative of the population of Zeeland, the sample's demographic
characteristics were weighted three-dimensionally: according to the population of the thirteen municipalities of Zeeland; by age; and gender. Data from
the Dutch Central Bureau for Statistics on the population distribution across
municipalities, age and gender was used as a reference point and 104 strata
and weighting factors were constructed. The values of the weighting factors
ranged between 0.4968 and 3.614. In general, values between 0.25 and 4.0
are perceived to be acceptable. A structured questionnaire was used, though
some questions provided for the possibility of adding qualitative responses.
The questionnaire was pre-tested on 25 respondents to make sure that all
response categories were as exhaustive as possible.

RESULTS

Affinity

The survey began with a question concerning the extent to which the residents of Zeeland feel connected with the province and its regions. A person's place of birth often determines to a large extent whether or not an

individual experiences a sense of place; that is, connectedness. Of the respondents, 70 per cent were born in Zeeland. Of the 30 per cent born elsewhere, a third of these had been brought up in Zeeland. Of all respondents, 57 per cent had spent their whole life in Zeeland. The Dutch refer to a resident of Zeeland as a 'Zeeuw'. As well as the formality of this title, it also describes a feeling of belonging. Respondents were asked to respond to the question of whether they considered themselves to be a Zeeuw, and if that was the case, to rate to what extent they considered themselves to be a Zeeuw. Of the respondents, 84 per cent considered themselves to be a Zeeuw, and 46 per cent of this 84 per cent replied that they considered themselves to be 100 per cent Zeeuw. The average level of 'Zeeuw-ness' (of the 84 per cent of the sample) was 87 on a scale of 100.

The respondents were also asked how and to what extent they felt connected with Zeeland. Three-quarters felt a strong or very strong connection with Zeeland. Of all respondents, 98 per cent felt connected, with only 2 per cent stating that they felt no affinity with Zeeland at all. Based on the survey results, it appears that the respondents have a great sense of affinity with Zeeland. An important question is whether such an insight could be leveraged to gather the populace behind Zeeland's brand identity and make residents 'live the brand' (Anholt 2002, p. 230; Ind 2004).

Zeeland's Cultural Identity

To investigate how residents define Zeeland's cultural identity, we applied Hofstede's (2001a) definition of culture. In selecting a symbol to represent Zeeland, nearly a third of the residents (30 per cent) chose the Deltaworks; 18 per cent opted for the Latin aphorism 'Luctor et emergo' ('I struggle and rise above'). It means that almost 50 per cent selected a symbol that bears a connection with the struggle against the sea, which has shaped Zeeland in its present state. The struggle against the sea is a very important narrative of Zeeland. Following these first two symbols, in third place were 'mussels' (11 per cent) and fourth 'dialect of Zeeland' (9 per cent).

Heroes, representing both the past and the present, can tell us a lot about a region's history. Hofstede (2001a) describes heroes as models of human behaviour; people with a high symbolic value, who are held in high esteem. We asked the residents to select three people from a list of heroes from the past and three from a list of contemporary heroes. In the category of heroes of the past, 87 per cent of the residents selected Dutch admiral Michiel de Ruyter, who led his country's fleet in the wars against England in the Golden Age. Annie M. G. Schmidt, a famous Dutch writer, received 26 per cent of the votes to occupy second position. A hero of today is the pop group Bløf, with 84 per cent of the votes, leaving behind the Dutch prime minister Jan Peter Balkenende with 26 per cent of the votes. The pop group Bløf could be a good ambassador for Zeeland, especially when targeting the younger population. On the other hand, Michiel de Ruyter may be seen as a person with a high symbolic value, who conveys to the contemporary Dutch people a sense of glory of Zeeland and the Netherlands in the Golden Age and has been held in high esteem internationally as well as in his native land.

Rituals are collective activities that are considered socially essential, but technically redundant in terms of reaching a desired goal (Hofstede 2001a). The residents of Zeeland were asked to choose from a list of rituals the one that they perceive as being unique to Zeeland. 'Tilting at the ring' (67 per cent) is a very typical ritual for Zeeland, with farmers on horseback trying to collect rings with a pole. Other notable rituals are the mussel festivities (66 per cent) and harbour festivities (38 per cent), both of which refer to the fishing industry and the importance of seafood, sea and harbours in Zeeland.

Based on the criteria that were applied, namely symbols, heroes and rituals, the respondents indicate that Zeeland's culture is primarily based on 'the battle against the sea', 'the province's rich heritage as a sea-trading and ruling region', and its fishery and agricultural sectors.

Residents' Perceptions on Experiencing Zeeland

Experiential perceptions were evoked by asking residents for their sensory and affective responses to location-based imagery, or how the residents of Zeeland see, hear, feel, smell and taste their own region. The affective responses to the photographic materials deserve attention in particular because these give an insight into the values system of the local populace. Table 6.1 shows that the three most popular images respondents associated with Zeeland were 'the seaside sensations of water and beach' (72 per cent), 'polder vistas (35 per cent) and 'the battle against the water' (34 per cent). The first two images were primarily associated with feelings of 'freedom', 'quiet' and 'space'. The feeling of 'enjoyment' associated with the image of 'the seaside sensations of water and beach' ranked first, whereas a 'holiday feeling' ranked fourth. Interestingly, Zeeland's residents feel simultaneously both at home and on holiday in their province. A major advantage of these two images is that, as a result of the values attached to them, the coast becomes connected with the hinterland. The third image – 'battle against the water' – was associated with feelings of 'admiration', 'wildness' and

TABLE 6.1 The three most-selected images and the top-5 emotional adjectives connected with them

1. The seaside sensations of water and beach (n = 3,450)		2. Polder vistas (n = 1,695)		3. Battle against the water (n = 1,636)	
1. Enjoyment	(n = 971)	1. Space	(n = 497)	1. Admiration	(n = 283)
2. Freedom	(n = 483)	2. Quiet	(n = 291)	2. Wildness	(n = 268)
3. Quiet	(n = 362)	3. Freedom	(n = 171)	3. Respect	(n = 251)
4. Holiday	(n = 278)	4. Beauty	(n = 166)	4. Fear	(n = 229)
5. Space	(n = 266)	5. Endlessness	(n = 159)	5. Battle	(n = 179)

Source: Photographs reproduced with the kind permission of Ruden Riemens.

'fear', which provides for a different angle in promoting Zeeland but still ties in with the characteristics of the region as they have been identified through the symbols and heroes.

The residents' feelings can function as an important source and base for the construction of a regional brand and a marketing approach that is based on the 'true' identity – the identity/image as perceived by the residents. In a way these feelings can be considered as values of the culture, for loading the regional brand.

The survey also asked residents what sensory and experiential perceptions, including colour, smell, noise and taste they associate with Zeeland. Blue, green and indigo are the colours respondents selected, and the 'sea', 'beach' and 'hay' are the smells they most commonly associate with Zeeland. Finally, respondents selected 'a quiet beach', 'the sound of a storm' and 'seagulls' as the noises they associate with Zeeland, and the taste of Zeeland was attributed to a meal of mussels. Overall, it can be concluded that the respondents' perceptions that ranked highest in the present survey all relate, in one way or another, to images of the coast (see Table 6.2).

TABLE 6.2 Multisensory elements of Zeeland, according to residents

Colour	%	Smell	%	Sound	%	Taste	%
Blue	45	Sea and beach	56	Sea and beach (quiet	39	Mussels	47
Green	25	Hay/fresh cut	18	beach; sun, waves,		Regional bun	24
Indigo	20	grass		wind)		Glasswort	6
Yellow	5	Seaweed	8	Wind/storm	22	(Marsh	
Orange	3	Cooked mussels	5	Seagulls	11	samphire)	
Violet	1	Manure, dung	5	Silence	9	Fish	5
Red	1	Onions	2	Sea and beach in	8	Regional	5
Black	1	Fried fish	2	summer (crowded		bull's eye	
White	0	Horses	1	beach, playing		Potatoes	3
		Woods	0	children)		Sea lavender	3
		French fries	0	Tractor, mowing-	6	Sugar beet	1
		Suntan lotion	0	and threshing		Fruit	1
		Barbecue	0	machine		Speculaas	1
		Exhaust gases	0	Water sports/rattling	1	(biscuits)	
		Industry	0	sails		Grain	1
		Other	2	Horses (hoof beats)	1	Cockles	1
				Industry and harbours	1	Asparagus	1
				Traffic	0	Other	1
				Music	0		
				Other	1		

CONCLUSION

In this chapter a 'resident perceptions' approach is introduced as a foundation to establishing a brand identity and gaining an insight to the regional and cultural identity of Zeeland. Important in this approach is that the identity of a region is established by its residents. Their meanings, experiences and feelings create a sense of place, an identity for Zeeland. The massive participation of Zeeland's residents in a survey on this identity reveals a high affinity and connectedness in the region where they live. The existence of a regional culture is supported by the presence of regional symbols, heroes, rituals and values. The sensory experiential approach for marketing purposes offers the possibility of enriching the projected identity/image so that it is based on a 'true' perceived identity. The findings of the study will be applied in the 're-loading' of Zeeland's brand identity.

CHAPTER 7

Case Flanders (Belgium): Place Identity Research

This chapter is based on the Master in Tourism thesis research work conducted by Stéphane Léonard, under the supervision of Robert Govers, at the Consortium University of Leuven. Stéphane successfully graduated in 2007, but his thesis was yet unpublished. The authors wish to thank him sincerely for his contribution to this book.

Belgium, with its capital Brussels, is a country divided into three main regions: the capital region of Brussels; French-speaking Wallonia in the south; and Dutch- (or Flemish-) speaking Flanders in the north. The population of Flanders is 6.1 million (on 1 January 2006, this was about 58 per cent of the Belgian population) and the region is known for the historic cities of Bruges, Ghent and Antwerp, and for its chocolate, beer and cafés. Although a federal state, some areas of governance are regionalized. Because of this autonomy, regions can outline their own policies and act as an equal partner to foreign governments. Particularly in the area of international advocacy, such as tourism promotion, export stimulation and attracting foreign investment, which are regional competencies, this sometimes creates confusion internationally when the awareness of Belgium, its regions and its state structure is limited. Additional confusion arises when, for example, foreign policy is both a federal as well as a regional competence. In the past this issue has been circumvented by having regional foreign promotion offices in neighbouring countries (the Netherlands to the north; France to the south; Germany and Luxembourg to the east; and, across the North Sea, the UK to the west) and Belgian offices with regions sharing space and cost, and joining forces to enter overseas markets.

However, since the regional parliamentary elections of 2004 and the federal parliamentary elections of 2007, the situation has changed. In recent years, expanded federalization of the state has gained importance on the political agenda in Flanders. This, for example, has resulted in the formation of a federal government to take more than a year, way into 2008, after the 2007 elections. An electoral minority with separatist sentiments has achieved power through party coalitions in the Flemish government. This has lead to increased pro-Flanders policies and actions; for example, in the establishment of what have been named 'Flemish houses' in long-haul markets such as New York and Beijing. Whether this makes sense from a brand awareness and perception perspective remains to be seen, but at least it should be established that there is such a thing as a Flemish regional identity (separate from a Belgian or supra-regional one) and that such an identity can be defined and communicated. Research into the resident perception of such a Flemish identity, and what it entails, is the subject of this chapter.

THE EXISTENCE OF A FLEMISH IDENTITY

In determining if it is useful to survey resident perceptions of local identity, it makes sense to establish whether there is existing evidence that such an identity in fact exists. In the political arena in Belgium today, this is obviously a subject of intense discussion, and even though we acknowledge that hierarchical layers of identity might exist, we shall not attempt to judge whether there is a dominant Belgian or Flemish identity, or what political consequences, if any, would be in the case of either of these. In other words, any delicate federal matters between communities in Belgian are far beyond the remit of this chapter. Nevertheless, looking at the various elements of identity, there seems to be supporting evidence for a unique and unifying Flemish identity.

Historically, based on the work by Kossmann-Putto and Kossmann (1997) and Vos (2002), it seems that Flanders is characterized by fragmentation, both in terms of the origins of rulers as well as internal territorial structures. The name Flanders first appears in 862, referring to the French district around Bruges. Through the centuries that followed, this region expanded under the County of Flanders, to include both Bruges and Ghent up to the border of present-day France. East of this county there was the Duchy of Brabant, around the axis of Antwerp and Brussels. Today, the Netherlands (Holland) and Belgium still include the provinces of North Brabant (in the south of the Netherlands) and Flemish Brabant (around Brussels).

The unification of Brabant and Flanders was first initiated in 1384 under the Burgundian dukes who united large parts of the present Benelux countries and Northern France. In the centuries that followed, control changed hands repeatedly among Austrian, Spanish and French powers, and many wars were fought on Belgian soil, causing it to be named 'the battlefield of Europe' (a reputation strengthened later by both world wars). Several unifications and separations of the Northern and Southern Netherlands (including Brabant and Flanders) were part of this upheaval. A separate Southern Dutch identity developed, based on counter-reformative Catholicism, historically grown public institutions and political solidarity as a buffer between super-powers. This culminated in a turbulent period around the 1800s, with a United States of Belgium that lasted only a year, before being recaptured, first by the Austrians and then by the French. This resulted in administrative simplification and the 'Frenchification' of public life in the upper class in the Southern Netherlands, including the northern provinces. After Napoleon Bonaparte's defeat at Waterloo, the Congress of Vienna created the United Kingdom of the Netherlands under King William of Orange in 1815. In the years that followed, the southern opposition of liberals and Catholics grew against the Dutch rule, leading to the final revolution of 1830, which created the present Belgian state and saw Leopold I installed as king in 1831 (see Figures 7.1 and 7.2 for maps of Flanders).

At first, in the new Belgian state, French was chosen as the official language, which soon led to the growth of a Flemish movement arising out of a concern for language and cultural equality, linked territorially to the north of the country. But only in the 1970s and 1980s did state reform result in true federalization, transferring significant areas of government competencies to the regions and communities. These successes made the Flemish movement virtually irrelevant as its role has been fulfilled increasingly by official substate nationalism by the Flemish authorities. At the time of writing, the dominant public opinion in Flanders rejects absolute Flemish

FIGURE 7-1 | Current map of Flanders

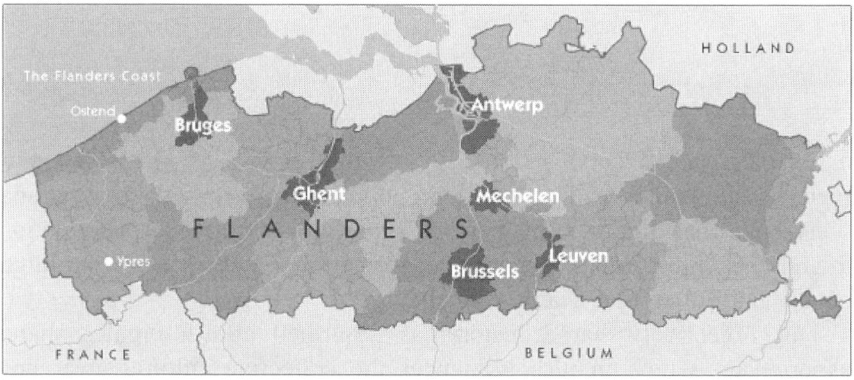

Source: www.visitflanders.co.uk/go/getting_there.

FIGURE 7.2 | **Map of the County of Flanders (16th century)**

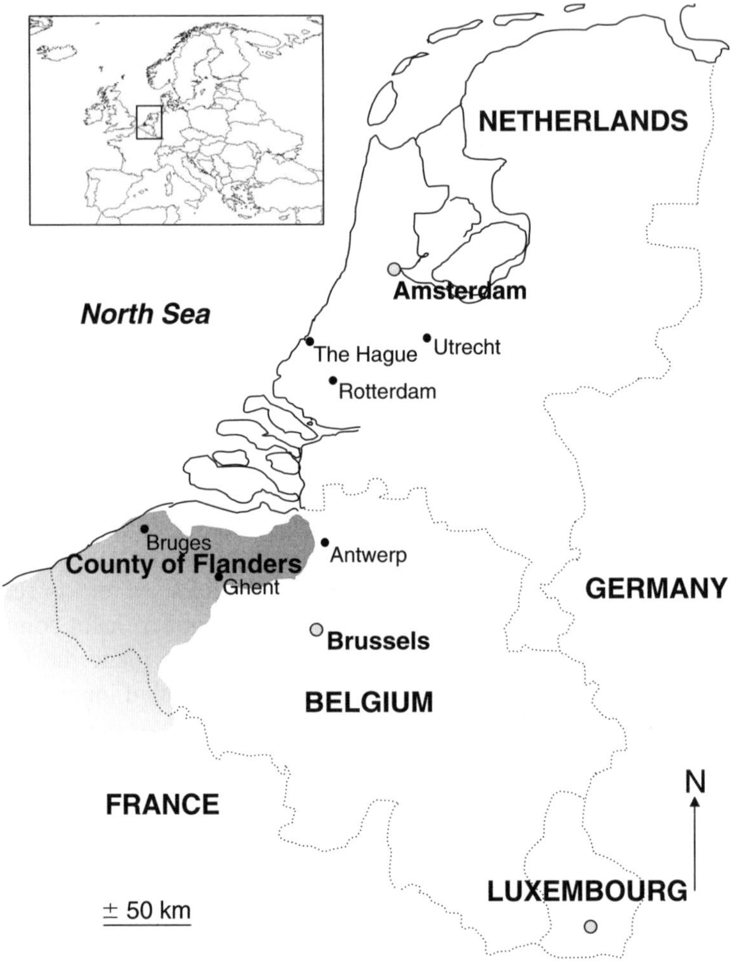

nationalism and accepts federal loyalty to Belgium. A small group of Flemish nationalists aside, the general population has no separatist inclinations and does not acknowledge a Flemish–Belgian contradistinction, though the failed federal government formations in 2007 and 2008 might have enhanced anti-Belgian sentiments.

This objectively-shared history, as described above, creates shared experiences, which in turn influences the collective cultural awareness and feelings of solidarity. But from a cultural identity perspective, the subjectively a posteriori construed symbolic past is often more important. The 'famous Flemish past' had already been committed to paper in Hendrik Conscience's novel, *The Lion of Flanders*, just after Belgian independence in 1838. The mythical reflection of Flemish greatness was found in the person of Robert III of Flanders (1249–17 September 1322), also called Robert of Bethune and nicknamed 'The Lion of Flanders', who was Count of Nevers 1273–1322 and Count of Flanders 1305–22. Conscience has his hero take part in the Battle of the Golden Spurs, near Kortrijk in southern Flanders, which in fact he never did. Nevertheless, the Battle of the Golden Spurs on 11 July 1302 was a heroic event as a successful folk uprising and the only Flemish victory ever over the French. In 1893, 11 July was nominated as the official celebration day of the Flemish community, regardless of the fact that present-day Flanders was not a political entity seven centuries ago, and that the arms were taken up by many armed forces from different ethnicities. People from Brabant and thirteenth-century Flanders, for example, were on opposing sides. Symbolically, Flanders is represented by an anthem and flag, both relying on the greatness of the lion. However, the lion as a symbol is far from exclusive, considering historical symbols in surrounding regions. The Flemish Hymn dates from a poetry contest in 1847 (a period in which many nationalist-minded writers, poets and artists in various European countries were busily taking up heroic characters from their countries' respective histories and myths, and making them into romantic symbols of national feeling and pride) and was chosen as the Flemish anthem in 1985.

It nevertheless shows that history and location have had a definite impact on the place identity of Flanders. But so has the geography, as flat and urbanized Flanders can easily be contrasted with the thickly forested hills and plateaux of the Walloon Ardennes that are more rugged and rocky, with caves and small gorges. Economically, Flanders has also expanded in recent years, focusing on a networked knowledge and information economy, with Walloon economic activities in heavy industries and mining stagnating. This is in fact one of the reasons for the political turbulence in Belgium at the time of writing.

Another distinctive element of Flemish identity is the unifying Dutch language, which signifies a cultural boundary with the French-speaking Belgian community. In fact, language has for long been an identity struggle in Flanders, as Belgium straddles the cultural boundary between Germanic and Latin Europe, as illustrated above. It means that Belgium has two communication environments with their own media and predominantly single-language education that facilitate the establishment and maintenance of two different frameworks of mental programming. In addition, there is no

significant interaction between the two language environments, as is illustrated by the fact that only a very small proportion of the Flemish population
watches French–Belgian television and vice versa (Ponette 2000). But also,
historically, the Dutch language has been a key element in the fight for
respect for the Flemish identity in Belgium, with two revised national language policies based on language battles – characterized by public unrest – in
the 1930s and 1960s (Beheydt 1993).

There are two assumptions to be made about the existence of a specific
Flemish 'inner mentality' or value system. Culturally, the two separate language environments with their own media and education system, as discussed above, have facilitated an autonomous transfer of values, norms
and ideas in the different regions. In the communication with Belgians
from other regions in daily life, the Flemish population is constantly confronted with these differences in mentality, which presumably brings an
awareness of a characteristic Flemish identity. On the other hand, from a
religious perspective, the Flemish have for long taken different stand-
points on social issues when compared to the Protestant North, the
Netherlands (where the same Dutch language is spoken). Even though
continued secularization and de-Christianization have reduced attention to
religious aspects of society, the strong Catholic background of the Flemish
still has an undeniable influence on the deep-seated value system. It provides evidence for the assumption that there is indeed a unique Flemish
mentality that is distinctively nestled between the French-speaking south
and the Dutch Protestant north.

This is illustrated through the European Values Studies (Halman 2001),
as presented in Table 7.1, which shows that, for the Flemish, the region is
more important than larger entities, when compared to opinions of residents
of other Belgian regions.

TABLE 7.1 Respondents' geographical attachment

Respondents' origin and age	Flanders		Wallonia		Brussels	
	18–30 yr	60 yr+	18–30 yr	60 yr+	18–30 yr	60 yr+
Municipality	58	60	49	56	28	35
Region	62	61	28	42	47	49
Belgium	49	49	58	67	54	62
Europe	15	12	33	20	29	36
The world	9	6	24	8	26	11

Note: Percentage of respondents indicating attachment, with first and second choice combined.

Finally, Table 7.2 lists the elements of Flemish identity based on several self-reflective literary sources (Carson 1974; Claeys and De Meulemeester 2000; Daems *et al*. 2000; De Roover and Ponette 2000; Heijl 2002) that also support the notion of a unique Flemish identity. There seems to be agreement between authors on some elements, such as the inner mentality or value system of the Flemish being Catholic, pacifist, hard-working and consensus-orientated. Also the Burgundian lifestyle; cycling, with the Tour of Flanders; the rich art and cultural patrimony; and typical gastronomic products, are all recurring items. The general category of art and cultural patrimony shelters items such as the art cities (Bruges, Ghent, Brussels, Antwerp and Leuven), Béguinages, belfries, diverse architecture, Flemish Primitives and later world-famous painters. Even though this literature study provides interesting points of departure for assessing the Flemish place identity, it seems to be limited in terms of its identification of symbols, heroes, great events and subjective experiential elements of which the Flemish are proud. It is these elements that are most useful as a way of defining brand identity of place, and hence an empirical study was undertaken to measure the resident perception of place identity in Flanders.

BOTTOM-UP FLEMISH PLACE IDENTITY SURVEY

In order to identify the place identity as defined by the Flemish themselves, a web survey was conducted among 969 respondents; a self-selection sample that was generated through links in online forums, and through associations and companies of students, friends and colleagues of the researchers. To stimulate response, survey participants were entered into a raffle draw, rewarding one winner with a weekend trip for two, selected from the Tourism Flanders catalogue. Obviously, with this kind of approach, the sample is not representative of the Flemish population. There tends to be an oversampling of young, higher-educated males, notwithstanding the fact that all age groups, Flemish provinces and educational backgrounds were covered, but not in proportion to the distribution of the Flemish population as a whole. In order to assess the extent to which this influenced the results, an analysis of variance was conducted to test differences in responses between different age groups, males and females, and respondents with different educational backgrounds. While regularly significant differences in judgements were recorded, these differences did not appear to have an affect on the ranking of items as presented in the results in Figure 7.4. Therefore, while the results presented in Figure 7.4 are not representative of the whole Flemish population, they can be

TABLE 7.2 Flemish identity according to self-reflective literature

	Carson (1974)	Claeys and De Meulemeester (2000)	Daems et al. (2000)	De Roover and Ponette (2000)	Heijl (2002)
Location/Geography	■ Beach, polders, Flat (region of) Kempen, Flemish hills, meandering rivers ■ Humid and misty	■ 68 km sandy beach ■ Good location in Europe	■ Geographical crossroads of cultures	■ Flat relief ■ Vegetation => high agricultural productivity ■ Mild climate	■ Ribbon development
Physical appearance	■ Densely built ■ Castles ■ Towers ■ Chapels ■ Lack of design and taste in common modern buildings	■ Good road infrastructure ■ Good public transport		■ Highly populated ■ Bad spatial planning ■ Strong urbanization	
Mentality	■ Devoted to own language ■ Government-averse ■ Contempt for discipline ■ Catholic ■ Indifferent to outward appearances ■ Conservative ■ Down-to-earth ■ Hard-working ■ Independent ■ (Too) adaptable	■ Pacifist ■ Respect for other cultures	■ International orientation ■ Pacifist	■ Catholic ■ Government-averse	■ Non-conformist ■ Modest ■ Compromise and consensus ■ Hard-working ■ Rest ■ Catholic

Rituals, traditions, behaviour	■ Devoted to home community ■ Fairs ■ Brass bands ■ Amusement ■ Cycling, pigeon racing, finching ■ Cafés	■ Gastronomy ■ Burgundian savoir-vivre ■ Hospitality ■ Speak foreign languages ■ Productive	■ Speak foreign languages ■ Festivals ■ Contemporary cultural life ■ Club life ■ Cycling ■ Pigeon racing ■ Social life	■ Burgundian hedonists ■ Traditional education ■ Well-educated ■ Speak foreign languages ■ Adaptability ■ Familiar with other cultures	■ Burgundian hedonists ■ Cycling, motocross, billiards, finching, pigeon racing ■ Fraudulent in relation to state ■ Well-educated ■ Devoted to home community ■ Cafés
Heroes	■ The fox Reinaert ■ Tijl Uilenspiegel		■ Eddy Merckx		■ Tijl Uilenspiegel ■ Pallieter
Symbols			■ Cycling Tour of Flanders ■ The Yser tower memorial	■ Flag ■ Anthem	■ The Flemish language ■ Cycling Tour of Flanders ■ Flemish draft horse
Artefacts	■ Art cities ■ Chips (not French but Flemish fries) Dutch doughnuts (oliebollen – oil balls), patisserie, chocolate, beer	■ Concentration of cultural patrimony	■ Exceptional cultural patrimony ■ Beer, chocolate, chips/fries, ox tongue, tomato with shrimps, Waterzooi (stew translates as 'watery mess'), eel, hotchpotch stew, casserole ■ Many good restaurants		■ Exceptional cultural patrimony ■ Contemporary art and literature ■ Beer, chips/fries, mussels, eel, asparagus, pensen sausages, Waterzooi, casserole, chicory, tomato with shrimps, meatloaf, patisserie

FIGURE 7.3 | **Level of regional attachment of the Flemish**

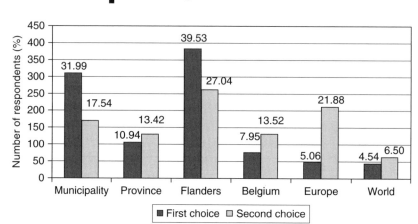

assumed to be highly correlated to potential results that would be generated with a utopian ideal sample.

The survey shows that, first, and indeed in line with the EU research presented in Table 7.1, the respondents feel highly attached to the Flemish region, more so than to provinces or to a feeling of nationalism towards Belgium, as illustrated in Figure 7.3. In response to the question regarding to which region respondents feel most attached, both as first as well as second choice, the connection with the Flemish region received the highest scores. Combined, two-thirds of all respondents indicate a sense of belonging to Flanders. Almost three-quarters of all respondents also indicate that they feel Flemish all or most of the time (with 18 per cent indicating that this is a feeling that they have only sometimes, and 9 per cent have seldom to never).

Of course, these scores could potentially be attributed to a self-selection bias in the web survey, assuming that, more so than others, the pro-Fleming is more likely to be inclined to participate in a survey that studies the self-perception of Flemish identity. This could be put in perspective, though, by emphasizing that there is also a predominance of Flanders in the second choice of respondents as well. This then contradicts the alleged self-selection bias, as one would assume that supporters of the Flemish movement would probably indicate their predisposition with Flanders as a first choice. The attachment to other regional entities also contradicts this self-selection bias assumption. For example, the devotion to the home community/village area – or parochialism, if worded with a negative connotation – as identified

FIGURE 7.4 | **Residents' perception of Flemish identity**

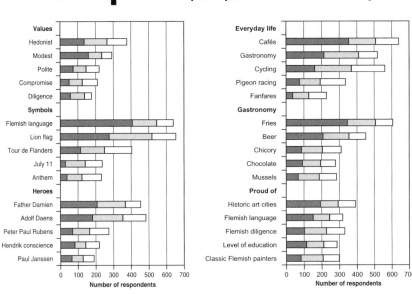

in Table 7.2, is also supported through the results of this survey, with a first and second choice combined score of close to 50 per cent.

This apparent attachment to a Flemish cultural identity is, of course, an important prerequisite for the validity of this research. It would not make any sense to ask residents about elements of their cultural identity, if there was no feeling of attachment to such an assumed identity. Therefore, the above observations are encouraging when it comes to assessing the validity of the elements of Flemish place identity as they are judged by the respondents. The results of the top-5 rankings in each category are presented in Figure 7.4. A recurring theme seems to be the Burgundian hedonist lifestyle, with good food and cafés with beer; as also represented by the work of the painter Rubens. Cycling, on the other hand, is also an important part of life in Flanders. What does not help in building a strong place brand is the fact that one of the most important values of the Flemish mentality is modesty. Many people in Flanders feel that this is one of the reasons why Flanders (or Belgium, for that matter) has not been able to build a strong image for itself.

Finally, the Burgundian lifestyle is also represented in an assessment of the resident' self-perception of Flemish iconography. Based on earlier work by Sinaeve (2005), who developed such an iconography of the Flemish landscape, respondents were presented with twenty images and asked which were most typically Flemish (on a scale of 1 to 10 for each image). Again, a picture of a typical cosy café market terrace was third in popularity. Other important themes were again the historical art cities and rustic rural landscapes with views of Flemish villages. Positive from a place branding perspective is the fact that negative environmental aspects, with images of chaotic spatial planning (or lack of such planning), inhospitable climate and heavy industry, received low scores. Respondents showed optimism in prioritizing positive elements over and above negative aspects. The only image with a failing grade was one that depicted the area around Brussels North railway station, which is characterized by a dynamic business environment, with high-rise buildings and modern service economy appeal. Such an image was not perceived to be typically Flemish, according to our respondents.

CONCLUSION

Through the analysis of secondary as well as primary data, this study supports the notion that there is such a thing as a unique and unifying Flemish identity, and that specific elements can be defined to describe that identity. Recurring themes are the Burgundian hedonist lifestyle and *savoir-vivre*, with good food, cafés, beer and the painter Rubens, but also historic art cities and cultural centres, Catholicism, Flemish language, cycling and rural landscape. Several elements of the international image of Flanders are also supported, as will be illustrated in Chapter 13. Even though the sample size is very small in that study, the few respondents who participated in the assessment of the image of Flanders indicated that it included elements such as historic buildings and old historic towns with cobbled streets; chocolate and beer; cafés and friendly people. The match between some of the elements in the above identity study and the image study in Chapter 13 is evident.

It seems to provide many elements for a differentiating brand positioning of Flanders. Nevertheless, this opportunity has, so far, not led to a decisive and coherent brand strategy. On the contrary, as in so many other places, Flanders, probably because of a reluctance on the part of public authorities or government agencies to make choices, is also stuck in a fragmented branding approach with brand identities that are based on generalizations and superficialities. In 2007, while Tourism Flanders (the tourist board) was working on its own brand strategy, the Flemish Minister for Governance, Foreign Policy, Media and Tourism launched a new logo with the slogan 'Flanders fits you' as an '*Appellation d'origine*', which says: 'This is from Flanders' emphasizing the diversity and dynamism of the region (Flemish

Department of Foreign Affairs 2007). Diversity and dynamism (with the exception, perhaps, of the Flemish place brand strategies) do not seem to be attributes that the literature and resident perception research attach to the Flemish identity; not to mention that numerous other regions and nations use similar adjectives. From our perspective, this was clearly a missed opportunity. The new destination brand of Tourism Flanders, with its core brand values of indulgence, charm, abundance and vibrancy (Tourism Flanders 2008), seems to make more sense.

Summary of Part 2

In a globalized world, places can utilize their, often unique, identities as a competitive advantage over other place brands. As emerging economies rush to take their positions as global hubs, such as our signature case Dubai, 'old' economies can potentially create a unique place brand positioning based on their established identities. Such place identities consist of structural elements such as location and history; semi-static elements such as size, physical appearance and personality; and colouring elements such as symbolism, behaviour and communication. How research into place identities can be useful for loading place brands is illustrated through our case studies on Flanders, Belgium, and Zeeland in the Netherlands. It also shows, however, that identities are perceived, constructed and influenced by political struggles and hence are not static, but rather are contested.

The authenticity of place identities is often contested as well, but we have to realize that there is not only the objective authenticity of the 'original, historic or real', but also processes of emerging authenticity and staged authenticity, often no less appreciated by visitors, tourists or travellers. In addition, experiential or existential authenticity is about people perceiving their experiences and social interactions as 'real' or meaningful, while constructed authenticity refers to how people co-create meanings that matter to them. The latter view of authenticity is what we as authors consider to be most relevant, because authenticity, in the end, is an individual judgement that is also based on people's self image. Together, hosts and guests, matching self-images and personalities, can co-create authentic meaningful experiences of identity.

Such identities are under pressure of globalization or McDonaldization/ Disneyization, but can also flourish as people are looking for a sense of place and belonging in a shifting world. This glocalization argument, where global flows are given local meaning, or where local identities receive wider attention and significance, can benefit place brands. This is illustrated in our case studies on Flanders, Belgium, and Zeeland in the Netherlands. In place branding, this balance between global significance and local meaning is often hard to establish and even harder to incorporate meaningfully in the brand strategies.

Such place brand strategies result in projected place images, through marketing and communication, using narratives and visuals. Linking this to a strong product offering in terms of tourism, trade, talent (attracting human capital), and treasury (attracting outside investment) can create a strong brand. This is illustrated clearly through the success of our signature case Dubai in building a global brand from the sand. However, a sustainable place brand, in our opinion, would link projected images and product offerings to the identity of place, because, over time, a sense of place is needed for hosts and guests to work together respectfully and effectively to co-create meaningful experiences; fake brands projecting fake experiences will be exposed.

Media and ICT are obviously important enablers for projecting place images, and with the growth of Web 2.0 and the convergence of media and ICT, online communities will play increasingly important roles in projecting place brand images, and thus the boundaries between overt induced agents (advertising, promotion, direct marketing) and organic or covert induced agents (communications under no control or limited control of place marketers) will blur increasingly. Nevertheless, in this noise of global mediascapes, meaning is still created through local narratives, traditions/rituals, myths, events, heroes, local culture (gastronomy, art, literature, popular culture), emblems, religions and languages. However, these meanings, as they are carefully selected, recontextualized and given an authoritative voice in projected images, are again politically constructed and contested.

Ultimately, projected images need to reflect rich place experiences, as the product offering of place and the services that it includes are really only facilitators for visitors, tourists, investors, traders, foreign workers and students, to consume place. This product offering, as with any service, is characterized as being intangible, inseparable (production and consumption take place simultaneously); heterogeneous (different individuals at different points in time receive varying levels of quality) and perishable (hotel rooms, trade and investment opportunities, places at college, new homes or jobs need to be filled as they become available on the market or revenue will be lost). Therefore, marketing this product offering requires global linkages, technology-infused service operations and virtual promotion of place brands for effective matching of demand and supply. However, in order to facilitate the projection of place identity, socialization and co-creation of personalized experiences, will also probably become more important. The human element in matching identities of place with product offerings and projected images is therefore essential, because if there is no alignment, a place brand strategy gap might appear. Dubai, as illustrated in our case study, is potentially at risk of this.

PART 3

Place Brand Performance

A new international division of labor, greater trade and more travel, the abstraction or removal of traditional activities from local communities: all these consequences of the global economy make available a new range and quality of experiences. At the same time, the disappearance of old sources of regional and local identity impoverishes others, leading to a new pursuit of authenticity and individualization. (Zukin 1991, p. 214)

If the place brand strategy is well designed, the first gap, as discussed in Part 2, might not occur. However, a strategy needs to be executed and many things can still go wrong. In that case, a place brand performance gap might occur, as will be explained below. In Part 2 we focused on place identity, product offering and projected image, and in Part 4, we shall focus on perceived image. In Part 3, as the second perspective from which we approach the place branding model, experience will take centre stage. Chapter 8 will show how consumption experience, physical and virtual, is a crucial element in place branding, and that building a product offering and an appropriate projected image in this context helps to bridge the potential place brand performance gap. In Chapter 9 we analyse the online communications of tourism actors in Dubai and evaluate how effective they are in projecting a consistent experience-based place image. Chapter 10 will then look at how experience branding is implemented in the province of Zeeland, in the Netherlands.

What we would like you to take away from this part of the book is to:

- Acknowledge that a place brand, in essence, represents a hedonic product that is the consumption experience of place, and hence place brands can be exposed on visitation.

- Appreciate that, when investors, tourists, traders, migrant workers or students experience places for themselves, this has a significant impact on their perceptions of place.

- Recognize that place experiences involve peoples' senses, mental imagery processes, emotions, social interactions and actions.

- Design optimal place brand experiences by 'imagineering' experience environments, through dialogue between (potential) visitors and experience networks (public and private parties involved in the place brand offering), in order to establish clear goals and expectations in terms of potential experiences that can be co-created.

- Understand that access to the experience networks allows the visitor to pick and choose and co-create a personal experience through active or passive involvement and relating to others, while finding a balance between challenges and personal skills.

- Appreciate that transparency facilitates the exchange of information and provision of feedback on progress of performance and risk assessments at touch points where sensory stimuli link perceptions to cognitive and affective processes, thus enhancing the brand.

- Contrast the physical experience of place to vicarious place experiences such as virtual worlds, social networks, television, movies, music, arts, travelling exhibitions, events, online videos and blogs.

- Distinguish vividness and interactivity (together facilitating telepresence) as important prerequisites for creating strong, vicarious place brand experiences.

- Identify the significance of visuals and narratives in the projection of rich place brand experiences, as exemplified by the projected image research on our signature case Dubai.

- Ultimately point out that place branding requires the effective management of human interaction in experience environments and their consistent marketing. If this is not the case, a place brand performance gap might occur, which seems to be an issue in our signature case Dubai.

CHAPTER 8

Place Brand Performance Elements

The quality of the place experience is derived from the interfacing between host and guest, the outcome of which can make or break the place brand image. Providing quality service encounters is an especially daunting challenge for places where the guest or new resident comes from a different cultural background. Cultural differences are likely to result in miscommunication, which in turn makes it harder for front-line staff to understand guests' expectations. Of course, repeated interaction between these hosts and guests will alleviate this problem through learning. Therefore, it is expected that familiarity with a certain place, and the level of involvement of the visitor with it, will influence the perceived image. The information acquired through personal experience or by visiting a place, forms the primary image, which may differ from the secondary image, which will be examined in Chapter 11. Indeed, some authors, such as Gartner and Hunt (1987), point out that post-visit image tends to be more realistic, complex and different from the pre-visit image, which is based on secondary sources of information. Echtner and Ritchie (1993) believe that the perceived images of travellers who are more familiar with a place is more holistic, psychological and unique, compared to first-time visitors, whose images are based more on attributes, functional aspects and common features.

Fakeye and Crompton (1991), however, emphasize the lack of agreement in literature about the impact of the actual experience on place image. Nevertheless, several empirical works in academic literature (Chon 1991; Fakeye and Crompton 1991; Milnam and Pizam 1995) demonstrate that perceived image is influenced by familiarity with, the number of visits to, and the length of stay at a destination. Beerli and Martín (2004a, p. 663) also explain that 'one of the factors related to personal experience is the intensity of the visit, or, in other words, the extent of an individual's interaction with the place'. This would affect travellers' perceived image as: 'the primary source of information formed by personal experience or visits will influence the perceived image depending on the number of visits and their duration, or on the degree of involvement with the place during the stay [measured by Beerli and Martín by the number of different places visited at the destination]' (2004a, p. 663). Therefore, to maintain a strong place brand image, standards of delivery and supply of the product offering as an involved consumption experience must be maintained everywhere, in every location visited by travellers, and at all times. Conversely, a strong place brand cannot be built on projected images alone, it needs to incorporate a high involvement experience concept – supported through infrastructure, projects, events and place development initiatives – in order to build a primary place image.

PLACE EXPERIENCE AS HEDONIC CONSUMPTION

Place experiences, facilitated through product and service offerings, are typically an example of hedonic consumption. Leemans (1994, p.210) argues that these 'are emotion-laden goods and services for which the consumption experience is an end in itself'. He discusses books as a hedonic product, but travel could also qualify as such, because of its emotion-intensive properties (Vogt and Fesenmaier 1998). In hedonic consumption, the experience is an end in itself (Hirschman and Holbrook 1982; Leemans 1994; Vogt and Fesenmaier 1998). Hirschman and Holbrook (1982, p. 92) emphasize the importance of multisensory, fantasy and emotive aspects of experiential or hedonic products (the 'three Fs': fantasies, feelings and fun – see Holbrook 2000, p. 178; Holbrook and Hirschman 1982).

Leemans later continues: 'factual information on objective and often physical characteristics of single items are much less important than the (holistic, non-attribute based) image that is built around items'. Urry (2002) clarifies and extends the argument that place experiences have a fundamental visual character, drawing an analogy with Michel Foucault's concept of the gaze. He develops the notion that there are diverse gazes, the visitor being a passive subject. Others prefer the alternative metaphor of 'performance', or the way Fairweather and Swaffield (2002, p. 294) describe it as 'the graded experience of the Elizabethan theatre ... in which some of the audience become active participants, some choose to remain detached spectators, and others move between the two. Furthermore, watching others in the audience perform becomes part of the experience'. So place experiences are also highly dependent on human interaction (see Chapter 4: Product Offering Based on Identity).

Summarizing, experiences seem to involve an interaction between the individual (see Chapter 11) and the physical or virtual and social environment, through:

- The senses, interacting with ...

- Imagery processes in the mind (cognitive processes linking perceptual observations to existing concepts, contexts and meanings, including processes of imagination creating fantasies), giving 'meaning'; and

- Generating emotions (affect); and

- Actions (conative reactions) –active participation or passive gazing – as well as ...

- Social interactions.

An experience that is '*autotelic*, or rewarding in and of itself', has been termed by Csikszentmihalyi (1995b, p. 8) as a state of *flow*:

> Artists, athletes, composers, dancers, scientists, and people from all walks of life, when they describe how it feels when they are doing something that is worth doing for its own sake, use terms that are interchangeable in their minutest details. This unanimity suggests that order in consciousness produces a very specific experiential state, so desirable that one wishes to replicate it as often as possible. (Csikszentmihalyi 1995a, p. 29)

This is what has been termed 'flow' or optimal experience. The flow experience is characterized by several dimensions: 'When a person's skill is just right to cope with the demands of a situation – and when compared to the entirety of everyday life the demands are above average – the quality of experience improves noticeably' (Csikszentmihalyi 1995a, p. 32). When the demands are too high, it results in a feeling of anxiety, but if the demands are too low, the person might get bored.

Other common characteristics of flow experiences include focused concentration and a distorted sense of time. People in flow commonly have no attention left to think of anything else. Also 'hours seem to pass by in minutes, and occasionally a few seconds stretch out into what seems to be an infinity' (Csikszentmihalyi 1995a, p. 33). Although in flow experiences clear goals and quick and unambiguous feedback on performance are needed, the goals are often just an excuse to make the experience possible: 'The mountaineer does not climb in order to reach the top of the mountain, but tries to reach the summit in order to climb' (Csikszentmihalyi 1995a, p. 33).

Characteristics of flow experiences are, according to Csikszentmihalyi (1997, pp. 111–13):

1. Clear goals.

2. Immediate feedback.

3. Balance between challenges and skills.

4. Action and awareness are merged.

5. Distractions are excluded from consciousness.

6. No worry of failure.

7. Self-consciousness disappears.

8. Distorted sense of time.

9. Activity becomes autotelic (an end in itself).

Csikszentmihalyi (1995b, p. 14) argues that 'whenever the quality of human experience is at issue, flow becomes relevant', hence its importance for branding place experiences. This is also supported by Cary (2004, p. 68) who argues that travellers' 'motivation and experiences centre upon the demand for leisure and the subsequent escape from boredom and anxiety. As a sacred journey, tourism foments the optimum conditions for experiencing a heightened state of being; or, for experiencing flow'. This illustrates why developing place experiences is such an intricate business. The demands on peoples' skills while visiting new places, when compared to everyday life, will be above average in most cases. This is likely to apply to any sort of travel, from package tours to adventure travel or temporary relocation to routine business travel, as demands are assessed relative to the person's everyday life, and different types of place experiences probably attract different markets with different domestic backgrounds, and hence different skills. As Cary (2004) suggests, many travellers report feelings of harmony with the environment, focused concentration, liminality, losing track of time, and the attractiveness of the act of travelling for its own sake.

At the same time it implies that visitors are often balancing on a thin line between boredom and anxiety. The latter in particular is often a cause of dissatisfaction. A trip is all too easily ruined if even the smallest thing goes wrong and the demands placed on the visitor exceed their skills.

Chapter 4 illustrated that services are heterogeneous (varying in quality every time a service is delivered) and inseparable (the customer consumes the product while it is being produced). Hence it is not surprising that, while the visitor is trying to balance his or her state of flow, moments of truth or touch-points in the service encounters often become disruptive. This is particularly true in place experiences, as high-contact service offerings. Social encounters between visitors and service personnel are decisive. While the visitor's experience is easily tipped over to a state of anxiety, the waiter, tour guide or steward is just going about his or her daily routines, often lacking an understanding of the traveller's state of mind. In virtual service encounters such problems will only be magnified, particularly when host and guest come from different cultural backgrounds, as people prefer remote communications with counterparts who have a similar background, vocabulary and training (Van Fenema 2002, p. 544). Local public and private actors need to appreciate these issues and act 'on-brand' in order to deliver the experience according to the brand's promise of value.

A PRODUCT OFFERING THAT DELIVERS THE PLACE EXPERIENCE

Places are really heterogeneous environments where experience networks of service providers and visitors co-create personalized consumption experiences (Prahalad and Ramaswamy 2004a, 2004b, 2004c, 2004d). Human interactions are essential in these environments, as a large part of place experiences, including the product delivery as a high customer contact service encounter, refers to interactions with other people, hosts with guests, but also to guests with other guests in a certain physical environment. Part of what is purchased in these experience environments (experiencescapes, according to O'Dell and Billing 2005) is a particular social composition of those serving in the front line as well as the social composition of other customers (Urry 2003, p. 17). Place experiences take place in what Go and Van Fenema (2006) refer to as social space. People interact and create meaning in a joint process based on concurrent or similar past experiences. Therefore interactions in social space do not necessarily have to take place in material space (at the physical destination) but can also take place remotely via the telephone or online. Place experiences, though still primarily created in material space, are therefore also partly constructed pre- and post-visit. Interaction with customer service employees while making the booking, for example, or when completing customer feedback surveys or talking to export agencies, are part of the social interaction and therefore endemic to the experience. It is not surprising that the service management and marketing literature repeatedly emphasizes the importance of front-line employees, whose work is also termed 'emotional work' or 'emotional labour' (Urry 2002, p. 62; Urry 2003, p. 17), particularly for service industries (Hoffman and Bateson 2002; Kotler *et al.* 2003; Lovelock 2002; Lovelock and Wright 2002; Zeithaml and Bitner 1996). Personalization in service encounters has therefore also received increased attention (Mittal and Lassar 1996).

While the host–guest encounter is essential, relationships with other visitors with whom one shares experiences (either family and/or acquaintances in the same travel party; social encounters or friendships established during the visit; or business contacts made during trade missions or meetings) influence the place experience as well. This takes place during the trip, but is also instrumental to the process of creating multisensory, emotional, historic or fantastic nostalgia prior to and after the visit. Because of the heterogeneity that characterizes the place experience environment and service performance in general, it is very difficult to set standards of service delivery and supply for the product offering. However, what we want to emphasize here is that the personal experience of service delivery and the intensity of the host–guest encounter (or lack thereof) is clearly related to the guest's perceived image. The interesting consequence is that offering visitors easy access and facilitating the co-opting of their competence may unlock the potential of a place to take the necessary steps to enhance service quality and influence perceived place image in a positive manner. What is often not appreciated enough by businesses in these experience environments or experiencescapes is that most people, while travelling, are out to enjoy themselves, to meet other people, explore new cultures and share with others. Through dialogue and the performance of genuine, what has been called, 'people-to-people' business, place experiences can be enhanced dramatically.

But, of course, experience environments also involve physical aspects, even though the 'world cities and hegemonic projects' literature (Archer 1997; Paul 2004; Rutheiser 1996; Yeoh 2005) acknowledges that 'most [of their] research misses the core insight that much of creating a world city lies in manipulating symbols, crafting images and shaping identities' (Paul 2004, p. 573); that is, place branding. In the branded place, land use, capital investment and construction, as well as image creation and/or preservation, 'are the core elements in building physical manifestations of the city's [or region's] (desired) global qualities and infusing festivals, sporting events, buildings, parks, squares, roads, even whole neighborhoods, with symbolic meaning' (Paul 2004, p. 573). This has also been referred to as 'place imagineering'. This creation of experience environments was invested in by Walt Disney Studios as they defined imagineering as 'combining imagination with engineering to create the reality of dreams' in their theme parks (The Imagineers 1998, cover text). Archer (1997, p. 326) identifies it as 'the construction, both physical and social, of a type of lived reality'. The same applies to place, as they 'attempt to connect to a global imaginary, while simultaneously appropriating the "cultural" realm as a means of maintaining a sense of unique identity' (Yeoh 2005, p. 947).

Chang and Lim (2004, p. 166) also acknowledge that places 'are "imagineered" by tourism planners and entrepreneurs ... such imaginative geographies include theme parks, heritage districts, conserved waterfronts and other leisure [or increasingly mixed-use] environments'. And Yeoh comments: 'Other [what have been referred to as] entrepreneurial landscapes ranging from whole new cities to sports complexes to host hallmark events and university campuses may also be read as instances of cultural production intended to fulfil the dual function of fuelling the nation's globalising ambitions on the one hand and producing new post-colonial citizens and shaping local sensibilities on the other' (Yeoh 2005, p. 951). The comparison between such entrepreneurial landscapes, or in particular our signature case Dubai, with Disney, is sometimes striking, as can be inferred from Archer (1997). Many of such spaces are controlled by private actors and dominated by entrepreneurialism. Those fortunate enough to 'get inside' often experience an environment seemingly without social conflict or problems. When inside, people seem to feel less guilty about spending money, as poverty appears not to exist. Even workers are seemingly happy, because they are trained to smile, but also, on average, they are treated well or at least are in a better position as contract workers than they would be 'back home'. It is about the creation of feel-good experience environments.

This is indeed the premise of the 'experience economy'. Schmitt (1999, 2003) argues that, in order to create consumer experiences organizations need to facilitate consumers sensing, feeling, thinking, acting and relating. Pine and Gilmore (Pine II and Gilmore 1999) argue that this involves entertainment, aesthetics, active escapism and education. The link with tourism experiences is not far-fetched if we consider Cohen's (1979) modes of entertainment; recharging energy; (staged) authenticity; rediscovering oneself; or ultimate nostalgia. Or Lengkeek's (2001) similar modes of amusement; change; interest; rapture; or mastering. All these typologies are considered on dimensions of being active versus passive or gazing/absorbing versus participating/immersing. But, according to Mossberg (2007), 'No matter what kind of tourism product we have in mind ... the tourist will be influenced by the experiencescape, wherein personnel, other tourists, physical environment, products/souvenirs and theme/story play a major role' (Mossberg 2007, p. 59). As we shall comment in Chapter 9, in business practice, limited reference is made to the experiential nature of places, particularly when considering multisensory references. According to Lindstrom (2005), linking the sensory consumption experience to the way in which consumers experience a brand, can be facilitated through the choice of pictures, colours, shapes, names, language, icons, sounds, behaviour, service, traditions, rituals and navigation.

Combining several theories that have been discussed above, there seem to be some common insights about how to guarantee value co-creation through optimal experiences. First, dialogue between (potential) visitors and the experience network (public and private parties involved in the place product offering) should facilitate the negotiation of appropriate expectations and the formulation of clear goals in terms of the types of experiences being sought. Second, transparency facilitates the exchange of information and provision of feedback on progress in service deliveries and risk assessments at touch-points where sensory stimuli link perceptions to cognitive and affective processes. Finally, access to the experience networks allows the visitor to pick and choose to co-create a personal experience through active or passive involvement and relating to others while finding a balance between challenges and personal skills.

EXPERIENCING PLACE IN ALTERNATIVE WAYS

A place experience cannot be tested or sampled prior to a visit, but there are other forms of hedonic consumption that can give a 'reality-like' insight into living place identity. Some examples are: social networks, online videos and blogs, movies, music, television shows, travelling exhibitions, events, literature, virtual worlds or other forms of popular culture. The influence of movies on place image and choice behaviour has received considerable attention in recent years: 'Leisure products such as books and movies increasingly trigger consumers to travel to certain places ([for example] ... Crocodile Dundee – Australia, The Beach – Thailand, Harry Potter – Great Britain, The Lord of the Rings – New Zealand [sic])' (Klooster et al. 2004, p. 2). For example, as a result of the success of the motion picture Troy, starring Brad Pitt, the Turkish city of Çanakkale, the location of ancient Troy, saw a 73 per cent increase in visitor numbers. This number increased further when the Trojan horse used in the film was reused as a visitor attraction. Elsewhere, New Zealand also benefited from movie exposure. Tourism is said to have increased as a result of its exposure as the backdrop for the movie trilogy *The Lord of the Rings*. Over 7 per cent of visitors to New Zealand were influenced by the movie. Hawaii's exposure in television shows (*North Shore*, *Hawaii* and *Lost*) and movies (*American Idol*) have helped to boost visitor numbers. However, place marketers should not make the mistake of thinking that these are autonomous agents that places cannot take advantage of or influence. In fact, Hawaii had to lobby actively and compete with other places in an effort to get producers to film on the island (Alcantara 2004).

In 1999, the *Economist* (1999) reported on major visitor attractions in the US Midwest that were put on the map by Hollywood. Many of these places were relatively unfamiliar to consumers until movies had people experience their unique identity at the cinema. Some examples are Winterset, Iowa in *The Bridges of Madison County*; Fort Hays in Kansas in *Dances with Wolves*; and The *Star Trek* Trek Fest in Riverside, Iowa, the claimed future birthplace of Captain Kirk, blessed by the television show's director, Gene Roddenberry.

As mentioned earlier, current developments show that place marketers increasingly try to turn previously autonomous agents into covert induced agents. These days, even celebrities are called to the rescue of places in crisis (Alcantara 2003). Also, museums can be useful providers of vicarious place experiences and a means of producing covert induced agents. The parallel between museum exhibitor and place marketer has been identified by Fesenmaier and MacKay: 'The roles of the museum exhibitor and destination marketer are paralleled by their efforts to control portrayal of culture and image. The planned exhibit and the constructed tourist destination image both represent a vision controlled by political ideologies' (Fesenmaier and MacKay 1996, p. 38).

Finally, as discussed briefly above, with current technology, virtual communities become interesting instruments in providing vicarious experiences: 'These communities may serve as extensions of the destination, and become colonies that revive destination-specific events (cultural, environmental etc.)' (Klooster *et al.* 2004, p. 7). The ultimate example in this Web 2.0 environment is a virtual world such as 'Second Life', where city centres have already been reconstructed in hyperreality. In 2007, the *Observer* newspaper selected that year's hottest place to visit: cyberspace (Bowes 2007).

Hirschman and Holbrook (1982, p. 92) emphasized the importance of multisensory, fantasy and emotive aspects of experiential or hedonic products (the 'three Fs': fantasies, feelings and fun (Holbrook 2000, p. 178; Holbrook and Hirschman 1982)). Consumers build up emotional arousals and mental multisensory imagery, either historic (based on prior experiences) or fantasy imagery, based on what they (expect to) taste, hear, smell, see or feel when consuming experiential products. Gretzel and Fesenmaier (2003, p. 51) argue that, in order to improve future place marketing strategies, sensory information should be communicated either through new emerging technologies such as virtual tours (possibly incorporating the development of sensors for taste, smell and touch) or using traditional forms such as metaphors and narratives. In online environments, Hoffman and Novak (1996, p. 61) and Shih (1998, p. 655) refer to this as 'vividness', which addresses the breadth and depth of the sensory information provided. Vividness, together with the interactivity of the internet, leads potentially to 'telepresence' (Hoffman and Novak 1996; Shih 1998), 'the extent to which consumers feel their existence in the virtual space' (Shih 1998, p. 658), or the extent to which they are able to experience what is presented through interactive and rich sensory information. According to Hoffman and Novak (1996) – as illustrated in Figure 8.1, this could eventually lead the consumer into a state of flow in itself (without the place consumption experience itself needing to happen). It seems hard to imagine a more effective way to create a strong place image prior to a visit.

As such, the above off-site place consumption experiences are obviously interrelated. Relevant movies and books are discussed in virtual communities, and museum-like exhibitions of 'the-making-of' will influence place image in their own way. At the same time, though, it is important to distinguish them from overt induced agents and autonomous agents, as discussed in Chapters 4 and 11.

PROJECTING PLACE EXPERIENCES: PICTURES AND TEXT

Despite being investigated empirically only sporadically in tourism research (Albers and James 1988; Fairweather and Swaffield 2002; MacKay and Fesenmaier 1997; Markwell 1997; Pritchard and Morgan 2001; Sternberg 1997), many have argued in conceptual theoretical papers for the critical analysis of photographs, as well as concentrating on textual and literary representations, in areas such as anthropology, sociology, geography and tourism and hospitality research, in particular (Cohen 1988; Feighey 2003; Garlick 2002; Human 1999; Ryan 1994, 2003). The relationship between photography and place experience has therefore received some interesting coverage, such as, for example, by Fesenmaier and MacKay (1996, p. 40): 'Photography represents a key vehicle for manipulating imagery by moulding what and how things are viewed. What potential tourists see as a replication of the real and as a credible source of information, is instead a "subjectively mediated content and composition"'

FIGURE 8.1 | A model of network navigation for virtual experiences

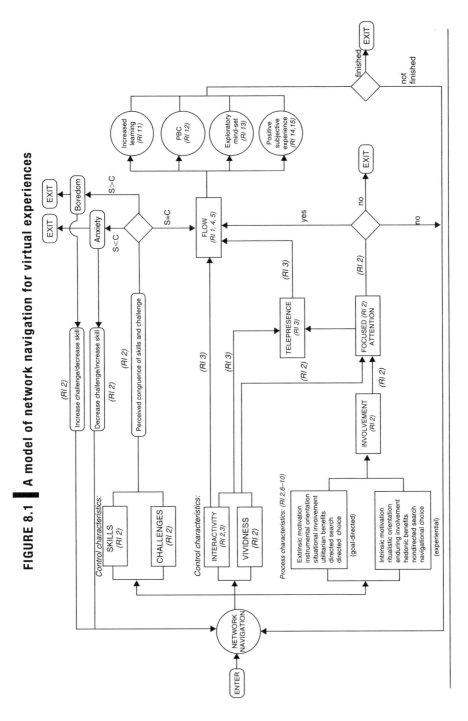

Notes: RI = Research issue; C = Challenges; S = Skills; PBC = Perceived Behavioural control.
Source: Hoffman, D. L. and Novak, T. P., 'Marketing in Hypermedia Computer-Mediated Environments: Conceptual Foundations'. Reproduced from *Journal of Marketing* 60 (July 1996), pp. 50–68 with kind permission.

(Albers and James 1988 in Fesenmaier and MacKay 1996, p. 40) Human (1999, p. 80) characterizes the relationship as being 'ambivalent'. 'Many destinations visited by tourists have a strong identity and sense of place, which is embodied in the history ... (culture) ..., physical form and social activity. However, photography selectively extracts from this multifaceted expression and reduces it to a series of icons. This distorts the identity and trivialises the place and contributes to the consuming nature of tourism.' On the other hand, through tourism, many places have been able to preserve at least something of their identity, culture and heritage, which otherwise might have been destroyed if it were not for the need of visitors' to experience them.

As has already been argued, place experiences can indeed be categorized as a form of hedonic consumption, where the experience is an end in itself (Hirschman and Holbrook 1982; Leemans 1994; Vogt and Fesenmaier 1998). Sternberg (1997, p. 951) in fact 'argues that tourism planning has as its central challenge the design of effective touristic experiences, and can find conceptual sources for this task in iconography'. Also Garlick (2002, p. 289) 'takes up this question of what role photography plays in determining the nature of touristic experience'. According to Sontag (2002, p. 3) this is a critical issue, as 'photographs, in teaching us a new visual code, alter and enlarge our notions of what is worth looking at and what we have a right to observe' and, at the same time, 'photographs really are experience captured, and the camera is the ideal arm of consciousness in its acquisitive mode'. From a brand perspective, Fesenmaier and MacKay (1996, p. 41) argue that 'since tourism is uniquely visual, photographs are considered paramount to successfully creating and communicating an image of a destination'. Rojek (1993, p. 130) remarked that television becomes 'the clearest embodiment of the replacement of reality with representation'.

On the other hand, developments may be seen as somewhat paradoxical; after all, 'don't tourists swim, climb, stroll, ski, relax, become bored perhaps, or ill; don't they go other places to taste, smell, listen, dance, get drunk, have sex?' (Saldanha 2002, p. 43) It brings us back to the gazing/absorbing versus participating/immersing discussion, but in any case, image seems central. Hirschman and Holbrook (1982, p. 93) also argue that, in the hedonic consumption perspective, 'the researcher is concerned not so much with what the product is as with what it represents. Product Image, not strict reality, is a central focus'. As explained later, in Chapter 11, narrative psychology contends that people have a natural propensity to organize information about experiences in story format. It also suggests that people relate their interpretations of experience to others by narrating, or telling stories (Dhar and Wertenbroch 2000; Padgett and

Allen 1997; Vogt and Fesenmaier 1998). Ideally, therefore, narratives included in place marketing material should represent such rich experiences and reflect multisensory, fantasy and emotional cues. Incorporating photographic material (as well as other visuals and sounds (Hoffman and Novak 1996; Shih 1998)) may contribute significantly to this: 'Although frequently conveyed as a stereotype, visuals in destination promotions are salient in early stages of destination evaluation and when the tourist's experience and/or involvement level is low. As such, destination decisions may be based on the symbolic elements of the destination (as conveyed in visual imagery) rather than the actual features' (Fesenmaier and MacKay 1996, p. 37).

This aspect of place image can be examined through the content analysis of publications about destinations and the beliefs that visitors share with others. For one thing, it can provide places with a better insight into the way in which they incorporate the authentic in relation to the identity of place in the online image projection so as to enhance its experiential nature. For example, Pritchard and Morgan (Pritchard and Morgan 2001), in their analysis of twenty-seven Welsh local tourism authority brochures, found significant differences in the projected images aimed at the UK market in comparison to those aimed at the US market. The 'Welshness' and amount of reference to local heritage was much more evident in the brochures aimed at the US market, while brochure content for the UK market seemed to focus on generic holiday attributes such as scenery and activities. There seems to be a tension between the desire to project imagery that provides an authentic identity of place, but at the same time commoditizes it for consumption, reflecting desirable experiences (or staged authenticity) (Cohen 1988, p. 371; MacCannell 1973).

This book examines, among other things, this tension between cultural identity and commoditization. In particular, there is a desire within the cultural community and public sector to project imagery that represents an authentic identity of place, whereas commercial interests are keen to stage authenticity (Cohen 1988, p. 371; MacCannell 1973) to represent desirable activities, or convenient commodities for consumption. As a result, we expect our investigation into the use of imagery and narratives by the tourism industry in Dubai, for example, to show differences between public and private institutions and different sectors of the industry, in terms of the images that they project online and the related perceptions of relevant decision-makers. Also, some stakeholders might not be heard at all, because, as was discussed in Chapter 4, imagery formation is negotiated, a political process reflecting power structures and ideology (Ateljevic and Doorne 2002; Jeong and Almeida Santos 2004;

Morgan and Pritchard 1998; Pritchard and Morgan 2001). 'Destination marketing organizations emit an authoritative voice in the visual and verbal context of their advertisements and travel brochures'; in so doing, the voices of residents may not be heard (Fesenmaier and MacKay 1996, p. 39).

This will be investigated in the case of Dubai in Chapter 9. Consequently, place branding is often built on 'one of the most important questions' already raised in the early 1980s by Boulding (1983): 'What do our decision-makers read? That is, what kind of image of the world do they have?' Investigating what is projected by various actors would give us insight into what part of the image of the world that they have, they want to 'appropriate' (Sontag 2002, p. 4). If, according to Sontag (2002, p. 3), 'the most grandiose result of the photographic enterprise is to give us the sense that we can hold the world in our heads – as an anthology of images' ('to collect photographs is to collect the world'), the presentation of these collections as assembled by private actors would represent their view of the world as they would like us, the public, to see it. As Boulding (1983) illustrates, 'It may be that a small nuclear catastrophe, for example, in the Middle East, would shock people to the point where there would be a restructuring of the human image and the national image.' Boulding must have been anticipating Huntington's 'The Clash of Civilizations' (Huntington 1993) using this metaphor, as Chapter 9 will illustrate the impact that recent events in the Middle East have had on the way in which Dubai projects its place image.

Taking this into account, different actors, public agencies versus private sector-specific companies, are hypothesized to have different objectives in terms of projecting a place image that will favourably affect their intended positioning and ultimately their customers' buying behaviour. One would anticipate that decision-makers within public agencies will utilize imagery and narratives that tend to be focused on authentic cultural identity, while private organizations might in fact try to avoid that, focusing more on commoditized experiences. 'The issue is,' as Long (1997) put it, 'how actors struggle to give meaning to their experiences through an array of representations, images, cognitive understandings, and emotional responses.'

CONCLUSION: THE PLACE BRAND PERFORMANCE GAP

In contrast to the consumption of goods that customers acquire for utilitarian benefits, the consumption of place is intangible and experiential in nature, involving emotions, feelings, drama and fantasies, and aims to satisfy primarily psychological benefits. Traditionally, researchers have viewed its labour-intensive character, the dependency on human interaction, and the involvement of a myriad of actors who participate in one way or another in the production, delivery and consumption of a total experience, as central issues. For example, consistency in service is often cited as being problematic, because any interruption in the delivery process will immediately affect service quality because of the simultaneous production and consumption.

Recently, therefore, the role of personalization in service encounters (Mittal and Lassar 1996) and the management of personalized experiences (Prahalad and Ramaswamy 2000, 2004a, 2004b, 2004c, 2004d) have received increased attention. Several guidelines are offered for service organizations to allow them to deal with service experience issues. First, places need to manage multiple channels or touch points of experience, such as vicarious experiences through popular culture and promotion/ advertising, social space experiences as well as the actual travel experience itself. The key challenge here will be 'to ensure that the nature and quality of the fulfillment, the personalized experience of the individual, is not different across the channels' (Prahalad and Ramaswamy 2000, p. 84). Second, places need to manage variety and evolution in service delivery. Customers 'judge a company's products not by their features but by the degree to which a product or service gives them the experiences *they* want' (Prahalad and Ramaswamy 2000, p. 85: emphasis added). Customization and knowledge about the place brand satisfaction and how it changes based on past experiences is therefore essential. Finally, shaping customers' expectations and place image is of crucial importance. This 'is not just about one-way communication by managers or advertising [of projected image]. It is about engaging current and potential customers in public debate' (Prahalad and Ramaswamy 2000, p. 86).

A limitation of much of the present research is that it seems to perceive place marketing organizations and businesses as 'command and control'-type organizations, where the focus has been on transaction cost theory, as opposed to the development of social interaction skills and trust. The latter are at the root of the emerging etiquettes of market forces and decision-making teams that are rapidly becoming the building blocks of the network economy. Organizational theory directed at the development of 'command and control'-type governance should be viewed as a myth in a world where uncertainty seems the only certainty. Specifically, even when the public sector and local businesses possess the 'right' information about visitor expectations and the perceived place image in the mind of the visitor is realistic, the delivery of the place experience can still be disappointing, affecting service quality, if service personnel are not empowered to deliver a truly personalized yet consistent service that co-opts the customer. Not much is needed to affect customer satisfaction negatively whenever organizations fail to do this (see Bigné *et al.* (2001) for the effect of quality on satisfaction), particularly in situations where host and guest come from different cultural backgrounds. When the value systems on which host and guest base their social expectations and behaviour are different, it makes it more difficult for front-line service employees to anticipate guests' expectations and accordingly offer a rapid response. As a result, the second place brand performance gap appears; that is, experience of delivery not being up to standard.

CHAPTER 9

Signature Case Dubai: Projected Image Research

This chapter will investigate online projected place image research, in terms of pictures and text, as discussed theoretically in Chapter 8 and reported by Govers and Go (2005). The research background is Dubai as described in Chapter 5. Dann (1996a) has argued that the visual and textual content of brochures are important in aiding a conceptualization of place, and that this has been studied in the literature. Fesenmaier and MacKay (1996, p. 41) also state that the 'analysis of media messages has been tackled from a variety of theoretical and disciplinary perspectives', and indeed text and pictures seem to have long been the main instruments of research (Uzzell 1984). Pritchard and Morgan's study (2001), discussed in Chapter 8, is similar to what will be reported here, though their approach was based on the content analysis of physical brochures. This section will therefore look at the online projected place image of Dubai, also in terms of pictures and text.

The UAE has the highest internet penetration rate in the region, with 37 per cent of its residents having online access (CIA 2008), compared to a world average of 21 per cent (Internet World Stats 2008). This is supported by the Emirate's drive to take up a strategic position in the new economy, endorsed by the creation of Dubai Internet City. The observations above show that this is bearing fruit. However, much more pertinent in this context is Dubai's dependency on international visitors when it comes to sustaining its drive towards economic diversification. European visitors constitute a large and growing market segment, being the primary source market, representing 32 per cent of the total market in 2007 (DTCM 2007d). On average, these visitors spend a whole day longer in Dubai compared to visitors from any other part of the world. According to the Yahoo! Summer Travel Survey in 2007, 61 per cent of Americans turn to the internet for vacation recommendations (Guntrum 2007). In Europe, the 2007 online travel market was worth €49.4 billion, represented 19.4 per cent of the market, according to the Centre for Regional and Tourism Research, Denmark (Marcussen 2008). This was up from €39.7 billion in 2006, when it represented 16 per cent of the market. Online travel sales in Europe increased by 24 per cent from 2006 to 2007. A further increase of about 18 per cent was expected during 2008, to about $58.4 billion (22.5 per cent of the market). Therefore, considering the advancement of Dubai in the online market place, and the importance of the European market, this study of Dubai's online projected place image is timely.

DATA COLLECTION

To sample the imagery, an online search was conducted to locate Dubai-based tourism company websites. Only Dubai-based websites were identified, under the assumption that these would belong to organizations that would generally be responsible for creating the projected place image of Dubai (more specifically, they would be the sources of the overt induced agents). Foreign intermediaries (tour operators and travel agents) and cybermediaries (such as Expedia, Lonely Planet or Travelocity) were not considered, as the government or industry in Dubai would not normally be able to influence the image projections by these actors directly. At best, these would be covert induced agents, using Dubai-based organizations as secondary sources of information. In practical terms, trying to include all non-organic information sources available on the Web would be an impossible task. As an indication, a Google search for 'Dubai AND tourism' yielded over five million results. Nevertheless, this research aimed at meeting the following research objective: 'To analyse the extent to which the projected images online correlate to the place identity: its authenticity, cultural heritage and natural resources.' The projected image would cover the online overt induced agents, not other online information sources, as they are outside the direct control of destination management.

Finding Dubai-based websites was done by screening the links detailed on local portals containing tourism directories, such as the Government of Dubai's Department of Tourism and Commerce Marketing (www.dubaitourism.co.ae); the Dubai Government Information and Services Portal (www.dubai.ae); AME-Info (www.ameinfo.com); UAE Interact (official website of the Ministry of Information and Culture in the UAE, at www.uaeinteract.com); and Emirates Internet &Multimedia (EIM) (the national internet provider at www.emirates.net.ae, part of the national telecommunications company Etisalat). Finally, a search on the keyword 'tourism' was conducted on the complete list of websites registered in Dubai as provided by the Abu Dhabi Chamber of Commerce and Industry (www.adcci.gov.ae/pls/uaesites/uae_web_sites_emirates).

Twenty websites were located and saved in a Favourites folder, using Microsoft Internet Explorer's 'Offline Web Pages' tool. The maximum number of three links deep from the websites' homepages was downloaded to hard disk, following only links within the same website, without specifying a disk space usage limit and including downloading of images. From the twenty websites, a total number of 3,600 JPEG and GIF files was collected. From these, 2,550 small images of less than 10 kilobytes were deleted immediately, under the assumption that these would include only buttons, icons, lines, banners and other design elements. Of the remaining 1,050 images, 74 were duplicates of the same image on the same website, and were therefore overwritten during cataloguing. Of the 976 viewed images, another 38 images were deleted as they consisted of banners, backgrounds and navigation menus. A further 433 images were excluded from the analysis for various reasons. These included: 11 images of poor quality, which made them difficult to analyse; 5 images of cargo at an airport or seaport, irrelevant to the locality; 8 images representing irrelevant business settings, not showing specific related facilities available in Dubai; 11 images of irrelevant objects not related to Dubai; 84 images consisting of logos, banners and ads; 48 geographic maps; 6 images of non-branded aircraft in flight and cars on non-Dubai roads; 83 images of other countries; 72 images of other Emirates; 42 press-related images; 44 images representing text; and 19 images of unknown individuals without context or within an irrelevant non-Dubai related context. The remaining 505 images included in the analysis were distributed as depicted in Table 9.1.

Subsequently, every page on every site was browsed manually and scanned superficially for its textual content. All full-text paragraphs of two or more sentences were cut and pasted into a separate Word document for every website. Most web pages were included, apart from pages that related to other Emirates; press sections; listings of hotel information, if not on the hotel website itself; listings of brief destination-related facts (such as exchange rates, telephone numbers, seasonal temperatures, holidays, languages, visa information); and bullet-pointed sections, unless part of a larger piece of text.

In this way, from the twenty websites, a total number of 92,485 words was collected, distributed as depicted in Table 9.1. In total, fifteen tour operators, three hospitality management companies, the destination marketing organization (Government of Dubai: Department of Tourism and Commerce Marketing (DTCM)) and the airport website were analysed.

TABLE 9.1 Sample distribution

		Private	Semi-governmental	Government	Total
Tour operator	No. of websites	13	2		15
	No. of images	255	47		302
	No. of words	26,075	16,156		42,231
Air transport	No. of websites		1		1
	No. of images		56		56
	No. of words		5,398		5,398
Hospitality	No. of websites	2	1		3
	No. of images	51	48		99
	No. of words	13,770	14,373		28,143
Destination marketing organization	No. of websites			1	1
	No. of images			48	48
	No. of words			16,709	16,709
Totals	No. of websites	15	4	1	20
	No. of images	306	151	48	505
	No. of words	39,845	35,927	16,709	92,481

Only the destination marketing organization was purely a government organization, but two tour operators, one hospitality management company and the airport are semi-governmental – part of the government control structure, but managed as private entities. Not surprisingly, the DTCM and the semi-governmental hospitality management company websites carried the greatest amount of text and images, corresponding to the total website size, these two being the largest of the websites analysed (16,709 words/48 images/30 MB; and 14,373 words/48 images/74 MB, respectively). The airport website had the greatest number of images (56), but not as much text, and was an average-sized website at 17 MB. Apart from one tour operator with a website of 18 MB (and 40 images), all other websites were smaller than 6 MB, six of them being smaller than 1 MB.

Apart from pictures and text, no other content, such as audio, video or experiential content (including stimuli affecting additional sensory modalities, such as tactile, proprioceptive or olfactory senses) (Hoffman and Novak 1996) was located on the websites sampled.

CONTENT ANALYSIS OF PICTURES

The need for researchers to embrace image-based research has been contended by Feighey (2003). The 505 images included in the analysis were content-analysed in terms of motifs (objects or appearances) and themes (or focal themes), as applied in other studies of place photography (Albers and James 1988; Markwell 1997; Sternberg 1997). Content analysis of motif was performed at three levels, as suggested by Sternberg (1997, pp. 957–9): first, identification of the actual objects (setting up what is staged); second, identifying the arrangement (which objects are shown together, or clustering); and third, identifying the contextualization (or the surrounding context).

At the outset, all the motifs appearing in every image were listed. Then, with each image being represented as one case (or a row) in the datafile, a separate dichotomous variable was created in SPSS for each object to indicate whether the specific object appeared in the picture or not (0 = no, 1 = yes). This allowed for the measurement of distribution and frequency, and for analysis of variance, treating the variable as an interval scale. Next, correlations between these variables were calculated, which would indicate if objects often appear together (positive correlation) or not (negative correlation). By doing this, objects were clustered by the level at which they correlate, identifying arrangement. Finally, the arrangements were correlated with contexts (such as desert, sea, creek) to identify contextualization and ultimately the focal theme of the image.

In a final note, it needs to be emphasized that visitors appearing in the images were not treated as 'objects' but as 'subjects' (Gallarza *et al.* 2002, p. 64). In none of the images analysed were visitors the major focal item. Rather, the appearance or absence of visitors in images was used as a way of distinguishing between gaze (Urry 2002) and experience (or performance) (Fairweather and Swaffield 2002; Garlick 2002; Urbain 1989) types of images. Fairweather and Swaffield (2002, p. 294) propose an interesting metaphor in this respect, using the graded experience of the Elizabethan theatre, 'in which some of the audience become active participants, some choose to remain detached spectators, and others move between the two. Furthermore, watching others in the audience perform becomes part of the experience'. In order to operationalize this, for arrangements in which visitors appeared, the focal theme was defined as being experiential, and in case of the absence of any tourists, the focal theme was defined as representations or reflections of objects and activities. Additional support for this was found in the concept of 'telepresence' (Hoffman and Novak 1996; Shih 1998), where it could be argued that the appearance of visitors in the images facilitates consumers projecting themselves into the actual experience.

CONTENT ANALYSIS OF TEXT

To analyse the textual element of the websites, we made use of CATPAC, a self-organizing artificial neural network software package used for content analysis of text. 'CATPAC is able to identify the most important words in a text and determine the patterns of similarity based on the way they are used in the text' (Woelfel 1998, p. 11). The theoretical foundation for CATPAC is based on an area of cognitive science, called neuroscience, a branch of psychology. Neuroscience is the study of the functioning of the nervous system, which includes the structures and functioning of the brain and its relationship to behaviour. Artificial neural networks are computing systems which mimic the brain through a network of highly interconnected, processing elements, giving them learning capabilities and enabling them to recognize, and to understand, subtle or complex patterns.

In simple terms, CATPAC produces a frequency table and proximity matrix for the most frequently used words in the text.

> Neural network software like CATPAC is modelled to operate like the structure of the human brain and like the human brain the software recognizes patterns of words and learns the regularities of co-occurrences or patterns. Moreover, if words are connected repeatedly the network will 'learn' the pattern, while patterns which are presented will seldom fade. The most frequently used words of a text build the nodes/neurons of the network. The relations between these words are defined by the co-occurring of the words in one unit. Connections between words co-occurring in a unit are strengthened, otherwise the connection values are reduced. (Züll and Landmann 2004, p. 2)

The unit of analysis is a sliding text window chosen by the researcher. Default window size is seven words. That is, CATPAC moves a window of seven words across the text and calculates word proximities based on the number of times words are found together (or not) within these frames. Alternatively, the window of analysis can be case-based. Here, CATPAC calculates word proximities based on the number of times respondents use words (or not) in each response to a question. The former approach was used in this study (a window of seven words), while the case-based approach is used in Chapter 13. The advantage of CATPAC over other software is that the researcher does not need to build a dictionary of words for which the software is to search (Züll and Landmann 2004). CATPAC will work with any and all words in the text; produce a frequency table; and then perform the neural network analysis on the top-X most frequently-found words. X (the maximum number of words to be included in the analysis) is to be defined by the researcher. However, words incorporated in an 'exclude' file are ignored. A default exclude file containing words such as articles, prepositions and other 'meaningless' words is provided with CAT-PAC, but the researcher can incorporate additional words of his/her own choice in the exclude file.

Summarizing, CATPAC identifies subtle and complex patterns in any documents or qualitative survey responses it processes, and is therefore ideal for analysing long pieces of text or a high quantity of qualitative data in order to identify the main concepts that authors of such texts or respondents are attempting to convey. It would take us beyond the object of this chapter to explain the detailed working of the program any further here, and the above explanation is a simplification, but for a good overview please refer to Woelfel and Stoyanoff (1993). Among others, Gretzel and Fesenmaier (2003), Ryan (2000) and Schmidt (2001) have advocated CAT-PAC as a valuable tool for content analysis. To obtain the results described below, five documents were content-analysed by CATPAC – one for each economic sector and one for the total population. Those words appearing with a minimum frequency, covering at least 2.5 per cent of the analysed content, were included in the results (ranging from 24 to 28 unique words, depending on the specific content of the text being reviewed). To determine patterns of similarity and central concepts, several hierarchical cluster analysis methods were applied to the proximity table produced by CATPAC in order to test coherence of the clustering solutions. As a result, the name 'Dubai' was excluded from analysis as this was obviously the most central word in all texts (representing 11.9 per cent of all words included in the analysis of the total text, compared to the second most frequent word, which represented 3.7 per cent). As Dubai correlated with almost every other concept in the text, it distorted the cluster analysis. Since it is obvious that the analysis relates to Dubai, there seemed to be no harm in excluding this word from the procedure, thus allowing better clustering results on the rest of the data. The outcomes reported in the next section are based on Ward's clustering method.

RESULTS

The content analysis of pictures and text was conducted separately. Nevertheless, results were strikingly similar. The rest of this chapter will report on the results of the content analysis of the pictures, followed by the results of the CATPAC analysis of the text, after which the Conclusion will pull observations together.

Pictures

Table 9.2 lists the results of the content analysis according to motifs, arrangement and contextualization. Motifs are clustered together with other motives with which they seem to often appear together (see Figure 9.1). The most frequently appearing motif is 'dining', followed by 'airport facilities'. The most frequently appearing context is that of a desert setting. Visitors appear in 24 per cent of the images, which suggests that, in general terms, the experiential nature of tourism is not often reflected in the projected imagery.

Someone who is unaware of the fact that Table 9.2 refers to Dubai, could read it as follows: it refers to an Arabic and Islamic country – mosques, palm trees, camels, dhows. In origin, it concerns a nomadic culture: monuments represent only 0.8 percent of images. The culture sustains a masculine order: pictures that include men (8.3 per cent), falconry, four-wheel drive vehicles and belly dancers. And finally, a tourist infrastructure has been put in place aimed at entertainment and leisure; the majority of pictures contain references to this. Hence Dubai seems to present its modern facilities, but does not distinguish its own unique identity. Table 9.2 could refer to many other places in the region. Dubai appears to be attracting visitors for its facilities and not for reasons based on a unique local or national identity.

Figure 9.1 shows the clustering of motifs and contexts using bivariate correlations as well as our own interpretation. There seem to be eight logical focal themes, which can then each be split into experiential or non-experiential themes depending on the presence or absence of visitors in the images.

Table 9.3 lists the fourteen focal themes (the themes of 'hospitality' and 'old and new' had no experiential dimension), their frequency and significant differences in distribution across sectors of the industry. Only 'cultural experience' was not significant at all, and 'reflections of old and new' and 'heritage experience' were only significant at 10 per cent. As was suspected earlier, only 26 per cent of images are experiential in nature. Most frequent focal themes are 'reflections of modern Dubai', 'hospitality facilities', 'leisure/recreational facilities and activities', 'reflections of culture' and 'outdoor activities', together making up almost two-thirds of the total number of images. This suggests that what is projected is very much facility-/activity-based. This is particularly true for the hospitality and transport

TABLE 9.2 Dubai website images content analysis results (n = 505)

Motif	Frequency Percentage of images in which motif appears	Arrangement Average no. of motifs in images that include this motif	Contextualization	
			Context in which cluster of motifs often appears	Percentage of images in which context appears
Dining (restaurant, bar, disco)	12.5	1.14		
Airport facilities	10.3	1.52		
Staff	4.6	2.22		
Modern shops/shopping malls	4.6	1.73		
Spa facilities	2.6	1.23		
Old fort	1.6	1.25		
Four-wheel drive vehicle	9.1	1.67	Mountains	3.2
Local Emirati men	8.3	2.45	Desert	16.0
Camp/picnic area	5.0	2.24		
Camels	4.2	2.57		
Sunset	1.6	2.38		
Artefacts (e.g. Arabic coffee pots, jewellery, jugs)	1.6	2.13		
Falcon	1.2	2.50		
Mosque	1.0	2.80		
Belly dancer	1.4	3.57		
Henna body painting	1.2	3.17		
Local Emirati girls/women	1.4	1.43		
Skyline	8.7	1.59		
Traditional dhow boat	4.8	2.20	Creek	9.1
Traditional architecture (e.g. Barasti houses, museum, wind towers, old Arabic doors)	4.8	1.70		
Hotel exterior	7.3	1.76		
Palm trees	6.7	2.62		
Water sports	5.5	1.71	Sea	8.1
Swimming pool	3.6	2.44		
Beach	3.6	2.39		
Gardens	2.0	2.80		
Hotel interior (non F&B, i.e. rooms/lobby)	3.8	1.11		

(Continued)

TABLE 9.2 Continued

Motif	Frequency Percentage of images in which motif appears	Arrangement Average no. of motifs in images that include this motif	Contextualization Context in which cluster of motifs often appears	Percentage of images in which context appears
Golf	3.6	1.78		
Golf club	1.8	2.56		
Souk	2.8	1.57		
Horse races	2.6	1.15		
Meeting, incentive, conference, exhibition facilities (MICE)	2.0	1.20		
Sport	1.6	1.63		
Wildlife	1.4	1.43		
Limousines	1.2	2.00		
Monuments	0.8	2.25		

FIGURE 9.1 | Dubai website focal themes of images through clustering of motifs

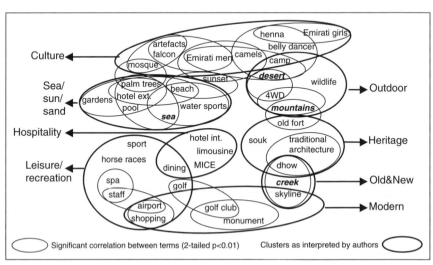

Note: Words in italics are contexts.

TABLE 9.3 Website focal themes and differences between sectors in Dubai (n = 505)

Focal theme	Freq. (%)	Hospitality (%)	Tour operators (%)	DMO (%)	Air transport (%)	F	p
	n = 505	n = 99	n = 302	n = 48	n = 56		
Leisure/ recreational facilities and activities	11.7	10.1[a]	10.6[a]	8.3[a]	**23.2**[b]	**2.8**	**0.040**
Experience modern Dubai	3.8	2.0[a]	0.3[a]	0.0[a]	**28.6**[b]	**45.3**	**0.000**
Reflection modern Dubai	17.4	7.1[a]	16.2[b]	**20.8**[c]	**39.3**[d]	**9.3**	**0.000**
Sea, sun, sand experience	3.4	2.0[a]	3.3[a]	**10.4**[b]	0.0[a]	**3.3**	**0.020**
Reflections of heritage	9.1	0.0[a]	**10.9**[b]	**27.1**[c]	0.0[a]	**12.6**	**0.000**
Reflections of culture	11.5	1.0[a]	**15.2**[c]	**16.7**[d]	5.4[b]	**6.2**	**0.000**
Outdoor activities	10.1	0.0[a]	**14.9**[b]	**12.5**[b]	0.0[a]	**8.8**	**0.000**
Outdoor experience	4.2	0.0[a]	**6.6**[b]	2.1[a]	0.0[a]	**4.0**	**0.008**
Reflections of old and new	2.2	0.0[a]	**3.6**[b]	0.0[a]	0.0[a]	**2.5**	**0.056**
Heritage experience	2.0	0.0[a]	**3.3**[b]	0.0[a]	0.0[a]	**2.3**	**0.077**
Hospitality facilities	13.1	**35.4**[b]	8.9[a]	4.2[a]	3.6[a]	**20.7**	**0.000**
Leisure/recreational experience	9.1	**30.3**[b]	4.3[a]	4.2[a]	1.8[a]	**25.6**	**0.000**
Sea, sun, sand facilities and activities	8.5	**19.2**[b]	7.6[a]	2.1[a]	0.0[a]	**7.8**	**0.000**
Cultural experience	3.8	1.0		2.1	5.4	1.2	0.326
Reflection of Dubai	40.2	8.1	46.0	64.6	44.6		
Facility- and activity-based	43.4	64.6	42.1	27.1	26.8		
Experience-based	26.1	35.4		22.5	18.8	35.7	

Note: Rows that contain significant variance between groups according to ANOVA's F-test are indicated in **bold type**. In these cases, means with a different superscripted letter (a, b, c, d) are significantly different at the 5 per cent level according to Duncan's post hoc test, while the letters indicate a within-row ranking (a are groups with the lowest means, d are groups with the highest means).

sectors. While they also have many experience-based images, these images show visitors making use of the leisure/recreational facilities and modern airport facilities, respectively. In fact, the hospitality and transport sectors had no images related to heritage, the outdoors or contrasts of old and new Dubai at all, and very few cultural images.

The promotion of the rich culture, heritage and identity of Dubai is therefore clearly left to the destination marketing organization, and to some extent the tour operators. In it (see the Culture cluster in Figure 9.1) we can recognize some of Hall's (1996, p. 627) elements of national identity, such as the emphasis on origins, continuity, tradition and timelessness (henna painting, falconry); the foundational myth (camels and camps in the desert); and the idea of a pure, original people or 'folk' (the Emirati men and women as depicted in these images), but also the invention of tradition (belly dancers). The fifth of Hall's elements, the narrative of the nation, can partly be found in the focal theme 'Heritage'.

Tour operators, while involved in cultural activities and the only ones projecting some heritage experiences, are primarily involved in outdoor activities, which represent largely what is called wadi- and dune-bashing (the idea of taking a four-wheel drive vehicle to its limits in small river beds in the mountains or on sand dunes). Finally, when performing an analysis of variance between private, semi-governmental and government organizations, there also proved to be a significant difference in the projection of the 'reflections of heritage' theme ($F = 12.3$, $p = 0.000$). This focal theme was present in 27 per cent of the imagery used by the government, compared to 9 per cent and 4 per cent for private and semi-government organizations, respectively.

Text

Table 9.4 displays the frequency list of unique words in the total text covering all websites. Based on the cluster analysis using the CATPAC proximity table, only four small clusters were identified: Arabian Desert Experience; Jumeirah International World (class) Hotel Facilities; Golf Club; and Shopping Centre. The other fourteen most frequently found words, could not clearly be clustered, probably because they were used in different contexts, in different parts of the text, coming from different types of sector-specific websites. This assumption is quite plausible, as analysis of the website texts per sector resulted in the identification of clear central concepts within each of the four documents, but different ones for different sectors (see Table 9.5). The most commonly used word in all the texts is, not surprisingly, the word 'desert', which is also part of one of the most

TABLE 9.4 Frequency list of unique words in all Dubai website text

Word	Freq.	%
Desert	298	6.4
International	290	6.2
Hotel	280	6.0
City	232	5.0
World	229	4.9
Arabian	222	4.8
Golf	219	4.7
Available	192	4.1
Facilities	178	3.8
Club	176	3.8
Jumeirah	174	3.7
Guests	172	3.7
Experience	166	3.6
Emirates	162	3.5
Day	155	3.3
Beach	153	3.3
Tour	151	3.2
Shopping	147	3.2
Water	146	3.1
Enjoy	143	3.1
Traditional	142	3.0
Group	137	2.9
Resort	131	2.8
Offers	130	2.8
Centre	120	2.6
Service	116	2.5

important central concepts, the Arabian Desert Experience. While this can be interpreted as a reference to Hall's (1996, p. 627) 'foundational myth', it is at the same time the only central concept in the overall analysis that can be linked initially to Hall's five elements of identity (two more can be found in Table 9.5 as being projected by the tourist board: the narrative of the nature of life in Dubai and its Arab origins). Another important central concept in the complete text is the combination of Jumeirah's International World (class) Hotel Facilities (Jumeirah is the geographical area of Dubai

TABLE 9.5 Central concepts of website content for sectors

Sector	Central concepts	Related words
Transport (5,398 words)	The airport	International airport *with* special *facilities* available *in 3* terminals
	Infrastructure	Gate(s) and business lounges
	Facilities	Duty free facilities and services located *in* concourse
	VIP facilities	Car *(parking and limo service)* at an *X-amount of* DHS *(local currency) cost per* day, *first*-class lounge and *hotel* rooms and *(business and medical)* centre
Tourist Board (16,709 words)	Purpose	*With chairman* Sheikh Maktoum *promotes* international tourism *for the* city *of Dubai*
	Heritage	Traditional life *around the* desert *and the* creek
	Modern Dubai	World-*class* modern shopping centres for visitors
	Cultural origin	Middle East, Arabian Gulf, United Arab Emirates
	Facilities	Golf club *and* available *tourist* facilities
	Outdoor	Bird species and water
Hospitality (28,143 words)	Properties 1	Jebel Ali golf resort, shooting *club* and spa
	Properties 2	Jumeirah International hotels and beach club *have* world-*class* facilities available *to* guests
	Dining	Experience and enjoy dining *in the* bars and restaurants located *close to the* rooms *or otherwise open for* day *visitors*
	Health club	Body and skin treatment
Tour Operators (42,235 words)	Sightseeing tour	Experience city tour: shopping, camels and the desert
	Incentives	World-*class* hotels and traditional Arabian adventures for groups *and your* guests
	Desert safari	Enjoy sand-dune drive and Arabic dinner at night
	Other activities	International golf club and water *sports,* tours and services *in the* Emirates

Note: Text in italics added by the researchers for clarity of reading.

where most of the resort hotels are situated). Of greater interest, though, are the differences in website content between the various economic sectors. This is shown in Table 9.5.

In line with the results from the content analysis of images on these same websites, it can be observed that the promotion of the rich culture, heritage and identity of Dubai is clearly left to the destination marketing organization, and to some extent the tour operators. The latter, despite being involved in cultural activities and the only ones projecting some heritage experiences, are primarily involved in outdoor activities and incentives. The transport and hospitality websites focus primarily on facilities and activities. While it is positive to observe that the hotels also mention guest experiences, this refers particularly to dining experiences.

What is striking is that, while there is limited reference to the experiential nature of tourism, no multisensory references, based on what we would (expect to) taste, hear, smell, see or feel when consuming these experiential products, are found in the texts. The words 'water' 'desert' and 'enjoy' probably come closest. It must be noted in this respect that, of course, pictures used on websites are an important part of the online projected place image: as visual cues. But even when taking into account the results of that part of the study, there is a general lack of reference to other sensory cues and emotions. They say that 'one picture is worth a thousand words', but a picture and description of a hotel room, restaurant or airport gate, for example, is not going to tell us much about the actual place experience one can expect at that particular, unique destination, in terms of the multisensory emotions that will be generated.

CONCLUSION

When analysing the projected identity through content analysis of websites in Dubai, we found that the representation of the identity of place, its culture and heritage is left to the government, the destination marketing organization and, in part, to tour operators. The vast majority of the unique elements of Dubai's identity are presented, but infrequently and largely by the destination marketing organization. While the government is trying to react to recent geopolitical events with projects and campaigns that are meant to illustrate the rich heritage of Dubai, private sectors, and particularly the hospitality and transport sectors, seem to be avoiding references to the local culture and heritage. As Fesenmaier and MacKay (1996, p. 42) argue: 'destination promotions commonly include people as tourists. An absence of local peoples may suggest denial of their existence and removal of relationships between the visiting at [sic and] local cultures'. The findings here suggest that this might apply to some economic sectors in Dubai, therefore both private sector and public sector appear to be working at cross purposes. In the case of the airport website, in particular, this is strange as it is the one most heavily involved in the media campaigns promoting Dubai's heritage. But even when it comes to the way that culture, heritage and identity are projected by the destination marketing organization, 'gaze'-type images are the norm, as opposed to experiential representations. At the same time, it will be difficult for the airport and hospitality industry in Dubai to reflect identity, as 80 per cent of the population and most of the labour as well as the management in the private sector consists of expatriates.

The results of this research clearly show that the way Dubai projects its place imagery lacks creativity and 'cross-border' thinking between actors, and therefore fails to reflect coherently its true place identity. Most of the projected imagery is fragmented in nature and product-based, showing the facilities and activities on offer. The experiential types of images that *are* found are those of fragmented experiences relating directly to the specific product offered by particular sectors (such as in 'dining experiences' or 'experience modern shopping facilities'). Therefore these experiential type images contribute in the main to the commoditization and consumption nature of place experiences. The use of photography to design effective (holistic) experiences, as suggested by Sternberg (1997) and Garlick (2002), seems to be very limited. The experiential nature of the 'consumption of place' is almost completely unrecognizable when one tries to interpret what is projected by tourism websites.

Hirschman and Holbrook (1982, p. 92) emphasize the importance of multisensory, fantasy and emotive aspects of experiential or hedonic products such as tourism. Yet, the way places project images of their product offering, such as, for example, on destination marketing websites (Gretzel and Fesenmaier 2003), is still:

> Focusing on communicating lists comprised of functional attributes such as price, distances and room availability. The design is based on a model of a rational and information seeking consumer which often results in simple activity based descriptions that reflect the supply side ... rather than an actual consumer's perceptions of tourism experiences. It is argued that this lack of an experiential mindset within the tourism industry is due largely to a lack of understanding of the nature of tourism experiences. (Gretzel and Fesenmaier 2003, p. 50)

Gretzel and Fesenmaier's conclusion is supported by the research findings presented in this chapter. One of the key challenges seems to be that the focus of private industry decision-makers is on maintaining visitor satisfaction levels and yield in their own very specific subdomain. The part of the image of the world that they perceive is often only related to the specific facilities and convenient commodities that they offer for consumption. Put differently, the private sector makes little or no effort to project place experiences that are embedded in a local context. They seem concerned neither with place identity nor how it should be projected. Therefore they often fail to incorporate the full potential of the prospective rich consumption experience that would match the visitors' perceived place image and the experience delivery they expect.

Gretzel and Fesenmaier (2003) showed that sensory information regarding consumer perceptions of places can be researched and bundled into sensory themes following specific patterns of association, which 'can be used to define coherent experiences sought after by certain groups of travelers'. Adding such vividness (Hoffman and Novak 1996; Shih 1998) would help to create telepresence, which would facilitate the consumer to experience place without having to fill in too many blanks. This proves that there is a world of opportunity for places to use the learning of the hedonic consumption domain to bridge the place brand performance gap between place brand strategy and place brand satisfaction; that is, the way that the place identity is reflected in the product offering, and the way it is communicated, in order to provide the rich place experience the visitor is seeking, based on a shared identity that has been projected by the destination (among others, through the media, websites, art and literature, historical narratives and prior experience with a culture other than one's own). Of course, with the current state of technology, it is still not easy to incorporate real stimulation of all the senses; touching and smelling are the least advanced elements of virtual reality, and even sounds are often left out. But the experiential nature of what is projected can be advanced even through well-written text alone, with clever references to the senses. An example of this will be presented in Chapter 13.

To do everything possible to create the right expectations through a strong projected image is crucial. If places fail to develop a design that is capable of dealing with local identity and the emerging transnational mediascapes, ethnoscapes and technoscapes, simultaneously, it risks the high probability of 'unbalanced' host–guest encounters. Consequently, visitors are likely to adjust their perceived place image and even to lower their expectations, based on their actual experiences. But what may be worse, at least from a place marketing perspective, is that they are likely to misinterpret and share perceptual inferences with other strangers, thereby creating a self-perpetuating spiral of misrepresentation in the image formation process. Therefore it is crucial that both the design of a shared identity and the construction of expectations are rooted in a sense of place. Ultimately, the quality of a place experience and sustainable host community development depends on the intelligent alignment of the perceived place image and projected identity. Our perceived image research on our signature case Dubai will be the area of research covered in Chapter 13.

CHAPTER 10

Mini Case Zeeland (The Netherlands): Place Experience

The authors wish to thank Gerard van Keken for his major contributions to this chapter; please also refer to Van Keken and Go (2006).

Culinary festivals and place experiences are uniquely positioned to integrate food and culture with the aim of regenerating authentic regional identities. In this sense, culinary experiences may be seen as a platform to foster a close encounter between host and guest, motivated by a common interest in the 'Other' and shared passions for food and drink, which are differentiated on the basis of regional identity and offer an opportunity to construct place brands. Culinary festivals and product offerings can stimulate the senses, arouse emotions, encourage social interaction and consumer involvement and inspire learning in aesthetic environments in order to create rich place experiences.

One aspect of this system of attractions are festivals, which Getz (cited in Derrett 2004, p. 32) highlights as 'unique leisure and cultural experiences, powerful travel motivators and facilitators of community pride and development'. Festivals and events provide authenticity and uniqueness, especially events based on inherent indigenous values; convenient hospitality and affordability; and with themes and symbols for participants and spectators. Derrett (2004) states that the more an event is seen by its host community as emerging from within rather than being imposed on them, the greater that community's acceptance of the event will be. There is growing interest in the notion that festivals and events represent the host community's sense of itself and sense of place. This requires a close reading of the host–guest relationship (Derrett 2004, p. 33).

Used as an example in this chapter is culinary tourism in Zeeland, discussed in Chapter 6 and a province in the south-west of the Netherlands. The choice of this province for culinary experiences as an example of place branding initiatives is not surprising, because Zeeland's identity is partly based on its past and present fishery and rural heritage. The province is still a major producer of seafood and regional agricultural products. According to several authors (Hall *et al.* 2003; Hjalager and Richards 2002) there is a very close relationship between gastronomy and local, regional and national identities. This part of Zeeland's identity, and the subsequent product development based on that identity, is captured by the photo survey and resident perception survey presented in Chapter 6.

The building of a gastronomic community, a culinary festival 'the taste of Zeeland' (in Dutch: 'De Smaek van Zeàland'), a culinary guidebook and a supporting marketing campaign, together with the policies of the province of Zeeland on fishery, agriculture and tourism, proves how the identity of a region can be constructed and branded. The goal of this identity construction is to create unique experiences for both hosts and guests, virtual and physical contact and encounters, and improve relations between the community of Zeeland and visitors.

EXPERIENCE BRANDING ZEELAND

As global competition between places increases, the search for distinct offerings becomes more intense. Gastronomy is seen as an important source for marketable images and experiences for visitors (Richards 2002, p. 4). Richards emphasizes that food has become an important factor in the search for identity. Food is one of our basic needs, so it is not surprising that it is also one of the most widespread markers of identity. We are what we eat, not just in a physiological sense, but also in a psychological and sociological sense. Food has been used as a means of forging and supporting identities, principally because what we eat and the way we eat are such basic aspects of our culture (Richards 2002, p. 5).

In particular, when place names are attached to products (also referred to as the 'origin effect'), eating the products is like experiencing the sense of place, and obviously even more so when consuming the product in its place of origin. Zeeland, for example, offers Zeeuwse mosselen (mussels from Zeeland); Oosterschelde lobster; eel from Lake Veere; Zeeuwse oysters; blackcurrants from Zuid-Beveland; and cheese from Schellach. Hughes (1995, cited in Richards 2002) points out that there is a notion of a natural relationship between a region's land, its climatic conditions and the character of the food it produces. It is this geographical diversity that provides for the regional distinctiveness in culinary traditions and the evolution of a characteristic heritage. The name Zeeland includes the two words 'Sea' and 'Land'; the culinary relevance is obvious.

FIGURE 10.1 | **Culinary festival 'De Smaek van Zeàland' held in Middelburg**

Source: Photograph reproduced with the kind permission of Gerard van Keken.

In its search for unique experiences emphasizing Zeeland's identity, the 'Foundation de Smaek van Zeàland' organizes an annual culinary festival called 'de Smaek van Zeàland' (the taste of Zeeland) (see Figure 10.1). The culinary event was, until 2006, based on the town square in front of Middelburg's Abbey, which created a unique medieval atmosphere. Since 2006, the event has been moved to the Middelburg yacht club. To enhance the experiential nature of the event, cooks prepare the food in an open kitchen in front of audience and are interviewed by a professional chef. Twenty restaurants participate in the event, together with almost twenty regional food producers and wholesalers, and many volunteers. Alongside the restaurants, where the public can enjoy the regional dishes and regional music, there is also a culinary market offering regional produce. The aims of the event are:

- to enhance regional/local awareness;

- to create unique Zeeland experiences;

- to create opportunities for local residents and visitors to meet;

- to promote Zeeland's gastronomy;

FIGURE 10.2 | Imaginative branding of folklore

Sources: Photographs reproduced with the kind permission of: (*left*) Anda van Riet, styling by Karina Leijnse; (*right*) Gerard van Keken.

- to stimulate co-operation and partnership; and

- to encourage innovation.

Over the years, the event has been a proven success through its appearance in many communication channels, such as a festival magazine, popular magazines, television and radio coverage, press lunches, and free publicity in all kinds of media as well as through the internet. There is a problem, however, in that the success is not lasting and results in brief encounters rather than lasting relationships. The success of the festival has not yet added very much to the overall brand positioning of Zeeland and the way it is experienced in the long run. The focus on culinary aspects was therefore enlarged to include a focus on cultural aspects as well. The celebration that took place in 2004 was extraordinary because of a fashion show that mixed older residents in their traditional folk costumes with young students from the Amsterdam Fashion Institute showing their designs based on these traditional costumes, on a catwalk of mussel shells. The atmosphere was further enhanced by combining a modern DJ and a large choir performing traditional songs about the sea.

But, for the future, new initiatives have to be developed in order to link the brand, the identity and the marketing of Zeeland. An integral marketing and promotion plan has already been made, including the formulation of product–market combinations and answering the question as to how these target groups can be 'touched' with the authentic charm of Zeeland. However, vicarious experiences, particularly the opportunities provided by the internet, should be incorporated. For example, a virtual

FIGURE 10.3 | New Zealand Edge

Source: With the kind permission of www.nzedge.com.

community site should be created where hosts and guests meet and share their passion and love for Zeeland. The site must be a place where one can find information, but also to get involved in online narratives, to get an idea of the true sense of place of Zeeland; in short, the possibility of sharing experiences. This should facilitate interactivity, the creation of new relationships; and getting to know (potential) visitors and their preferences and interests. Eventually, a community will be built around 'The taste of Zeeland' as a brand. Zeeland could follow the example of the 'New Zeeland' in the South Pacific (discovered in 1642 by the Dutch explorer Abel Tasman), where New Zealanders Brian Sweeney and Kevin Roberts (CEO of Saatchi and Saatchi, and author of Lovemarks 2005) created New Zealand Edge (www.nzedge.com). This online community instils a new way of thinking about New Zealand's identity, people, stories, achievements and place in the world. It aims to strengthen identity and foster the global community of New Zealanders. These pointers (identity and 'compatriation') are substantiated online through stories of New Zealand heroes who have made their mark on world culture; a features section that covers contemporary New Zealand achievements and issues through essays, forums and features; and a media page which surveys New Zealand as featured in the world's online media.

ENCOUNTERS OF HOST AND GUEST

The resident perception survey of Zeeland's identity, as presented in Chapter 6, provides us with a theoretical foundation for the chosen direction of the place-brand-inspired product development. Three resident perception statements of the identity of Zeeland combined the seaside sensations of water and beach; polder vistas; and the battle against the water, and together provide an excellent opportunity to demonstrate Zeeland's unique and distinct positioning and create experiences for Zeeland's residents as well as for visitors. Traces of other statements such as 'folklore and nostalgia' and 'the intimacy of the hinterland' can also be found in the experience concept, through the participation of residents who still wear traditional folk costumes, and by allowing the event to remain small-scale and refined, creating a unique event. The taste of Zeeland is a good example of an experience concept where visitors as guests, and Zeeland's' residents as hosts, meet Zeeland's cultural identity as well as each other.

In a polyinclusive world this means that 'virtual encounters' (providing information, online narrative, virtual communities, Web 2.0; or specifically, vicarious experiences) should arouse consumer expectations in people's minds, so that a desire for a physical visit is stimulated and eventually (pseudo)-relations (in social space) are established. This should result in satisfied guests who love to return to Zeeland for gastronomic and other experiences, and have a shared history of interaction with their hosts. The experiences at the Abbey and yacht club in Zeeland have to be unique, pleasant, personal, aesthetic and engaging in various ways, as we have been taught through the wisdom of 'the experience economy'.

All actors, a network of companies, restaurants and accommodation providers, public organizations, volunteers and residents in general are important 'software' creating the event. They are crucial elements in making the taste of Zeeland a success, positioning Zeeland as a gastronomic region. Important in this regard is the imagined and experienced hospitality, which can be described as 'a contemporaneous human exchange, which is voluntarily entered into, and designed to enhance the mutual well-being of the parties concerned through the provision of accommodation, and/or food and/or drink (Brotherton 1999, p. 168).

Two aspects are relevant here: 'the human exchange' and the 'mutual well-being of the parties'. But a crucial aspect is missing in this definition.

The offering as defined here is only focusing on material things such as accommodation, food and drink. Just as important, or possibly more so, are the immaterial components such as the atmosphere, the constructed identity and its authenticity, emotions and the personal attention of people. These create the feeling of wellbeing and should be an integral part of human experience. It is such a push that enables people to move out of their every-day 'environmental bubble' and open up to the possibility of a 'close encounter of host and guest'.

Too often, these close encounters are missing. Culinary events, where both residents and visitors have to sit next to each other (which is why benches are preferred to individual chairs), create excellent opportunities for experiencing (pseudo-)encounters, long-term relationships and shared experiences. Here, people eat their meals, get to know each other, under-stand each other's culture and share their thoughts. A culinary event like 'the taste of Zeeland' can be seen as the host community's sense of itself and sense of place, providing a unique and authentic experience.

CONCLUSION

The research of resident perceptions of Zeeland's identity, as described in Chapter 6, proved to be a good starting point for constructing and decon-structing old and new identities. As globalization, homogenization and stan-dardization have an impact on localities and fast food continues to conquer the world, another trend is noticeable in regionalism, uniqueness, authentic-ity and 'slow' food. Culinary experiences are strongly connected with a region's identity and are an excellent opportunity to construct these new identities. Zeeland, a peripheral region in the Netherlands, is using culinary experiences in its place branding. Culinary festivals are a good opportunity to construct and enhance a regional identity in the globalized world. Festivals can be used to represent the host community's sense of itself and sense of place, as Derrett (2004) has suggested. The festivals can be used to create close encounters between host and guest, by creating opportunities to meet and develop a shared history of interaction. Contacts and encounters can be constructed in the information space (internet) where a pre-taste might be provided, leading to a physical visit with a real taste. The festivals can be used as a tool to draw visitors out of their environmental bubble and to get to know the host's and the region's culture, heritage, stories and gas-tronomy. The sharing of these experiences between hosts and guests might lead to a shared passion and love for the destination, which might lead to a culinary and cultural community in both the information space and the social space, with a mix of encounters and (pseudo-)relations.

Summary of Part 3

Brands represent products and services, but a place, even though it provides a certain product – offering tourism services, investment and trade opportunities, jobs, housing, education and health care systems – in essence it is an environment in which visitors can co-create personal experiences. A place brand therefore represents a hedonic product that is consumed not for any material benefits that it might bring, but for the psychological stimuli – sensory cues, emotions, fantasies – that it generates. Therefore, whatever reputation the brand strategy attempts to build, if it is not realistic, the brand will be exposed when target customers finally visit the place. Place experience, then, always has an impact on the perceived image, because even if perceptions are realistic, they tend to be simplistic and superficial.

Place experiences are about people's interactions with their physical, virtual and social environments through their senses, stimulating imagery processing in the mind, giving 'meaning', and generating emotions and actions as well as social interactions. Combining several theories that have been discussed above, there seem to be some common insights about how to guarantee brand value co-creation through optimal experiences. First, dialogue between (potential) visitors and the experience network (public and private parties involved in the place product offering) should facilitate the negotiation of appropriate expectations and the formulation of clear goals in terms of the types of experiences being sought. Second, transparency facilitates the exchange of information and provision of feedback on progress in service deliveries and risk assessments at touch points where sensory stimuli link perceptions to cognitive and affective processes. Finally, access to the experience networks allows the visitor to pick and choose, and co-create a personal experience through active or passive involvement and relating to others while finding a balance between challenges and personal skills. Creating such environments based on a worthwhile experience concept is also referred to as 'imagineering'. This has been illustrated through the case of Zeeland, in the Netherlands.

A place experience cannot be tested or sampled prior to a visit, but there are other forms of hedonic consumption that can give a 'reality-like' insight into the living place's identity. For example, virtual worlds, social networks, television, movies, music, arts, travelling exhibitions, events, online videos and blogs can provide vicarious experiences. The tremendous impact of movies on tourism arrivals, for example, has been acknowledged repeatedly. In order to build effective vicarious experiences, vividness, which addresses the breadth and depth of sensory information provided, and interactivity, are important prerequisites, as they facilitate telepresence.

In this, visuals and narratives are essential elements for projecting rich place brand experiences. Careful selection and consistent use across channels will help to build reputation, but is also a challenge, with different actors (particularly public versus private parties) designing their messages according to their own objectives. This is illustrated clearly in our case study on projected images of Dubai. Ultimately, place branding requires the effective management of human interactions in experience environments and how consistently they are marketed, otherwise a place brand performance gap might occur, as seems to be an issue in our signature case Dubai.

PART 4

Place Brand Satisfaction

Our image of the world is not uniformly certain, uniformly probable, or uniformly clear. Messages, therefore, may have the effect not only of adding to or of reorganising the image. They may also have the effect of clarifying it, that is, of making something which previously was regarded as less certain more certain, or something which was previously seen in a vague way, clearer. Messages may also have the contrary effect. They may introduce doubt or uncertainty into the image. (Boulding 1956, p. 10)

Place branding is all about managing reputation, so therefore Part 4 will focus entirely on aspects of perceived image. In Part 2, the first of three perspectives on the 3-gap place branding model, we focused on place identity and projected image, while in Part 3, experience took centre stage. In Part 4, we shall focus on how place brand reputation is built through the perceived images of millions of individuals around the world. Chapter 11 illustrates how perceptions, being individual and influenced by many processes, create personal expectations that place brands need to fulfil to avoid the occurrence of a place brand satisfaction gap. Chapter 12 will show how traditional image research is insufficient, and Chapter 13 provides in-depth insight into new and innovative image research methods.

What we would like you to take away from this part of the book is to:

- Appreciate that where place brands attempt to build reputation from the supply side, images are personal constructs, the sum of beliefs, ideas and impressions in the minds of individuals on the demand side.

- Categorize elements of place image as cognitive, affective or conative as well as attribute-based versus holistic, functional versus psychological, and common versus unique.

- Evaluate the many different ways in which perceived image can be studied, as illustrated through our case studies of the Netherlands and Dubai.

- Recognize that, as place image is a personal construct, it is not the objective perception of place, but rather of the relationship between place and the individual (self-congruity).

- Identify, as a result, how images are influenced through cultural background and social, personal and psychological characteristics of the individual and his/her identity.

- Consider that as well as overt induced agents (marketing) and organic agents (experience), as discussed earlier, image is largely impacted by autonomous agents or what is reported in the news media in terms of temporal environmental and situation influences, such as economic conditions, political circumstances, technological advancements and social changes, which is illustrated in our research on perceived image for case Dubai, among others.

- Consider how one other source has tremendous impact on place image, namely word of mouth or the online 'word of mouse' (solicited or unsolicited organic agents).

- Recommend that the place brand should build consistent and realistic images, because these images create the expectations that need to be met when visitors experience the place. If not, a place brand satisfaction gap might occur, as could be the case in some markets for Dubai.

CHAPTER 11

Place Brand Satisfaction Elements

The formation of image has been described by Reynolds (1965, p. 69), as one of the first commentators, as the development of a mental construct based on a few impressions chosen from a flood of information. In the case of place image, this 'flood of information' has many sources, including promotional sources (advertising and brochures), the opinions of others (family/friends, travel agents), media reporting (newspapers, magazines, television news reporting and documentaries) and popular culture (motion pictures, literature); 'Furthermore, by actually visiting the destination, the image will be affected and modified based upon first hand information and experience' (Echtner and Ritchie 2003, p. 38).

As Reynolds (1965, p. 70) states: 'often, of course, the word "image" is used as equivalent to reputation ... what people believe about a person or an institution, *versus* character, what the person or institution actually is'. The latter could also be referred to as identity, as discussed in Chapter 4. We shall focus now on the image as the mental construct of the tourist, migrant worker, investor or trader. The following sections will expand on what Ryan (2000, p. 121) states the visitor to be; that is, 'a voyeur whose very presence is a catalyst for action in both the meta and narrow narrative; an interpreter of experience within personal constructs of meaning, but able to discard those meanings in ludic moments ... Within this framework of analysis the place becomes a locus of selected meanings'. However, a challenge for hosts that attract culturally different groups of visitors is to exploit those few impressions in order to mould perceptions and thereby raise the right expectations. The further away and the more culturally different the visitor, the harder the task of influencing the perceived place image will be. As explained by McCabe and Stokoe (2004, p. 604): 'The changing nature and character of places, together with adapting modes of leisure consumption and commercialization of locales, have shifted the ways in which meanings are attached to places.' The way in which people do this is the subject of the following section.

PERCEIVED PLACE IMAGE

With regard to experiential products, people are involved in an ongoing search for information (Leemans 1994, p. 23). By collecting information, the consumer creates an image or 'mental prototype'(Tapachai and Waryszak 2000, p. 37) of what the experience might be like. As place experiences are intangible, images become more important than reality (Gallarza *et al.* 2002, p. 57) and the place images projected in information space will have a great influence on the place images as perceived by consumers. The latter are generally accepted (Echtner and Ritchie 1991, 1993, 2003; Padgett and Allen 1997, p. 50; Tapachai and Waryszak 2000, p. 38) to be based on attributes, functional consequences (or expected benefits), and the symbolic meanings or psychological characteristics consumers associate with a specific place (or service). As a consequence, projected images influence place positioning and ultimately location choice behaviour.

There appears to be a consensus among authors that the place image research stream has emerged from Hunt's work of 1971 (Gallarza *et al.* 2002, p. 58; Hunt 1975). 'From this time onwards, there have been numerous and varied approaches to its study', totalling 65 works, between 1971 and 1999, as identified by the thorough synoptic work of Gallarza *et al.* (2002) and of Pike (2002) ,who reviewed 142 papers. One influential study was published by Echtner and Ritchie (1991, 1993, 2003). Through their research, Echtner and Ritchie concluded that:

- Place image should be envisioned as having two main components: those that are attribute based and those that are holistic.

- Each of these components contains functional (or more tangible) and psychological (or more abstract) characteristics.

- Place images can also range from those based on 'common' functional and psychological traits to those based on more distinctive or even unique features, events, feelings or auras.

This illustrates that there are many aspects involved in formulating the total place image in the mind of the (potential) visitor. The three-dimensional model envisaged by Echtner and Ritchie is depicted in Figure 11.1, together with some examples for four of the six components. The common-versus-unique dimension is missing in this example for Nepal, but it normally

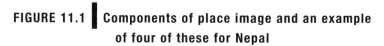

FIGURE 11.1 | Components of place image and an example
of four of these for Nepal

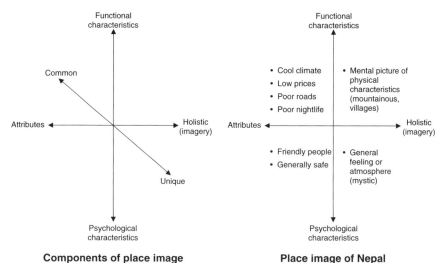

Components of place image   **Place image of Nepal**

Source: Reproduced from Echtner and Ritchie (1991), with the kind permission of the *Journal of Tourism Studies*.

identifies whether image aspects are unique for the specific destination, or shared by others as well.

It is apparent that, similar to the earlier discussion about the 'true' identity of place (see the section on Identity and Culture in Chapter 4), 'the' place image does not really exist either. Different projections and perceptions are individual or community constructions, and different individuals and communities might have different or fragmented insights. Arguably, it would be better to refer to the 'dominant view', which would normally correspond more or less to the identity of place in line with sociologist Stuart Hall's narrative of the nation. Therefore, when we refer to 'the' place image, what is really meant is the 'dominating image', or the tendency to stereotype place. Nevertheless, for the sake of readability, we refer mainly to 'the' image, as if it were a single concept, keeping in mind that it is in fact an individualized construct, which incorporates many variations and interpretations.

Because of the complexity of the construct of place image, Echtner and Ritchie (1991, 1993, 2003) proposed a combination of structured and unstructured methodologies to measure place image. They proposed open-ended questionnaires to capture holistic components and more distinctive or unique features of the place image. Second, an attribute-based

TABLE 11.1 ▐ A taxonomy of procedures for measuring place image

Statistical procedure				Data collection	Authors
I. MULTIVARIATE METHODS	Information reduction procedures	FACTOR ANALYSIS METHODS	Principal components analysis	Lk 5 Lk 5 Lk 7 Lk 7 Lk 10 SD 7	Ahmed (1991; 1996) Baloglu (1997) Baloglu & McCleary (1999) Walmsley & Young (1998) Sternquist (1985) Fakeye & Crompton (1991) Muller (1995) Driscoll *et al.* (1994)
			Factor analysis	Lk 7 Lk 7 SD 5 Lk 6	Crompton et al. (1992) Schroeder (1996) Opperman (1996a, 1996b) Guthrie & Gale (1991) Crompton (1979) Echtner & Ritchie (1993)
			Correspondences analysis	Yes/No Yes/No	Calantone *et al.* (1989) Eizaguirre & Laka (1996)
		Multidimensional scaling		Lk 5 Lk 7 2nd technique Rk 12 SD 7	Gartner (1989) Goodrich (1982) Guthrie & Gale (1991) Haahti (1986) Baloglu & Brinberg (1997)
		Grouping	Cluster analysis	2nd technique DS 5	Muller (1995) Embacher & Buttle (1989)
	Dependence analysis		Multiple regression	Lk 7	Dadgostare Isotalo (1995)
			Log-linear	2nd technique	Eizaguirre & Laka (1996)
			Conjoint analysis	Rk 4	Carmichael (1992)
			Analysis of variance (ANOVAS, MANOVAS;...)	Lk 5 Lk5 SD7 2nd technique 2nd technique 2nd technique	Chon (1992) Baloglu & McCleary (1999) Schroeder (1996) Crompton (1979) Gartner & Hunt (1987) Baloglu (1997) Fakeye & Crompton (1991 Ahmed (1991; 1996)
		Correlations analysis		2nd technique	Dadgostare Isotalo (1995)
II. Bivariate methods	T-Test and others			Lk 7 SD 5 Lk 5 2nd technique 2nd technique 2nd technique	Chon (1991) Gartner & Hunt (1987) Borchgrevink & Knutson (1997) Fakeye & Crompton (1991) Driscoll *et al.* (1994) Ahmed (1991) Muiller (1995) Reilly (1990) Opperman (1996a, 1996b) Schroeder (1996)

Notes: SD = semantic differential; Lk = Likert scale; Categorical data: Yes/No; Rk = Ranking order. When studies developed successive algorithms of the transformed data, the name of the author(s) appears repeated in two or more sections. In these cases, the data collection method is cited with the first technique and '2nd technique' appears in the data collection column, in the second citation.
Source: Table and listed references reprinted from Gallarza *et al.* (2002), with the kind permission of Elsevier. (Full details of the references can be found there.)

eight-factor scale was produced to measure place image performance across destinations. Most studies to date emphasize only the second attribute-based approach to assessing place image, as is illustrated in Table 11.1. Gallarza *et al.* (2002, p. 67) conclude that: 'for the most part, there is a combination of multivariate and bivariate techniques, with a greater or lesser presence of qualitative techniques in the preliminary steps. Very few studies use qualitative methods as the main technique. Among all collection procedures, the seven-point Likert Scale is the most commonly used'. Such studies must, however, be limited because they cannot capture the holistic nature and subjective perspective of the individual, nor a place's unique characteristics of the image (Echtner and Ritchie 2003; Tapachai and Waryszak 2000). As Bigné *et al.* (2001, p. 611) state: 'the sum of the attribute scores is not an adequate measurement of the overall image'. The ideas presented by Van Riel (1996) in the corporate image domain, referred to in Chapter 2, would support this reasoning, as one would at least need to take into account the level of consumer elaboration of the image.

While Echtner and Ritchie (1993, p. 12) claim that their approach can be used to compare and contrast most, if not all, place images, one needs to realize that places and their types of offering can be classified into many different categories: as a mass versus niche tourism destination; as a meeting, conference or exhibition location; a cultural hotspot; or as a business, investment or employment hub. When considering all common and unique image characteristics, each category has a long list of specific attributes attached to it. Morgan (1999), for example, created a rating system for beach destinations that included forty-nine attributes for beaches alone. The categorization of destinations is normally set by the researcher (with very few studies comparing two or more different types of places), but consumers' perceptions of what type of place is being considered and what the boundaries are, might not be so clear (Gallarza *et al.* 2002, p. 65). Cho and Fesenmaier (2000) targeted their enquiry on small-scale eco-tourism as the object of their virtual tour research. The ingredients for such a virtual eco-tour would be relatively easy to assess. However, would it also be applicable in a metropolitan context – if, for example, the Amsterdam or London place marketers decided to create a virtual tour to promote their 'product offering'? Within the metropolitan context, the list of potential attributes to be considered would be much more complex. And to add to the confusion, what if a place such as Dubai were to be included in such a study? It has developed an impressive metropolitan presence, but attracts many tourists as a beach resort, though it offers cultural attractions and opportunities to escape into the desert, as well tremendous investment, employment and trade opportunities. How would one assess the image to be projected in a virtual tour for a place like that?

In recent years, calls for more pluralistic approaches to understanding place image formation have become louder (Feighey 2003; Jenkins 1999; MacKay and Couldwell 2004). Some, for example, have begun to use photographs (Dann 1996b; MacKay and Couldwell 2004; MacKay and Fesenmaier 1997; Markwell 1997). In the research on retail store image, the use of scales has long been criticized, based on the observation that 'people are encouraged to respond to characteristics that do not necessarily comprise the image they have of the store being studied' (Kunkel and Berry 1968, p. 25), and 'It has been suggested that a more appropriate measurement would be achieved by the use of unstructured instruments, followed by content analysis and coding of responses' (McDougall and Fry 1974, p. 54). In this way, 'the respondent is free to discuss only that which is relevant to his image of the store' (Kunkel and Berry 1968, p. 25). Related and alternative methods have been deployed in the research projects as presented in several of the case study chapters in this book, as we believe, as stated earlier, that holistic experiential and unique aspects of image are much more important than common attributes.

VISITOR IDENTITY AS IMAGE SELF-FOCUS

The interpretation of the many aspects involved in the formulation of place image in the mind of the visitor will differ between places and the types of visitors they attract (attributes differ according to object (type of place) and subject (person), as Gallarza *et al.* (2002, p. 62) put it). The latter is also referred to in the literature as 'self-focus', where the affective evaluations are not a description of the object, but of the relationship between the person and the object (Leemans 1994). Sirgy and Su (2000) emphasize the importance of 'self-congruity' it this context, which involves a process of matching a visitor's self-concept to the place image. A study by MacKay and Fesenmaier (2000) provides empirical evidence to support the notion that the manner in which people view place images is mediated by cultural background, for one thing. Cultural background determines people's values, ideals, norms, beliefs and folk wisdom (Arnould *et al.* 2003, p. 77). It would seem logical to assume that these will in turn have an impact on people's perceptions of places. The classic work by Hofstede (2001b), for example, found important differences in work-related values across forty national cultures.

It is generally accepted in the literature that, in the people's minds, the perceived place image is formed by two (Baloglu and Brinberg 1997; Baloglu and McCleary 1999; Embacher and Buttle 1989) or three (Dann 1996b; Gartner 1993) 'distinctly different but hierarchically interrelated components: cognitive, affective and [according to some] conative' (Gartner 1993, p. 193). These are all processes of awareness, according to Csikszentmihalyi (1995a, p. 19), who also identified attention (senses) and memory as the other two structural elements of human consciousness; 'Cognitive evaluations refer to the beliefs or knowledge about place attributes whereas affective evaluation refers to feelings toward, or attachment to it' (Baloglu and McCleary 1999, p. 870). According to Gartner (1993, p. 196), 'the affective component of image is related to the motives one has for destination selection'. The conative component, on the other hand, 'is the action component which builds on the cognitive and affective stages' (Dann 1996b, p. 49).

If self-congruity occurs, perceived place image would surely also be mediated by socio-demographic characteristics, cultural background, personal identity and psychological consumer characteristics, which is supported by Baloglu and McCleary (1999, p. 870) (see also Consumer Behaviour (Arnould *et al.* 2003; Blackwell *et al.* 2000)). Beerli and Martín (2004a, p. 678; 2004b, p. 623) provide evidence for this, as they have established empirically that: (i) motivations (as affective psychological characteristics) influence the affective component of image; (ii) the experience of travel (as in learning as a psychological characteristic) has a significant relationship with cognitive and affective images; and (iii) the socio-demographic and personal characteristics (gender, age, level of education, occupation, country of origin and social class) influence the cognitive as well as the affective assessment of image. However, it has to be stated that these conclusions need to be treated with caution, as most hypotheses in Beerli and Martín's study were only partially maintained; a specific model of causality was not constructed, and generalization of results was only permitted within the context of the case study of Lanzarote.

Nevertheless, Echtner and Ritchie (1993, p. 9) do not disagree with the idea that measuring the common attributes of place image is not sufficient, as individuals can hold different interpretations of perceived image. They found that answers to open-ended questions were a rich additional source needed to complement scale items, as they provided more descriptive, distinctive and detailed impressions. For example, 'when one scale item measures the degree of perceived friendliness, the open-ended questions revealed the differences in the way this friendliness was manifest – in Jamaica as outgoing and fun, whereas in Japan as reserved and formal' (Echtner and Ritchie 1993, p. 9).

Fairweather and Swaffield (2002, p. 294), also support the notion that there is significant variation in the way individuals interpret a uniform place image. Help in understanding this can be sought in the literature on destination choice processes in tourism studies. Major contributions to this have been made by Crompton (Ankomah *et al.* 1996; Um and Crompton 1990); and Woodside (Sirakaya and Woodside 2005; Woodside and Lysonski 1989). For a detailed overview of existing literature on destination choice modelling, see Sirakaya and Woodside (2005). The most commonly used model (one of 'the grand models' according to Sirakaya and Woodside (2005, p. 818)) involves five stages: (i) need recognition; (ii) information search; (iii) alternative evaluation and selection; (iv) purchase; and (v) outcomes (or post-purchase behaviour)

(Blackwell *et al.* 2000, ch. 3). Dellaert (1999) distinguishes six phases: (i) research, information search; (ii) composition, or the mental integration of different travel components; (iii) transaction, or purchase; (iv) creation, or production; (v) consumption; and (vi) evaluation, or post-purchase behaviour. It could be assumed that perceived place image will change as people go through these various processes. At the same time, however, Decrop and Snelders (2004) found that travel planning is an ongoing process, entailing much adaptability and opportunism, where fantasy and emotions also play an important role. Hence this departs from traditional rational decision-making models and supports the notion that, with regard to experiential products, people are involved in an ongoing search for information (Leemans 1994, p. 23; Vogt and Fesenmaier 1998, p. 553). As a result, the need recognition, information search, and alternative evaluation and selection processes might prove to be more dynamic and non-sequential in the decision-making process of selecting the place to visit for leisure, business or employment, as they are in other non-hedonic product purchase decisions.

Another approach to place choice modelling involves choice sets (Um and Crompton 1990; Woodside and Lysonski 1989): 'The concept postulates that there is a funneling process which involves a relatively large initial set of destinations being reduced to a smaller late set, from which a final destination is selected' (Ankomah *et al.* 1996, p. 138). The choice set model is depicted in Figure 11.2. The late set (referred to by others as the 'evoked set' (Sirakaya and Woodside 2005, p. 825) includes those places a traveller considers as probable places to visit. This set can be subdivided into an action set, comprising those places on which a potential visitor has taken some action, such as requesting brochures or visiting websites; and an inaction set of places, for which the individual took no further action. If a person does not have sufficient information to make an evaluation on a certain place, it will ultimately be placed in the inert set. Places in individuals'

FIGURE 11.2 ▌ Choice set model

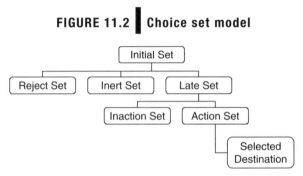

Source: Reprinted from Ankomah *et al.* (1996), p. 139, with the kind permission of Elsevier.

reject sets have been excluded from consideration because they have received a negative evaluation (Ankomah *et al.* 1996, p. 139).

It can be assumed that perceived place image changes as consumers move destinations from one set to another. This is also supported by Ankomah *et al.* (1996), who found empirical evidence to support the notion that the accuracy of cognitive distance estimation (as a possible component of perceived image – see Table 12.1) varies among choice sets. However, at the same time, Sirakaya and Woodside (2005, p. 829) propose that 'revisions occur to such consideration sets in a dynamic process as consumers move mentally toward making commitment and rejection decisions; [and] ... consumers are able to easily report intention probabilities to visit alternatives in consideration sets and these probabilities are revised dynamically'. Therefore, linking changes in perceived place image to altered choice sets will be a challenging task, and much of it is likely to depend on situational constraints (Sirakaya and Woodside 2005, p. 826). Not much research has been reported in this area, but our research on the case of the Netherlands presented in Chapter 12 will show that traditional attribute-based place image research seems to be incapable of establishing such a relationship between destination choice modelling and image. Therefore, evaluating alternative methodologies for measuring place image was a priority in the case research presented in this book.

As soon as effective standardized methodologies for measuring perceived place image become available (as illustrated above, much has been written but without achieving general agreement), evaluating the relationship between destination choice modelling and perceived place image will be a vast area of research. This, however, is not the focus of this book, and to avoid measurement issues relating perceived place image change to the progression within the different destination choice stages or formation of choice sets, the research presented in some of the case study chapters in this book will focus primarily on pre-choice perceived image in general (which in itself constitutes a gap in the existing literature). Because, as several authors have concluded, the evaluation of the place experience will certainly influence the image, and modify it (Bigné *et al.* 2001; Chon 1991; Echtner and Ritchie 1993; Fakeye and Crompton 1991).

TEMPORAL ENVIRONMENTAL OR SITUATIONAL INFLUENCES

Temporal environmental or situational influences will also change people's perceptions in the short term (Gartner and Hunt 1987) These are referred to as 'autonomous agents' by Gartner (1993, p. 201–3). Beerli and Martín (2004a, p. 667), based on the work of Gartner, attempted to measure the impact on place image of autonomous agents. They first highlighted guidebooks, news, articles, reports, documentaries and programmes about the place in the media. Later however, they combine these roughly into two variables related to 'tourist guidebooks' and 'news and popular culture'. In fact, news and popular culture were considered by Gartner (1993, p. 201) to be 'two [different] sub-components in the autonomous category'. Obviously, these components can take many different forms and it would be impossible to try and list them exhaustively, as will be illustrated by the examples that follow.

The distinction between autonomous and induced agents might also not always be clear, as place marketers can influence the impact of temporal environmental and situational factors through public relations, crisis management and lobbying (Gartner 1993, p. 202). This was illustrated in Chapter 8, when we examined covert induced agents. The difference is that overt induced agents (as discussed in Chapter 4) are initiated by place marketers (or one or more of the place marketing stakeholders) as proactive interventions, while responses to autonomous agents can only be reactive. Finally, covert induced agents are somewhere in the middle, with place marketers attempting to influence otherwise autonomous processes that influence media agendas. This can be quite relevant, as Gartner (1993, p. 203) states: 'news and popular culture forms of autonomous image formation, because of their high credibility and market penetration, may be the only image formation agents capable of changing an area's image dramatically in a short period of time'. One of the reasons for this may be that news does not age well, and major events often receive massive attention in a relatively brief period of time. However, without reinforcement over time, images are likely to revert back to what they were before. This can be either positive or negative, but whatever the case, one would expect that place marketers would want to influence this process. That is why covert induced agents are becoming increasingly important, and the nature of many previously autonomous agents have been changed to become covert induced agents.

Nevertheless, Beerli and Martín (2004a) found that, as far as the autonomous sources are concerned, there seemed to be little impact on perceived image. However, again, it needs to be emphasized that Beerli and Martín measured only post-visit image. It is expected that autonomous agents will have a larger impact in pre-visit image formation, compared to post-visit perceptions, which are more likely to be influenced by organic agents (experience), as has been illustrated in earlier chapters. It will be obvious to most researchers that the role of the media, together with other temporal and environmental influences, cannot be ignored in the context of image formation. In particular with the internet and the current reach of mass media, and how people are influenced by these (Magala 2001), major events (significant political, economic, technological or social events) will affect what people observe and read. Subsequently, perceptions will change: 'One of the most common Autonomous image formation agents is news reporting. Generally destination area promoters have no control over what appears in a news story and the projected image is based on someone else's interpretation of what is happening in the area' (Gartner 1993, p. 201). Often, therefore, place marketing can be a demanding job.

Recent examples of the tragic impact that major news events and their coverage in the news can have on places are obvious. The 2004 Indian Ocean tsunami; the appalling terrorist attacks in various parts of the world; and the lethal SARS outbreak are, of course, examples that stand out. Sometimes it is not even the catastrophe itself that is to blame for deterring visitors, but the way it is blown out of proportion in the press. To illustrate this in case of SARS, tourism professionals were addressing the phenomenon with SIP (SARS Induced Panic) to illustrate that, not the virus itself, but the subsequent dramatization in the press was to blame for the rapid decline in international travel to the affected regions.

These situational and transient circumstances could be of great influence on place image, and therefore also on choice behaviour. However, many of these can be positive, unexpected and dormant. A good example was in the press in 2002. According to a survey of British tourist boards, the 'Queen Mother effect' had boosted the number of visitors to the UK and helped erase memories of the foot and mouth crisis. The *Telegraph* newspaper (e-tid 2002) reported that the results of the survey by MICG, a London-based tourism conference organizer, suggested that the Queen Mother's funeral had had more success than official marketing campaigns in encouraging visitors back to Britain. Bookings rose by nearly 20 per cent in Cumbria, one of the areas worst hit by foot and mouth decease, while Cornwall showed a similar increase, and many hotels reported occupancy levels close to pre-2001 rates. These examples illustrate how temporal, environmental or situational influences can have a dramatic short-term effect on perceived place image, and it is acknowledged that organizing mega-events such as the Olympic Games or World Cup soccer not only facilitate memorable place experiences, but they also have a dramatic effect on place image through the coverage they receive in the media (Nielsen 2001). Some of these changes and events will, of course, also have a longer-term impact on place image by changing a destination's identity, as described in the place brand strategy section in Chapter 4.

SHARED MEANING THROUGH NARRATIVES

Place image is formed in what Go and Van Fenema (2006) refer to as mind or knowledge space. 'We develop and express routines and experiences that are communicated ... through stories and scripts ... processed and enhanced by other human beings.' People interact and share meaning, and subsequently shape each others' perceptions of objects and places. In Gartner's terminology these are called Solicited or Unsolicited Organic Agents (1993, pp. 203–4) and referred to in Figure 3.1 as word of mouth and word of mouse (Riedl *et al.* 2002), the latter being a contemporary reference to people communicating and willingly or unwillingly collaborating online, such as through the use of e-mail, newsgroups, collaborative filtering, personalized websites, blogs, chat rooms or audio/video and pictures (digitalized, accompanied or not by peoples comments, remarks and critiques); specifically, Web 2.0.

Because of the unique characteristics of services (such as their intangibility and the difficulty of quality control – see Chapter 4), consumer decision-making in tourism is often associated with perceived financial and emotional risks: 'In these high-risk situations, word-of-mouth or personal information sources are more influential than impersonal media sources' (Sirakaya and Woodside 2005, p. 827). In relation to these organic agents, Beerli and Martín (2004a, p. 677) state that 'the fact that word of mouth is considered to be the most believable and truthful communication channel, together with the fact that it also significantly influences the cognitive image, means that it is important that the messages transmitted in the markets of origin match the reality of the destination'. In other words, as we stated earlier, the projected image must be realistic. If not, public and private actors will struggle to satisfy visitors who arrive at their destination with glorified expectations (see also the Conclusion, below). This in turn will have a negative effect on the image they will transmit by word of mouth on their return home, causing clashes with other induced sources of image formation.

A lot of these processes now also occur online, for example, in virtual travel communities (Wang and Fesenmaier 2002, 2003, 2004a, 2004b; Wang *et al.* 2002). Dellaert (1999) argues that, with the internet, consumers become involved in the production and assemblage process, sharing information with others. The possibility of many-to-many communication could greatly affect branding strategies because it allows individuals to influence place images directly by sharing detailed experiential information with others. There should therefore be great potential in combining the enabling capabilities of expanded computer processing power and the internet with methodologies of content analysis as applied in the research area of narrative and social psychology. As places offer experiential products, as do most services (Dhar and Wertenbroch 2000; Padgett and Allen 1997; Vogt and Fesenmaier 1998), consumers try to organize a complex sequence of events and their reactions to these events (and the information gathered) into a meaningful whole. Understanding this is the province of narrative psychology, which contends that people have a natural propensity to organize information about experiences in story format. It also suggests that people relate their interpretations of experience to others by narrating, or telling stories. Nevertheless (as has been the case in place image research) the predominant explanation of psychological functioning has focused almost entirely on paradigmatic research, rather than considering the narrative mode. In other words, past research has considered consumers as rational thinkers rather than storytellers (Padgett and Allen 1997). Given the experiential nature of place visitation, this supports the notion that the assumptions of the narrative mode of thought may be more promising in place image research than those of the paradigmatic mode of thought, which is not divergent from current academic opinion (McCabe and Stokoe 2004; Padgett and Allen 1997; Tapachai and Waryszak 2000). The narratives people share will therefore be the focus of research when it comes to measuring the perceived place image of our signature case Dubai, as presented in Chapter 13.

CONCLUSION: PLACE BRAND SATISFACTION GAP

The result, at the end of this section, is a perceived place image built up from an extensive set of customer expectations, be it functional or psychological, attribute based or holistic, or based on common traits or unique features. The extent to which the actual place experience meets or exceeds these expectations will determine the level of visitor satisfaction (Bigné *et al.* 2001; Chon 1990; Govers and Go 1999). As MacInnes and Price (1987, p. 481) put it: 'even if the actual outcome is favourable, it is likely to differ from the imagined outcome. Deviations of the actual outcome from the imagined outcome give rise to surprise.' So one reason why visitors might leave the host dissatisfied may be because they are reading from a different script (Bateson 2002; Hubbert *et al.* 1995; Schoemaker 1996). In other words, their expectations might be unrealistic. These deviations are an important cause of customer dissatisfaction. So one way in which visitors become disappointed is when a place brand satisfaction gap occurs. This takes place when the perceived place image and the visitors' expectations are unrealistic and therefore clash with the real identity of the place and its product offering as experienced through consumption. This might occur if an unrealistic or incomplete place image has been projected, or people's interpretation of the place images is distorted because of temporal environmental or situational influences, interaction with others, or the person's own identity (selective attention and retention). This is illustrated by Fairweather and Swaffield (2002, p. 293), who found that place image 'also sets up criteria for negative evaluation. The promotional image is largely skewed towards a set of favourable experiences. When visitors encounter settings or experiences that differ markedly from their expectations, their evaluations can be very negative'. This is more likely to happen with culturally diverse groups of visitors, which would be supported by MacKay and Fesenmaier (2000). If the cultural setting of a place is completely different from that of the visitor's home country, the experience is more likely to hold surprises if the promotional image is skewed than in the case of a place where the culture is similar.

In another paper, Fesenmaier and MacKay (1996, p. 37) argue that a distorted image can also have a negative effect on the destination's residents: 'For residents, an image based on a false reality generates and perpetuates a lie with which the residents must live; thereby, robbing a culture of its authenticity.' This in itself will again have a negative effect on 'visitor satisfaction as place brand performance deteriorates. In other words, this illustrates that visitors might also become dissatisfied because the actual experience might not correspond to what was rightfully expected because of an inadequate place brand performance. Kitchin (2003, p. 17) calls this the 'belief gap'. This was discussed in more detail in Chapter 8, but perhaps here we have to clarify this difference between the place brand satisfaction gap and the place brand performance gap.

Bigné et al. (2001) discuss in detail the relationship between perceived image and evaluative assessments such as perceived quality and customer satisfaction and their respective influence on post-purchase behaviour, measured by intention to return to and recommend a destination (much of this also based on the work by Oliver (1999) who discusses such issues within a wider marketing theory context). As Bigné et al. (2001, p. 608) argue, these aspects relate to the visitors' view rather than that of the providers. Hence it fits logically into the lower part of the place branding model, which was under scrutiny above (see Figure 3.1). The providers' perspective relates to the place brand strategy gap; the place brand satisfaction gap determines customer satisfaction; and finally, the place brand performance gap determines perceived quality, as discussed in Chapter 8. This is supported directly by Bigné et al. (2001) and Oliver (1999) as they explain the difference between quality and satisfaction, the former being more specific, about particular attributes and key aspects of service delivery, while the latter is based on more holistic judgements based on predictions. In other words, one focuses on 'image' while the other focuses on perceived experience of actual service delivery. The impact of both of these on behavioural aspects such as repeat visits and willingness to recommend the place to others, are more conative elements that are outside the range of this book. From the perceived image perspective, the emphasis in this book lies primarily on assessing place image pre-visit and on evaluating alternative methods for doing so, both of which are major gaps in existing research. Sources of pre-visit image (induced, organic or autonomous agents) and differences according to cultural, social and personal characteristics will be studied in the next few chapters.

CHAPTER 12

Case The Netherlands: Perceived Image Research

As discussed in great detail in Part 1 and here in Part 4, a strong place image means perceived superior customer value and consequently positively influences buying behaviour (Tapachai and Waryszak 2000). Therefore, we wanted to identify whether, regardless of places' unique features and holistic auras, the common attribute-based approach would be able to measure the effectiveness of place brand marketing efforts aimed at (re)positioning place image among different groups with different levels of product familiarity. If that were found to be the case, the problem of measuring consumer evaluations of place images, be it on- or offline, would be fairly limited. Therefore, arising from this discussion, the following theoretical assumptions needed to be confirmed in this case research:

- Traditional quantitative attribute based place image research can be used to identify the content of perceived images and subsequently determine effectiveness of place brand marketing;

- It is possible to rate place brand images based on attribute based research.

In order to assess this, a study was conducted among the Dutch population, to measure their image of the Netherlands as a domestic tourism destination (Govers and Go 2003).

RESEARCH BACKGROUND

An empirical study was commissioned by the former Dutch domestic tourism organization, the Dutch Foundation on Tourism and Recreation AVN (AVN for short). The foundation, which was later integrated in the national tourist board, was in the past a co-operation between the Dutch

Automobile Association (ANWB), the Netherlands Bureau for Tourism (NBT) – which is the Dutch national tourism organization, and the Tourist Information Offices (VVVs). The AVN was concerned about the sustainable development of domestic tourism and recreation in the Netherlands. It was involved in many activities, such as trade fairs, consumer shows, direct mailing of brochures, the distribution of travel guides, organization of familiarization trips, and the enhancement of media exposure. In order to practice marketing in a responsible manner, AVN decided to measure, on a regular basis, the effectiveness of its marketing efforts. Such a marketing effectiveness monitor would offer two important benefits:

(i)　It would provide stakeholders with a reasonable degree of 'transparency' in the marketing affairs of the AVN, and would therefore possibly pre-empt many time-consuming enquiries from stakeholders; and

(ii)　It would provide a 'success indicator', which would enable the AVN to measure to what extent their efforts gained results by changing the destination's image.

SURVEY METHOD

Carman (1990) suggests that consumer expectations change with the extent to which consumers are familiar with the service rendered, therefore the study population, was divided into the following four groups, based on awareness and patronage levels as indicated in the AIDA-model (creating Awareness, Interest, Desire and Action) (Ster and Wissen 1987):

Group 1　Those consumers who have no experience of, and are not familiar with the Netherlands as a holiday destination.

Group 2　Those who are aware of, but show no interest in the Netherlands as a holiday destination.

Group 3　Those who show an interest, but are not active tourists in their own country.

Group 4　Those who are actively experiencing the Netherlands as a destination for domestic tourism.

As stated earlier, attribute scores, and therefore perceptions of the domestic place image, were obviously expected to differ between these four groups.

Attributes were identified in a management session through a Bernstein (1984) discussion (as suggested by Van Riel, 1996, p. 63). Place marketers were asked to mention those attributes of the 'Dutch tourism and recreation'-product that play an important role in determining the organization's communication activities. In a subsequent discussion, the total number of attributes was reduced to eight essential values, which all participants considered to be important and are believed to contribute to the identity of the Netherlands as a holiday destination for the various AVN target groups. In the place image measurement literature, it is not uncommon to have such unstructured approaches in in-depth interviews or focus groups with industry professionals, in order to identify image attributes (Gallarza *et al.* 2002). Alternatively, consumers themselves could be asked to identify attributes through unstructured approaches first, before applying the quantitative approaches using scales. A third option, sometimes applied in the literature, is to perform a review of promotional material from the place being studied, in order to identify the relevant attributes (Beerli and Mart°n 2004b, p. 624). The latter two approaches were not considered here, assuming that AVN management, as heavily involved professionals, would, as a team, be able to predict the potential outcomes of the other approaches.

Table 12.1 lists the attributes identified in the fourth column along with results from other studies consulted at the time the methodology was formulated (first three columns). It shows that scales are comparable and the literature agrees, particularly with Echtner and Ritchie's (1993) place image measurement scale, discussed earlier, but also with other studies if compared with Table 12.2 (matched with Table 12.1 in its last column).

The attributes identified were used as a basis for the AVN marketing effectiveness monitor, which would potentially be integrated into a longitudinal research panel, called CVO – the Dutch Continuous Holiday Research panel. Prior to this, however, two surveys were conducted as a reliability/validity test and reference (t = 0) measurement, identifying attribute scores as a base reference for indexing future place image perceptions among the four AIDA target groups (different groups with different levels of product awareness and patronage as described above). The way the sampling was conducted for these two surveys is shown in Figure 12.1.

With AVN's customer database being readily available, it was a logical choice to use this as the sampling frame for quota sampling AIDA groups 2, 3 and 4 for the monitor pre-test measurement. For detailed reference, the responses are listed by sampling frame in Table 12.3. But, as one of the objectives of the monitor for AVN was to provide a 'success indicator', enabling AVN to measure to what extent their efforts obtained results through changing the destination's image, it was essential for the population sample to include a sufficient number of respondents with a minimum level of awareness concerning AVN's activities (Group 1), in order to be able to attribute perceptual changes to AVN's efforts. Therefore, for the first survey, additional respondents in Group 2 and all those in Group 1

TABLE 12.1 Place image attributes

Common place image attributes (Echtner and Ritchie 1993, pp. 3–13)	Destination choice attributes, based on tourists' perceptions of European countries (Haahti and Yavas 1983, pp. 34–42)	Netherlands' strengths, based on NBT's place image research (AVN 1995, p. 14)	Image attributes identified through this study's Bernstein discussion	Compared with the most commonly used attributes as listed in Table 12.2
	Accessibility	Close by	Good accessibility	Accessibility Transportation
Interest/ adventure	Entertainment and night life Facilities for sports	Variation in a small area Biking/ water sports	Variation in activities	Various activities Nightlife and entertainment Shopping facilities Sports facilities Relaxation v. Massific[ation].
Natural state	A peaceful and quiet holiday	Water/dunes/ polder	Variation in scenery	Landscape, surroundings Nature Originality
Inexpensiveness	Good value for money	Inexpensive	Possibilities for any budget range	Price, value, cost
Tourist facilitation		Easy to organize	Well organized	Information available Accommodation
Resort atmosphere/ climate			Opportunities in all seasons	Climate
Cultural distance Lack of language barrier	Cultural experience	Familiar	Familiar	Cultural attractions Gastronomy Safety Social interaction Residents receptiveness
Comfort/security	Friendly and hospitable people	Easy to get information	High service standard	Service quality

Sources: See column headings in table.

Place Brand Satisfaction

TABLE 12.2 The most common attributes used in place image studies

Authors	Various activities	Landscape, surroundings	Nature	Cultural attractions	Nightlife and entertainment	Shopping facilities	Information available	Sport facilities	Transportation	Accommodation	Gastronomy	Price, value, cost	Climate	Relaxation vs Massific	Accessibility	Safety	Social interaction	Resident's receptiveness	Originality	Service Quality
	Functional																		*Psychological*	
1. Crompton (1979)									X			X	X	X		X		X		
2. Goodrich (1982)		X		X	X			X		X	X				X			X		
3. Stemquist (1985)		X		X	X	X		X		X	X				X			X		
4. Haahti (1986)		X	X	X	X			X				X			X	X		X	X	
5. Gartner and Hunt (1987)		X	X					X		X			X					X		
6. Calantone and al. (1989)	X	X		X	X	X		X	X			X			X		X	X		
7. Gartner (1989)		X	X	X	X			X										X		
8. Embacher and Buttle (1989)	X	X		X								X	X	X		X	X			
9. Guthrie and Gale (1991)	X			X			X	X				X	X	X	X	X		X	X	X
10. Ahmed (1991)		X	X	X	X	X		X							X			X		
11. Chon (1991)		X	X	X	X				X	X	X	X				X	X	X	X	
12. Fakeye and crompton (1991)	X	X	X	X	X	X	X	X	X	X	X	X	X	X	X			X		
13. Crompton et al. (1992)	X		X		X							X	X		X			X	X	X
14. Carmichael (1992)	X											X			X			X		
15. Chon (1992)	X	X		X	X		X			X	X				X	X		X		X
16. Echtner and Ritchie (1993)		X	X	X	X	X	X	X	X	X	X	X	X	X	X	X	X	X	X	X
17. Driscoll and al. (1994)	X	X		X	X	X						X	X			X		X	X	X
18. Dadgostar and Isotalo (1995)			X	X	X	X		X		X	X				X		X			
19. Muller (1995)		X		X	X	X				X	X	X	X	X	X	X		X		
20. Eizaguirre and Laka (1996)						X		X	X	X		X			X	X		X		
21. Schroeder (1996)		X	X	X	X	X		X		X	X	X			X			X	X	
22. Ahmed (1996)		X	X	X	X	X		X										X		
23. Oppermann (1996a, 1996b)		X		X	X				X	X	X	X	X				X			X
24. Baloglu (1997)		X	X	X	X	X		X	X	X	X	X				X		X	X	
25. Baloglu and McCleary (1999)		X		X	X			X		X	X	X	X				X	X		
Total	8	19	12	18	17	15	3	16	8	14	15	16	12	12	12	10	7	20	7	4

Source: Table and listed reference reprinted from Gallarza *et al.* 2002, with the kind permission of Elsevier.

were selected through another quota sample, identifying non-domestic travellers via the telephone using automated random calling via the national telephone directory CD-ROM, until a total number of 300 responses had been collected.

FIGURE 12.1 ▮ Survey sample designs and travel behaviour, awareness and patronage

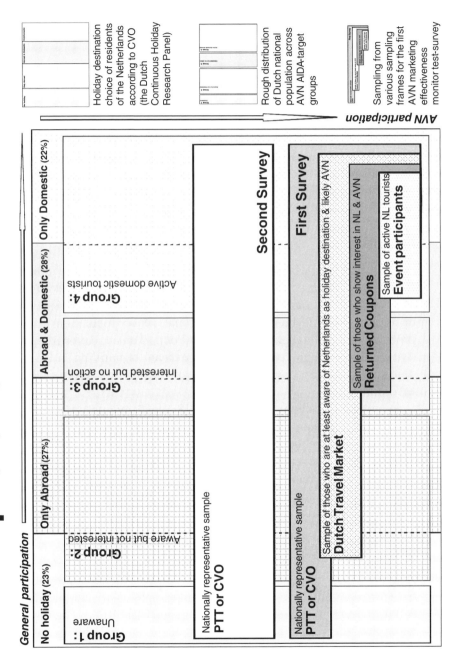

TABLE 12.3 Sampling frames for first measurement

Sampling frame	Sample	Response
Addresses from returned coupons in a cycling magazine	200	75
Addresses from returned coupons in a special issue on recreational cycling	200	85
Addresses from returned coupons in a cultural magazine	200	93
Addresses from returned coupons in a hiking magazine	200	81
Two address directories of participants of the annual national cycling event	400	142
Total (response rate = 40 per cent)	1200	476

Because of results obtained from this latter sample, however, it was later decided to proceed with the second survey using a national representative sample across all AIDA groups. The first survey showed that even among those respondents who had not taken more than one domestic holiday during the previous three years, more than 25 per cent were aware of AVN, and even interested or participating in its activities. Assuming that such a level of awareness could be extrapolated to the whole population, and would probably be even higher among AIDA Groups 3 and 4, national representative samples were proved to be a feasible means of fulfilling all the research objectives. For the second survey, therefore, sampling decisions were made accordingly.

In the first measurement (using the different sampling frames to identify different target groups), the results showed significant differences in place image between frequent domestic travellers and Dutch tourists who never patronize their own country (for specific details, see Govers and Go 1999). However, the second survey, using the nationally representative sample, failed completely to identify such differences. The latter results are discussed in more detail below.

DATA COLLECTION

A total of 510 respondents were interviewed by telephone, targeting a national representative stratified random sample using automated random calling through the national telephone directory CD-ROM. The sample was controlled for geographical spread, matching the population distribution in the country; 57.6 per cent of respondents were women. Principal component analysis with Varimax rotation was performed on thirty-two items for the total sample of measurements, as shown in Table 12.4.

TABLE 12.4 Results of factor analysis on thirty-two items measuring place image

Items	Factor loading	Factor name	Eigen-value	Percentage var. exp. (cumulative)	Cronbach Alpha
Places of interest and historic sites	0.68				
Tourist and recreational attractions/events	0.45	Variation in activities			0.68
Entertainment and nightlife					
Cycling, hiking and water sports	0.65		9.19	32.8 (32.8)	
Natural beauty and countryside	0.70				
Accommodation in variety of nice settings	0.47	And scenery			0.76
Urban beauty	0.61				
Variety, both countryside as well as cities	0.74				
Opportunities for any budget	0.84	Possibilities for any			
Opportunities in adequate price brackets	0.80	budget	1.42	5.05 (37.9)	0.88
Entertainment to suit everybody's purse	0.87				
Also with little money it can be pleasant	0.75				
Safe	0.74				
Familiar	0.68	Familiar	1.02	3.63 (41.5)	0.71
Cosy	0.48				
Nice holiday atmosphere	0.47				
Range of accommodation and packages	0.42				
Information accessibility	0.68	Well			0.66
Organizational capabilities	0.47	organized			
Info and help from organizations such as VVV	0.56		2.38	8.5 (50.0)	
Service and quality	0.55				
Standards of facilities	0.54	High service			
Satisfying customer needs	0.56	standard			0.74

(Continued)

TABLE 12.4 Continued

Items	Factor loading	Factor name	Eigen-value	Percentage var. exp. (cumulative)	Cronbach Alpha
Customer concern, e.g. child friendliness	0.54				
For any season	0.70	Opportunities			
Opportunities despite the climate	0.54	in all seasons	1.16	4.15 (54.2)	0.77
Bad weather facilities	0.56				
Also in fall and winter enough to offer	0.68				
Itineraries					
Accessibility of tourism destinations		Good accessibility			0.63
Signposting					
Easy to reach destination					

While some factors were combined in the factor analysis, they were retained as separate factors in the analysis because of their satisfactory Cronbach Alphas (over 0.65). The accessibility attribute was not included in the factor analysis as two out of four items were changed as a consequence of unsatisfactory results in the first survey. Although Cronbach Alpha for this factor still raises concern, it was increased from only 0.56 in the first survey. Only the 'entertainment and nightlife' item had to be removed because of unsatisfactory results. In the subsequent analysis, each respondent's score on the eight image attributes was calculated by the geometric average of the corresponding four items for each attribute.

RESULTS

Figure 12.2 portrays the image attribute scores for the four AIDA groups earlier identified. Analysis of variance only shows significant differences in scores for the 'opportunities in all seasons' attribute. Apparently those people that are aware but show no interest in the Netherlands as a possible tourism destination, view the weather conditions as one of the main inhibiting factors for domestic tourism. Surprisingly however, all other

FIGURE 12.2 | Place image among four different awareness and patronage groups

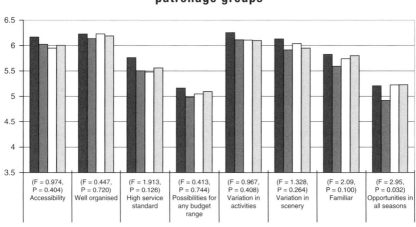

attributes show no significant differences between different groups of consumers with different levels of awareness and patronage. Even an overall average 'school mark' on a 1-to-10 scale does not significantly differ between groups.

In another effort to identify place image differences, two groups of tourists were formed: one group of domestic tourists, who had not gone abroad during the previous three years, but went on holiday in the Netherlands more than twice; and a group of international tourists with reverse characteristics. However, t-tests between the two groups provided the similar results; there were no real differences apart from the 'weather attribute'. In a final attempt, cluster analysis was used to create three groups of respondents with relatively high, medium and low scores on all attributes; that is, groups with a strong, weak and intermediate image of the Netherlands as a tourism destination. Again, however, contrary to what was expected, no differences in socio-demographic characteristics or leisure travel behaviour were identified.

Unfortunately, we were deceived by the first survey into observing expected differences between the four AIDA groups. In fact, the findings of the second survey prompted us to take another, closer look at the results of the first survey. This showed that the observed differences between the AIDA groups were attributable primarily to variations in perceptions between those respondents who were not interested in the Netherlands as a tourist destination (they were either aware of it or not; that is, Groups 1 and 2 combined), and those who were interested, frequent domestic travellers, and those who were interested but not active (Groups 3 and 4). Retrospectively, these first survey findings could be rationalized in two ways:

- The use of two different contact methods for collecting the data in the first survey: respondents selected from the AVN customer database, mainly those in Groups 3 and 4, received the questionnaire through the post using the AVN direct mail system, while all other respondents, mainly in Groups 1 and 2, were contacted by telephone; and

- Sampling frame bias: as illustrated in Figure 12.1 above, the respondents in the various AIDA groups in the first survey were selected from different sampling frames, with customer contact data originating from different sources. Earlier assumptions that these consumers would be representative of the rest of the population of 'domestics travel enthusiasts' (Groups 3 and 4) would have to be rejected and, concluded, quite to the contrary, that the sampling frames contained particular groups of consumers (such as 'domestic hiking and biking trips enthusiasts') with their own distinctive domestic place image perceptions.

This was supported by an analysis of variance of the total sample (the first and second surveys taken together), which showed clearly that differences in place image perception were to be attributed primarily to sampling frame membership (and related variations in contact method) compared to most other respondent characteristics (neither in terms of demographics, nor in leisure travel behaviour or AIDA group membership). This showed that the first survey was flawed, and that the results of the second, nationally representative survey, were to be regarded as the true measurement of place image perception across the population, as defined in this research study.

Consequently, what is apparent is that the theoretical assumptions posed earlier do not hold, as the results of the second survey clearly show the inappropriateness of the measurement scale. While there might be mediating variables involved, such as chauvinism, destination proximity or domestic versus international tourism, ultimately the scale proved to be incapable of identifying a relationship between consumer perception of place image and destination choice behaviour.

CONCLUSION

As mentioned earlier, it is widely agreed in the literature that image influences buying behaviour, and therefore mediates marketing effectiveness (Echtner and Ritchie 1993; MacKay and Fesenmaier 2000; Padgett and Allen 1997; Sirgy and Su 2000; Tapachai and Waryszak 2000). However, summarizing the results of the above study, the eight-factor place image measurement scale that was developed based on a literature review as well as an expert focus group, is incapable of identifying differences in perceptions between groups with different levels of product awareness and patronage. Therefore, these results reject the hypothesis and it has to be assumed that the traditional multi-attribute system is inadequate for measuring place image.

It seems that, because of the factor analysis applied in the multi-attribute approach, the resulting image characteristics lose their uniqueness, and are reduced to 'hygiene factors', or the minimum requirements that tourism destinations need to fulfil. The subjective perspective of individuals seems to be lost. Any destination needs to provide a satisfying level of 'things to do', 'nice scenery', 'affordability' and 'tourist facilitation'. However, the interpretation of these aspects will differ largely between destinations and the types of visitors going to them (attributes differ according to object (type of place) and subject (consumer) as Gallarza *et al.* (2002, p. 62) put it. As discussed in Chapter 11, the latter is also referred to in the literature as 'self-focus', where the affective evaluations are not a description of the object, but rather of the relationship between the consumer and the object (Leemans 1994). Sirgy and Su (2000, p. 340) emphasize the importance of 'self-congruity' it this context, which 'involves a process of matching a tourist's self-concept to a destination visitor image'.

Capturing nuances and self-congruity can be very relevant. This can be illustrated by returning briefly to the context of Dubai, which is promoting itself as a tourist destination internationally, to consumers who are not familiar with Islamic societies, but also, at the same time, to those who are. It would be of interest to identify the extent to which consumers are prejudiced based on prior information – for example, contained in travel guidebooks – but also particularly in the news and cultural media, such as in novels or motion pictures, or from visits to museums elsewhere. For example, the perception that Western consumers have of the Arabian Gulf has obviously been affected by the events of 11 September 2001, and at the time, for the first time in history, the internet had a major impact on this. It illustrates the increasing ephemerality of place images. As the events in New York and Washington unfolded, people anywhere in the world, at a distance or close by, were able to read first-hand, up-to-date reports of what was happening. When the telephone system collapsed, the internet came through: 100 million US internet users sent or received e-mails expressing concern after the terrorist attacks. Almost 23 per cent received concerned e-mails from overseas (Lebo 2002). If people were unable to follow the course of events on television, they turned to the Web. Reuters reported that the number of visitors to internet news sites soared tenfold after the attacks. CNN.com said it was serving 9 million page views per hour after the attacks occurred, in comparison with its normal traffic of 11 million page views per day. A spokeswoman said it was the largest amount of traffic they had ever had (Reuters 2001).

All these unique and transient circumstances could be of great influence on place image and therefore destination choice behaviour. As another example, a major cultural event in the Netherlands celebrating the painter Vermeer attracted far more visitors from France than had been anticipated 100,000, compared to only 6,000 visiting a similar event celebrating Rembrandt (Vervoorn 2000). This success in the French market was later attributed to the fact that a study of Vermeer was part of the postwar French high school curriculum, something that had not been anticipated during the planning and operational stages of the event.

These examples emphasize the complex, relativistic (people have different perceptions) and dynamic (changing over time and geographical distance) (Gallarza *et al.* 2002, p. 69) nature of place image and the fact that it is therefore very hard to measure, particularly when using only common multi-attribute quantitative measurement systems across destinations.

Based on the presented empirical and anecdotal evidence, it needs to be contended that structured methodologies can be effective for measuring the common and attribute-based components of image, (but) are not useful for capturing the unique and holistic components (Echtner and Ritchie 1993, p. 5; Echtner and Ritchie 2003; Tapachai and Waryszak 2000, p. 37). As commonality of attributes across destinations and consumers is limited, research that does not incorporate uniqueness and holistic images is insufficient. Returning to Kierkegaard, the subjective truth of the individual seems to be more important than the objective common attributes.

As a result of the above findings, a constructivist approach was perceived to possibly be the right alternative (Ryan 2000). Or, in other words, we thought that a deconstructionist, postmodern approach, which included 'some kind of struggle with the fact of fragmentation, ephemerality, and chaotic flux' (Harvey 1989, p. 117), might lead to greater success. As with the radical changes created by business process re-engineering, the use of IT might also lead the way in deconstructing place image, challenging the assumptions that have long existed, resulting in an emerging new IT-based place image measurement paradigm. The potential of combining the enabling capabilities of expanded computer processing power and the internet with methodologies of content analysis as applied in the research area of narrative psychology was perceived to be the way to move forward. A supplementary study on the place image of Dubai in comparison to other destinations was therefore based on open-ended free elicitation of tourists' stories about destinations. This research is discussed in the next chapter.

CHAPTER 13

Signature Case Dubai: Perceived Image Research

As a consequence of the unsatisfactory findings of the traditional approach to measuring perceived place image, as shown in Chapter 12, we have developed an alternative methodology (Govers *et al.* 2007a, 2007b), which will be presented in this chapter. In earlier chapters, arguments were put forward for the formulation of a qualitative phenomenographic approach, built on the premise of the narrative mode of thought of consumers and their ways of perceiving, retaining and interpreting hedonic consumption experiences. Free elicitation of descriptive adjectives for place image assessment has been contended by Reilly (1990). It was assumed that, if this was done with the co-operation of major online travel agents and/or place marketing websites that have large numbers of unique visitors, sufficient data could be assembled to quantify these unstructured data, using computerized content analysis (Weber 1990) through artificial neural network analysis software (Woelfel 1998; Woelfel and Stoyanoff 1993). With the growth of the internet, breakthrough opportunities were and are provided for place image research, removing resource, time and practical research restrictions that prevented such large-scale unstructured approaches in the past.

SURVEY METHOD

As an alternative methodology, respondents were asked to elaborate, in story format, on their expected travel experience when travelling to one of seven sample destinations they had never visited before. Visitors to the virtual travel community Travellerspoint.com were able to participate in this research. The project focused on the image of Dubai, compared to other places that are in some way either similar or particularly contrasting. The global comparative study included places such as the Canary Islands, Flanders (Belgium), Florida, Morocco, Singapore and Wales. Travellerspoint.com, with, at the time, nearly half a million 'unique' visitors a month and 20,000 members from 200 countries; would, it was hoped, generate a good response from all over the world. To maximize response rates, all participants were automatically eligible to win the grand prize raffle draw: a free holiday to Dubai.

Until recently, it would have been virtually impossible to analyse the large quantity of qualitative data this approach generates, as a researcher would have had to wade through hundreds of thousands of words and code them. Then, to assure reliability of the results, at least two other colleagues would have had to go through the same process, creating serious time- and human-power demands on limited resources. However, today, with computerized neural network content analysis software such as CATPAC (as also applied in the analysis on signature case Dubai in Chapter 9), these types of constraints have been eliminated. With respondents submitting their written accounts online, the data is already in digital format, and therefore the time involved in data entry and analysis is reduced significantly, from several months, if not years, to only a few days. However, at the same time, it is possible to criticize these types of approaches on several counts.

First, most require that respondents translate imagery processing into a discursive mode (such as verbal responses), confusing even more the distinction between the processing modes. Moreover, individual differences in verbosity or vocabulary can influence the nature of this translation. In addition, studies that ask individuals to detail imagery scenarios may not be assessing the extent of detail contained in the image, but rather the subjects' abilities to control their image to enable details to be specified (MacInnes and Price 1987, p. 485).

In addition, the level of detail provided by unstructured methodologies is highly variable, as it depends upon the verbal and/or writing skills of the individuals used in the study, their willingness to provide multiple responses, and their knowledge base of the product (McDougall and Fry 1974). Furthermore, because of the qualitative nature of the data, statistical analyses of the results are limited. In particular, comparative analyses across several products are not facilitated by unstructured methodologies (Echtner and Ritchie 2003). The latter, however, can be overcome with the use of recent technologies for automated content analysis. The former issue of verbosity, vocabulary and writing skills was partly dealt with through thorough automatic spelling and grammar checking, and pre-reading of all texts, but it is acknowledged that this issue forms a potential limitation of this study. Again, CATPAC was used for the analysis, this time using a case-based approach, as opposed to a sliding window of seven words (see Chapter 9).

QUESTIONNAIRE

The central question of the survey questionnaire was of such importance, providing only one chance to elicited correct responses from participants, that it was decided to set-up a Delphi-type discussion with experts first, in order to guarantee an optimal formulation of the question. The following experts were included in the Delphi panel:

- Dimitrios Buhalis, Deputy Director, International Centre for Tourism and Hospitality Research (ICTHR), School of Services Management, Bournemouth University

- Daniel R. Fesenmaier, Professor and Director, National Laboratory for Tourism and eCommerce, Temple University, Philadelphia

- Matthias Fuchs, Director, e-Tourism Competence Centre Austria, and Professor, European Tourism Research Institute, Mid Sweden University

- William C. Gartner, Professor of Applied Economics, Board Chair of the International Academy for the Study of Tourism, University of Minnesota

- Ulrike Gretzel, Assistant Professor, Department of Recreation, Park and Tourism Sciences, Texas A&M University

- Jafar Jafari, Founding Editor, Annals of Tourism Research, Department of Hospitality and Tourism, University of Wisconsin-Stout

- Jamie Murphy, Associate Professor in Electronic Marketing, Business School, The University of Western Australia

- Karl Wöber, Associate Editor of Information Technology and Tourism, President, MODUL University Vienna

Delphi participants were first given general information about the research set-up and about the first page of the questionnaire that would be provided to respondents (see Exhibit 13.1).

EXHIBIT 13.1 First page of the image survey questionnaire

Complete this survey and win a luxury trip to Dubai! To join and win, tell us your story.

This survey is part of a research project sponsored by the University of Leuven, the largest and oldest university in Belgium, and the Rotterdam School of Management, Erasmus University, the Netherlands, a premier business school.

Courtesy of KLM Royal Dutch Airlines and Jebel Ali International Hotels, Dubai, we can offer this stunning prize to one lucky winner:

- An economy class ticket from any KLM serviced point in the world, via Amsterdam to Dubai.

- 7 nights at the 5-star Jebel Ali Golf Resort & Spa, a member of 'The Leading Hotels of the World' and part of Jebel Ali International Hotels, featuring its own golf course, over 13 restaurants and bars, a shooting club, horse riding stables, spa, and various other wet and dry sports facilities.

- On top of that, Travellerspoint will add 500 EUROs in spending money, if the winner is a member of Travellerspoint (membership is free, register now).

Notes

- Data you provide is treated anonymously and we guarantee complete protection of your privacy.

- All responses must be in English, otherwise your participation will be invalid.

- The answers you give do not influence your chance of winning the prize. The winner will be drawn through a random lottery.

- The 3 page survey should not take you long, we estimate no more than 10 minutes.

Please indicate which of the following destinations you have ever visited before by ticking the Checkbox:

☐ Canary Islands

☐ Dubai (United Arab Emirates)

☐ Flanders (Belgium)

☐ Florida

☐ Morocco

☐ Singapore

☐ The Netherlands

☐ Wales

Subsequently, Delphi participants were told that, based on the future survey response to the first page, a central question would be put forward. The initially proposed formulation of the central question, as forwarded to Delphi participants in the first round of Delphi feedback, is presented in Exhibit 13.2. Destination X would be substituted by a random pick of one of the sample destinations that the survey respondent would indicate not to have visited before. Delphi participants were then asked to do the following:

'Please read this question carefully and let me know, by replying to this e-mail, what you think? Should it be formulated differently, expanded, reduced, or otherwise revised? I have asked seven other expert colleagues elsewhere to do the same and after everyone has replied, I will try to incorporate responses and come back to you for a final time with the revised formulation.'

EXHIBIT 13.2 Initial wording of central image survey question as proposed in the Delphi discussion

Imagine that you would decide next week to visit Destination X. What images or other immediate thoughts come to mind? Tell us your story. What do you think your experience in Destination X would be like; what would you expect to see, or feel, hear, smell, taste?

Please give us as much detail as you can, but do not do any specific research and do not look up additional information that you do not have right now; just try to express the thoughts that you have at this very moment, positive or negative. We want you to tell us what you think this trip would really be like. We are NOT asking you to describe your ideal or dream trip in Destination X, just an experience in Destination X that could easily become a reality if you wanted it to. If you do not know much about Destination X, your story will probably be relatively short; but if you already have very clear ideas about Destination X, your story might be very long. Whatever the case may be, we would be very grateful if you would take a few minutes of your time right now and share your ideas about Destination X with us in the space below.

Remember, there is no right, wrong or best model answer. We want you to tell us what your own ideas are about Destination X, and NOT what you think we want to hear. There will be NO jury assessment of the best story or anything like that. The content of your response will have no impact whatsoever on your chance of winning the grand prize. All participants in this survey will have an equal chance of winning, as the winner will be drawn through a random lottery, regardless of the answers provided to the questions in this survey.

Please relate your story of your stay in Destination X in the space below:

After receiving all comments from Delphi participants in the first round, the central question was reformulated accordingly and sent back to the participants again. After a second round of incorporating comments, the second page of survey questionnaire was finalized, as shown in Exhibit 13.3.

The length as well as complexity of the wording of the central question was reduced significantly, while retaining the main elements that the probing contained:

- Pre-visit perceived place image;

- Experiential in nature, shared through story-telling; and

- Including sensory information.

EXHIBIT 13.3 Final wording of page two of the image survey questionnaire resulting from the Delphi discussion

Imagine that next week you will visit Destination X for the first time. Tell us your story. What do you think your experience in Destination X would be like? What images and thoughts immediately come to mind? What would you expect to see, or feel, hear, smell, taste there?

Without any research or additional information, kindly be spontaneous and share with us whatever thoughts come to your mind right now, whether positive or negative. Make your response as detailed or as brief as you like, there are no limits, but try to write in story format; using complete sentences, not just single words.

If you know little about Destination X, your story will probably be short. If you already have clear ideas about Destination X, your story might be very long. But remember, there is no right, wrong or best model answer; simply express your own ideas about Destination X, and NOT what you think we want to hear. The content of your response will have NO impact whatsoever on your chance of winning the grand prize.

Share your ideas about Destination X with us right now, in the space below:

Finally, a third (and last) page was added to the questionnaire to obtain some additional details about respondents, such as:

- Information sources on which their perception was based (also through an open-ended question).

- Attitude towards the one selected sample destination on a ten-point scale ranging from: 10 – Extremely positive, would definitely want to go there; to 1 – Extremely negative, will definitely never want to go there.

- Intention to visit any of the eight sample destinations within two years, as an indication of choice-set membership and prior information search.

- Socio-demographic variables, including country of residence; homeland (if different from country of residence); number of countries ever visited; age, family life cycle situation; income, education, occupation, gender.

COMPARATIVE CASES

For the selection of cases, it was of primary concern to ensure that the study could determine commonalities and differences among destinations using the methodology. Therefore, as wide a range of case studies as possible was required. Preferably, they would include places that had appeared in earlier image, branding, or other literature. The samples had to have some potential overlapping attributes among them, but also differences in other elements, in order to guarantee the best results in assessing convergent and discriminant validity. In addition, destinations had to be identifiable to a global audience. However, the actual selection of cases was in fact not crucial to the contribution of the study, as long as they seemed to provide the basis on which the usefulness of the methodology could be assessed. Hence, the selection process was the result of a combination of considerations.

First, Dubai, Flanders (Belgium) and the Netherlands were included, for obvious reasons.

Second, some case studies were selected because of their striking resemblance to Dubai in one way or another:

- The Canary Islands compare to Dubai as an exotic 'sea, sun, sand' destination.

- Flanders could be positioned as a complete opposite to Dubai, in terms of its pace identity.

- Florida compares to Dubai in terms of being the entertainment capital in the region, as illustrated through the development of Dubailand.

- Singapore compares to Dubai as a rapidly developed city state and financial and trade centre in the Orient, contrasting modernity and tradition.

- Morocco compares to Dubai as a new exotic destination with an Arabian heritage and expansive desert ecology.

- The Netherlands compares to Dubai with its image of being a regional destination and entertainment centre where much is possible.

- Wales is, as was Flanders, a complete opposite of Dubai.

Third, in March 2004, *National Geographic Traveler* reported on a destination scorecard study conducted by Leeds Metropolitan University (Tourtellot 2004). The survey convened a global panel of 200 experts in a variety of fields: ecology, sustainable tourism, geography, urban and regional planning, travel writing and photography, historic preservation, cultural anthropology, and archaeology. The experts were asked to 'evaluate only those places with which they were familiar, using six criteria weighted as appropriate to each destination: environmental and ecological quality; social and cultural integrity; condition of historic buildings and archaeological sites; aesthetic appeal; quality of tourism management; and the outlook for the future' (Tourtellot 2004, p. 67). Judgements were then indexed on a 1–100 scale indicating the overall level of stewardship at each of the 115 destinations included by *National Geographic Traveler*. Some of the case studies included in this chapter were among the destinations reported on by Tourtellot (2004), such as:

- The Canary Islands, which received a low ranking with 52 points (the lowest score being 41).

- Florida, more specifically, Key West, which ended up somewhere at the bottom with 42 points.

- Morocco, more specifically Fez historic centre, which received a high score of 71 (the highest score being 82).

- The Netherlands, which received an average score of 65.

This illustrates the attempt to incorporate a sample destination from every category of top, middle and low scores.

Third, several of the selected destinations have been described as case studies in the literature on destination branding:

- Florida, best practice (Ritchie and Ritchie 1998).

- Morocco, bad practice (Polunin 2002).

- Singapore, best practice (Ooi 2004).

- Spain (Canary Islands), best practice (Morgan and Pritchard 2004).

- Wales, best practice (Pride 2004; Pritchard and Morgan 1998; Pritchard and Morgan 2001).

The referenced literature provides us with additional information regarding the brand identity of some of the case studies, which would prove useful in interpreting the survey results. Pritchard and Morgan (2001) identified those aspects that define Welsh identity, through the analysis of existing branding campaigns, marketing efforts and consumer research. They include, for the overseas market:

- Language (*Cymraeg*);

- Celtic heritage and fascinating history;

- Myths and legends;

- Welsh emblems: such as the daffodil, the leek, the Welsh dragon and national flag;

- Musical tradition;

- Arts, crafts and entertainment;

- Castles; and

- Friendly people.

Morocco was discussed by Polunin (2002, p. 4):

Sometimes outsiders are the saboteurs. Morocco thought it had come up with a winning strapline, 'A Feast for the Senses', supported by stunning visuals of the Moroccan countryside and culture. Initially it was widely accepted. However, it had to be dropped when German tour operators told the tourist board that they wanted a sun and sea product for their clients.

The identity of Singapore is summarized by Ooi (2004, p. 247) through the Singapore Tourism Promotion Board's Destination Marketing brief:

'New Asia – Singapore' expresses the essence of today's Singapore: a vibrant, multicultural, sophisticated city-state where tradition and modernity, East and West meet in harmony; a place where one can see and feel the energy that makes New Asia – Singapore the exemplar of the dynamism of the South-East Asia region.

Additional considerations for destination selection included the wish to obtain a global spread with destinations from all continents, considering that the survey itself was to be conducted on a global scale. Also, the relative global awareness of the destination and its basic perimeters and characteristics should be relatively easy to assess by a global audience. For example, popular destination branding case studies such as Australia, Western Australia and New Zealand were considered, for a general global audience, to be either too 'big' and heterogeneous, or too difficult to delineate.

Half way the data-collection stage, when 400 responses had been collected, it was decided to exclude four of the destinations – the Canary Islands, Morocco, the Netherlands and Wales – from the survey, with the aim of increasing the responses to the remaining four case studies. This led to the following sample population.

SAMPLE

For the survey, a total of 1,198 responses was collected. Most respondents replied to e-mail newsletters sent out via Travellerspoint.com and later also by MeetURplanet.com, and TrekShare.com, advertising the survey to the roughly 33,000 members of these three websites. This would indicate a response rate of 3.6 per cent, though it is very difficult to be conclusive on that, as it is impossible to know exactly how many people read the newsletters and/or saw the additional banner ads on the above websites as well as on Mytripjournal.com and iTravelnet.com.

For one thing, it was concluded that the survey did not generate enough responses (32) for the Netherlands and hence that destination was excluded from the analysis. After data quality evaluation and cross-checking of completeness of answers, 1,102 useable questionnaires were retained in the analysis. These provided a total of 111,000 words of place image descriptions – roughly on average 100 words per respondent, with no significant differences between destinations. Figure 13.1 shows the split of the sample according to the destinations on which respondents provided feedback. Obviously, Dubai was over-sampled, being the central case of reference in this research.

Figure 13.2 shows the distribution of the sample according to age. Not surprising, this being an online study, the younger age group up to 30 years of age is relatively overrepresented; 54.7 per cent of respondents were female.

Table 13.1 provides an overview of the countries of residence of respondents. Based on country of residence, the sample was subdivided according to continent. This is depicted in the left hand column of Table 13.2.

Respondents were also asked to indicate their country of origin or 'homeland' if different from the country of residence; 18 per cent of

FIGURE 13.1 | Sample across destinations (number of respondents
providing feedback per destination)

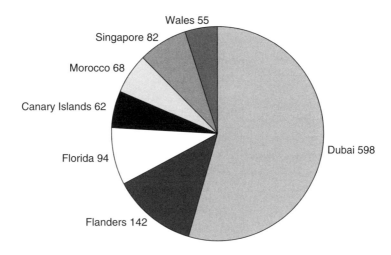

FIGURE 13.2 | Sample according to age of respondent (percentages)

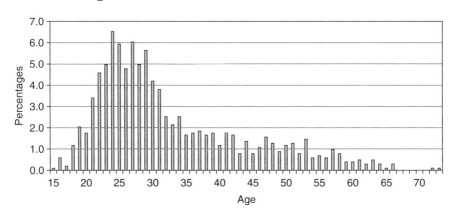

respondents indicated a different country than their country of residence as their homeland. However, the migration between continents in the sample is limited to 12.8 per cent. Major continental migration representing more than 1 per cent of the sample involves Europeans and Asians who have moved to North America; Asians and Australasians who have moved to

TABLE 13.1 Countries of residence of respondents

Country	N	Country	N	Country	N
United States	204	Russian Federation	5	Bermuda	1
Belgium	133	Thailand	5	Botswana	1
Australia	107	Uganda	5	Brunei Darussalam	1
United Kingdom	105	Hungary	4	Chile	1
Canada	75	Japan	4	Congo	1
Netherlands	40	Saudi Arabia	4	Côte d'Ivoire	1
India	31	United Arab Emirates	4	Croatia	1
Malaysia	29	Cameroon	3	Cyprus	1
South Africa	21	Egypt	3	Estonia	1
Singapore	20	Peru	3	Ethiopia	1
Ireland, Republic of	17	Poland	3	Faeroe Islands	1
New Zealand	12	Portugal	3	Jamaica	1
France	11	Slovenia	3	Kenya	1
Spain	11	Taiwan	3	Korea, Republic of	1
Sweden	11	Turkey	3	Kuwait	1
Finland	10	Algeria	2	Latvia	1
Italy	10	Austria	2	Malta	1
Nigeria	10	Bangladesh	2	Nicaragua	1
Germany	9	Czech Republic	2	Oman	1
Indonesia	8	Denmark	2	Puerto Rico	1
Norway	8	Ecuador	2	Qatar	1
Pakistan	8	Israel	2	Seychelles	1
Switzerland	8	Macedonia	2	Slovakia	1
China	7	Mauritius	2	Sri Lanka	1
Ghana	7	Moldova, Republic of	2	St Helena	1
Greece	7	Morocco	2	Sudan	1
Hong Kong	6	Panama	2	Tunisia	1
Iran (Islamic Republic of)	6	Romania	2	Uruguay	1
Mexico	6	Suriname	2	Venezuela	1
Philippines	6	Tanzania, United Rep. of	2	Yemen, Republic of	1
Argentina	5	Bahamas	1	Zambia	1
Brazil	5				

Europe; and North Americans and Europeans who have moved to Asia. The continental split of the sample according to country of origin is considered to be the reference for cultural background in this research study, based on ethnicity (Arnould *et al.* 2003, p. 75). This follows the work of Hofstede

TABLE 13.2 Sample across continents

	Residency (%)	Cultural background (%)
Europe	39.5	37.9
North America	26.5	26.0
Asia	13.9	14.1
Australasia	11.2	12.6
Africa	6.3	6.6
Middle and South America	2.6	2.7

(2001b), who also studies cultural differences between nation states and measures cultural values across continents. Hofstede is often criticized for this, as 'nations are not the best units for studying cultures' (Hofstede 2001b, p. 73; Hofstede 2003, p. 812). However, they are usually the only kinds of units available for comparison. Hofstede (2003, p. 812) argues: 'Nation states cannot be equated with national cultures, but does this render conclusions about cultural differences based on nation-level data invalid?'. Since the purpose of this research was not to measure cultural background or cultural differences per se, but to assess whether cultural background has an effect on perceived image and in what way country of origin was considered to be an appropriate estimation of cultural background. This is represented in the right-hand column of Table 13.2. Of course, if a respondent did not indicate a different 'homeland', the country of origin is considered also to be the country of residence.

Figure 13.3 shows the number of countries respondents have visited previously. On the one hand, 8 per cent of respondents report never having been abroad, while at the other extreme, a further 8 per cent of respondents has visited more than thirty-five countries. Figure 13.4 distributes the sample according to income, family life cycle situation, and occupation. The respondents in the sample are very well educated, with 80.7 per cent holding a college or university degree or equivalent, and 16.7 per cent completed upper secondary senior high schooling. Obviously, this sample is not representative for the world population, or even the online world population. It needs to be emphasized, however, that this research did not intend to provide a global representative description of the perceived image of the sample destinations. Instead, it aimed to test an alternative methodology for assessing perceived image and subsequently to identify differences across destinations. At the same time, its objective was to discover variations in perceived image depending

FIGURE 13.3 | Number of countries visited

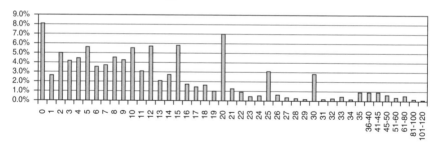

FIGURE 13.4 | Sample according to income, family life cycle and occupation

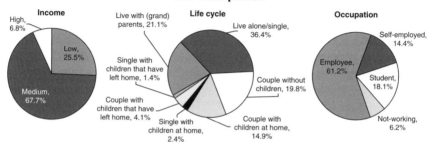

on the cultural background and socio-demographic characteristics of respondents. Therefore, bias in sample selection was not perceived to be a major issue.

RESULTS

Using neural network content analysis software, the totality of qualitative responses for each destination was content analysed in order to find the most frequently used meaningful words describing perceived place image elements. These are listed in Table 13.3. The detailed description of the content analysis procedure followed to obtain these results is presented in Appendix I. The content of Table 13.3 speaks for itself, but, interestingly, the destination-specific literature, on which the selection of the sample destinations was based (see the section 'Comparative Cases' above), is confirmed. In the *National Geographic Traveler* study on destination stewardship (Tourtellot

2004), the Canary Islands and Florida received low scores. In our study, these are the only two destinations that respondents perceived to be particularly 'touristy'. As far as reported image attributes is concerned, our findings also match the branding literature. The identity of Wales summarized in aspects such as historic, castles, scenic, natural beauty and friendly people is confirmed in our research. References to the Welsh language (7 times), musical tradition (twice) and even the leek as the Welsh emblem (once) were also found, but not frequently enough to appear in the dominating image. Myths and legends and arts and crafts were not mentioned as image attributes, but we need to emphasize that only 55 responses were collected for Wales. The sabotaged slogan for Morocco – 'A Feast for the Senses' – does not appear to be all that misplaced. At least, according to our findings, the second most important image attribute for Morocco relates to smell. People indeed seem to relate Morocco to strong sensual images of the smell of spices, aromatic Arabic food and fragrances, heat and colourful surroundings. These are unique aspects that apply specifically to Morocco, even when compared to Dubai, where these images are far less dominant. It seems that the Moroccan tourist board was on the right track until the German tour operators misused their market power. As far as Singapore is concerned, the essence of today's Singapore being a vibrant, multicultural, sophisticated city-state where tradition and modernity, East and West, meet in harmony, also seems to be well reflected in the perceived image as identified in our study.

Referring back to Table 12.1, several common attributes that appear repeatedly across destinations can also be identified. These include image components such as, for example, the physical and natural surroundings (buildings/architecture and nature/sea); cultural distance; weather/climate conditions; activities on offer (such as shopping or water sports); and tourist facilitation (such as hotels). However, for each destination, very specific unique image components can also be identified, such as, in the case of Dubai, the desert; wealth; luxury; life in the streets; the smell of various fragrances; sand; oil; and camels. Some components are holistic (such as the Arab and Muslim culture) while others are attribute based (the availability and quality of beaches). Some are functional (such as shopping), while others are more psychological (such as the friendliness of the people). This seems to confirm the theory developed by Echtner and Ritchie (1991, 1993, 2003), discussed in Chapter 11. Nevertheless, the results also show that the importance of unique image components should not be underestimated. More explicitly, for most of the sample destinations included in this study, one or two unique negative image components were identified. For example, in the case of Dubai, over 14 per cent of respondents made reference to the position of women in Muslim/Arab societies. Several misperceptions seem to exist, such as the need for female visitors to cover their hair in Dubai; or women not being allowed to drive cars; or the idea that one will not see many women in the streets and public places in Dubai. Also in the case of Dubai, 21 per cent of respondents made comments along the lines of 'I have never been there or to that region/never visited/never heard of'. The same was found for the destinations of Flanders and Wales. This seems to indicate a general lack of knowledge about the destinations, the comments made being an excuse for not being able to provide much detail about the places in question. Additional analysis of the data, by searching for the phrase 'do not know' confirmed this. Indexing this phrase by the number of times it was used by the equivalent of 100 respondents showed an index of 11.2 for Dubai, 12 for Flanders, and 16.4 for Wales, while the index for the Canary Islands and Florida was 3, and Singapore scored 6. This indicates that it was harder for respondents to control their perceived image for the first three destinations; or, in other words, these are not very strong place brands. In other cases, particular destinations were found to be specifically touristy or to suffer from distinctive bad weather conditions. Such misperceptions and negative image components would obviously demand active involvement from place marketers in order to try to change such public perceptions. Unfortunately, when utilizing the generally applied traditional attribute-based place image research methodologies, such unique negative components would never be identified.

The same applies to the ephemeral character of image, as illustrated by the case of Florida. Taking into consideration that the fieldwork for this survey was conducted during the autumn of 2004, many references were made to hurricanes, obviously because of the intensive media reporting of the effects of hurricane Frances. It is doubtful that such perceptions would still dominate if this survey had been conducted six months earlier or later. This illustrates the effects of temporal environmental and situational influences.

The subjectivity and individual private nature of image is also illustrated. For Dubai, the most frequently mentioned image component, 'hot weather', was still only mentioned by fewer than 30 per cent of respondents. This seems to indicate that, while stereotypical mental images exist, the act of perceiving is a purely individual affair. Many differences exist among consumers, as will be illustrated later. Hence it is not surprising that measuring only common attribute scales does not explain destination choice behaviour, as was concluded in Chapter 12.

Also, the experiential nature of tourism was clearly identified. It seemed to be natural for respondents to make comments along the lines of: 'hear the waves of the sea', 'feel the heat', 'experience the busy streets', 'smell the

TABLE 13.3 Image descriptions for seven sample destinations

DUBAI (n = 598; words = 63,918)	Percentage of 3,706 meaningful words	Percentage of respondents
HOT (warm weather/heat/warm climate)	5.8	28.6
CULTURE (as in different, local culture)	5.4	27.1
HOTEL (famous/7-, 6-, 5-star/luxury/expensive hotels)	6.0	26.9
BUILDING (as in amazing/special architecture/buildings)	5.6	25.9
DESERT	6.0	25.4
SHOP (shops/shopping)	5.5	24.9
ARAB (Arabic/Arabian)	5.4	24.6
MODERN	4.7	23.7
RICH (wealth/wealthy/rich)	4.6	22.6
NEVER (never been there/visited/heard of)	3.8	21.1
LUXURY (luxurious)	2.9	15.9
WOMAN (as in the position of women in Muslim/ Arab countries)	3.5	14.2
SMELL (smell of spices/food/fragrances/heat)	2.8	13.2
WATER (water/sea)	2.5	13.0
MARKET(S)	2.3	12.7
BEACH(ES)	2.3	11.5
STREET (busy /lively/people in the street)	2.3	11.0
MUSLIM	2.5	10.9
SAND	2.2	10.6
OIL	1.8	9.7
CAMEL(S)	1.6	9.2

CANARY ISLANDS (n = 62; words = 6,419)	Percentage of 314 meaningful words	Percentage of respondents
BEACH(ES)	12.1	48.4
ISLAND(S)	14.3	38.7
WATER (water/sea)	9.6	32.3
HOT (warm weather/heat/warm climate)	5.4	25.8
SUN (sunny/sunshine)	6.1	24.2
SPAIN (Spanish)	6.7	22.6
TOURIST (as in touristy)	4.8	21.0
HOTEL (comfortable/nice/good/luxurious/fancy hotel)	3.8	17.7
SAND	3.8	16.1
CULTURE (as in different, local culture)	3.2	12.9
BLUE (blue water/skies)	2.9	11.3
NATURE (natural)	2.9	9.7

(Continued)

TABLE 13.3 Continued

FLANDERS (n = 142; words = 13,260)	Percentage of 661 meaningful words	Percentage of respondents
BELGIUM (Belgian)	20.1	53.5
BUILDING (old/historic buildings/architecture)	5.9	22.5
CHOCOLATE(S)	6.7	21.8
EUROPE (European)	3.9	16.2
CULTURE (as in different, local culture)	4.2	15.5
HISTORY (historic)	4.1	15.5
OLD (as in old town/buildings/castles)	4.4	14.8
STREET (cobbled/narrow/winding streets)	4.2	14.8
FRENCH	4.5	14.1
NEVER (never been there/visited/heard of)	3.5	14.1
SHOP (shops/shopping)	4.1	14.1
BEER	3.5	12.0
CAFÉ(S)	2.61	2.0
FRIENDLY (as in friendly people)	2.7	11.3

FLORIDA (n = 94; words = 7,964)	Percentage of 454 meaningful words	Percentage of respondents
BEACH(ES)	16.7	53.2
HOT (warm weather/heat/warm climate)	9.7	35.1
SUN (sunny/sunshine)	8.6	30.9
DISNEY (Disneyland/Disneyworld)	6.6	29.8
MIAMI	7.7	26.6
AMERICA (American/Americans)	6.6	25.5
EVERGLADES	4.6	21.3
WATER (water/sea)	5.5	21.3
HURRICANE(S)	3.1	14.9
TOURIST (as in touristy)	3.3	13.8
NATURE (natural)	2.4	11.7
PALM (palm tree(s))	2.4	11.7
WHITE (white beach/houses/paving)	2.6	11.7

WALES (n = 55; words = 4,811)	Percentage of 236 meaningful words	Percentage of respondents
GREEN	8.5	32.7
RAIN (rains/rainy)	7.6	27.3
HILLS	5.9	25.5

(Continued)

TABLE 13.3 Continued

NATURE (natural)	7.2	25.5
PUB	6.4	25.5
CASTLE(S)	5.5	21.8
COUNTRYSIDE	5.5	21.8
NEVER (never been there/visited/heard of)	5.5	21.8
BUILDING (old/historic buildings/architecture)	5.5	20.0
FRIENDLY (friendly people)	4.7	18.2
VILLAGE(S)	4.7	18.2
OLD (as in old buildings/castles)	4.2	16.4
COLD (as in cold weather)	3.8	14.5
WALK (walking/long walks)	4.2	14.5
SHEEP	3.8	12.7

MOROCCO (n = 68; words = 7,763)	Percentage of 374 meaningful words	Percentage of respondents
HOT (warm weather/heat/warm climate)	8.0	32.4
SMELL (smell of spices/food/fragrances/heat)	7.0	32.4
CULTURE (as in different, local culture)	6.7	26.5
SPICE (spices/spicy)	5.6	26.5
DESERT	5.6	25.0
COLOUR (colours/colourful)	4.8	23.5
BUILDING (old/beautiful buildings/architecture)	3.5	17.6
ARAB (Arabic/Arabian)	3.7	16.2
MARKET(S)	3.2	16.2
STREET (busy/lively/people in the street)	4.5	16.2
CASABLANCA	4.0	14.7
MUSLIM	3.5	14.7
AFRICA(N)	3.2	13.2
SUN (sunny/sunshine)	2.7	13.2
CAMEL(S)	2.9	11.8
TEA	3.2	10.3

SINGAPORE (n = 82; words = 8,298)	Percentage of 401 meaningful words	Percentage of respondents
MODERN	9.0	31.7
CULTURE (as in variety of local culture)	8.2	30.5
CLEAN	6.7	29.3
STREET (busy /lively/people in the street)	7.7	26.8

(Continued)

TABLE 13.3 Continued

ASIA(N)	6.7	25.6
BUILDING (as in high-rise buildings/special architecture)	5.7	24.4
HOT (warm weather/heat/warm climate)	5.0	18.3
FRIENDLY (friendly people)	3.5	17.1
SMELL (smell of spices/food/fragrances/heat)	3.2	15.9
BUSY	3.0	14.6
DIFFERENT (as in different culturally)	4.0	14.6
SHOP (shops/shopping)	4.2	14.6
HOTEL (nice/luxurious hotels)	3.0	13.4
MIX (cultural mix)	4.2	13.4
AIRPORT (busy/clean/modern airport)	3.0	12.2
CHINESE	3.5	12.2
COLOUR (colours/colourful)	2.7	12.2
EAST (as in Orient)	2.7	11.0
EXOTIC	2.7	11.0

spices in the street markets and souks'. The most vivid example of a well-written experiential-type description of place was, ironically enough, provided by one of the respondents, prior to visit, and not in Chapter 9 by one of the organizations projecting destination Dubai. Below is an excerpt from this:

The first thing I notice when I get out of the plane in Dubai is the noise, everyone talking in Arabic at the same time, men, women, children, every one enthusiastically speaking to one another. When I take my taxi to the hotel I can hear the mosques calling people to take their prayers, I can see prayer mats placed everywhere around the city and men kneeling on them and placing their heads towards the floor. I can smell the spices when we drive through the market, extraordinary smells of saffron and cinnamon. When we drive across the city I can see mosques and other beautiful white buildings mixed with sky scrapers and modern office buildings. Everywhere I can see rich sheiks coming out of their limousines and entering their offices. But when we drive through the poor areas I can see starving children begging beside the road. In here I feel lucky and ashamed of being from the Western world. We quickly drive past the poor area and I put my feelings of shame in the back of my mind when I see my glorious hotel, red mat placed on the floor and golden onion shaped towers touching the sky. When I enter the hotel I start my cultural lessons and cover myself with a long sleeved top and a long skirt. I enter the new world and a new adventure.

Although this would prove to be a perceived image susceptible to correction post-visit (or a place brand satisfaction gap seems to occur here) multisensory experiential elements seem to be at least as important as gazing (for example, at buildings/architecture or people). Again, this seems to be difficult to capture in attribute-based scales, as experiential remarks often refer to very specific unique and characteristic expectations related to a particular destination.

Clustering of Destinations

Differences between common and unique characteristics are illustrated in Figure 13.5. After identifying the list of meaningful words (or image components) as identified in Table 13.3, the total text of all 1,102 responses was fed back into CATPAC. The program was instructed to analyse the text, searching only for the keywords from Table 13.3, plus the reference names of the destinations involved. In this way, CATPAC would identify which words are often used together and in reference to what destinations. The complete paired comparison similarities matrix for the sixty-seven image components plus seven destination reference names was fed into the perceptual mapping tool ThoughtView, provided as a CATPAC extension. The result is a three-dimensional model of which a snapshot from one angle is depicted in Figure 13.5.

Obviously, it is suboptimal to interpret a three-dimensional model on paper, but nevertheless Figure 13.5 should provide a good insight into the usefulness of this methodology. Sample destinations have been underlined and their corresponding image attributes clustered through the use of ellipses. Ellipses are dashed as the boundaries are porous; that is, they do not definitely include or exclude specific components, particularly as dimensions are difficult to interpret in this two-dimensional snapshot. What seems to happen is that image components that are place specific or unique characteristics move towards the boundaries, while common characteristics move towards the centre as they are shared by multiple destinations. Consequently, the most specific image components for Dubai are clustered closely together in the top-left-hand corner of the diagram. As there are more responses in the sample for Dubai (600 compared to 500 for the other six destinations), the unique characteristics for Dubai cluster closely together as their concordance is much stronger than for the other destinations because they appear together more often. These unique characteristics include hot weather, modern versus old, Arabian culture, and the position of women.

FIGURE 13.5 | **Perceptual map of destinations and their image components**

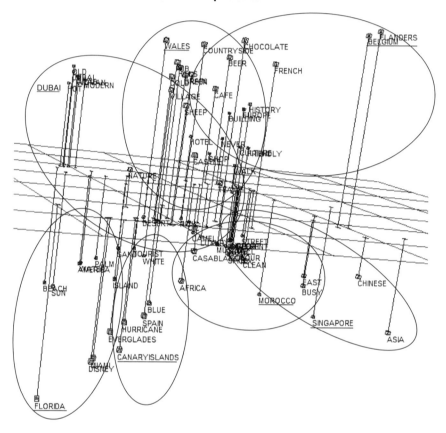

Fuzzy-set theory (Viswanathan and Childers 1999; Wedel and Steenkamp 1991) seems to be a useful frame of reference here, as it contends that products (tourist destinations) can be relatively similar on some characteristics, while being different on others. For example, Dubai shares many of its characteristics with Morocco (such as climate, desert, camels, street markets and aromas), but is different in its modernity, wealth and luxury, characteristics that it shares with Singapore. Also, being located in the Middle East, the position of women seems to be more of an issue here than in Morocco. Based on such an approach, Florida and the Canary Islands seem to cluster more closely together, as do Wales and Flanders, while Singapore and Dubai stand out more distinctively.

As common attributes cluster more closely together in the centre, it might prove useful in future research to combine the methodology applied here with attribute scales for these common characteristics, in order to identify the relative position of destinations on these attributes. As argued by many (Feighey 2003; Jenkins 1999; MacKay and Couldwell 2004), a combination of measurement techniques seems to be the best approach. The above approach, new in this field, has proved to be useful in identifying unique characteristics and as a means of mapping destinations relative to each other.

Sources of Information

Respondents were also asked to indicate on what information sources their perceptions were based. This was also done through an open question, the responses to which were analysed in a similar manner as the image responses, using CATPAC. The most frequently mentioned sources of information, referred to by at least 3 per cent of respondents (35 or more), are listed in Table 13.4. The middle column categorizes the information source according to Gartner's (1993) typology. This illustrates the tremendous importance of covert induced and autonomous agents – vicarious place experiences and temporal environmental and situations influences – through television, literature, internet, pictures and movies. Eleven of the nineteen information sources listed in Table 13.4 include such agents. Also, television as a source of image construction clearly occupies a dominant position, next to direct travel experiences (organic agents), which are obviously the most valuable and rich sources of all.

In addition, Table 13.4 also emphasizes the massive importance of solicited and unsolicited organic agents; that is, word of mouth (mentioned by over a quarter of respondents) and word of mouse (the internet being in fifth place). Despite this being an online research study, the internet still does not seem to occupy a dominant position, even though most respondents are active internet users (mainly members of virtual travel communities). However, the convergence of the media and ICT will make this point irrelevant in the future (Werthner and Klein 1999, p. 69). Pure overt induced agents such as advertising appear only in sixteenth position, being mentioned by just 4 per cent of respondents. However, if television is ranked as information source number one, of course, the logical question to ask is to what extent advertising has been consumed as part of this vicarious place experience, without consciously registering it as such. Nevertheless, Table 13.4 seems to confirm all relationships predicted in our place branding model.

The importance of the various information sources to the different sample destinations has also been assessed through analysis of variance. The

TABLE 13.4 Information sources

Source	Agents	Mean (%)
Television	Covert Induced and Autonomous	23.5
Travel (elsewhere/in region)	Organic	23.0
Friends	Solicited and Unsolicited Organic	19.1
Magazines	Covert Induced and Autonomous	13.4
Internet	Covert Induced, Autonomous and Organic	8.4
Books	Covert Induced and Autonomous	8.1
Pictures	Covert Induced and Autonomous	7.9
People (other people)	Solicited and Unsolicited Organic	7.4
Movies	Covert Induced and Autonomous	6.9
Stories	Covert Induced and Autonomous	6.6
Experience	Organic	5.8
News	Autonomous	5.7
Imagination	Organic	5.4
Newspaper	Autonomous	4.5
National Geographic Channel	Covert Induced and Autonomous	4.2
Advertisements	Overt Induced	4.0
Articles	Covert Induced and Autonomous	3.8
Media	Covert Induced and Autonomous	3.7
Documentaries	Covert Induced and Autonomous	3.5

results, which are striking in some cases, are reported in Table 13.5. The tremendous importance of vicarious place experiences through television, movies and magazines is overwhelming in the case of Florida. Also, news reporting is relatively important when referring to Florida, but this could be a confirmation of the transitory effects of autonomous agents such as the media coverage of hurricane Frances at the time. News reporting seems to be of little importance for Wales, however. For Dubai, word of mouth appears to be of particular relevance, as are the media in general to some extent. The latter might not be surprising considering the establishment of Dubai Media City. Movies have had a particular impact on the image of Morocco, but the top four information sources are mentioned remarkably less frequently in the case of Flanders. This seems to support the notion that the image of Flanders is less developed than for other destinations. Again, these results also seem to confirm the influence of all types of agents on the image formation process, but more importantly they emphasize its dynamic and ephemeral nature.

TABLE 13.5 Information sources for each of seven sample destinations

	Dubai (%)	Flanders (%)	Florida (%)	Canary Islands (%)	Morocco (%)	Singapore (%)	Wales (%)	F	p
Television	24.1^c	8.5^a	52.1^d	8.1^a	16.2^b	26.8^c	29.1^c	**12.85**	**0.000**
Travel	23.9	14.8	21.3	24.2	27.9	26.8	23.6	1.26	0.275
Friends	**24.2**^{c}	6.3^a	13.8^b	19.4^b	17.6^b	14.6^b	12.7^b	**5.03**	**0.000**
Magazines	15.1^c	2.8^a	24.5^d	6.5^b	10.3^b	15.9^c	10.9^b	**4.93**	**0.000**
Internet	10.0	6.3	7.4	8.1	5.9	4.9	5.5	0.92	0.482
Books	7.4	7.0	12.8	1.6	11.8	9.8	10.9	1.51	0.172
Pictures	8.2	5.6	8.5	3.2	4.4	14.6	9.1	1.56	0.156
People	6.0	5.6	8.5	14.5	7.4	11.0	10.9	1.61	0.141
Movies	4.3^a	4.9^a	19.1^d	3.2^a	16.2^c	7.3^a	10.9^b	**6.99**	**0.000**
Stories	5.5	7.0	5.3	11.3	5.9	9.8	10.9	1.11	0.355
Experience	4.8	9.9	1.1	9.7	4.4	9.8	5.5	2.25	0.037
News	7.0^b	2.1^a	**12.8**^{c}	1.6^a	1.5^a	4.9^a	**0.0**^{a}	**3.65**	**0.001**
Imagination	5.0	7.0	2.1	8.1	4.4	7.3	7.3	0.80	0.571
Newspaper	5.2	2.8	7.4	3.2	2.9	3.7	1.8	0.85	0.531
NGC	3.5	3.5	5.3	6.5	8.8	3.7	3.6	0.95	0.461
Advertisements	5.7	0.0	2.1	3.2	2.9	1.2	5.5	2.26	0.036
Articles	5.7	0.0	2.1	3.2	2.9	1.2	5.5	1.20	0.303
Media	5.7	0.7	3.2	0.0	1.5	0.0	3.6	2.80	0.010
Documentaries	4.7	2.8	4.3	0.0	0.0	2.4	1.8	1.36	0.226

Note: Rows that contain significant variance between groups according to ANOVA's F-test are indicated in **bold type**. In these cases, means with a different superscripted letter (a, b, c, d) are significantly different at the 5 per cent level according to Duncan's post hoc test, while the letters indicate a within-row ranking (a are groups with the lowest means; d are groups with the highest means).

Differences between Respondents for Destination Dubai

Differences based on cultural background have been estimated using country of origin (or 'homeland') as a reference. Countries have subsequently been clustered by continent (for a detailed justification, see the section headed 'Sample', above). The results of analysis of variance are shown in Table 13.6. Several significant differences in the perceived image of Dubai are indicated in bold type. It appears that, in particular, Europeans suffer from extravagant expectations about Dubai as a travel destination. Their perception of Dubai as a leisure destination offering luxury, fancy hotels, sea, sun and sand, is most vivid. Dubai as a shopping paradise is also recognized

TABLE 13.6 Perceived image of Dubai according to cultural background

Dubai (n = 598; words = 63,918)	North America (n = 168)	Latin America (n = 23)	Europe (n = 200) (%)	Africa (n = 42) (%)	Asia (n = 80) (%)	Australasia (n = 75) (%)	F (%)	p (%)
HOT	25.0[b]	17.4[a]	37.0[c]	14.3[a]	22.5[b]	26.7[b]	**3.11**	**0.009**
CULTURE	28.0	34.8	29.0	26.2	20.0	33.3	0.85	0.512
HOTEL(S)	19.6[b]	30.4[b]	34.5[c]	14.3[a]	36.3[c]	21.3[b]	**3.78**	**0.002**
BUILDING(S)	27.4	26.1	29.0	11.9	23.8	24.0	1.16	0.326
DESERT	22.6	30.4	32.0	21.4	25.0	29.3	1.06	0.382
SHOP(S)	17.9[a]	13.0[a]	29.0[b]	28.6[b]	36.3[c]	22.7[b]	**2.79**	**0.017**
ARAB	26.8[b]	30.4[c]	33.5[c]	11.9[a]	32.5[c]	22.7[b]	**2.08**	**0.067**
MODERN	25.0	17.4	29.5	9.5	26.3	22.7	1.71	0.130
RICH	27.4	21.7	28.5	21.4	16.3	26.7	1.09	0.365
NEVER	20.8	26.1	23.0	19.0	21.3	20.0	0.17	0.975
LUXURY	10.1[a]	13.0[a]	28.5[b]	2.4[a]	12.5[a]	9.3[a]	**7.69**	**0.000**
WOMAN	19.0[c]	26.1[d]	15.5[c]	0.0[a]	10.0[b]	12.0[b]	**2.87**	**0.014**
SMELL	14.9	17.4	13.5	7.1	10.0	17.3	0.75	0.584
WATER	8.9[a]	17.4[a]	20.0[a]	11.9[a]	12.5[a]	14.7[a]	**1.96**	**0.082**
MARKET(S)	15.5[b]	13.0[b]	12.5[b]	14.3[b]	6.3[a]	24.0[c]	**2.19**	**0.054**
BEACH(ES)	10.1[a]	26.1[c]	14.5[b]	4.8[a]	10.0[a]	8.0[a]	**1.97**	**0.081**
STREET(S)	9.5	17.4	13.0	7.1	6.3	16.0	1.28	0.270
MUSLIM	10.7	17.4	12.5	11.9	11.3	4.0	1.05	0.386
SAND	10.1	21.7	13.0	11.9	3.8	9.3	1.68	0.138
OIL	14.9	4.3	10.0	11.9	5.0	14.7	1.54	0.176
CAMEL(S)	6.5	13.0	11.5	4.8	6.3	12.0	1.14	0.339

Note: Rows that contain significant variance between groups according to ANOVA's F-test are indicated in **bold type**. In these cases, means with a different superscripted letter (a, b, c, d) are significantly different at the 5 per cent level according to Duncan's post hoc test, while the letters indicate a within-row ranking (a are groups with the lowest means; d are groups with the highest means).

by Europeans, but this is more evident to people from Asia, who are also quite aware of the impressive hotels that are located in Dubai. The Arab identity of Dubai is commented upon more often by Europeans and Asians. Most striking, but not surprising, is the fact that in particular respondents from the Americas, and to a lesser extent Europeans, comment on the position of women in Dubai. This is much less an issue to Asians and no issue at all to Africans. Of course, this can easily be explained from a religious perspective as well as the fact that these issues have been receiving

TABLE 13.7 Perceived image of Dubai according to gender

Dubai (n = 598; words = 63,918)	Female (n = 305) (%)	Male (n = 258) (%)	t	p
HOT	28.4	26.7	0.43	0.666
CULTURE	29.4	26.0	0.90	0.371
HOTEL(S)	28.7	26.4	0.62	0.535
BUILDING(S)	27.1	24.8	0.61	0.545
DESERT	24.4	29.8	−1.44	0.152
SHOP(S)	28.7	22.1	**1.80**	**0.072**
ARAB	27.1	30.6	−0.93	0.354
MODERN	25.7	26.0	−0.06	0.951
RICH	29.0	22.5	**1.78**	**0.076**
NEVER	25.7	18.2	**2.16**	**0.031**
LUXURY	17.5	14.3	1.02	0.309
WOMAN	23.1	5.4	**6.30**	**0.000**
SMELL	16.8	10.5	**2.21**	**0.027**
WATER	13.2	16.3	−1.03	0.305
MARKET(S)	16.2	12.8	1.14	0.256
BEACH(ES)	11.9	11.6	0.09	0.926
STREET(S)	14.5	7.8	**2.58**	**0.010**
MUSLIM	10.9	10.9	0.01	0.988
SAND	10.9	10.9	0.01	0.988
OIL	9.9	14.0	−1.47	0.143
CAMEL(S)	10.6	7.0	1.51	0.132

Notes: Rows that contain significant variance between groups according to t-tests are indicated in **bold type**.

increased attention in the Western media. It seems that many misperceptions exist, which are attributed to the Middle East or Arab world being seen as one homogeneous entity, while in fact, as the analysis of signature case Dubai in Chapter 5 has shown, significant heterogeneity exists. These results seem to confirm many of the points made by Said (1981).

Table 13.7 reports on the analysis of variance according to gender. Again, several significant differences are found. Women are more likely to comment on Dubai as a rich shopping paradise. Also, references to experiential aspects of street markets, and the fragrances and spices one would expect to smell there, are more often attributed to women. Most importantly, though, but again not surprising, is the fact that it is mainly women who comment on the position of women in Dubai. Apparently, it is not just a general perception, but a particular concern that probably needs to be addressed. If more than a quarter of the women in the West hold these (mis)perceptions, it probably inhibits a quarter of the market from travelling to Dubai for that reason, as the majority of leisure travel involves couples and families (DTCM 2000, p. 27). Of these travel parties, the female members might have a large impact on decision-making if such perceptions prevail. Surprising, though, is the fact that it is also women that more often comment that they have never heard of Dubai or visited the region. This would again confirm the existence of stereotypical generalizations.

Respondents were also asked to indicate, on a 10-point scale, what their attitude was towards the sample destination as a travel destination. Ranging from 10 – 'extremely positive, would definitely want to go there' to 1 – 'extremely negative, will never want to go there', Dubai received an average score of 8. To measure direct intention to visit, respondents were subsequently asked if they planned to visit the sample destinations within the next two years, answering yes or no. To measure the impact of attitude and intention to visit on image, correlation coefficients between these variables and the various image attributes were calculated. Those respondents whose attitude was less positive about Dubai and those who thought they were less likely to visit were more likely to comment on the hot weather in Dubai ($r = -0.146$, $p < 0.000$), the wealth in Dubai ($r = -0.162$, $p < 0.000$) and the position of women ($r = -0.095$, $p = 0.023$).

Travel experience was also measured by asking respondents to indicate how many countries in the world they had visited previously. For those respondents commenting on Dubai, the number was 12.7 on average. To measure the impact of travel experience on image, correlation coefficients between this variable and the various image attributes were calculated. Those respondents with more travel experience were more likely to be informed about Dubai's modernity ($r = 0.131$, $p = 0.001$) and wealth ($r = 0.115$, $p = 0.005$) built up from oil revenues ($r = 0.119$, $p = 0.004$) and the fact that it is near the sea ($r = 0.106$, $p = 0.009$).

These results confirm that self-focus and differences according to cultural background, personal and psychological characteristics do exist, though the research set-up was not focused primarily towards identifying such differences, and hence associations are often weak. These results should therefore be confirmed through future research and be treated as indicative qualitative assessments, precisely according to the objectives of the study.

CONCLUSION

Chapter 12 illustrated the inadequacy of prevailing methodologies for measuring perceived place image. Through the use of the standard common attributes identified in the literature and corroborated by destination marketing organization management in the Netherlands, we were unable to explain differences in destination choice behaviour among Dutch consumers. Based on the AIDA model, we identified four groups of consumers: those who frequently spend their holidays within their own country; those who would consider spending their holiday in their own country, but do not; those who always tend to go abroad on their holidays and for whom a domestic holiday is not an option; and finally, those who have not even considered where to go on holiday, such as consumers that do not travel at all, or infrequently. Contrary to our expectations, the perceived image of the Netherlands as a domestic holiday destination did not differ significantly across these four groups. This contradicted the literature, which states that perceived place image determines consumer preference, and subsequently destination choice behaviour. The logical explanation for these unexpected results was to assume that the common attributes that were identified had been reduced to hygiene factors and were incapable of measuring subjective perceptions of individuals and self-congruity.

Nevertheless, based on the subsequent study, in which we applied a phenomenographic approach as described in Chapter 13, we conclude that, as far as perceived place image measurement is concerned, we should not dismiss common attribute scales completely. In our second study of perceived image, we allowed respondents to express their perceived image in free-text form. The use of neural-network-based computerized content analysis software enabled us to achieve a thorough and objective analysis of this vast amount of qualitative data, at the same time allowing for quantification and the application of statistical procedures. The results produce a vivid three-dimensional picture of the differences and commonalities between seven sample destinations, including Dubai. For each destination, unique characteristics are identified, but common attributes across destinations are also observed. The limitation of our second approach is that common attributes move towards the centre of our three-dimensional clustering space, as these attributes are shared by several of the destinations that were included in the study. This makes it virtually impossible to assess the relative positions of different destinations on these common attributes. Hence, this is where attribute scales would appear to be useful, to allow for an importance-performance analysis (Go and Govers 1997) of destinations on such common attributes.

Our phenomenographic analysis proves to be useful and valid, though. Face validity is evident when examining Table 13.3, as it reveals no unexpected or peculiar findings for any of the seven destinations. Discriminant validity is also apparent, as differences between destinations are clearly identified. Based on the application of fuzzy-set theory, we were able to establish 'family resemblance' between destinations on some attributes, while others clearly represented distinctive unique attributes for the different sample destinations. As expected, Wales and Flanders are positioned closer together, as are the Canary Islands and Florida, while Singapore and Dubai stand out more individually, though they share characteristics of modernity as rapidly developing city-states. The Canary Islands and Florida compare to Dubai as sea, sun and sand destinations, while Morocco compares to Dubai as an exotic destination with an Arabian heritage and a desert habitat.

Convergent validity is established through the confirmation of image attributes in literature. The elements of the brand identity of Wales as identified by Pritchard and Morgan (2001) are largely confirmed, as is the 'essence of today's Singapore', according to Ooi (2004). Morocco proves to have tremendous opportunities for projecting and formulating a unique product offering with a strong local identity. Our research confirms that the intended branding campaign as discussed by Polunin (2002), focusing on Morocco's tourism potential based on its identity of being 'a feast for the senses', was well chosen. We observed that differentiating affective perceptions are already present in many consumers' perceived images of Morocco. Motion pictures have done the country a favour in this respect, and they provide good opportunities for projecting consistent images across channels by exploiting these vicarious experiences. It is regrettable that a destination's positive efforts towards achieving such a positioning are being sabotaged by outsiders who base their judgement on myopic, short-term profit maximization perspectives. As a result, in the case of Morocco at least, it is the major tour operators that contribute much to the commoditization of place and cause destinations to be dependent on short-term trends and market fluctuations.

However, despite the results appearing to be valid, considering the sample size relative to the global scale of the analysis, the reliability of the content of the results can be questioned. We cannot guarantee that a repeated application of our methodology, with a different sample, will generate exactly similar results. In other words, the perceived images we found in our research are not likely to be fully representative for the whole population. However, it was not our primary goal to generate such representative results. Our objectives were twofold. First we intended to test the methodology, by exploring the extent to which perceived image descriptions for each destination individually could be measured and confirmed in the literature, as well as differences between destinations identified based on fuzzy-set theory. Second, we intended to test whether differences in perceived image across different market segments based on cultural background and personal and psychological characteristics, could be confirmed using this methodology. With reference to our argumentation above, we can conclude that the results of our analysis have contributed successfully to our objectives.

Our phenomenographic analysis also clearly provides preliminary confirmation that the various components in the bottom half of the place branding model indeed have their influence on perceived image. Self-congruity is an issue, as differences in perceived image across cultural groupings and gender classes are confirmed. Contrary to Beerli and Martín (2004a) we also find that secondary sources of information are of tremendous importance. In particular, covert induced and autonomous agents have a dramatic influence, as over 60 per cent of information sources mentioned by our respondents involve these types of agents. Vicarious experiences, such as motion pictures, television and literature, are mentioned by respondents. Even the National Geographic Channel is mentioned. Autonomous agents, such as news coverage, newspapers and television in general, which represent the most important source of information, are also acknowledged by respondents. The media in general therefore have a tremendous influence. However, the role of the internet was less important than we expected considering the sampled population. Nevertheless, as media and ICT will converge in the future (Werthner and Klein 1999, p. 69) both will have a significant impact on image formation (Magala 2001).

At the same time, we need to support Beerli and Martín (2004a) in their conclusion that organic agents (that is, primary sources of information) are essential as well. The second most relevant source of information to which respondents refer is their own travel experiences or those of others. Hence, also solicited and unsolicited agents, word-of-mouth from friends and others, are highly relevant. The influence that various image formation agents have on perceived image also varies across destinations. Motion pictures have been mentioned specifically in relation to Morocco and Florida, where, in the latter case, also television in general is an extremely relevant image formation agent. The case of Florida illustrates the ephemeral character of images and the dynamic influence that autonomous agents such as news reporting can have on the model. Solicited and unsolicited organic agents seem to be particularly significant with reference to Dubai.

The experiential nature of tourism is also clearly identified. Respondents seem to have no difficulty referring to mental imagery of things they expect to hear, smell, taste or see; in particular, unsolicited references to specific colours for several destinations being of interest. Again, it is striking that this is particularly true in the case of Morocco, where the destination marketing organization had apparently wisely chosen to focus on such elements. Also, affective social aspects of the place experience and the related image appear to be of relevance, as expected. References to friendly people, the local culture or the touristic nature of a destination are made frequently. Of unique relevance here is the fact that respondents in the West, especially female respondents, commented on the position of women in Dubai and their concern about social restrictions that might possibly apply.

Our findings therefore confirm many of our assumptions and substantiate the place branding model. However, as a final remark we conclude that, as a result of the methodology applied, causal relationships between the various image formation agents and the content of the image, or the way in which agents change the image, are not identified. Our research provides preliminary evidence of the existence of the various components in the model. It is left for future research to test the causal relationships statistically.

Summary of Part 4

It is often stated that place brand management is the same as reputation management, and that the owners of trademarks are not the owners of the brands, because, as Simon Anholt puts it, the brand image resides 'in the mind of the consumer ... in a remote, secure, distributed location' (Anholt 2007, pp. 5–6). Place brand management, indeed, attempts to build reputation from the supply side, but images are personal constructs, defined as the sum of beliefs, ideas and impressions in the minds of individuals on the demand side. Images also consist of cognitive (information processing), affective (emotional) and conative (action) elements. In addition, place image should also be envisioned as having two main components: those that are attribute based and those that are holistic. Each of these components contains functional (or more tangible) and psychological (or more abstract) characteristics. Place images can also range from those based on 'common' functional and psychological traits to those based on more distinctive or even unique features, events, feelings or auras.

There are many different ways in which place image can be measured, but in our case regarding the Netherlands we have shown that purely quantitative traditional methods are insufficient. In a subsequent study, in which we have measured global perceptions of the image of Dubai in comparison with other destinations such as Morocco, Wales, Florida, Singapore, Flanders and the Canary Islands, we have tried and tested a new qualitative method that, at the same time, allows for large-scale application and testing through quantitative techniques. Through the application of a global internet survey and computerized content analysis, we have been able successfully to cross boundaries of qualitative versus quantitative methods of place image research, thus opening up new opportunities for the future.

As place image is a personal construct, it is therefore not an objective description of place but rather an individual perception of a person's relationship to a place. This is referred to as self-focus or self-congruity. This idea is supported by early modern philosophy, as we have seen, because we do not know for certain if there is an outside world; all we have is information through our senses and our mental constructions. Therefore, the image that someone has of a place is influenced by the person's cultural background and social, personal and psychological characteristics;, or specifically, his/her identity. Also, as well as overt induced agents (marketing) and organic agents (experience), as discussed earlier, image is largely impacted by autonomous agents or what is reported in the news media in terms of temporal environmental and situation influences, such as economic conditions, political circumstances, technological advances and social change. All this is clearly illustrated in our research on perceived image and case Dubai, among others. The global image of Dubai changes from continent to continent, and differs between male and female consumers. In addition, it is shown that neither the image of Dubai, nor that of the other selected cases, is significantly affected by destination marketing and promotion. Autonomous, covert induced and organic agents are far more important.

Finally, as in any experiential product, what also are essential agents for changing perceived images are the experiences that people share with others; that is, word-of-mouth or word-of-mouse – the online variant exchanged through virtual communities, online reviews, videos and blogs. These are also referred to as solicited of unsolicited organic agents. Building consistent and realistic images is therefore a major challenge for place branding, but is paramount, because these images create the expectations that need to be met when visitors experience place. If they are not, a place brand satisfaction gap might occur, as could be the case in some markets for Dubai, where stereotypes and clichés sometimes seem to prevail.

PART 5

Conclusion

A national brand strategy determines the most realistic, most competitive and most compelling strategic vision for the country, and ensures that this vision is supported, reinforced and enriched by every act of communication between the country and the rest of the world. (Anholt 2003, p. 11)

When countries change, it can take a long time for damaging, left-over stereotypes to disappear. Branding works when it projects and reinforces a changing reality – but it can be counter-productive if it is not rooted in fact. (Olins 1999)

It has taken us three parts of a book to describe, in detail, and with the necessary underpinning, research and examples, our dynamic place branding model, from a 3-gap perspective. What is still lacking is a model that can be applied in order to attempt to bridge the gaps. Such a model will be presented in Chapter 16, but not until after we have briefly revisited the three gaps and their implications in Chapter 14, and the applied perspective through our signature case Dubai in Chapter 15.

What we would like you to take away from this last section of the book is to:

- Appreciate that people are not purely rational decision-makers, and that the affective and social elements of human conduct are often underestimated.

- Brand places with projected images and product offerings that are embedded in local uniqueness and identity, incorporating the processes of both globalization and localization.

- Consider the need for renewed social interactions and rich co-created experiences.

- Emphasize the importance of multisensory information.

- Recommend co-operation and co-creation between public and private, supply and demand, as well as local and global actors.

- Reflect on the need for Dubai to bridge gaps.

- Analyse a place brand through perceived identity and perceived and projected image research;

- Design a place brand essence with its brand identity, experience concept and value match.

- Implement a place brand through construction, co-operation and communication.

CHAPTER 14

The 3-Gap Place Branding Model

In this book, we have deconstructed the place branding model from a theory development angle, presenting this from a 3-gap perspective: three ways in which the strength of a place brand, as experienced in the host–guest encounter, between, most often, culturally diverse groups, might be affected.

- Gap 1, where the unique place identity can be a sustainable competitive advantage, but the challenge is to build a product offering and place brand using this uniqueness and projecting it through consistent narratives.

- Gap 2, where, while hosts have a similar reading of the place brand as guests, the implementation and performance in delivering the place experience might be 'off-brand', resulting in disappointing performance.

- Gap 3, where the perceived place image is skewed because of different cultural interpretations of the projected images, situational influences or biased word-of-mouth. In such a case, the place experience might be 'on-brand', but fails because the guest has a different reading of the place brand.

By undertaking a thorough review and integration of the existing literature, we have examined both the antecedents of the model in the philosophy and immediate discipline of marketing at the interface of ICT, as well as the components that constitute the model itself. Several recurring themes can be identified.

Probably the most important conclusion must be that past research has major limitations in so far as it assumes that on both the demand and supply sides we are dealing with rational decision-makers. Consumers, organizations and individuals in co-operative networks have been treated as homogeneous groups whose decision-making is based on similar cognitive processes aimed at utility optimization. A lack of appreciation of the affective and social elements of human conduct in past research has allowed us to identify important shortcomings that have had major impacts on the way we look at the place branding model. Some of the most important observations we would like to re-emphasize before we draw our final conclusion in Part 5, are listed here.

First, we have argued that, from a place brand strategy perspective and under conditions of commoditization, local public and private actors need to embed their projected images and product offering within local uniqueness and identity. Semi-static and colouring elements of identity are crucial, as they allow for subjective interpretation and hence lead to power struggles and political hijacking. The ongoing discussion in the literature about the degree to which the identity of place, the unique resources and capabilities that form the competitive advantage of a destination, are 'authentic', seems to be patronizing and irrelevant; at least, as far as our assessment of the level of objective authenticity is concerned. We believe that the only valid assessment of authenticity is to measure the extent to which people co-create things that matter to them. By people, here, of course, we refer to the actors directly involved in the process – visitors, local residents and front-line service personnel – not public agencies and actors aiming to include and exclude people in line with their political objectives, nor local business or multinational management companies and intermediaries concerned primarily with yield maximization. Of course, we appreciate that this might be a naïve perspective, as economic and political realities cannot be ignored. However, what really matters is that place identities are safeguarded from the perils of commoditization through foreign intermediaries and from exploitation by local and multinational businesses and political leadership with hidden agendas.

Nevertheless, the international community and academia should not take the high road and argue that progress and modernization 'is not for them', except when it is convenient to them. In this sense, places have turned into arenas where international imagery is seen to have filled the void left by colonialism, to exert cultural power and thereby construct both peoples and places. Co-operation, public involvement, alliances, coalitions and partnerships are the way forward; this is referred to by Van Gelder (2008) as 'Place 2.0'.

This exertion of cultural power has been enforced by the process of globalization, where the global flows of finance, information technology, images and international labour and management are believed to have led to a process of 'McDonaldization'. Fortunately, others have identified the opposite reaction – localization – where local groups are in search of an identity and secure moorings in a world dominated by ephemerality and extravagant expectations. We believe that culture, heritage and tourism can build on each other, in order to provide places with a sustainable competitive advantage. By joining forces they can assist in the sustainable development of modern urban functions. Identity can be projected by a focus on local narratives, traditions (either historical or invented), artefacts, local language, and a sense of who the people are – 'the folks' – that populate a place. For businesses operated by multinational management companies utilizing international labour – organizations that are therefore firmly rooted in the network of global flows, detached from the locales in which they operate, and projecting ephemeral images – this might prove to be a major challenge. Nevertheless, for the local public authorities, it is important to recognize these issues. At the same time, we need to clarify that, of course, these elements of identity do not have to be 'old' – they could refer, just as well to current traditions, modern society and contemporary art and popular culture. The point is that whatever is rooted in local identity should, in most cases, establish uniqueness. That, one hopes, provides for a sustainable flow of international visitor arrivals, trade and investment, thus breeding cultural understanding and respect for local resources, while also bringing in foreign currency. Both of these can subsequently be employed to further invest in local resources and the construction of modern functions to help local residents. Hence, it also facilitates social sustainability.

This leads us to a second important observation that needs to be carried forward from this chapter: the need for renewed social interaction. The main benefit of technology is not, as many have argued, its ability to increase efficiency and reduce transaction costs, but rather its application in the facilitation of social exchange, innovation and the management of multiple channels of experiences, such as the increasing importance of vicarious experiences. An important source of potential dissatisfaction in the host–guest encounter is the way in which service delivery and supply fulfil (or fail to fulfil) expectations. Services in general are problematic because of their intangibility, perishability and heterogeneity. But in place experiences in particular, where production and consumption also take place simultaneously, and where hosts and guests often have different cultural backgrounds, this is a major issue. Past management practices and the literature have focused on rational solutions to this, such as the formalization of operating procedures, standardization, and training and education orientated towards the perfecting of basic skills. Now that technology is able to replace or streamline many of the manual operations involved, service delivery has (and will) become increasingly characterized by detached and clinical processes. This is particularly true when it involves remote interactions. Hence several authors have argued for a renewed personalization of the service encounter and a process of co-opting the customer. As we have seen, an important component of perceived image involves affective elements.

In many cases, these are likely to relate to interpersonal expectations and feelings. As the actual place experience also influences perceived image, as do vicarious experiences – which will in turn have a major impact on the perceived images of others through word-of-mouth, it is crucial that places recognize this need for social interaction and rich co-created place experiences.

This also relates to a third important observation we want to put forward, involving the way in which place experiences are projected. Compared to physical goods, where utilitarian benefits are often important, place experiences are hedonic in nature, where emotions, fun and fantasy play important roles. In other words, affective elements become more important than rational considerations, which emphasizes the importance of multisensory information. The actual physical place experience at the destination involves seeing, smelling, feeling and hearing, thereby building a rich perceptual image of the immersive experience. To project this in virtual environments holds many challenges. Real vividness of projected experiences, facilitating telepresence, is hard to achieve, and, based on our literature review, we need to conclude a priori that this issue is largely misunderstood. There is a focus on practical, rational elements of destination choice behaviour and marketing, and in online environments in particular these elements seem to prevail. Booking dates, prices, climatic conditions, availability, facilities and activities, accessibility, currencies and languages spoken are just some examples of attributes that generally seem to receive the most attention.

Fourth, from a supply perspective, an important observation to make is that, again, it seems that there is a void in the body of knowledge when it comes to understanding the human element of place branding and co-operation in relation to place image projection. Irrational processes based on stereotyping and subjective interpretation, lack of trust, myopic views and social prejudice seem to be much more important than the literature has appreciated thus far. For example, we anticipate that public- and private-sector bodies differ markedly in their objectives and the way they project images of place. However, public and private interests might be more connected than has been appreciated to date. Such connection is increasingly important because of a growing complexity of decision-making faced by both public and private interests, as a result of the interrelation of several strategic challenges – one of which being how to project a place experience. In this context, public and private interests tend to have different views of a situation and define problems differently. However, divergence may be interpreted as a productive force, if people, through debate and interaction, learn from one another.

Also, on the demand side, past research measuring perceived place brand image has focused on methodologies that fail to incorporate many of the affective elements of perceived image. Each destination, as well as each individual consumer, is unique. Focusing on common attributes across destinations, and common measurement scales across different groups of consumers, will inevitably fail to recognize many of the subtle differences, unique characteristics and holistic impressions that determine consumer preferences and destination choice behaviour. By integrating a large variety of sources in literature, we have tried to identify the many elements in the place branding model that have a dynamic influence on perceived image. These include the self-focus of the individual consumer; temporal environmental and situational influence; word-of-mouth; Web 2.0; vicarious experiences; and, of course, the actual place experience itself. This seems to provide evidence for our assertion that the process of place branding is much more subtle and subjective than it appears to be in much of the existing image measurement literature. Therefore, in our case study research, we have decided, both in our research on projected image (supply side), as well as with regard to perceived image (demand side), to use an existentialist constructivist approach, based on the content analysis of pictures and text and resulting in an interpretation of subjective meaning. Here again, it is the technology that has facilitated the ability to do that, using innovative research techniques that open up novel opportunities.

Finally, through the 3-gap place branding model, we have also attempted to illustrate that perceived image and the way it is influenced by the personal experience of service delivery and the host–guest encounter, cannot be understood properly without studying the configuration of power in the context of place, and concepts such as 'staged authenticity' (McCannell 1973) and the identity construction of place. Therefore, we have presented a detailed analysis of signature case Dubai and its identity, and an empirical analysis of the way in which it projects its image online. Apart from providing empirical support for our theoretical observations, it allows us to determine to what extent the gaps, as formulated in our model, can be identified in a specific research setting.

CHAPTER 15

Signature Case Dubai: Research Conclusions

From an applied perspective, the analysis of projected and perceived images has allowed us to identify several aspects concerning the nature of the gaps in the place brand strategy of Dubai. Three main issues have been identified that are relevant to this strategy,. First, while the public sector, and in particular the destination marketing organization, aims to project the uniqueness, culture and heritage of Dubai, the private sector is focusing on promoting modern tourism and business facilities. In many cases, we even suspect a denial of the existence of local people and a removal of the relationships between the guests and the local culture. Hence, the various players are working at cross purposes and should realize that public and private interests are more connected than they have appreciated thus far. The interrelationship of strategic challenges and place branding, particularly as far as the need to project consistent images is concerned, has become more important with the expansion of global media and the proliferation of ICT (Magala 2001). Convergence of the two will only accelerate this process.

Second, the experiential nature of place consumption is hardly reflected at all in the projected image of Dubai. Ironically, the best experiential descriptions of Dubai – those that include rich information about what one would expect to see, hear, smell or taste there – are provided by some of our respondents who have never in fact visited Dubai, and not by the texts that we analysed in our discussion in Chapter 9. Much can be learned from the hedonic consumption literature and academic research in the field of place marketing, which found that sensory information regarding consumer perceptions of places can be researched and bundled into sensory themes according to specific patterns of association. Some of our results related to perceived image seem to confirm this. In an online environment in particular, when projecting virtual experiences, adding such vividness would help to create telepresence. Place marketers would be wise to acknowledge the fact that consumers are not purely rational decision-makers and affective perceptions are indeed of tremendous importance.

Third, the factors that have contributed to Dubai's success, as have been identified in literature, seem to be particularly relevant within the context of global flows. However, we are unsure if the same applies to the local setting. This is illustrated by the fact that the tourism industry, particularly the transport and hospitality sectors in Dubai, have failed to support the efforts of the destination marketing organization in projecting the uniqueness of Dubai. These companies themselves operate primarily in the space of global flows, detached from local reality. Progression in Dubai is rapid, economic growth has been remarkable and modernization is taking place at an unprecedented rate. This has been illustrated by the way in which new technologies have been adopted and aspects of globalization localized. Tourism itself has led to rapid development, but also brought along social issues. It would be advisable for the Dubai government to study the impact that these processes have had on the local population, and determine the extent to which the sense of identity among the population can provide opportunities for an enriched brand identity.

From a place brand satisfaction perspective, several other issues were pinpointed. First, the perceived image of Dubai in general seems to be stereotypical and based on generalizations about the Middle East and Muslim society, such as those suggested by Said (1981). References are made to general characteristics such as Arab culture, Muslim religion, desert, camels, oil and sand. More specific and unique attributes relevant to Dubai, such as the royal family, pearling, dhows, the creek, the *majlis*, falconry, calligraphy, poetry, henna painting and wind towers, to name just a few, are not mentioned at all, or perhaps just once or twice among 600 respondents. Ironically, when referring to dancing, the only references found related to the perception of belly dancing being indigenous to the region, which in fact it is not; this involves an invented tradition created for the sake of commercialization by private actors. While these perceptions are not dominant and hence do not appear in the results of our research described in Chapter 13, it is illustrative of the fact that place imagery has sometimes filled the void left by colonialism. The only uniquely dominant image that does exist is that of Dubai being a modern wealthy city providing luxurious facilities as a sea, sun and sand destination that combines leisure with extensive shopping facilities. It is these extravagant expectations that dominate, particularly from the point of view of respondents in Europe. Another far less dominant image, which is shared with Morocco and holds promise for projecting uniqueness, relates to the souks, where respondents report images of smells and fragrances in busy street markets.

In that sense, Dubai should be on its guard not to fall prey to Western intermediaries and multinational management companies that want to exert cultural power and construct place identity through tourism, as has happened in the case of Morocco. The myopic views and orientation towards the short-term yield maximization of such players leads only to the projection of ephemeral images and the creation of simulacra environments. This in turn would merely result in further commoditization of destination Dubai.

Our analysis also allowed for some particularly negative image attributes to be identified; two in the case of Dubai. First, for many respondents it proved difficult to offer any mental representations of Dubai, suggesting that Dubai does not have a very strong image internationally, at least not when compared to some of the other sample destinations included in our studies presented in this book, such as Florida, Morocco or Singapore. Second, women in Western societies in particular have misperceptions about the position of women in Dubai. They are concerned about the need for women tourists to cover their hair; or women not being allowed to drive cars; or the idea that one will not see many women in the streets and public places. Such social issues need to be addressed and it would help, for example, to start a public debate on the role of women in Dubai's society. Co-opting the customer could be a good approach towards correcting these distorted images. Providing opportunities for potential and first-time visitors to discuss cultural issues with front-line employees, and managing consistency across experiences, online and offline and through the media, in order to provide subtle cues towards an ideal place brand image, seem to be important measures that need to be implemented in Dubai.

Finally, from a place brand performance perspective, while not specifically examined in our research, we anticipate that most first-time visitors to Dubai will be surprised. Taking into account the inconsistency of projected images and the incomplete generalized and distorted perceived image, it is highly unlikely that the actual place experience will be in line with expectations. This does not mean that customer satisfaction levels will automatically be negative – that depends on relative performance compared to expectations. This, however, was not part of our research objectives, but past research has provided ample proof of the fact that perceived images change dramatically during and after a visit. Because of this existing evidence, we concentrated on the perceived image prior to a visit, but it would be an interesting area of research in the case of Dubai to assess the place brand performance gap. Because, adding to the challenges of destination Dubai is the fact that much of the private sector is operated and managed almost exclusively by expatriate workers and executives, who are themselves firmly positioned in the space of global flows, but often ignorant of the local identity, cultural origins, habits, traditions and heritage of Dubai, and the local population. All three gaps, as we have been able to identify and portray them in the case of Dubai, therefore need to be bridged. Some suggestions for doing this are provided in Chapter 16.

How to Build Strong Place Brands that Bridge Gaps

As Polunin explains (2002, p. 3) 'branding starts with self analysis; with understanding and defining the product personality. It then shifts to communicating this personality to the target market ... It cannot be fabricated and turned on to please a market because it will soon be found out as false when it fails to deliver'. This illustrates that, while branding might be a way to facilitate bridging the gaps, false branding will make things worse:

> Nike and Coke – sports shoes and fizzy drinks – had the advantage of being able to start with a blank sheet of paper on which to create their personalities and to make themselves 'human'. Destinations, however, are very human from the start, with personalities moulded and constrained by history and preconceptions. Places consist of a broad, heterogeneous range of personalities that will cause confusion and are likely to resist being shoehorned into a homogeneous mould. But if branding is to work, there must be a common cause and consensus among stakeholders. The long process of consulting, co-opting and involving stakeholders, followed by distilling from their input the essence of a place's personality, is probably the toughest part of the destination branding exercise. (Polunin 2002, p. 3)

Destination personality and brand personality are related concepts that emphasize the idea that places, particularly in the branding process, can effectively have human personality characteristics attached to them (Ekinci and Hosany 2006). This facilitates the bridging of emotional connections between consumers and nations, cities and regions, but for us, there is more to it. Brand personality is part of the brand essence, or, as referred to by others, the brand expression (Van Gelder 2003). This includes, fundamentally, the brand identity, which incorporates the brand roots, values, vision, scope, name, visual identity, behaviour and the narratives of place (Dinnie 2008; Van Gelder 2003). In addition to that, the place brand essence should

FIGURE 16.1 | Gap-bridging place branding guide

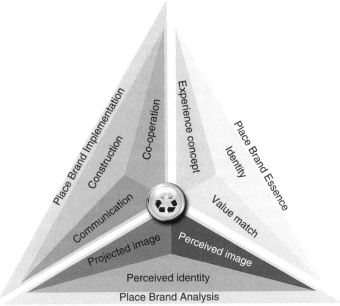

be built on a value match between place identity and the type of audience the place is attempting to attract, which could also be referred to as brand positioning. Finally, the brand essence involves, as with any brand, a reference to the quality and service characteristics of the economic offering. While this is often forgotten, when brands are sometime perceived as purely virtual entities, this link to the actual offering is also essential in place branding. But as places offer mainly hedonic consumption experiences as opposed to physical products, we argue that the place brand essence should involve the formulation of an experience concept; that is, a vision about the characteristics of the place experience that people can expect as visitors. This, then, is also the element that builds brand personality. To implement this place brand essence triangle, several elements are needed. An experience concept requires the construction of events, infrastructure, icons. In other words, place branding cannot be based on communication alone; it requires actual product development. Such building of place experiences and consistent projection of the brand essence requires the co-operation of many stakeholders, and finally, of course, consistent communication. All this, however, has to be supported by thorough research and analysis at the base, looking at place identity, and projected and perceived images, as we have illustrated in this book. This whole set of elements in our gap-bridging place branding guide is depicted in Figure 16.1 and will be elaborated on in this chapter.

PLACE BRAND ANALYSIS

Bridging the gaps begins by studying the identity of place. Points of departure can be found in Table 16.1. Useful secondary sources are historical literature, museums, historians, or academics with local knowledge. However, as we illustrated through several studies in Part 2, resident perception surveys of local identity might also prove useful. Surveys can be based on input from secondary sources (as we have done), but also qualitative preliminary investigations or larger-scale qualitative primary research could be beneficial. The Zaltman Metaphor Elicitation Technique (ZMET), using pictures (similar to our Zeeland study) or objects, could be very powerful (Christensen and Olson 2002; Zaltman 2002). Because of the character and objectives of such research, it is quite attractive for the media to become involved and possibly link it to contests and publicity stunts; hence stimulating response and local involvement. Of course, this might incur political risks and therefore requires thorough reflection and subtle propositions.

In terms of perceived place image, it has been stated that many academics have acknowledged the relevance of this research area in the past, and have tried to measure place image by applying multi-attribute systems, using quantitative common measurement scales (Echtner and Ritchie 2003; Gallarza *et al.* 2002). However, Chapter 13 proved these traditional multi-attribute systems to be incapable of measuring differences in place image among different groups of consumers that show unequal levels of destination preference (that is, based on this method, tourists who visit a destination regularly do not report a different perceived image of that destination, compared to non-visitors). Therefore, multi-attribute approaches on their own seem to be inadequate in measuring place image or visitors' ratings of places, and alternative methods should be evaluated. As a result, we were compelled to agree with current thought in literature (Padgett and Allen 1997; Tapachai and

TABLE 16-1 Constructive elements of identity

Structural	Semi-static	Changing signifiers	Colouring elements
Location	Size	Great events/Great heroes	Past symbolism
History	Physical appearance	Food/Architecture/Arts/Literature/ Popular culture	Past behaviour
	Inner mentality	Language/Traditions/Rituals/Folk	Communication

Waryszak 2000), which concludes that the narrative mode of thought may be more promising than the paradigmatic mode. In a supplementary study, we used open-ended free elicitation of tourists' stories about places, and applied neural network based computerized content analysis procedures to generate the results. These proved to be satisfactory and capable of solving some of the issues related to common attribute scales, but for future research a combination of the two approaches is most likely to yield the best results.

In terms of projected place image, we used content analysis of pictures and text to analyse online marketing communications of twenty Dubai-based websites, including the majority of the most influential actors in the various tourism sectors. This has also been applied, though generally through manual analysis, to content analysis of brochures, travel guides, press clippings and other sources in which places are represented. This has proved useful in identifying how not only local stakeholders but, for example, also the international press and travel professionals, project images of place. For more insight into relevant methods and applications of research, we refer back to Chapters 5, 7, 9 and 13.

DESIGNING THE PLACE BRAND ESSENCE

The essence of the place brand is well defined by Gnoth (2002). What is required is to 'develop sets of shared values, quality standards and pricing signals even in the face of local, regional and national competition among industry participants themselves' (Gnoth 2002, p. 270). It is about the relationship between place identity (including attractions), experience and visitor. Gnoth also provides some examples:

> The features can be described through terms that usually refer to a personality. Tourists' (symbolic) interactions with these attributes become the characteristics of the experience which, in turn, define qualities of services that support the experience. For example, a large part of the experience of destination New Zealand is typified by the outdoors, wilderness, insular weather and agriculture, particularly sheep farming. These features translate into service experiences of human warmth, rugged but cosy surroundings, simplicity, hardiness, independence and peace. The experience of, say, urban France may be characterised by sophistication, relaxed style, *laissez faire* [italics in original] and indulgence. These attributes that emerge from the interplay of people in their environment form part of the attraction as well as attributes of the brand. Branding the attraction is the first level of destination branding activity. [The primary brand is then extended to the essential supporting services.] The network of each service industry helps shape the service delivery channel and the final service product through both tangibles and

intangibles. A hotel, for example, is built from materials that are supplied from quarries, timber yards and manufacturers of hotel fittings and furnishers. Likewise, tour operators may be using tour buses or boats built in the country and restaurants provide food supplied by local produce markets ... Extending the brand to essential services is the second level of branding, while extending it to the directly supporting primary and secondary industries is the third. Products and services involved here relate to food grown and processed in the country, including wine, but also technological products such as snow skis and ski lifts. (Gnoth 2002, pp. 270–1)

'The results are numerous opportunities for the generation of unique experiences that are associated with uniquely presented (branded) products and services' (Gnoth 2002, p. 273). Go (2003, p. 26) suggests several other ways in which to use experience marketing to co-opt customers into the brand story through symbols and rituals. The first, and simplest, way is to buy off-the-shelf stories – for example, by sponsoring athletes, popular culture or a Formula 1 team (such as Dubai is doing). Alternatively, a second approach could be to organize events on location. The Camel trophy is a good example related to Dubai, but travelling museum exhibitions might be a good alternative for destinations. A third possibility lies in the realization that the brand story could in fact be propagated by customers themselves, such as in the example of Harley Davidson. A fourth alternative is to create a (virtual) community where customers and partner organizations can get involved in the composition of the brand story (Klooster *et al.* 2004). Creating such a virtual community is not as easy as some of the popular marketing literature might suggest though (Valck 2003, p. 5). The creation of a virtual community is a complex business. One cannot force the birth of a community; one can only feed it. However, the way in which communities can be fed is currently being revolutionized, as will be discussed in the next section.

But the role of festivals and events in promoting place identity has also been acknowledged (Jeong and Almeida Santos 2004; Kotler *et al.* 1993). In the case of Dubai, the shopping festivals, and particularly the Ramadan festival and Eid and national day celebrations, have been important vehicles for representing Dubai's distinctiveness as a regional centre for leisure, tourism, entertainment and trade, but at the same time always heavily promoting its national heritage and Arab culture. As discussed, one of the centres of activity during these festivities is always the Heritage Village, a place where (emergent) authentic local culture can still be witnessed. However, as illustrated in Chapter 9, this is generally not acknowledged by the travel and hospitality industries, who seem to prefer to sell what they know – the traditional sea–sun–sand destination. Hence the potential value of including festivals as part of the experience concept in a well-orchestrated branding strategy. A challenge, however, would be to export these popular events abroad, in order to involve potentially interested consumers pre-visit and to create a real attachment to the destination, even before they have travelled there. Examples are, of course, the World Expos, Chinese New Year celebrations around the world, and embassy involvement in themed cultural events whenever possible.

One major concern that many stakeholders in place branding processes express, is the question of how a coherent and unique brand can facilitate marketing processes aiming at diverse target groups (the value match). This is one of the reasons why, as we exemplified earlier in this book, many places eventually opt for brand values that include meaningless references to diversity, dynamics, heterogeneity and 'finding all you might ever want in one place'. Such brands, of course, allow for all stakeholders involved (destination marketing organizations, export and foreign investment agencies, or trade organizations) to continue business as usual with their own marketing programmes without needing to worry about their activities being 'on-brand' or not.

As we have abundantly sought to argue, however, such brands do not seem to be very effective in linking the sense of place to a strong and meaningful perceived image. In other words, such brands are ineffective, as the idea of place branding was invented to create perceived uniqueness of place in a globalizing world as opposed to being all things to all people. Brands need to create a unique positioning based on the identity of place in order to link projected and perceived images effectively. So how should places deal with the tension between creating such a unique brand positioning on the one hand, but still allow for traditional marketing activities aimed at specific target groups?

For this, Christian Laesser (2008) introduced the useful concepts of 'territory related tasks' and 'product related tasks' of place marketing. Territory related tasks are aimed at image creation and communication in relation to a clearly defined geographical space, benefiting all service providers and diverse (potential) customers of a given political territory or entity, based on a neutrality/inclusion principle. This could clearly involve place branding initiatives, including a common brand identity with specific brand values, visuals, narratives, colours, fonts, tone-of-voice, and logo and slogan, as well as an overall experience concept (script). Product-related tasks would then include marketing initiatives aimed at bundling offers towards marketable products, benefiting selected and suitable service providers that match product related requirements based on a sector/subsector and segmented market exclusion principles (value match). Of course, based on the existence of a long-term place branding programme, short-term product marketing initiatives would have to be assessed in terms of the extent to which they are 'on-brand' or not. This links strategy with tactical programmes and an 'umbrella' brand approach, supported by Hankinson (2007), but still allows for flexibility and creativity within specific marketing initiatives. Brand architecture decisions are highly relevant in this context.

PLACE BRAND IMPLEMENTATION

As was alluded to in the previous paragraph, strong place brands need to be constructed; with physical elements, which could create the reason for changing or enhancing symbolism, behaviour and communication, as actions speak louder than words. Experience concepts and brand associations need to be materialized in infrastructural or cultural projects, events, museums or travelling exhibitions. In other words, it requires co-ordinated innovation aligned to the place brand strategy (Anholt 2007; Kavaratzis and Ashworth 2005; Van Gelder and Allan 2006, p. 7). As Anholt put it: 'don't talk unless you have something to say' (Anholt 2007, p. 34).

With place branding, this century seems to have introduced the importance of 'landmarks' (Kavaratzis 2005, p. 5), what we refer to as 'experience icons'. Icons and created world wonders ancient and modern – the remaining Egyptian, Greek, Mayan and Inca structures; the Great Wall of China; the Taj Mahal; the Empire State Building, the Golden Gate Bridge, the Eiffel Tower, Big Ben, the Statue of Liberty; the statue of Christ the Redeemer overlooking Rio de Janeiro; or the Petronas Towers in Kuala Lumpur– seem to have been rooted in religious, power or security concerns. However, in the twenty-first century, many new icons are being built for the consumption experience. Perhaps one of the first – relevant to our signature case – was the Burj Al Arab in Dubai, which, as a hotel and leisure complex, opened its doors just before the start of the new millennium. It put Dubai on the world map as a tourist destination and global hub years before most of the other megaprojects in Dubai were announced. Other known examples that are often used as best practices in relation to place branding, and that could be categorized as experience icons, are the Guggenheim in Bilbao, the Palm Islands in Dubai, and Beijing's Bird's Nest and Water Cube. Does this indicate that consumption experience is the new religion heralding the experience economy? Perhaps not, if we consider the fact that the Roman Coliseum and other amphitheatres were built millennia ago. Nevertheless, allowing for these few exceptions and the fact that experience icons such as Las Vegas and the Disney parks have been around for a while, place branding based on experience icons seems to be the new strategy for many places, if we consider additional examples such as, for instance, the Millennium Dome, Eden project and the London Eye in Britain; the Shanghai Expo in China; or the Autostadt in Germany.

Of course, this does not mean that there can be no place branding without iconic projects. Many, if not most, countries, regions or cities already accommodate unique and worthwhile experience environments or cultural assets, sometimes undeveloped or perceived by local people as uninteresting. By attaching value matched experience concepts to them and developing them through imagineering, renovation, accessibility programmes, edutainment remodelling and/or upgrading through events and festivals, such resources can be exploited in order to enhance place brand positioning for attracting tourists, talent, investors and trade. The many successful waterfront developments and revitalization projects in some of the world's major cities are examples of this.

But, regardless of the importance of physical appearance, of course, if places want to maintain their image in the future, communication will become increasingly important as well. With technology, information space is expanding at what appears to be the speed of light, and getting one's message across to the right consumer at the right time will be essential. The same technology will be able to facilitate that, however, and places need to start preparing themselves to be able to manage their narratives and project consistent images through the right channels, but in a flexible and customized manner. This can be done through content management systems (Valck 2003).

Content management is a method aimed at the collection, co-ordination, control and dissemination of information in targeted online channels, in an integrated and flexible manner. Information is linked and organized to form a consistent narrative through the use of metadata. Additionally, the use of metadata allows users to customize their application of the information (Valck 2003, p. 26). Metadata is basically data about data, such as author, title, date created, subject and keywords: 'Metadata describes how and when and by whom a particular set of data was collected, and how the data is formatted. Metadata is essential for understanding [and processing] information stored in data warehouses' (Internet.com 2008). On the internet, the technology used is RDF, short for Resource Description Framework.

RDF is a general framework for describing a website's metadata, or the information about the information on the site. It provides interoperability between applications that exchange machine-understandable information on the World Wide Web. RDF details information such as a site's sitemap, the dates when updates were made, keywords that search engines look for, and the web page's intellectual property rights. Developed under the guidance of the World Wide Web Consortium, RDF was designed to allow developers to build search engines that rely on the metadata and to allow internet users to share website information more readily. RDF relies on XML (Extensible Markup Language – a specification for creating custom markup languages) as an interchange syntax, creating an ontology system for the exchange of information on the Web (Internet.com 2008: http://www.webopedia.com/TERM/M/metadata.html), allowing for the proliferation of Web 2.0.

But to share the content of data warehouses with consumers, in today's information-overloaded society, is the most challenging part of the narrative management and communication processes. Just having a website will not be sufficient in the future. Of course, for consumers who have already positioned a destination in their action-set (see Chapter 11) and are actively searching for detailed information, the increasingly rich site content of destination marketing organizations will be very useful. However, places should want to create a strong and consistent brand, and manage diversity of perceptions across the whole population, regardless of which phase of the destination choice process a consumer is in, or in what choice set the destination is placed. In fact, one would preferably want to try to achieve a more favourable positioning. In the early phases of the consumer decision-making process, or with consumers with low levels of awareness, this is probably not done through the destination's own website. It is more likely that the media, intermediaries and cybermediaries, virtual travel communities, review and blogging sites (Web 2.0) and portals will have a large influence on this process (Magala 2001). So how to push one's content and consistent communications through these channels, and how to control user-generated content? The internet technology of RSS feeds might be useful in this respect.

RSS, short for RDF Site Summary or Rich Site Summary (an XML format for syndicating Web content), is potentially the way to move forward. Syndicating is the sharing of content among different websites: 'The term is normally associated with licensed content such as television programs and newspaper columns' (Internet.com 2008: http://webopedia.com/TERM/I/syndication.html). 'A website that wants to allow other sites to publish some of its content creates an RSS document and registers the document with an RSS publisher. A user that can read RSS-distributed content [feeds] can use the content on a different site. Syndicated content includes such data as news feeds, events listings, news stories, headlines, project updates, excerpts from discussion forums or even corporate information' (Internet.com 2008: http://www.psionplace.com/articles/2005/10/2005-10-18-Avantgo-Mobilizes-RSS-print.html). Even blog content can be fed into

RSS, making mass consumer-to-consumer communication even more accessible, further encouraging active bloggers.

This technology would allow place marketers to manage content all the way through to the consumers' desktops and mobile devices, supporting a strong branding strategy and management of diverse perceptions. Combined with other technologies such as provided through ambient intelligence, that would allow for completely customized but consistent content feeding and customer communication. Ambient Intelligence was already predicted by Toffler in 1980 when he introduced the concept of the 'intelligent environment'. It is based on the premise that all consumer electronics, even the most inexpensive devices, are becoming intelligent with embedded computing power. Today, mobile devices, cars, refrigerators and other appliances have the capacity to process information, and in the future even clothes, or ultimately our body, will have embedded (artificial) intelligence. Then, if fixed and mobile communication could be integrated in a seamless way; if these devices could be linked to this basic infrastructure and embedded in their surroundings; if value added services could be incorporated; and if these could be set up in such a way that they could be made to understand the people they serve, a world of ambient intelligence would have been created. 'Such a world may be conceived as a huge distributed network consisting of thousands of embedded systems that support users with easy, intelligent and meaningful interaction, that satisfy their personal needs for information, communication, navigation, and entertainment' (Loonstra *et al.* 2004, p. 96).

What it will do is allow 'the network stakeholders to sense and respond to individual customers' expectations and take measures that provide exclusive access to any source of information, at any place and time, resulting in increased purchase volumes and user loyalty' (Loonstra *et al.* 2004, p. 96). But, of course, if customers' locations, expectations, connectedness and profiles are known, it provides great opportunities also to push customized and balanced information. This would allow places to narrate their story and communicate this in a customized way, dealing with, but at the same time leveraging, diverse perceptions. As an example for Dubai: it would not matter that large resorts attempt to 'recruit', 'sign up' and 'lock up' customers within the boundaries of their holiday bubbles encapsulated in global flows. An ambient intelligent world would recognize a traveller on arrival, possibly even before, and if the traveller were to be identified not just as a sea–sun–sand devotee, but as a potentially culturally or otherwise interested tourist, the place marketer could try to use push technology to encourage the person to break away from their bubble and learn more about the place as a whole. A richer experience, and hence a stronger place brand, might ensue. In 1980, Toffler saw an emerging trend towards de-massification of the media, which would result in a 'blip culture', where fewer and fewer people seek the larger picture. The over-supply of information has caused people to settle for 'blips' of information, which they then attempt to string together in a sensible manner to account for changes in their environment. Since the mid-1990s or so, through the expansion of the internet and the rapid diffusion of technology, this trend has developed firmly into today's blip culture. However, in future, the same technology, supported through ambient intelligence, might just be the antidote to its own 'negative side-effects'. Connected computers 'can sift vast masses of data to find subtle patterns. It can help assemble "blips" into larger, more meaningful wholes' (Toffler 1980, p. 174). Through this, places should try to tell their story, or even to co-create it in social networks, by designing message, conflict, characters and plot (Fog *et al.* 2005).

But 'brands need to be managed and controlled. It thus becomes a focal issue as to who controls and manages a country brand, especially if its potential national brand extensions – the service providers together with their potential partners from primary and secondary industries – lack community, vision and control' (Gnoth 2002, p. 267). 'Consulting, co-opting, and involving stakeholders, followed by distilling from their input the essence of a place's personality, is probably the toughest part of the destination branding exercise' (Polunin 2002, p. 3), but it will be essential to bridge the place brand strategy gap. This is illustrated by Jeong and Almeida Santos (2004), who studied the cultural politics of festivals and the political nature of place identity, where they found that dominant groups can use such vehicles to consolidate their privileged social status by including and excluding other groups in the construction of regional identity. Of course, this is not a desirable situation and will eventually collapse in the face of globalization. It is important that everyone is heard, and that all stakeholders, interest groups and layers of society are involved. Co-operative brands are stronger brands (Cai 2002).

Kitchin (2003, p. 19) supports the notion that it is the people who create the brand. He comments on the proposition that organizations can attach authenticity to brands when he states that 'authenticity cannot be attached to brands any more than humanity can. People attach themselves to people' ... and ... 'people love people, not soap powder' (when referring to Kevin Roberts' (2005) *Lovemarks*). Some contend that place brand communities are the way forward (Gnoth 2002; Klooster *et al.* 2004). Also, Van Rekom (1994a, 1994b) argues that the people on the shop floor, the employees of all the businesses and organizations involved in delivering the place experience, are of crucial importance. He argues that, within a corporate communication context, the whole production chain should be involved in communicating the brand mentality, and all the men and women involved should share the values and goals that differentiate the place.

Nevertheless, as Polunin rightfully argues, this is a complicated process. As he states (2002, p. 5), in many existing cases of branding: 'the emotional gap, between product personality and customer feeling, does not appear to have been bridged' (one might notice the parallel between this statement and the gap between the product offering and perceived image as presented in this book). Anholt (2002, p. 234) not only explains how branding might help to improve the tourism product, but at the same time how tourism might help in 'branding the nation ... by encouraging first-hand experience of the country through tourism'. Furthermore, Anholt argues that: 'just as corporate branding campaigns, if properly done, can have a dramatic effect on the morale, team spirit and sense of purpose of the company's own employees, so a proper national branding campaign can unite a nation in a common sense of purpose and national pride' (2002, p. 234).

Nicholas Ind refers to this as 'living the brand' (Ind 2003, 2004), while Hankinson (2004, 2007) refers to place brands as relational networks linking customers, services providers and other stakeholders. This will help in bridging the place brand performance gap, as it will guide the local actors and their employees in delivering the right experience in the right way. Anholt stresses the great importance of national culture as part of the branding exercise, as it is 'irreplaceable and uncopiable because it is uniquely linked to the country itself; it is reassuring because it links the country's past with its present; it is enriching because it deals with non- commercial activities; and it is dignifying because it shows the spiritual and intellectual qualities of the country's people and institutions' (Anholt 2002, p. 236).

What is needed is the creation of a 'community of practice', in which people learn at the intersection of community, social practice, meaning and (cultural) identity (Wenger 1998). 'Communities of practice come together around common interests and expertise – whether they consist of first-line managers or customer service representatives, neurosurgeons or software programmers, city managers or home-improvement amateurs. They create, share and apply knowledge within and across the boundaries of teams, business units, and even entire companies – providing a concrete path toward creating a true knowledge organisation' (Wenger *et al*. 2002, cover text). An example of a typical community of practice, relevant to the research context of Dubai, is the traditional *majlis*, still common today in the Gulf States (see Chapter 5). As an institution where common interests can be discussed by people from different walks of life and from different stakeholder groups, the *majlis* seems to be the perfect example of a community of practice that has been sustained over time, while in Western society these types of traditional cultural foundations have disappeared (Wenger *et al.* 2002, p. 5). As Wenger *et al.* suggest, we need to cultivate our communities of practice as a ways to consult, co-opt and involve stakeholders and create common ground (based on the creation, sharing and application of common knowledge). The brand community, as first suggested by Gnoth (2002) and later Klooster *et al.* (2004), indeed seems to be a promising concept for the fruitful application in the place branding context.

'It is not communities of practice themselves that are new, but the need for organisations to become more intentional and systematic about "managing" knowledge, and therefore to give these age-old structures a new, central role in the business' (Wenger *et al.* 2002, p. 6). 'For it is only through value-oriented, networked cooperatives and shared vision that a place brand community can evolve. A [place] brand community is here understood as a heterogeneous group of service producers who give a sense of homogeneity of experience to tourists through employing the same brand attributes during service production'(Gnoth 2002, p. 269). Klooster *et al.* (2004) approach brand communities as distributed community-based knowledge initiatives (Wenger *et al.* 2002, chs 6 and 9) and discuss their requirements based on Wenger, from a poly-inclusive perspective. 'The success of the destination brand community depends on the commitment and development of shared vision between the different stakeholders. This is a difficult process since all stakeholders operate in their own local context, holding different values and perspectives and only limited resources to interact with other stakeholders and develop a common ground, that is to say, a sense of community' (Klooster *et al.* 2004, p. 12). In mind space, 'to provide value for participation, the identity of the destination brand community should be closely aligned with strategic priorities of the different stakeholders' (Klooster *et al.* 2004, pp. 14, 124; Wenger *et al.* 2002, p. 217):

A strong community fosters interactions and relationships based on mutual respect and trust. Social space refers to the development of interpersonal relationships that reinforce commitment and trust between individuals. Reciprocity is of major importance within a community. Without it, the community is unlikely to sustain ... The levels of participation are very organic as stakeholders are constantly evaluating their goals and looking for new ways in which the community can contribute to their individual needs and those of the collective. Rather than force participation, successful communities 'build benches' for those on the sidelines, for example through a (digital) newsletter or website with the latest news [as well as private spaces for personal networking]. (Klooster *et al.* 2004, p. 16; Wenger *et al.* 2002, pp. 57, 133)

'Information space is able to support both social and mind space. By putting community related information on the internet (as website content or database documents), members can catch up with the latest news whenever they want ... Discussion boards and who-does-what facilities make dispersed "invisible" members visible, bringing the community alive in an online environment' (Klooster *et al.* 2004, p. 16; Wenger *et al.* 2002, p. 127). 'Material space facilitates gatherings where the community members can communicate face-to-face with each other. Face-to-face contact is the richest form of communication, providing space for stake-holders to build trust and share complex knowledge through (informal) discussions, and brainstorm sessions' (Klooster *et al.* 2004, p. 17; Wenger *et al.* 2002, p. 130). Through well-cultivated brand communities it is hoped that places can build sustainable brand identities, create meaning and generate the knowledge that can be managed through the processes discussed in the previous section: 'In other words, the required network structures to be formed in the industry to sustain a branding exercise need to develop a brand community that creates communication and interaction patterns which overcome the lack of a powerful channel captain' (Gnoth 2002, p. 277).

Maathuis (1999, p. 229) discusses how a corporate brand can be transferred to business units and products. When place brands prove to have the same properties as a trade brand, it would be an interesting issue to address the 'transmittability' of such brands in a place branding context. Could the brand community create not only a strong place brand, but at the same time facilitate the 'transmittability' of this brand to the various stakeholders and value chain members, as suggested by Gnoth? Whatever the case, if the place marketers are able to formulate a compelling and comprehensive brand story, which mobilized all (or many) of its emotional, multisensory and fantastic elements based on the identity of place, it should:

- Facilitate in projecting the right place image through marketing communication;

- Direct the creation of the right product offering, particularly the way it is delivered by guiding the stories that hosts share with guests; and

- Exploit the value of positive word-of-mouth/word-of-mouse by providing subconscious or real cues that create common stories for consumers to share.

This would help to bridge the three gaps as discussed.

FINAL THOUGHTS

This part of the book has argued that the gravity and frequency of the instances in which the three gaps are exposed can be reduced through thorough place branding. First of all, branding is a process of soul searching. The place marketers, in consultation with government and private industry actors, should formulate the identity of the place, its strategic personality and positioning. From this, a coherent place experience should be assembled, including a communications strategy that includes consistent narratives, supported by visuals. This facilitates a process in which the projected place image is consistent and in line with reality, bridging the place brand strategy gap. If, apart from paid advertising, good use is made of covert induced agents, this can help in bridging the place brand satisfaction gap, as perceived place images will create the right expectations. Finally, as industry is involved in the process and the projected image should be in line with the identity of the place, front-line employees will, it is hoped, be united and guided in their daily interaction with visitors. This, of course, supported by appropriate brand-related selling strategies, service performance standards, a process of co-opting customers, and promotion activities, helps to bridge the place brand performance gap. The ways in which the success of these strategies in bridging the image gaps can be measured, and to what extent these assumptions about the usefulness of branding hold true, is an important and fertile area for future research.

The contributions made by this book cover two specific domains. First, the innovative methodology of computerized content analysis based on neural network technology, as applied in the research case studies, proved to generate good results. It opens up opportunities for future research in many areas. It also proved to be useful for identifying unique attributes of place image at the same time, while traditional methodologies based on attribute scales have major limitations in that respect. On the other hand, common characteristics across destinations were also identified and our methodology proved to be incapable of measuring relative preference of places on the basis of such common attributes. Therefore, we suggest that a progression towards a standardized place image measurement methodology should be based on the combination of both these methodologies.

Second, we have contributed to the formulation of a generic but dynamic place branding model. All the relationships suggested in the model, based on literature review and integration in this book, proved to be identifiable in the empirical results in cases. Hence, the model is now grounded in (quantified) qualitative data. The causality of some of the relationships presented in the model has already been studied and confirmed in past research, but others might still need more extensive quantitative substantiation. Further research can concentrate on this.

Major conclusions on the nature of the gaps for signature case Dubai will be of interest to similar rapidly-developing places in the Orient, but it is obviously hard to generalize. For example, the discontinuity between private- and public-sector projected images is clearly an issue in Dubai. While we expect this is the case in many places, our research does not provide firm proof. Also, the intercultural issues identified in the perceived image, such as the misperceptions in the West on the nature of Muslim society in Dubai, will be of interest to similar places, but cannot be generalized automatically. However, we need to emphasize that it was, and is not, our intention to be able to provide universal results on the nature of the gaps. Our intention was, and our contribution is, to be able to identify whether there are gaps and how these can be identified, without limiting ourselves to the unsatisfactory methodologies that have been applied in the literature thus far. The case of Dubai was a means to an end to establish the model's relationships, which can only be achieved when seen in context. While the specific content of this context might be of interest to the destination involved and other similar rapidly developing regions or city-states in the Orient, it is not of concern to the general progression of science within this research area. Scientifically, it is not the content of the findings that is of interest here. What does constitute our contribution to the body of knowledge in this area of research in general is the fact that we have been able to produce these findings, our ability to identify gaps, and the way in which we have done that.

We hope that this research and our modelling design approach will also contribute in a broader context by helping others to appreciate the complexity involved in place branding, and to provide a lever for place marketers to enhance their impact. Purely rational approaches to strategic marketing management and the application of information and communication technology are insufficient. Moreover, to consider the consumer to be a purely rational decision-maker is also a fallacy. If places want to bridge their gaps and make sure that customer satisfaction and a fulfilling host–guest encounter prevail, they have to build trust, include elements of social awareness in their image projections, and behave in line with who and what they really are, or build uniqueness based on identity.

Appendix 1: Suggested Reading

This book focuses on sound methods and designs for the development of effective place branding. It draws on and includes a thorough examination of many important works. As the reader may wish to explore further, we provide a list, which is not exhaustive, of the main sources listed alphabetically.

Anholt, S. (2007) *Competitive Identity: The New Brand Management for Nations, Cities and Regions*, Basingstoke: Palgrave Macmillan.

Baker, B. (2007) *Destination Branding for Small Cities*, Portland, Ore.: Creative Leap Books.

Dinnie, K. (2008) *Nation Branding: Concepts, Issues, Practice.* Oxford: Butterworth-Heinemann.

Ind, N. (2004) *Living the Brand: How to Transform Every Member of Your Organization into a Brand Champion*, London: Kogan Page.

Kapferer, J.-N. (2004) *The New Strategic Brand Management: Creating and Sustaining Brand Equity Long Term*, 3rd edn, London: Kogan Page.

Lindstrom, M. (2005) *Brand Sense: How to Build Powerful Brands Through Touch, Taste, Smell, Sight and Sound*, London: Kogan Page.

Morgan, N., Pritchard, A. and Pride, R. (eds) (2004) *Destination Branding: Creating the Unique Destination Proposition*, 2nd edn, Oxford: Elsevier.

Olins, W. (1999) *Trading Identities: Why Countries and Companies Are Taking On Each Other's Roles.* London: The Foreign Policy Centre.

Van Gelder, S. (2003) *Global Brand Strategy: Unlocking Brand Potential Across Countries, Cultures and Markets.* London: Kogan Page.

Also:

Journal of Place Branding and Public Diplomacy, Palgrave. Available at: www.placebranding.com.

APPENDIX II: SURVEY CONTENT ANALYSIS PROCEDURE

This Appendix reports the procedure used to conduct an analysis of the responses to the free-elicitation open-ended questions in the survey hosted on Travellerspoint.com.

As a first step, all the text was checked for correct spelling.

Subsequently, seven text files were created, one for each destination, which included all responses for that particular destination. The survey did not generate enough responses (32) for the Netherlands and therefore that destination was excluded from the analysis.

A first word frequency analysis was processed using the standard CATPAC exclude file. For each destination, the 160 (maximum capacity of CATPAC) most frequently used words were identified from all the responses. Based on these lists, several recodes were conducted. If plural and singular of the same word appeared, plural was changed to singular. Words with similar meaning were recoded to one standard. In that way, for example, the following recodes were incorporated:

- HIGH BUILDINGS, ARCHITECTURE and SKYSCRAPERS became BUILDING;
- WARM WEATHER, WARM CLIMATE, GOOD WEATHER and HEAT became HOT;
- BAD WEATHER, RAINS and RAINY became RAIN;
- SEA became WATER;
- WEALTH and WEALTHY became RICH;
- DUNES became DESERT;
- DISNEYLAND and DISNEYWORLD became DISNEY;
- HISTORICAL became HISTORY.

This procedure was repeated several times until the lists of the top-160 most frequently used words stabilized.

Subsequently, for the top 40 most frequently used words in responses for each destination, commonality across destinations was checked. The idea was that words that did not immediately reflect a particular meaning, and were common across destinations, would not yield any particular descriptive image component of specific destinations. Such words, if they appeared in the top-40 lists of at least four out of the seven destinations, were incorporated in the CATPAC exclude file. This was done with the following words:

- AROUND
- BEAUTIFUL
- CITY
- EXPECT
- FIND
- FIRST
- KNOW
- LITTLE
- LIFE
- LIVE
- LOCAL
- PEOPLE
- PLACE
- REALLY

- TIME
- TRAVEL
- VISIT

Also, references to the specific destinations were added to the exclude list, in order to exclude them from the analysis. Later, by selecting the specific files for analysis, it would in itself be clear to what destination the analysis was referring. Hence the following terms were added to the exclude list:

- MOROCCO
- MOROCCAN
- DUBAI
- CANARY ISLANDS
- FLANDERS
- FLEMISH
- CANARY
- FLORIDA
- SINGAPORE
- NETHERLANDS
- WALES

The above actions were necessary in order to exclude any dominant, non-value-adding terms from the analysis. This is important in neural-network-based text analysis, as otherwise all unique words will seem to be connected through this one dominant term, which in itself does not add to the interpretability of the results. CATPAC builds a network of relationships among words used in the analysis, but if one of these is a dominant word that is used all the time (for example, the reference to the destination in question), then everything will appear to be linked. As all other words link to the dominant concept, they also link to each other through the total network of nodes. Hence, different groupings of concepts cannot be identified and the analysis yields little useful information. By eliminating the above 'meaningless' words, the remaining words will generate a more descriptive image.

Subsequently, the actual analysis of the seven text files was conducted. Below are the results for each destination. Each time a word is included in the analysis it means that it appears in at least 10 per cent of the responses. After the first round of analysis, ORESME, a non-hierarchical clustering tool included in CATPAC, was used to identify 'meaningless' words for each destination separately. If words did not appear to provide a specific contextual meaning for the destination, they were excluded from further analysis if ORESME generated no connection between such a term and the other words in the analysis. For example, the word GREAT appeared in the lists of only three destinations (and hence was not excluded from the start). But this word does not in itself provide any specific meaning. It would only get meaning in context (great weather, great food, great buildings, etc.). However, if ORESME tells us through cluster analysis that there is no link between the word 'GREAT' and any other concept, then it is best to exclude that word altogether, as it would not add to the interpretability of the results. In that way several words were identified for each destination specifically. This is reported in the following sections. If, after the final analysis, there were still words included of which the meaning was not completely apparent, the TestSTAT Search/Concordance tool was used to read the full context of the specific parts of the responses in which the words had been used. This is a useful means through which to gain an enhanced understanding of results. Sometimes this led to additional specifications of the particular meaning of words, while in other cases words were still excluded from further analysis if the meaning appeared to be ambiguous and non-value-adding. This is also reported below.

DUBAI

Frequency list using common exclude file:

TOTAL WORDS	4,283	THRESHOLD	0.000
TOTAL UNIQUE WORDS	31	RESTORING FORCE	0.100
TOTAL EPISODES	598	CYCLES	1
TOTAL LINES	2865	FUNCTION	Sigmoid (−1 − +1)
		CLAMPING	No

DESCENDING FREQUENCY LIST				ALPHABETICALLY SORTED LIST				
			CASE	CASE			CASE	CASE
WORD	FREQ	PCNT	FREQ	PCNT	WORD	FREQ	PCNT	FREQ	PCNT

WORD	FREQ	PCNT	CASE FREQ	CASE PCNT	WORD	FREQ	PCNT	CASE FREQ	CASE PCNT
COUNTRY	310	7.2	190	31.8	ARAB	200	4.7	147	24.6
DESERT	222	5.2	152	25.4	BEACH	84	2.0	69	11.5
HOTEL	222	5.2	161	26.9	BUILDING	207	4.8	155	25.9
HOT	216	5.0	171	28.6	CAMEL	58	1.4	55	9.2
BUILDING	207	4.8	155	25.9	COUNTRY	310	7.2	190	31.8
SHOP	204	4.8	149	24.9	CULTURE	200	4.7	162	27.1
ARAB	200	4.7	147	24.6	DESERT	222	5.2	152	25.4
CULTURE	200	4.7	162	27.1	DIFFERENT	132	3.1	90	15.1
WORLD	200	4.7	148	24.7	EXPERIENCE	132	3.1	103	17.2
MODERN	174	4.1	142	23.7	FEEL	90	2.1	73	12.2
RICH	171	4.0	135	22.6	GREAT	123	2.9	94	15.7
NEVER	139	3.2	126	21.1	HOT	216	5.0	171	28.6
DIFFERENT	132	3.1	90	15.1	HOTEL	222	5.2	161	26.9
EXPERIENCE	132	3.1	103	17.2	LOOK	84	2.0	71	11.9
WOMAN	131	3.1	85	14.2	LUXURY	109	2.5	95	15.9
GREAT	123	2.9	94	15.7	MARKET	84	2.0	76	12.7
LUXURY	109	2.5	95	15.9	MIDDLEEAST	91	2.1	78	13.0
SMELL	102	2.4	79	13.2	MODERN	174	4.1	142	23.7
WATER	94	2.2	78	13.0	MUSLIM	91	2.1	65	10.9
WONDERFUL	92	2.1	75	12.5	NEVER	139	3.2	126	21.1
MIDDLEEAST	91	2.1	78	13.0	OIL	65	1.5	58	9.7
MUSLIM	91	2.1	65	10.9	RICH	171	4.0	135	22.6
FEEL	90	2.1	73	12.2	SAND	83	1.9	65	10.9
UAE	88	2.1	72	12.0	SHOP	204	4.8	149	24.9
STREET	85	2.0	66	11.0	SMELL	102	2.4	79	13.2
BEACH	84	2.0	69	11.5	STREET	85	2.0	66	11.0
LOOK	84	2.0	71	11.9	UAE	88	2.1	72	12.0
MARKET	84	2.0	76	12.7	WATER	94	2.2	78	13.0
SAND	83	1.9	65	10.9	WOMAN	131	3.1	85	14.2
OIL	65	1.5	58	9.7	WONDERFUL	92	2.1	75	12.5
CAMEL	58	1.4	55	9.2	WORLD	200	4.7	148	24.7

ORESME analysis led to the exclusion of the following words:

- DIFFERENT
- FEEL
- LOOK
- MIDDLE EAST
- UAE
- WONDERFUL

Final Analysis

TOTAL WORDS	3,706	THRESHOLD	0.000
TOTAL UNIQUE WORDS	25	RESTORING FORCE	0.100
TOTAL EPISODES	598	CYCLES	1
TOTAL LINES	2865	FUNCTION	Sigmoid (-1 — +1)
		CLAMPING	No

DESCENDING FREQUENCY LIST

WORD	FREQ	PCNT	CASE FREQ	CASE PCNT
COUNTRY	310	8.4	190	31.8
DESERT	222	6.0	152	25.4
HOTEL	222	6.0	161	26.9
HOT	216	5.8	171	28.6
BUILDING	207	5.6	155	25.9
SHOP	204	5.5	149	24.9
ARAB	200	5.4	147	24.6
CULTURE	200	5.4	162	27.1
WORLD	200	5.4	148	24.7
MODERN	174	4.7	142	23.7
RICH	171	4.6	135	22.6
NEVER	139	3.8	126	21.1
EXPERIENCE	132	3.6	103	17.2
WOMAN	131	3.5	85	14.2
GREAT	123	3.3	94	15.7
LUXURY	109	2.9	95	15.9
SMELL	102	2.8	79	13.2
WATER	94	2.5	78	13.0
MUSLIM	91	2.5	65	10.9
STREET	85	2.3	66	11.0
BEACH	84	2.3	69	11.5
MARKET	84	2.3	76	12.7
SAND	83	2.2	65	10.9
OIL	65	1.8	58	9.7
CAMEL	58	1.6	55	9.2

ALPHABETICALLY SORTED LIST

WORD	FREQ	PCNT	CASE FREQ	CASE PCNT
ARAB	200	5.4	147	24.6
BEACH	84	2.3	69	11.5
BUILDING	207	5.6	155	25.9
CAMEL	58	1.6	55	9.2
COUNTRY	310	8.4	190	31.8
CULTURE	200	5.4	162	27.1
DESERT	222	6.0	152	25.4
EXPERIENCE	132	3.6	103	17.2
GREAT	123	3.3	94	15.7
HOT	216	5.8	171	28.6
HOTEL	222	6.0	161	26.9
LUXURY	109	2.9	95	15.9
MARKET	84	2.3	76	12.7
MODERN	174	4.7	142	23.7
MUSLIM	91	2.5	65	10.9
NEVER	139	3.8	126	21.1
OIL	65	1.8	58	9.7
RICH	171	4.6	135	22.6
SAND	83	2.2	65	10.9
SHOP	204	5.5	149	24.9
SMELL	102	2.8	79	13.2
STREET	85	2.3	66	11.0
WATER	94	2.5	78	13.0
WOMAN	131	3.5	85	14.2
WORLD	200	5.4	148	24.7

WARDS METHOD

```
ARAB.........<<<<<<<<<<<<<<<<<<<<<<<
             <<<<<<<<<<<<<<<<<<<<<<<
COUNTRY.....<<<<<<<<<<<<<<<<<<<<<<<<  (excl. ambiguity: arab/hot/modern coun-
                                      try)
             <<<<<<<<<<<<<<<<<<<<<<<
HOT........<<<<<<<<<<<<<<<<<<<<<<<
             <<<<<<<<<<<<<<<<<<<<<<<
MODERN......<<<<<<<<<<<<<<<<<<<<<<<
             <<<<<<<<<<<<<<<<<<<<<<<
EXPERIENCE.....<<<<<<<<<<<<<<<<<<<<<  (excl. ambiguity)
             <<<<<<<<<<<<<<<<<<<
GREAT.........<<<<<<<<<<<<<<<<<<<<<  (excl. ambiguity)
             <<<<<<<<<<<<<<<<<<<
WOMAN...........<<<<<<<<<<<<<<<<<<  (position of women)
                      <
BEACH....................<<<<<<<<<<
                      <<<<<<<<<<
MUSLIM..................<<<<<<<<<<
                      <<<<<
```

```
HOTEL.............<<<<<<<<<<<<<<<< (famous  /  7,6,5-star/luxury/expensive
                                   hotel)
                 <<<<<<<<<<<<<<<<
LUXURY...........<<<<<<<<<<<<<<<<
                 <<<<<<<<
SHOP.....................<<<<<<<<<
                 <<<<<<<<<
WATER...................<<<<<<<<<<
                 <<<<
CAMEL................<<<<<<<<<<<<<
                 <<<<<<<<<<<<<
DESERT...............<<<<<<<<<<<<<
                 <<<<<<<<<<<<
SAND..................<<<<<<<<<<<<
                 <<<<<
OIL..............<<<<<<<<<<<<<<<<<
                 <<<<<<<<<<<<<<<<
RICH.............<<<<<<<<<<<<<<<<<
                 <<
BUILDING...................<<<<<<<
                 <<<<<<<
CULTURE...........<<<<<<<<<<<<<<<< (as in different, local culture)
                 <<<<<<<<<<<<<<<<
WORLD.............<<<<<<<<<<<<<<<< (excl. ambiguity)
                 <<<<<<<<<
NEVER....................<<<<<<<<< (never been there/visited/heard of)
                 <<<
MARKET.............<<<<<<<<<<<<<<<
                 <<<<<<<<<<<<<<
STREET.............<<<<<<<<<<<<<<< (busy/lively/people in the street)
                 <<<<<<<<<<<<<
SMELL.................<<<<<<<<<<<<< (smell of spices/food/fragrances/heat)
```

CANARY ISLANDS

Frequency list using common exclude file:

TOTAL WORDS	347	THRESHOLD	0.000
TOTAL UNIQUE WORDS	21	RESTORING FORCE	0.100
TOTAL EPISODES	62	CYCLES	1
TOTAL LINES	290	FUNCTION	Sigmoid (-1 — +1)
		CLAMPING	No

DESCENDING FREQUENCY LIST					ALPHABETICALLY SORTED LIST				
			CASE	CASE				CASE	CASE
WORD	FREQ	PCNT	FREQ	PCNT	WORD	FREQ	PCNT	FREQ	PCNT
ISLAND	45	13.0	24	38.7	BEACH	38	11.0	30	48.4
BEACH	38	11.0	30	48.4	BLUE	9	2.6	7	11.3
WATER	30	8.6	20	32.3	CULTURE	10	2.9	8	12.9
SPAIN	21	6.1	14	22.6	DAY	17	4.9	12	19.4
SUN	19	5.5	15	24.2	DOWN	9	2.6	7	11.3
DAY	17	4.9	12	19.4	FEW	13	3.7	10	16.1
HOT	17	4.9	16	25.8	HOT	17	4.9	16	25.8
NICE	17	4.9	12	19.4	HOTEL	12	3.5	11	17.7
TOURIST	15	4.3	13	21.0	ISLAND	45	13.0	24	38.7
SMALL	14	4.0	10	16.1	NATURE	9	2.6	6	9.7
FEW	13	3.7	10	16.1	NICE	17	4.9	12	19.4
HOTEL	12	3.5	11	17.7	NIGHT	9	2.6	7	11.3
SAND	12	3.5	10	16.1	PALM	9	2.6	7	11.3
PROBABLY	11	3.2	8	12.9	PROBABLY	11	3.2	8	12.9
WEATHER	11	3.2	10	16.1	SAND	12	3.5	10	16.1
CULTURE	10	2.9	8	12.9	SMALL	14	4.0	10	16.1
BLUE	9	2.6	7	11.3	SPAIN	21	6.1	14	22.6
DOWN	9	2.6	7	11.3	SUN	19	5.5	15	24.2
NATURE	9	2.6	6	9.7	TOURIST	15	4.3	13	21.0
NIGHT	9	2.6	7	11.3	WATER	30	8.6	20	32.3
PALM	9	2.6	7	11.3	WEATHER	11	3.2	10	16.1

ORESME analysis led to the exclusion of the following words:

- FEW
- PROBABLY
- SMALL

TOTAL WORDS	314	THRESHOLD	0.000
TOTAL UNIQUE WORDS	18	RESTORING FORCE	0.100
TOTAL EPISODES	62	CYCLES	1
TOTAL LINES	290	FUNCTION	Sigmoid (-1 — +1)
		CLAMPING	No

```
DESCENDING FREQUENCY LIST                    ALPHABETICALLY SORTED LIST
                        CASE CASE                              CASE CASE
WORD          FREQ PCNT FREQ PCNT    WORD          FREQ PCNT FREQ PCNT
------------  ---- ---- ---- ----    ------------  ---- ---- ---- ----
ISLAND         45 14.3   24 38.7     BEACH          38 12.1   30 48.4
BEACH          38 12.1   30 48.4     BLUE            9  2.9    7 11.3
WATER          30  9.6   20 32.3     CULTURE        10  3.2    8 12.9
SPAIN          21  6.7   14 22.6     DAY            17  5.4   12 19.4
SUN            19  6.1   15 24.2     DOWN            9  2.9    7 11.3
DAY            17  5.4   12 19.4     HOT            17  5.4   16 25.8
HOT            17  5.4   16 25.8     HOTEL          12  3.8   11 17.7
NICE           17  5.4   12 19.4     ISLAND         45 14.3   24 38.7
TOURIST        15  4.8   13 21.0     NATURE          9  2.9    6  9.7
SMALL          14  4.5   10 16.1     NICE           17  5.4   12 19.4
HOTEL          12  3.8   11 17.7     NIGHT           9  2.9    7 11.3
SAND           12  3.8   10 16.1     SAND           12  3.8   10 16.1
WEATHER        11  3.5   10 16.1     SMALL          14  4.5   10 16.1
CULTURE        10  3.2    8 12.9     SPAIN          21  6.7   14 22.6
BLUE            9  2.9    7 11.3     SUN            19  6.1   15 24.2
DOWN            9  2.9    7 11.3     TOURIST        15  4.8   13 21.0
NATURE          9  2.9    6  9.7     WATER          30  9.6   20 32.3
NIGHT           9  2.9    7 11.3     WEATHER        11  3.5   10 16.1
```

```
WARDS METHOD

BEACH....<<<<<<<<<<<<<<<<
         <<<<<<<<<<<<<<<<
SPAIN....<<<<<<<<<<<<<<<<
         <<<<<<<<<<<<<<<<
SUN......<<<<<<<<<<<<<<<<
         <<<<<<<<<<<<<<<<
NICE.......<<<<<<<<<<<<<<<<  (excl. ambiguity: nice beach, nice sun, nice
                            weather)
           <<<<<<<<<<<<<<
DOWN........<<<<<<<<<<<<<<   (excl. ambiguity)
            <
BLUE...........<<<<<<<<<     (blue water/skies)
               <<<<<<<<
SAND...........<<<<<<<<<
               <<<
CULTURE............<<<<<<    (as in different, local culture)
                   <<<<<<
DAY..............<<<<<<<<    (excl. ambiguity)
                 <<<<<<<
NIGHT..........<<<<<<<<<<    (excl. ambiguity)
               <<<<<<<<<
SMALL..........<<<<<<<<<<    (excl. ambiguity)
               <<<<<<<
HOTEL.............<<<<<<<    (comfortable/nice/good/luxurious/fancy hotel)
                  <<
HOT...........<<<<<<<<<<
             <<<<<<<<<<<
WEATHER........<<<<<<<<<<<   (relates to hot)
               <<<<
ISLAND.......<<<<<<<<<<<<
             <<<<<<<<<<<<
WATER.......<<<<<<<<<<<<<
            <<<<<
NATURE.......<<<<<<<<<<<<
             <<<<<<<<<<<
TOURIST.......<<<<<<<<<<<<
```

FLANDERS

Frequency list using common exclude file:

TOTAL WORDS	863	THRESHOLD	0.000
TOTAL UNIQUE WORDS	28	RESTORING FORCE	0.100
TOTAL EPISODES	142	CYCLES	1
TOTAL LINES	632	FUNCTION	Sigmoid (-1 +1)
		CLAMPING	No

DESCENDING FREQUENCY LIST					ALPHABETICALLY SORTED LIST				
			CASE	CASE				CASE	CASE
WORD	FREQ	PCNT	FREQ	PCNT	WORD	FREQ	PCNT	FREQ	PCNT
BELGIUM	133	15.4	76	53.5	BEER	23	2.7	17	12.0
COUNTRY	46	5.3	29	20.4	BELGIUM	133	15.4	76	53.5
CHOCOLATE	44	5.1	31	21.8	BUILDING	39	4.5	32	22.5
BUILDING	39	4.5	32	22.5	CAFE	17	2.0	17	12.0
GREAT	32	3.7	20	14.1	CHOCOLATE	44	5.1	31	21.8
FRENCH	30	3.5	20	14.1	COUNTRY	46	5.3	29	20.4
GOOD	30	3.5	22	15.5	CULTURE	28	3.2	22	15.5
OLD	29	3.4	21	14.8	DAY	22	2.5	15	10.6
SMALL	29	3.4	24	16.9	ENJOY	27	3.1	21	14.8
TOWN	29	3.4	16	11.3	EUROPE	26	3.0	23	16.2
CULTURE	28	3.2	22	15.5	EXPERIENCE	17	2.0	15	10.6
LOOK	28	3.2	19	13.4	FEEL	22	2.5	20	14.1
STREET	28	3.2	21	14.8	FRENCH	30	3.5	20	14.1
ENJOY	27	3.1	21	14.8	FRIENDLY	18	2.1	16	11.3
HISTORY	27	3.1	22	15.5	GOOD	30	3.5	22	15.5
SHOP	27	3.1	20	14.1	GREAT	32	3.7	20	14.1
EUROPE	26	3.0	23	16.2	HISTORY	27	3.1	22	15.5
BEER	23	2.7	17	12.0	HOTEL	22	2.5	18	12.7
NEVER	23	2.7	20	14.1	LOOK	28	3.2	19	13.4
NICE	23	2.7	21	14.8	NEVER	23	2.7	20	14.1
TRIP	23	2.7	19	13.4	NICE	23	2.7	21	14.8
DAY	22	2.5	15	10.6	OLD	29	3.4	21	14.8
FEEL	22	2.5	20	14.1	SHOP	27	3.1	20	14.1
HOTEL	22	2.5	18	12.7	SMALL	29	3.4	24	16.9
WORLD	21	2.4	17	12.0	STREET	28	3.2	21	14.8
FRIENDLY	18	2.1	16	11.3	TOWN	29	3.4	16	11.3
CAFE	17	2.0	17	12.0	TRIP	23	2.7	19	13.4
EXPERIENCE	17	2.0	15	10.6	WORLD	21	2.4	17	12.0

ORESME analysis led to the exclusion of the following words:

- DAY
- ENJOY
- EXPERIENCE
- GOOD
- GREAT
- LOOK
- NICE
- TRIP

TOTAL WORDS	661	THRESHOLD	0.000
TOTAL UNIQUE WORDS	20	RESTORING FORCE	0.100
TOTAL EPISODES	142	CYCLES	1
TOTAL LINES	632	FUNCTION	Sigmoid (-1 — +1)
		CLAMPING	No

DESCENDING FREQUENCY LIST

WORD	FREQ	PCNT	CASE FREQ	CASE PCNT
BELGIUM	133	20.1	76	53.5
COUNTRY	46	7.0	29	20.4
CHOCOLATE	44	6.7	31	21.8
BUILDING	39	5.9	32	22.5
FRENCH	30	4.5	20	14.1
OLD	29	4.4	21	14.8
SMALL	29	4.4	24	16.9
TOWN	29	4.4	16	11.3
CULTURE	28	4.2	22	15.5
STREET	28	4.2	21	14.8
HISTORY	27	4.1	22	15.5
SHOP	27	4.1	20	14.1
EUROPE	26	3.9	23	16.2
BEER	23	3.5	17	12.0
NEVER	23	3.5	20	14.1
FEEL	22	3.3	20	14.1
HOTEL	22	3.3	18	12.7
WORLD	21	3.2	17	12.0
FRIENDLY	18	2.7	16	11.3
CAFE	17	2.6	17	12.0

ALPHABETICALLY SORTED LIST

WORD	FREQ	PCNT	CASE FREQ	CASE PCNT
BEER	23	3.5	17	12.0
BELGIUM	133	20.1	76	53.5
BUILDING	39	5.9	32	22.5
CAFE	17	2.6	17	12.0
CHOCOLATE	44	6.7	31	21.8
COUNTRY	46	7.0	29	20.4
CULTURE	28	4.2	22	15.5
EUROPE	26	3.9	23	16.2
FEEL	22	3.3	20	14.1
FRENCH	30	4.5	20	14.1
FRIENDLY	18	2.7	16	11.3
HISTORY	27	4.1	22	15.5
HOTEL	22	3.3	18	12.7
NEVER	23	3.5	20	14.1
OLD	29	4.4	21	14.8
SHOP	27	4.1	20	14.1
SMALL	29	4.4	24	16.9
STREET	28	4.2	21	14.8
TOWN	29	4.4	16	11.3
WORLD	21	3.2	17	12.0

WARDS METHOD

```
BEER..........<<<<<<<<<<<<<<<
              <<<<<<<<<<<<<<<
SHOP..........<<<<<<<<<<<<<<<
                    <<<<<<<<
FRIENDLY.............<<<<<<<<
                      <<<<<
OLD.........<<<<<<<<<<<<<<<<<
              <<<<<<<<<<<<<<<
STREET.......<<<<<<<<<<<<<<<<< (cobbled/narrow/winding streets)
              <<<<<<<<<<<<<<<
TOWN..........<<<<<<<<<<<<<<<< (excl. ambiguity)
                       <<
BELGIUM....<<<<<<<<<<<<<<<<<<<
              <<<<<<<<<<<<<<<<
COUNTRY....<<<<<<<<<<<<<<<<<<< (excl. ambiguity)
              <<<<<<<<<<<<<<<<
BUILDING....<<<<<<<<<<<<<<<<<< (old/historic buildings)
                    <<<<<<<<<
FEEL...........<<<<<<<<<<<<<<< (excl. ambiguity)
              <<<<<<<<<<<<<<
HISTORY........<<<<<<<<<<<<<<<
              <<<<<<<<<<<<<
FRENCH...........<<<<<<<<<<<<<
                     <<<
CHOCOLATE................<<<<<
                        <<<<<
CULTURE...........<<<<<<<<<<<< (as in different, local culture)
                  <<<<<<<<<<<<
NEVER.............<<<<<<<<<<<< (never been there/visited/heard of)
                     <<<<<<<
HOTEL.................<<<<<<< (excl. ambiguity)
                       <
CAFE....................<<<<
                       <<<<
EUROPE..............<<<<<<<<<
                    <<<<<<<<<
SMALL..............<<<<<<<<<< (excl. ambiguity)
                   <<<<<<<<<<
WORLD..............<<<<<<<<<< (excl. ambiguity)
```

FLORIDA

Frequency list using common exclude file:

TOTAL WORDS	541	THRESHOLD	0.000		
TOTAL UNIQUE WORDS	25	RESTORING FORCE	0.100		
TOTAL EPISODES	94	CYCLES	1		
TOTAL LINES	388	FUNCTION	Sigmoid (-1 — +1)		
		CLAMPING	No		

DESCENDING FREQUENCY LIST				ALPHABETICALLY SORTED LIST				
			CASE	CASE			CASE	CASE
WORD	FREQ	PCNT	FREQ	PCNT	WORD	FREQ	PCNT	FREQ	PCNT

WORD	FREQ	PCNT	CASE FREQ	CASE PCNT	WORD	FREQ	PCNT	CASE FREQ	CASE PCNT
BEACH	76	14.0	50	53.2	AMERICA	30	5.5	24	25.5
HOT	44	8.1	33	35.1	BEACH	76	14.0	50	53.2
SUN	39	7.2	29	30.9	COURSE	11	2.0	10	10.6
MIAMI	35	6.5	25	26.6	DISNEY	30	5.5	28	29.8
AMERICA	30	5.5	24	25.5	ENJOY	13	2.4	13	13.8
DISNEY	30	5.5	28	29.8	EVERGLADES	21	3.9	20	21.3
NICE	26	4.8	19	20.2	GOOD	13	2.4	12	12.8
WATER	25	4.6	20	21.3	GREAT	12	2.2	10	10.6
EVERGLADES	21	3.9	20	21.3	HOT	44	8.1	33	35.1
WORLD	20	3.7	15	16.0	HOUSES	13	2.4	10	10.6
MIND	19	3.5	13	13.8	HURRICANE	14	2.6	14	14.9
TOURIST	15	2.8	13	13.8	MIAMI	35	6.5	25	26.6
HURRICANE	14	2.6	14	14.9	MIND	19	3.5	13	13.8
WEATHER	14	2.6	11	11.7	NATURE	11	2.0	11	11.7
ENJOY	13	2.4	13	13.8	NICE	26	4.8	19	20.2
GOOD	13	2.4	12	12.8	PALM	11	2.0	11	11.7
HOUSES	13	2.4	10	10.6	PROBABLY	12	2.2	11	11.7
STATE	13	2.4	10	10.6	STATE	13	2.4	10	10.6
GREAT	12	2.2	10	10.6	SUN	39	7.2	29	30.9
PROBABLY	12	2.2	11	11.7	TOURIST	15	2.8	13	13.8
WHITE	12	2.2	11	11.7	WATER	25	4.6	20	21.3
WONDERFUL	12	2.2	10	10.6	WEATHER	14	2.6	11	11.7
COURSE	11	2.0	10	10.6	WHITE	12	2.2	11	11.7
NATURE	11	2.0	11	11.7	WONDERFUL	12	2.2	10	10.6
PALM	11	2.0	11	11.7	WORLD	20	3.7	15	16.0

ORESME analysis led to the exclusion of the following words:

- COURSE
- ENJOY
- GOOD
- GREAT
- HOUSES
- STATE
- WONDERFUL

TOTAL WORDS	454	THRESHOLD	0.000		
TOTAL UNIQUE WORDS	18	RESTORING FORCE	0.100		
TOTAL EPISODES	94	CYCLES	1		
TOTAL LINES	388	FUNCTION	Sigmoid (-1 — +1)		
		CLAMPING	No		

DESCENDING FREQUENCY LIST					ALPHABETICALLY SORTED LIST				
			CASE	CASE				CASE	CASE
WORD	FREQ	PCNT	FREQ	PCNT	WORD	FREQ	PCNT	FREQ	PCNT
--------	-----	-----	-----	-----	-----	-----	-----	-----	-----
BEACH	76	16.7	50	53.2	AMERICA	30	6.6	24	25.5
HOT	44	9.7	33	35.1	BEACH	76	16.7	50	53.2
SUN	39	8.6	29	30.9	DISNEY	30	6.6	28	29.8
MIAMI	35	7.7	25	26.6	EVERGLADES	21	4.6	20	21.3
AMERICA	30	6.6	24	25.5	HOT	44	9.7	33	35.1
DISNEY	30	6.6	28	29.8	HURRICANE	14	3.1	14	14.9
NICE	26	5.7	19	20.2	MIAMI	35	7.7	25	26.6
WATER	25	5.5	20	21.3	MIND	19	4.2	13	13.8
EVERGLADES	21	4.6	20	21.3	NATURE	11	2.4	11	11.7
WORLD	20	4.4	15	16.0	NICE	26	5.7	19	20.2
MIND	19	4.2	13	13.8	PALM	11	2.4	11	11.7
TOURIST	15	3.3	13	13.8	PROBABLY	12	2.6	11	11.7
HURRICANE	14	3.1	14	14.9	SUN	39	8.6	29	30.9
WEATHER	14	3.1	11	11.7	TOURIST	15	3.3	13	13.8
PROBABLY	12	2.6	11	11.7	WATER	25	5.5	20	21.3
WHITE	12	2.6	11	11.7	WEATHER	14	3.1	11	11.7
NATURE	11	2.4	11	11.7	WHITE	12	2.6	11	11.7
PALM	11	2.4	11	11.7	WORLD	20	4.4	15	16.0

```
WARDS METHOD

AMERICA..........<<<<<<<<<<<
                 <<<<<<<<<<<
HURRICANE........<<<<<<<<<<<
                 <<<<<<<
WORLD.............<<<<<<< (excl. ambiguity)
                 <<<<<
PROBABLY.............<<<<<<< (excl. ambiguity)
                 <<<<<<<
TOURIST.............<<<<<<< (as in touristy)
                 <<<
MIND.................<<<<<< (excl. ambiguity)
                 <<<<<<
NICE.............<<<<<<<<<< (excl. ambiguity: various meanings incl. nice
                           weather)
                 <<<<<<<<<<
WEATHER..........<<<<<<<<<< (excl. ambiguity, incl. hot weather)
                 <<<<
PALM.............<<<<<<<<<
                 <<<<<<<<<
WHITE.............<<<<<<<<< (white beach/houses/paving)
                 <<
BEACH.........<<<<<<<<<<<<<
                 <<<<<<<<<<<<<
SUN...........<<<<<<<<<<<<<<
                 <<<<<<<<<<<<<
HOT...........<<<<<<<<<<<<<
                 <<<<<<<<<<<
WATER...........<<<<<<<<<<<
                 <
DISNEY......<<<<<<<<<<<<<<<<
                 <<<<<<<<<<<<<<<
MIAMI.......<<<<<<<<<<<<<<<<
                 <<<<<<<<<<<<<<
EVERGLADES...<<<<<<<<<<<<<<<
                 <<<<<<<<<<<<<<
NATURE........<<<<<<<<<<<<<<
```

MOROCCO

Frequency list using common exclude file:

TOTAL WORDS	485	THRESHOLD	0.000
TOTAL UNIQUE WORDS	31	RESTORING FORCE	0.100
TOTAL EPISODES	68	CYCLES	1
TOTAL LINES	344	FUNCTION	Sigmoid (-1 — +1)
		CLAMPING	No

DESCENDING FREQUENCY LIST					ALPHABETICALLY SORTED LIST				
			CASE	CASE				CASE	CASE
WORD	FREQ	PCNT	FREQ	PCNT	WORD	FREQ	PCNT	FREQ	PCNT
COUNTRY	32	6.6	23	33.8	AFRICA	12	2.5	9	13.2
HOT	30	6.2	22	32.4	AIR	10	2.1	10	14.7
SMELL	26	5.4	22	32.4	ARAB	14	2.9	11	16.2
CULTURE	25	5.2	18	26.5	BUILDING	13	2.7	12	17.6
DIFFERENT	25	5.2	19	27.9	CAMEL	11	2.3	8	11.8
DESERT	21	4.3	17	25.0	CASABLANCA	15	3.1	10	14.7
SPICE	21	4.3	18	26.5	COLOUR	18	3.7	16	23.5
COLOUR	18	3.7	16	23.5	COUNTRY	32	6.6	23	33.8
DAY	17	3.5	13	19.1	CULTURE	25	5.2	18	26.5
STREET	17	3.5	11	16.2	DAY	17	3.5	13	19.1
CASABLANCA	15	3.1	10	14.7	DESERT	21	4.3	17	25.0
EXPERIENCE	15	3.1	12	17.6	DIFFERENT	25	5.2	19	27.9
ARAB	14	2.9	11	16.2	DOWN	10	2.1	9	13.2
MAYBE	14	2.9	10	14.7	ENJOY	11	2.3	9	13.2
NICE	14	2.9	10	14.7	EXPERIENCE	15	3.1	12	17.6
BUILDING	13	2.7	12	17.6	FEEL	10	2.1	9	13.2
MUSLIM	13	2.7	10	14.7	HOT	30	6.2	22	32.4
AFRICA	12	2.5	9	13.2	LONG	10	2.1	8	11.8
MARKET	12	2.5	11	16.2	MARKET	12	2.5	11	16.2
PROBABLY	12	2.5	10	14.7	MAYBE	14	2.9	10	14.7
TEA	12	2.5	7	10.3	MUSLIM	13	2.7	10	14.7
TOURIST	12	2.5	10	14.7	NEVER	11	2.3	8	11.8
WORLD	12	2.5	10	14.7	NICE	14	2.9	10	14.7
CAMEL	11	2.3	8	11.8	PROBABLY	12	2.5	10	14.7
ENJOY	11	2.3	9	13.2	SMELL	26	5.4	22	32.4
NEVER	11	2.3	8	11.8	SPICE	21	4.3	18	26.5
AIR	10	2.1	10	14.7	STREET	17	3.5	11	16.2
DOWN	10	2.1	9	13.2	SUN	10	2.1	9	13.2
FEEL	10	2.1	9	13.2	TEA	12	2.5	7	10.3
LONG	10	2.1	8	11.8	TOURIST	12	2.5	10	14.7
SUN	10	2.1	9	13.2	WORLD	12	2.5	10	14.7

TOTAL WORDS	374	THRESHOLD	0.000
TOTAL UNIQUE WORDS	22	RESTORING FORCE	0.100
TOTAL EPISODES	68	CYCLES	1
TOTAL LINES	344	FUNCTION	Sigmoid (-1 — +1)
		CLAMPING	No

ORESME analysis led to the exclusion of the following words:

■ ENJOY
■ FEEL
■ MAYBE
■ NEVER

- NICE
- EXPERIENCE
- PROBABLY
- TOURIST
- WORLD

DESCENDING FREQUENCY LIST					ALPHABETICALLY SORTED LIST				
WORD	FREQ	PCNT	CASE FREQ	CASE PCNT	WORD	FREQ	PCNT	CASE FREQ	CASE PCNT
COUNTRY	32	8.6	23	33.8	AFRICA	12	3.2	9	13.2
HOT	30	8.0	22	32.4	AIR	10	2.7	10	14.7
SMELL	26	7.0	22	32.4	ARAB	14	3.7	11	16.2
CULTURE	25	6.7	18	26.5	BUILDING	13	3.5	12	17.6
DIFFERENT	25	6.7	19	27.9	CAMEL	11	2.9	8	11.8
DESERT	21	5.6	17	25.0	CASABLANCA	15	4.0	10	14.7
SPICE	21	5.6	18	26.5	COLOUR	18	4.8	16	23.5
COLOUR	18	4.8	16	23.5	COUNTRY	32	8.6	23	33.8
DAY	17	4.5	13	19.1	CULTURE	25	6.7	18	26.5
STREET	17	4.5	11	16.2	DAY	17	4.5	13	19.1
CASABLANCA	15	4.0	10	14.7	DESERT	21	5.6	17	25.0
ARAB	14	3.7	11	16.2	DIFFERENT	25	6.7	19	27.9
BUILDING	13	3.5	12	17.6	DOWN	10	2.7	9	13.2
MUSLIM	13	3.5	10	14.7	HOT	30	8.0	22	32.4
AFRICA	12	3.2	9	13.2	LONG	10	2.7	8	11.8
MARKET	12	3.2	11	16.2	MARKET	12	3.2	11	16.2
TEA	12	3.2	7	10.3	MUSLIM	13	3.5	10	14.7
CAMEL	11	2.9	8	11.8	SMELL	26	7.0	22	32.4
AIR	10	2.7	10	14.7	SPICE	21	5.6	18	26.5
DOWN	10	2.7	9	13.2	STREET	17	4.5	11	16.2
LONG	10	2.7	8	11.8	SUN	10	2.7	9	13.2
SUN	10	2.7	9	13.2	TEA	12	3.2	7	10.3

WARDS METHOD

```
AFRICA.................<<<<<<<<
                      <<<<<<<<
DESERT.................<<<<<<<<
                      <<<<
COUNTRY.............<<<<<<<<<<<<< (excl. ambiguity)
                      <<<<<<<<<<<<
DAY.................<<<<<<<<<<<<< (excl. ambiguity)
                      <<<
ARAB.................<<<<<<<<<<
                      <<<<<<<<<<
MUSLIM...............<<<<<<<<<<
                      <<<<<<
CULTURE.............<<<<<<<<<<<< (as in different, local culture)
                      <<<<<<<<<<<
DIFFERENT...........<<<<<<<<<<<< (excl. ambiguity)
                      <<
BUILDING.................<<<<<< (old / beautiful buildings)
                      <<<<<<
CASABLANCA..............<<<<<<<<
                      <<<<<<<
SUN.....................<<<<<<<<
                      <<<<<
STREET................<<<<<<<<<< (busy/lively/people in the street)
                      <<<<<<<<<
```

```
TEA...................<<<<<<<<<<
                              <
AIR.............<<<<<<<<<<<<<<< (excl. ambiguity: smell in the air/hot air)
                <<<<<<<<<<<<<<<
LONG............<<<<<<<<<<<<<<< (excl. ambiguity)
                <<<<<<<<<<<<<<<
COLOUR.......<<<<<<<<<<<<<<<<<<<
                <<<<<<<<<<<<<<<<<
SMELL.......<<<<<<<<<<<<<<<<<<<<< (smell of spices/food/fragrances/heat)
                <<<<<<<<<<<<<<<<<<
SPICE.......<<<<<<<<<<<<<<<<<<<<
                <<<<<<<<<<<<<<<<<
DOWN.........<<<<<<<<<<<<<<<<<<< (excl. ambiguity)
                <<<<<<<<<<<<<<<<<
HOT...........<<<<<<<<<<<<<<<<<<
                <<<<<<<<<<<<<<<<
MARKET.........<<<<<<<<<<<<<<<<<
                <<<<<<<<<<<<<<
CAMEL.............<<<<<<<<<<<<<
```

SINGAPORE

Frequency list using common exclude file:

TOTAL WORDS	443	THRESHOLD	0.000
TOTAL UNIQUE WORDS	24	RESTORING FORCE	0.100
TOTAL EPISODES	82	CYCLES	1
TOTAL LINES	384	FUNCTION	Sigmoid (-1 — +1)
		CLAMPING	No

	DESCENDING FREQUENCY LIST					ALPHABETICALLY SORTED LIST			
			CASE	CASE				CASE	CASE
WORD	FREQ	PCNT	FREQ	PCNT	WORD	FREQ	PCNT	FREQ	PCNT
MODERN	36	8.1	26	31.7	AIRPORT	12	2.7	10	12.2
CULTURE	33	7.4	25	30.5	ASIA	27	6.1	21	25.6
STREET	31	7.0	22	26.8	BIG	14	3.2	12	14.6
ASIA	27	6.1	21	25.6	BUILDING	23	5.2	20	24.4
CLEAN	27	6.1	24	29.3	BUSY	12	2.7	12	14.6
COUNTRY	27	6.1	23	28.0	CHINESE	14	3.2	10	12.2
BUILDING	23	5.2	20	24.4	CLEAN	27	6.1	24	29.3
HOT	20	4.5	15	18.3	COLOUR	11	2.5	10	12.2
HIGH	17	3.8	11	13.4	COUNTRY	27	6.1	23	28.0
MIX	17	3.8	11	13.4	CULTURE	33	7.4	25	30.5
SHOP	17	3.8	12	14.6	DIFFERENT	16	3.6	12	14.6
DIFFERENT	16	3.6	12	14.6	EAST	11	2.5	9	11.0
NICE	16	3.6	11	13.4	EXOTIC	11	2.5	9	11.0
BIG	14	3.2	12	14.6	FRIENDLY	14	3.2	14	17.1
CHINESE	14	3.2	10	12.2	GREAT	12	2.7	9	11.0
FRIENDLY	14	3.2	14	17.1	HIGH	17	3.8	11	13.4
SMELL	13	2.9	13	15.9	HOT	20	4.5	15	18.3
AIRPORT	12	2.7	10	12.2	HOTEL	12	2.7	11	13.4
BUSY	12	2.7	12	14.6	MIX	17	3.8	11	13.4
GREAT	12	2.7	9	11.0	MODERN	36	8.1	26	31.7
HOTEL	12	2.7	11	13.4	NICE	16	3.6	11	13.4
COLOUR	11	2.5	10	12.2	SHOP	17	3.8	12	14.6
EAST	11	2.5	9	11.0	SMELL	13	2.9	13	15.9
EXOTIC	11	2.5	9	11.0	STREET	31	7.0	22	26.8

ORESME analysis led to the exclusion of the following words:

- BIG
- GREAT
- NICE

TOTAL WORDS	401	THRESHOLD	0.000
TOTAL UNIQUE WORDS	21	RESTORING FORCE	0.100
TOTAL EPISODES	82	CYCLES	1
TOTAL LINES	384	FUNCTION	Sigmoid (-1 — +1)
		CLAMPING	No

```
     DESCENDING FREQUENCY LIST              ALPHABETICALLY SORTED LIST
                          CASE CASE                           CASE CASE
   WORD            FREQ PCNT FREQ PCNT    WORD          FREQ PCNT FREQ PCNT
   ---------       ---- ---- ---- ----    ---------     ---- ---- ---- ----

   MODERN           36  9.0   26 31.7     AIRPORT        12  3.0   10 12.2
   CULTURE          33  8.2   25 30.5     ASIA           27  6.7   21 25.6
   STREET           31  7.7   22 26.8     BUILDING       23  5.7   20 24.4
   ASIA             27  6.7   21 25.6     BUSY           12  3.0   12 14.6
   CLEAN            27  6.7   24 29.3     CHINESE        14  3.5   10 12.2
   COUNTRY          27  6.7   23 28.0     CLEAN          27  6.7   24 29.3
   BUILDING         23  5.7   20 24.4     COLOUR         11  2.7   10 12.2
   HOT              20  5.0   15 18.3     COUNTRY        27  6.7   23 28.0
   HIGH             17  4.2   11 13.4     CULTURE        33  8.2   25 30.5
   MIX              17  4.2   11 13.4     DIFFERENT      16  4.0   12 14.6
   SHOP             17  4.2   12 14.6     EAST           11  2.7    9 11.0
   DIFFERENT        16  4.0   12 14.6     EXOTIC         11  2.7    9 11.0
   CHINESE          14  3.5   10 12.2     FRIENDLY       14  3.5   14 17.1
   FRIENDLY         14  3.5   14 17.1     HIGH           17  4.2   11 13.4
   SMELL            13  3.2   13 15.9     HOT            20  5.0   15 18.3
   AIRPORT          12  3.0   10 12.2     HOTEL          12  3.0   11 13.4
   BUSY             12  3.0   12 14.6     MIX            17  4.2   11 13.4
   HOTEL            12  3.0   11 13.4     MODERN         36  9.0   26 31.7
   COLOUR           11  2.7   10 12.2     SHOP           17  4.2   12 14.6
   EAST             11  2.7    9 11.0     SMELL          13  3.2   13 15.9
   EXOTIC           11  2.7    9 11.0     STREET         31  7.7   22 26.8
```

WARDS METHOD

```
AIRPORT.................<<<<<<< (busy/clean/modern airport)
                        <<<<<<<
SHOP....................<<<<<<<
                        <<<<
COLOUR..............<<<<<<<<<<
                    <<<<<<<<<<
FRIENDLY..........<<<<<<<<<<<<
                  <<<<<<<<<<<<
SMELL............<<<<<<<<<<<<<< (smell of spices/food/fragrances/heat)
                 <<<<<<<
EXOTIC.................<<<<<<<
                      <<<
CHINESE...........<<<<<<<<<<<<
                  <<<<<<<<<<<<
MIX...............<<<<<<<<<<<< (cultural mix)
                  <<<<<<<<<
EAST.................<<<<<<<<< (as in Orient)
                     <<<<<<
DIFFERENT...............<<<<<< (as in different culturally)
                        <<
ASIA...........<<<<<<<<<<<<<<<
               <<<<<<<<<<<<<<
CULTURE........<<<<<<<<<<<<<<<< (as in variety of local culture)
               <<<<<<<<<<<<<<
COUNTRY.........<<<<<<<<<<<<<< (excl. ambiguity)
                <<<<<
BUILDING.......<<<<<<<<<<<<<<<<
               <<<<<<<<<<<<<<<<
MODERN.........<<<<<<<<<<<<<<<<
               <<<<<<<<<<<
```

```
HIGH...............<<<<<<<<<<<  (excl. ambiguity: incl. high buildings)
                         <
BUSY.........<<<<<<<<<<<<<<<<<
             <<<<<<<<<<<<<<<<<
CLEAN......<<<<<<<<<<<<<<<<<<<
             <<<<<<<<<<<<<<<<<
STREET.....<<<<<<<<<<<<<<<<<<<<  (busy/lively/people in the street)
              <<<<<<<<<<<<<<<<<
HOT.........<<<<<<<<<<<<<<<<<<<
               <<<<<<<<<<<<<<<
HOTEL.........<<<<<<<<<<<<<<<<<  (nice/luxurious hotels)
```

WALES

Frequency list using common exclude file:

TOTAL WORDS	282	THRESHOLD	0.000
TOTAL UNIQUE WORDS	22	RESTORING FORCE	0.100
TOTAL EPISODES	55	CYCLES	1
TOTAL LINES	228	FUNCTION	Sigmoid (-1 — +1)
		CLAMPING	No

DESCENDING FREQUENCY LIST					ALPHABETICALLY SORTED LIST				
			CASE	CASE				CASE	CASE
WORD	FREQ	PCNT	FREQ	PCNT	WORD	FREQ	PCNT	FREQ	PCNT
COUNTRY	20	7.1	15	27.3	BUILDING	13	4.6	11	20.0
GREEN	20	7.1	18	32.7	CASTLES	13	4.6	12	21.8
RAIN	18	6.4	15	27.3	COLD	9	3.2	8	14.5
NATURE	17	6.0	14	25.5	COUNTRY	20	7.1	15	27.3
PUB	15	5.3	14	25.5	COUNTRYSIDE	13	4.6	12	21.8
HILLS	14	5.0	14	25.5	EXPERIENCE	10	3.5	8	14.5
NICE	14	5.0	10	18.2	FRIENDLY	11	3.9	10	18.2
BUILDING	13	4.6	11	20.0	GOOD	10	3.5	8	14.5
CASTLES	13	4.6	12	21.8	GREEN	20	7.1	18	32.7
COUNTRYSIDE	13	4.6	12	21.8	HILLS	14	5.0	14	25.5
WELSH	13	4.6	6	10.9	NATURE	17	6.0	14	25.5
NEVER	12	4.3	12	21.8	NEVER	12	4.3	12	21.8
FRIENDLY	11	3.9	10	18.2	NICE	14	5.0	10	18.2
VILLAGE	11	3.9	10	18.2	OLD	10	3.5	9	16.4
EXPERIENCE	10	3.5	8	14.5	PROBABLY	10	3.5	8	14.5
GOOD	10	3.5	8	14.5	PUB	15	5.3	14	25.5
OLD	10	3.5	9	16.4	RAIN	18	6.4	15	27.3
PROBABLY	10	3.5	8	14.5	SHEEP	9	3.2	7	12.7
WALK	10	3.5	8	14.5	VILLAGE	11	3.9	10	18.2
WEATHER	10	3.5	9	16.4	WALK	10	3.5	8	14.5
COLD	9	3.2	8	14.5	WEATHER	10	3.5	9	16.4
SHEEP	9	3.2	7	12.7	WELSH	13	4.6	6	10.9

ORESME analysis led to the exclusion of the following words:

- EXPERIENCE
- NICE
- PROBABLY

TOTAL WORDS	236	THRESHOLD	0.000
TOTAL UNIQUE WORDS	18	RESTORING FORCE	0.100
TOTAL EPISODES	55	CYCLES	1
TOTAL LINES	228	FUNCTION	Sigmoid (-1 — +1)
		CLAMPING	No

```
    DESCENDING FREQUENCY LIST                 ALPHABETICALLY SORTED LIST
                          CASE CASE                               CASE CASE
WORD              FREQ PCNT FREQ PCNT    WORD              FREQ PCNT FREQ PCNT
----------------- ---- ---- ---- ----    ----------------- ---- ---- ---- -----
COUNTRY            20  8.5   15  27.3    BUILDING           13  5.5   11  20.0
GREEN              20  8.5   18  32.7    CASTLES            13  5.5   12  21.8
RAIN               18  7.6   15  27.3    COLD                9  3.8    8  14.5
NATURE             17  7.2   14  25.5    COUNTRY            20  8.5   15  27.3
PUB                15  6.4   14  25.5    COUNTRYSIDE        13  5.5   12  21.8
HILLS              14  5.9   14  25.5    FRIENDLY           11  4.7   10  18.2
BUILDING           13  5.5   11  20.0    GOOD               10  4.2    8  14.5
CASTLES            13  5.5   12  21.8    GREEN              20  8.5   18  32.7
COUNTRYSIDE        13  5.5   12  21.8    HILLS              14  5.9   14  25.5
WELSH              13  5.5    6  10.9    NATURE             17  7.2   14  25.5
NEVER              12  4.3   12  21.8    NEVER              12  4.3   12  21.8
FRIENDLY           11  4.7   10  18.2    OLD                10  4.2    9  16.4
VILLAGE            11  4.7   10  18.2    PUB                15  6.4   14  25.5
GOOD               10  4.2    8  14.5    RAIN               18  7.6   15  27.3
OLD                10  4.2    9  16.4    SHEEP               9  3.8    7  12.7
WALK               10  4.2    8  14.5    VILLAGE            11  4.7   10  18.2
WEATHER            10  4.2    9  16.4    WALK               10  4.2    8  14.5
COLD                9  3.8    8  14.5    WEATHER            10  4.2    9  16.4
SHEEP               9  3.8    7  12.7    WELSH              13  5.5    6  10.9
```

WARDS METHOD

```
BUILDING...........<<<<<<<<<< (old/historic buildings)
                   <<<<<<<<<<
VILLAGE............<<<<<<<<<<
                   <<<<<<<<<<
GOOD...............<<<<<<<<<< (excl. ambiguity)
                   <<<<<
CASTLES...........<<<<<<<<<<<
                   <<<<<<<<<<<
OLD...............<<<<<<<<<<<<
                   <<<<<<<<<<<<
PUB...............<<<<<<<<<<<<
                   <<
COUNTRY........<<<<<<<<<<<<<<< (excl. ambiguity)
                <<<<<<<<<<<<<<
GREEN.......<<<<<<<<<<<<<<<<<
            <<<<<<<<<<<<<<<<<
HILLS.......<<<<<<<<<<<<<<<<<
            <<<<<<<<<<<<<
NATURE..........<<<<<<<<<<<<<
                <<<<<<
RAIN.........<<<<<<<<<<<<<<<
             <<<<<<<<<<<<<<<
WALK.........<<<<<<<<<<<<<<<
             <
COLD..................<<<<<<<
                      <<<<<<<
WEATHER...............<<<<<<< (excl. ambiguity: incl. cold weather)
                      <<<<
COUNTRYSIDE.....<<<<<<<<<<<<<
                <<<<<<<<<<<<<
SHEEP...........<<<<<<<<<<<<<
                <<<
FRIENDLY.............<<<<<<<< (friendly people)
                     <<<<<<<<
WELSH................<<<<<<<< (excl. ambiguity)
                     <
NEVER............<<<<<<<<<<<< (never been there/visited/heard of)
```

BIBLIOGRAPHY

Aaker, D. A. (2001) *Strategic Market Management* (6th edn), New York: Wiley.

Aaker, D. A. and Joachimsthaler, E. (2000) *Brand Leadership*, New York: Free Press.

Albers, P. C. and James, W. R. (1988) Travel Photography: A Methodological Approach, *Annals of Tourism Research*, 15(1): 134–58.

Alcantara, N. (2003) Stars to the Rescue, *eTurbo News*, May 30. Available at: http://www.travelwirenews.com.

Alcantara, N. (2004) Movies and Television Shows Help Boost Tourism, *eTurbo News*, July 14; Available at: http://www.travelwirenews.com.

Alhemoud, A. M. and Armstrong, E. G. (1996) Image of Tourism Attractions in Kuwait, *Journal of Travel Research*, 34(4): 76–80.

Al Maktoum – H.H. Sheikh Mohammed bin Rashid (2001) Speech at the World Economic Forum. Available at: http://www.sheikhmohammed.ae/english/events/ template/template.asp?nn=12; accessed 30 September 2004.

AME Info (2003) Aptec Moves to Boost Market Share as UAE Mobile Phone Penetration Extensively Outpaces Landlines. Available at: http://www.ameinfo.com/news/Detailed/ 25056.html; accessed 21 October 2003.

Anderson, B. (1991) *Imagined Communities* (2nd edn), London: Verso.

Anholt, S. (2002) Foreword, *Brand Management* (Special Issue: Nation Branding), 9(4–5) April: 229–39.

Anholt, S. (2003) *Brand New Justice: The Upside of Global Marketing*, Oxford: Butterworth-Heinemann.

Anholt, S. (2004) Nation Brands and the Value of Provenance, in N. Morgan, A. Pritchard and R. Pride (eds), *Destination Branding: Creating the Unique Destination Proposition* (2nd edn), Oxford: Elsevier, pp. 26–39.

Anholt, S. (2007) *Competitive Identity: The New Brand Management for Nations, Cities and Regions*, Basingstoke: Palgrave Macmillan.

Ankomah, P. K., Crompton, J. L. and Baker, D. (1996) Influence of Cognitive Distance in Vacation Choice, *Annals of Tourism Research*, 23(1): 138–50.

Appadurai, A. (1996) *Modernity at Large: Cultural Dimensions of Globalization*, Minneapolis, Minn.: University of Minnesota Press.

Archer, K. (1997) The Limits to the Imagineered City: Sociospatial Polarization in Orlando, *Economic Geography*, 73(3): 322–3.

Arnould, E., Price, L., and Zinkhan, G. M. (2003) *Consumers* (2nd edn), Boston, Mass.: McGraw-Hill/Irwin.

Ashworth, G. J. (1991) *Heritage Planning: Conservation as the Management of Urban Change*, Groningen, Netherlands: Geo Pers.

Ashworth, G. J. (2007) Heritage, Tourism and the Tourist: On Bridging the Gaps in the Uses of Pasts, *Paper presented at the International Symposium on Heritage, Tourism, Planning and Design Practices (Visiting the Past, Discovering the Limes)*, Utrecht, Netherlands, 11–12 October.

Ashworth, G. J. and Dietvorst, A. G. J. (1995) Conclusion: Challenge and Policy Response, in G. J. Ashworth and A. G. J. Dietvorst (eds), *Tourism and Spatial Transformations*, Wallingford: CAB International, pp. 329–40.

Ateljevic, I. and Doorne, S. (2002) Representing New Zealand: Tourism Imagery and Ideology, *Annals of Tourism Research*, 29(3): 648–67.

Atkinson, R. L., Atkinson, R. C., Smith, E. E., and Hilgard, E. R. (1987) *Introduction to Psychology* (9th edn), Orlando, Fla.: Harcourt Brace Jovanovich.

AVN (1995) *Middle–Long Term Plan 1996–1998 (In Dutch)*, Voorschoten: Stichting Toerisme en Recreatie AVN.

Baloglu, S. and Brinberg, D. (1997) Affective Images of Tourism Destinations, *Journal of Travel Research*, 35(4): 11–15.

Baloglu, S. and McCleary, K. W. (1999) A Model of Destination Image Formation, *Annals of Tourism Research*, 26(4): 808–89.

Bateson, J. (2002) Consumer performance and quality in services, *Managing Service Quality*, 12(4): 206–9.

Beerli, A. and Martín, J. D. (2004a) Factors Influencing Destination Image, *Annals of Tourism Research*, 31(3): 657–81.

Beerli, A. and Martín, J. D. (2004b) Tourists' Characteristics and the Perceived Image of Tourist Destinations: A Quantitative Analysis – A Case Study of Lanzarote, Spain, *Tourism Management*, 25(5): 623–36.

Beheydt, L. J. (1993) De toekomst van het Nederlands: een nieuwe taalstrijd (The Future of Dutch: A New Language Battle), in L. J. Beheydt *et al.* (eds) *Tussen taal en staat (Between Language and State)*, Leuven: Davidsfonds, pp. 73–94.

Bernstein, D. (1984) *Company Image and Reality*, Eastbourne: Holt, Rinehart & Winston.

Bigné, J. E., Sánchez, M. I. and Sánchez, J. (2001) Tourism Image, Evaluation Variables and After Purchase Behaviour: Inter-relationship, *Tourism Management*, 22(6): 607–16.

Birkigt, K. and Stadler, M. M. (1986) *Corporate Identity: Grundlagen, Funktionen, Fallspielen*, Landsberg an Lech: Verlag Moderne Industrie.

Bitner, M. J., Brown, S. W. and Meuter, M. L. (2000) Technology Infusion in Service Encounters, *Academy of Marketing Sciences*, 28(1): 138–49.

Blackshaw, P. (2004) *Buzz-Informed Predictions for 2005*, ClickZ Network, December 14. Available at: http://www.clickz.com/experts/brand/cmo/print.php/ 3446711; accessed 15 Decembr 2004.

Blackwell, R. D., Miniard, P. W. and Engel, J. F. (2000) *Consumer Behavior* (9th edn), Fort Worth, Tx.: Harcourt College Press.

Blain, C., Levy, S. E. and Ritchie, J. R. B. (2005) Destination Branding: Insights and Practices from Destination Management Organizations, *Journal of Travel Research*, 43(4): 328–38.

Bloch, M., Pigneur, Y. and Steiner, T. (1996) The IT-enabled Extended Enterprise, Applications in the Tourism Industry, in S. Klein *et al.* (eds), *Proceedings of the International Conference on Information and Communication Technologies in Tourism, ENTER1996*, Innsbruck, January, Vienna/New York: Springer Verlag.

Boorstin, D. J. (1962) *The Image*, London: Weidenfeld & Nicolson.

Boulding, K. E. (1956) *The Image*, Ann Arbor, Mich.: University of Michigan Press.

Boulding, K. E. (1983) Lecture 2: 'Weapons Technology and National Defense', Lecture Series, International Institute for Applied Systems Analysis, Laxenburg, Austria.

Bowes, G. (2007) This Year's Hottest Destination: Cyberspace, *Guardian*. (*Observer* Escape section), 18 March. Available at: http://travel.guardian.co.uk/article/2007/mar/18/travelwebsites. escape; accessed 27 April 2007.

Britton, R. A. (1979) The Image of the Third World in Tourism Marketing, *Annals of Tourism Research*, 6(3): 318–29.

Brotherton, B. (1999) Towards a Definitive View of the Nature of Hospitality and Hospitality Management, *International Journal of Contemporary Hospitality Management*, 11(4): 16–17.

Burdett, A. L. P. (ed.) (2000) *Records of Dubai 1761–1960*, Cambridge Archive Editions Series, Vol. 2, Cambridge University Press.

Butler, R. W. (1980) The Concept of the Tourist Area Cycle of Evolution: Implications for Management of Resources, *Canadian Geographer*, 24(1): 5–16.

Butler, T. (2005) *Dubai's Artificial Islands Have High Environmental Cost. The Price of 'The World': Dubai's Artificial Future*, Mongabay, August 23. Available at: http://news.mongabay.com/2005/0823-tina_butler_dubai.html; accessed 7 July 2008.

Cai, L. A. (2002) Cooperative Branding for Rural Destinations, *Annals of Tourism Research*, 29(3): 720–42.

Carman, J. M. (1990) Consumer Perceptions of Service Quality: An Assessment of the SERVQUAL Dimensions, *Journal of Retailing*, 66(1) Spring: 33–55.

Carson, P. (1974) *The Fair Face of Flanders*, Gent: Story-Scientia.

Cary, S. H. (2004) The Tourist Moment, *Annals of Tourism Research*, 31(1): 61–77.

Castells, M. (1996) *The Information Age: Economy, Society and Culture, Vol. 1: The Rise of the Network Society*, Cambridge, Mass.: Blackwell.

Castells, M. (1997) *The Information Age: Economy, Society and Culture, Vol. 2: The Power of Identity*, Cambridge, Mass: Blackwell.

Chang, T. and Lim, S. (2004) Geographical Imaginations of 'New Asia–Singapore', *Geografiska Annaler: Series B, Human Geography*, 86(3): 165–85.

Cho, Y. and Fesenmaier, D. R. (2000) A Conceptual Framework for Evaluating the Effects of a Virtual Tour, in D. R. Fesenmaier, S. Klein and D. Buhalis (eds) *Proceedings of the International Conference on Information and Communication Technologies in Tourism* (pp. 314–23), ENTER 2000, Barcelona, Spain, April, Vienna/New York: Springer Verlag.

Chon, K.-S. (1990) The Role of Destination Image in Tourism: A Review and Discussion, *Revue de Tourisme*, 45(3): 2–9.

Chon, K.-S. (1991) Tourism Destination Image Modification Process: Marketing Implications, *Tourism Management*, 12(1): 68–75.

Christensen, G. L. and Olson, J. C. (2002) Mapping Consumers' Mental Models with ZMET, *Psychology & Marketing*, 19(6): 477–502.

CIA (2008) *CIA World Factbook: United Arab Emirates*, US Central Intelligence Agency, November 30. Available at: https://www.cia.gov/library/publications/the-world-factbook/geos/ae.html; accessed 19 May 2008.

Claeys, U. and De Meulemeester, K. (2000) Toerisme en identiteit (Tourism and Identity), in L. Abicht *et al.* (ed.) *Hoe Vlaams zijn de Vlamingen (How Flemish Are the Flemish)?*, Leuven: Davidsfonds, pp. 58–61.

Clawson, M. and Knetsch, J. L. (1966) *Economics of Outdoor Recreation*, Baltimore, Md.: Johns Hopkins Press.

CNN (2008) Undercover Cops Order Dubai Beach Coverup, *CNN International*, 14 July. Available at: http://edition.cnn.com/2008/WORLD/meast/07/14/dubai. beach.ap/index. html; accessed 16 July 2008.

Cohen, E. (1979) A Phenomenology of Tourist Experiences, *Sociology*, 13(2): 179–201.

Cohen, E. (1988) Authenticity and Commoditization in Tourism, *Annals of Tourism Research*, 15(3): 371–86.

Cohen-Hattab, K. and Kerber, J. (2004,) Literature, Cultural Identity and the Limits of Authenticity: A Composite Approach, *International Journal of Tourism Research*, 6(2): 57–73.

Colliers International (2007) *Global Office Real Estate Review 2007* (Research report).

Cooper, C., Fletcher, J., Gilbert, D. and Wanhill, S. (2000) *Tourism: Principles and Practice* (2nd edn), R. Shepherd (ed.), Harlow: Pearson.

Cooper, K. J. (1997) Beaches Scarcely Bare in Muslim Maldives, *The Washington Post*, Washington, 20 May: A12.

Cooper, P. J. (2003) Dubai 2003, the Real Story!, *AME-Info*, 17 June. Available at: www.ameinfo.com/25190.html; accessed 25 June 2003.

Crompton, J. L. (1979) An Assessment of the Image of Mexico as a Vacation Destination and the Influence of Geographical Location upon that Image, *Journal of Travel Research*, 14(4): 18–23.

Csikszentmihalyi, M. (1995a) The Flow Experience and Its Significance for Human Psychology, in M. Csikszentmihalyi and I. S. Csikszentmihalyi (eds) *Optimal Experience: Psychological Studies of Flow in Consciousness*, Cambridge University Press, pp. 15–35.

Csikszentmihalyi, M. (1995b) Introduction. in M. Csikszentmihalyi and I. S. Csikszentmihalyi (eds) *Optimal Experience: Psychological Studies of Flow in Consciousness*, Cambridge University Press, pp. 3–14.

Csikszentmihalyi, M. (1997) The Flow of Creativity, in M. Csikszentmihalyi (ed.) *Creativity: Flow and the Psychology of Discovery and Invention*, New York: Harper Perennial, pp. 107–26.

Daems, S., Peeters, J, and van Doren, J. (2000) *Vlaanderen, een goed bewaard geheim (Flanders, a Well Kept Secret,)* Antwerp: Pandora.

Dann, G. M. S. (1996a) *The Language of Tourism: A Sociolinguistic Perspective*, Wallingford: CAB International.

Dann, G. M. S. (1996b) Tourists Images of a Destination: An Alternative Analysis, *Journal of Travel and Tourism Marketing*, 5(1/2): 41–55.

Davies, P. (2004) Dynamic packaging: the future for Lastminute.com, *TravelMole*, November 25 Available at: http://www.travelmole.com/news_detail.php?news_id =102307; accessed 14 December 2004.

Decrop, A. and Snelders, D. (2004) Planning the Summer Vacation: An Adaptable Process, *Annals of Tourism Research*, 31(4): 1008–30.

Dellaert, B. G. C. (1999) The Tourist as Value Creator on the Internet, in D. Buhalis and W. Schertler (eds) *Proceedings of the International Conference on Information and Communication Technologies in Tourism*, pp. 66–76, ENTER 1999, Innsbruck, January, Vienna/New York: Springer Verlag.

De Roover, P. and Ponette, E. (2000) Vlaamse identiteit. Een standpunt (Flemish Identity. One Perspective) in L. Abicht *et al.* (eds) *Hoe Vlaams zijn de Vlamingen (How Flemish Are the Flemish?)*, Leuven: Davidsfonds, pp. 9–20.

Derrett, R. (2004) Festivals, Events and the Destination, in I. Yeoman *et al.* (eds) *Festival and Events Management: An International Arts and Culture Perspective*, Oxford: Elsevier, pp. 32–52.

Dhar, R. and Wertenbroch, K. (2000) Consumer Choice between Hedonic and Utilitarian Goods, *Journal of Marketing Research*, 37(1): 60–71.

Dietvorst, A. G. J. and Ashworth, G. J. (1995) Tourism Transformation: An Introduction, in G. J. Ashworth and A. G. J. Dietvorst (eds) *Tourism and Spatial Transformations*, Wallingford: CAB International, pp. 1–12.

Dinnie, K. (2008) *Nation Branding: Concepts, Issues, Practice*, Oxford: Butterworth-Heinemann.

Dredge, D. and Jenkins, J. (2003) Destination Place Identity and Regional Tourism Policy, *Tourism Geographies*. 5(4): 383–407.

DTCM (2000) *Dubai Visitor Survey 1998/99,* Dubai: Government of Dubai, Department of Tourism and Commerce Marketing, April.

DTCM (2002) *Dubai Gross Domestic Product at Factor Cost by Economic Sector,* Government of Dubai, Department of Tourism and Commerce Marketing, Operations & Marketing Division – One Stop Information Center. Available at: http://www.dubaitourism.co.ae; accessed 25 June 2003.

DTCM (2003) *Heritage & Diving Village,* Government of Dubai, Department of Tourism and Commerce Marketing. Available at: http://www.dubaitourism.co.ae/ www/Business/diving_village.asp; accessed 25 June 2003.

DTCM (2007a) Dubai Hotels Discharge Half a Billion Kilos of CO2, *Dubai Weekly Newsletter*,2(92), Dubai: Government of Dubai, Department of Tourism and Commerce Marketing.

DTCM (2007b) *Dubai International Visitor Survey 2006/07,* Dubai: Government of Dubai, Department of Tourism and Commerce Marketing.

DTCM (2007c) Dubai Police Cracks on Vices, *Dubai Weekly Newsletter,* 2(91) Dubai: Government of Dubai, Department of Tourism and Commerce Marketing, 6 December.

DTCM (2007d) *Hotel Statistics,* Government of Dubai: Department of Tourism and Commerce Marketing. Available at: http://www.dubaitourism.com/EServices/ HotelStatistics/tabid/167/language/en-US/Default.aspx; accessed 10 October 2007.

DTCM (2008) Sheikh Mohammad lauds DTCM's emiratisation efforts, *Dubai Weekly Newsletter,* 2(102), Dubai: Government of Dubai, Department of Tourism and Commerce Marketing, 24 April.

Dubai Chamber (2007) Dubai Nominal GDP 2006, *Dubai Economic Bulletin,* 4(36): 6.

Dubai Palm Developers LLC (2003) *The Palm: Live the Eighth Wonder,* Dubai,. Available at: www.thepalm.co.ae.

Dubai Tourism Development Company (2003) *Dubailand,* Dubailand General Information Press Release and Investor Brochure in Info-Pack CD-ROM.

Echtner, C. M. and Ritchie, J. R. B. (1991) The Meaning and Measurement of Destination Image, *Journal of Tourism Studies,* 2(2): 2–12.

Echtner, C. M. and Ritchie, J. R. B. (1993) The Measurement of Destination Image: An Empirical Assessment, *Journal of Travel Research,* 31(4): 3–13.

Echtner, C. M. and Ritchie, J. R. B. (2003) The Meaning and Measurement of Destination Image, *Journal of Tourism Studies,* 14(1): 37–48.

Economist, The (1999) Movie Tourism in the USA Midwest..., 30 October.

Economist Intelligence Unit (2007) *World Investment Prospects to 2011: Foreign Direct Investment and the Challenge of Political Risk,* New York: Economist Intelligence Unit.

Ekinci, Y. and Hosany, S. (2006) Destination Personality: An Application of Brand Personality to Tourism Destinations, *Journal of Travel Research,* 45: 127–39.

Embacher, J. and Buttle, F. (1989) A Repertory Grid Analysis of Austria's Image as a Summer Vacation Destination, *Journal of Travel Research,* 28(3): 3–23.

e-tid (Travel and Hospitality Industry Digest) (2002) Royal Funeral Raises Britain's Profile, *e-tid.com,* 31 May. Available at: www.e-tid.com/viewarticle. asp?id=17975; accessed 22 June 2002.

Fairweather, J. R. and Swaffield, S. R. (2002) Visitors' and Locals' Experiences of Rotorua, New Zealand: An Interpretative Study Using Photographs of Landscapes and Q Method, *International Journal of Tourism Research,* 4(4): 283–97.

Fakeye, P. C. and Crompton, J. L. (1991) Image Differences Between Prospective, First-Time, and Repeat Visitors to the Lower Rio Grande Valley, *Journal of Travel Research,* 30(2): 10–6.

Featherstone, M. and Lash, S. (1995) Globalization, Modernity and the Spatialization of Social Theory: An Introduction, in M. Featherstone, S. Lash and R. Robertson (eds) *Global Modernities,* London: Sage, pp. 1–24.

Feighey, W. (2003) Negative Image? Developing the Visual in Tourism Research, *Current Issues in Tourism,* 6(1): 76–85.

Fesenmaier, D. and MacKay, K. (1996) Deconstructing Destination Image Construction, *Revue de Tourisme,* 51(2): 37–43.

Flemish Department of Foreign Affairs (2007) *Brand Objectives,* Flemish Government. Available at: http://docs.vlaanderen.be/buitenland/logo/logo-objectives.htm; accessed 23 July 2008.

Fog, K., Budtz, C. and Yakaboylu, B. (2005) *Storytelling: Branding in Practice,* Berlin: Springer.

Fonda, D. (2006) Inside Dubai Inc., *Time,* 6 May.

Fridgen, J. D. (1984) Environmental Psychology and Tourism, *Annals of Tourism Research,* 11(1): 19–39.

Fukuda-Parr, S. (2004) *Human Development Report 2004: Cultural Liberty in Today's Diverse World,* Human Development Report Series, New York: United Nations Development Programme (UNDP). Available at: http://stone.undp.org/ hdr/reports/global/2004/.

Gabr, H. S. (2004) Attitudes of Residents and Tourists Towards the Use of Urban Historic Sites for Festival Events, *Event Management,* 8(4): 231–42.

Gallarza, M. G., Gil Saura, I. and Calderón Garcia, H. (2002) Destination Image: Towards a Conceptual Framework, *Annals of Tourism Research,* 29(1): 56–78.

Garlick, S. (2002) Revealing the Unseen: Tourism, Art and Photography, *Cultural Studies,* 16(2): 289–305.

Gartner, W. C. (1993) Image Formation Process, *Journal of Travel and Tourism Marketing,* 2(2/3): 191–215.

Gartner, W. C. and Hunt, J. D. (1987) An Analysis of State Image Change over a Twelve-Year Period (1971–1983), *Journal of Travel Research,* 25(2): 15–19.

Gibson, O. (2001) Arab Websites See Traffic Soar, *Guardian,* 9 October. Available at: http://media.guardian.co.uk/newmedia; accessed 23 June 2002.

Gilmore, F. (2002) A Country – Can It Be Repositioned? Spain – The Success Story of Country Branding, *Brand Management,* 9(4–5): 281–93.

Gilmore, J. H. and Pine II, B. J. (2007) *Authenticity: What Consumers Really Want,* Boston, Mass.: Harvard Business School Press.

Gnoth, J. (2002) Leveraging Export Brands Through a Tourism Destination Brand, *Brand Management (Special Issue: Nation Branding),* 9(4–5) April: 262–80.

Go, F. M. (2003) Experience Marketing: Implications for Business, *Markeur,* 2: 24–7.

Go, F. M. and Govers, R. (1997) The Asian Perspective: Which International Conference Destinations in Asia Are the Most Competitive?, *CEMS Business Review,* 2(1): 57–65.

Go, F. M. and Haywood, M. (2003) Marketing of the Service Process: State of the Art in the Tourism, Recreation and Hospitality Industries, in C. P. Cooper (ed.), *Aspects of Tourism: Classic Reviews in Tourism,* Clevedon: Channel View Publications, pp. 87–114.

Go, F. M. and Pine, R. (1995) *Globalization Strategy in the Hotel Industry,* New York: Routledge.

Go, F. M. and Van Fenema, P. C. (2006) Moving Bodies and Connecting Minds in Space: It Is a Matter of Mind over Matter, *Advances in Organization Studies* 17: 64–78.

Go, F. M., Govers, R. and Heuvel, M. v. d. (1999) Towards Interactive Tourism: Capitalising on Virtual and Physical Value Chains, in W. Schertler (ed.) *Proceedings of the International Conference on Information and Communication Technologies in Tourism,* pp. 11–24, ENTER 1999, Innsbruck, January, Vienna/New York: Springer Verlag.

Go, F. M., Lee, R. M. and Russo, A. P. (2004) e-Heritage in the Globalizing Society: Enabling Cross-Cultural Engagement through ICT, *Information Technology & Tourism*, 6(1): 55–68.

Government of Dubai (2007) *Highlights, Dubai Strategic Plan 2015*, Dubai. Available at: www.dubai.ae.

Govers, R. and Go, F. M. (1999) Achieving Service Quality through the Application of Importance-Performance Analysis, in P. Kunst, J. Lemmink and B. Strauss (eds), *Service Quality and Management*, Focus Dienstleistungsmarketing Series (eds M. Kleinaltenkamp, *et al.*) Wiesbaden: Gabler.

Govers, R. and Go, F. M. (2003) Deconstructing Destination Image in the Information Age, *Information Technology & Tourism*, 6(1): 13–29.

Govers, R. and Go, F. M. (2005) Projected Destination Image Online: Website Content Analysis of Pictures and Text, *Information Technology & Tourism*, 7(2): 73–90.

Govers, R., Go, F. M. and Kumar, K. (2007a) Promoting Tourism Destination Image, *Journal of Travel Research*, 46(1): 15–23.

Govers, R., Go, F. M. and Kumar, K. (2007b) Virtual Destination Image: A New Measurement Approach, *Annals of Tourism Research*, 34(4): 977–97.

Graham, R. (1980) The Middle Eastern Muddle, *The New York Review of Books*, 27(16). Available at: www.nybooks.com/articles/7268; accessed 8 September 2004.

Greenwood, D. J. (1977) Culture by the Pound: An Anthropological Perspective on Tourism as Cultural Commoditization, in V. L. Smith (ed.), *Hosts and Guests*, Philadelphia, Penn.: University of Pennsylvania Press, pp. 129—39.

Gretzel, U. and Fesenmaier, D. R. (2003) Experience-based Internet Marketing: An Exploratory Study of Sensory Experiences Associated with Pleasure Travel to the Midwest United States, in A. Frew, M. Hitz and P. O'Connor (eds), *Proceedings of the International Conference on Information and Communication Technologies in Tourism*, pp. 49–57, ENTER 2003, Helsinki, January, Vienna/New York: Springer Verlag.

Gulf News (2001) Step to Get Historical Buildings Registered as World Heritage Sites..., Dubai, 19 November. Available at: www.gulfnews.com.

Gulf News (2003) Dubai to Host Meet on Architectural Conservation, Dubai, 26 February: 37.

Guntrum, K. (2007) Yahoo! Travel Shapes Up for Summer with Innovative Personalized Trip Recommendations and More Travel Deals, *Yahoo!*, 9 May. Available at: http://yhoo.client.shareholder.com/press/releasedetail.cfm?ReleaseID =241644; accessed 3 June 2008.

Haahti, A. and Yavas, U. (1983) Tourists' Perceptions of Finland and Selected European Countries as Travel Destinations, *European Journal of Marketing*, 17(2): 34–42.

Hall, M., Sharples, L., Mitchell, R., Macionis, N. *et al.* (2003) *Food Tourism Around the World: Development, Management and Markets*, Oxford: Butterworth-Heinemann.

Hall, S. (1996) The Global, the Local, and the Return of Ethnicity, in S. Hall (ed.), *Modernity: An Introduction to Modern Societies*, Oxford: Blackwell, pp. 613–19.

Hallowell, E. M. (1999) The Human Moment at Work, *Harvard Business Review*, 77(1): 58–66.

Halman, L. (2001) *The European Values Study – A Third Wave: Source Book of the 1999/2000 European Values Study Surveys*, Tilburg: WORC.

Hammer, M. (1990) Reengineering Work: Don't Automate, Obliterate, *Harvard Business Review*, 68(4) July–August: 104–12.

Hankinson, G. (2004) Relational Network Brands: Towards a Conceptual Model of Place Brands, *Journal of Vacation Marketing*, 10(2): 109–21.

Hankinson, G. (2007) The Management of Destination Brands: Five Guiding Principles Based on Recent Developments in Corporate Branding Theory, *Brand Management*, 14(3): 240–54.

Harvey, D. (1989) *The Condition of Postmodernity: An Enquiry into the Origins of Cultural Change,* Oxford: Basil Blackwell.

Heard-Bey, F. (2001) The Tribal Society of the UAE and Its Traditional Economy, in I. Al Arab and P. Hellyer (eds) *United Arab Emirates: A New Perspective,* London: Trident Press, pp. 98–116.

Heijl, M. (2002) *Een Hollander verkent Vlaanderen (A Dutchman Scouts Flanders,)* Leuven: Van Halewyck.

Henderson, J. (2006) Destination Development: Singapore and Dubai Compared, *Journal of Travel & Tourism Marketing,* 20(3/4): 33–45.

Hirschman, E. C. and Holbrook, M. B. (1982) Hedonic Consumption: Emerging Concepts, Methods and Propositions, *Journal of Marketing,* 46(3): 92–101.

Hjalager, A. and Richards, G. (2002) *Tourism and Gastronomy,* London/New York: Routledge.

Hoffman, D. L. and Novak, T. P. (1996) Marketing in Hypermedia Computer-Mediated Environments: Conceptual Foundations, *Journal of Marketing,* 60 (July): 50–68.

Hoffman, K. D. and Bateson, J. E. G. (2002) *Essentials of Services Marketing: Concepts, Strategies, & Cases* (2nd edn), Fort Worth, Tx.: Harcourt College Publishers.

Hofstede, G. (2001a) *Allemaal Andersdenkenden: Omgaan met Cultuurverschillen (Working with Cultural Differences),* Amsterdam: Contact.

Hofstede, G. (2001b) *Culture's Consequences: Comparing Values, Behaviors, Institutions and Organizations across Nations,* (2nd edn), Thousand Oaks, Calif.: Sage.

Hofstede, G. (2003) What Is Culture? A Reply to Baskerville, *Accounting, Organizations and Society,* 28(7–8): 811–13.

Holbrook, M. B. (2000) The Millennial Consumer in the Texts of Our Times: Experience and Entertainment, *Journal of Macromarketing,* 20(2) December: 178–92.

Holbrook, M. B. and Hirschman, E. C. (1982) The Experiential Aspects of Consumption: Consumer Fantasies, Feelings, and Fun, *Journal of Consumer Research,* 9(2): 132–40.

HRG (2008) *HRG Unveils 2007 Hotel Survey,* Hogg Robinson Group, Press release, 14 February. Available at: http://hoggrobinsongroup.hrgworldwide.com/ Portals/40/Documents/ MediaCentre/HRG_press_releases/2008/HRG_Hotel_survey2007.pdf; accessed 2 June 2008.

HSBC (2001) Oil Production, Revenue and Public Finance in the GCC, *HSBC Economic Bulletin* (HSBC Bank). Available at: http://www.uae.hsbc.com/hsbc/ uae_wel/economic-bulletins; accessed 29 September 2004.

Huang, J. (2001) Future Space: A New Blueprint for Business Architecture, *Harvard Business Review,* 79(4): 149–58.

Hubbert, A. R., Sehorn, A. G. and Brown, S. W. (1995) Service Expectations: The Consumer Versus the Provider, *International Journal of Service Industry Management,* 6(1): 6–20.

Human, B. (1999) Kodachrome Icons: Photography, Place and the Theft of Identity, *International Journal of Contemporary Hospitality Management,* 11(2/3): 80–4.

Hunt, J. D. (1971) *Image: A Factor in Tourism,* Unpublished Ph.D. dissertation, Fort Collins, Colorado State University (cited in Gartner and Hunt (1987)).)

Hunt, J. D. (1975) Image as a Factor in Tourism Development, *Journal of Travel Research,* 13(3): 1–7.

Huntington, S. P. (1993) The Clash of Civilisations, *Foreign Affairs,* 72(3): 22–8.

Imagineers, The (1998) *Walt Disney Imagineering: A Behind the Dreams Look at Making the Magic Real by the Imagineers,* New York: Hyperion.

Ind, N. (2003) Inside Out: How Employees Build Value, *Journal of Brand Management,* 10(6): 393–402.

Ind, N. (2004) *Living the Brand: How to Transform Every Member of Your Organization into a Brand Champion,* London: Kogan Page.

Internet World Stats (2008) Internet Usage Statistics – The Big Picture: World Internet Users and Population Stats, *Internet World Stats,* 28 May. Available at: http://www.internetworld-stats.com/stats.htm; accessed 19 June 2008.

Jansen-Verbeke, M. (2004) Urban Policies for Cultural Tourism: Critical Issues in Destination Management, in P. Burns (ed.), *Conference Proceedings. Global Frameworks and Local Realities: Social and cultural identities in making and consuming tourism* (CD-ROM), Eastbourne, 9–10, University of Brighton.

Jenkins, C. L. (2004) Overcoming the Problems Relating to Seasonality: The Case of Dubai, in R. MacLellan *et al.* (eds) *Proceedings. Tourism: State of the Art II* (CD-ROM), Glasgow, 27–30 June, The Scottish Hotel School, University of Strathclyde.

Jenkins, O. H. (1999) Understanding and Measuring Tourist Destination Images, *International Journal of Tourism Research,* 1(1) January/February: 1–15.

Jeong, S. and Almeida Santos, C. (2004) Cultural Politics and Contested Place Identity, *Annals of Tourism Research,* 31(3): 640–56.

Johnson, G. and Scholes, K. (1999) *Exploring Corporate Strategy* (5th edn), Harlow: Pearson.

Jumeirah International (2003) *Madinat Jumeirah.* Available at: www.jumeirahinternational.com/madinat/; accessed 25 June 2003.

Kapferer, J.-N. (2004) *The New Strategic Brand Management: Creating and Sustaining Brand Equity Long Term* (3rd edn), London: Kogan Page.

Kavaratzis, M. (2005) Place Branding: A Review of Trends and Conceptual Models, *The Marketing Review,* 5(4): 329–42.

Kavaratzis, M. and Ashworth, G. J. (2005) City Branding: An Effective Assertion of Identity or a Transatory Marketing Trick?, *Tijdschrift voor Economische en Sociale Geografie,* 96(5): 506–14.

Keillor, B. D. and Hult, G. T. M. (1999) A Five-Country Study of National Identity: Implications for International Marketing Research and Practice, *International Marketing Review.* 16(1): 65–82.

Kelly, K. (1999) *New Rules for the New Economy: 10 Radical Strategies for a Connected World,* New York: Penguin Books.

Kemerling, G. (2001) *History of Western Philosophy,* Available at: http://www.philosophypages.com/hy/index.htm; accessed August 2004.

Kim, H. and Richardson, S. L. (2003) Motion Picture Impacts on Destination Image, *Annals of Tourism Research,* 30(1): 216–37.

Kitchin, T. (2003) *On Being Human: Devlivering Values in the Relationship Age,* Available at: http://www.beyond-branding.com/essays.htm; accessed 28 May 2004.

Klein, N. (2000) *No Logo: Taking Aim at the Brand Bullies,* New York: Picador USA.

Klooster, E. van 't, Go, F. M. and Baalen, P. van (2004) Exploring Destination Brand Communities: A Business Model for Collaboration in the Extremely Fragmented Tourism Industry, Paper presented at the 17th Bled eCommerce Conference, Bled, Slovenia, 21–23 June, eCommerce Center, University of Maribor.

Kossmann-Putto, J. A. and Kossmann, E. H. (1997) *De Lage Landen: geschiedenis van de Noordelijke en Zuidelijke Nederlanden (The Low Countries: History of the Northern and Southern Netherlands,)* Rekkem: Ons Erfdeel.

Kotler, P. (2000) *Marketing Management: The Millennium Edition* (10th edn), Upper Saddle River, NJ: Prentice Hall.

Kotler, P. and Gertner, D. (2002) Country as Brand, Product, and Beyond: A Place Marketing and Brand Management Perspective, *Brand Management (Special Issue: Nation Branding),* 9(4–5) April: 249–61.

Kotler, P., Bowen, J. and Makens, J. (2003) *Marketing for Hospitality & Tourism*, (3rd edn), Upper Saddle River, NJ: Prentice Hall.

Kotler, P., Haider, D. H. and Rein, I. (1993) *Marketing Places: Attracting Investment, Industry, and Tourism to Cities, States, and Nations*, New York: The Free Press.

Kriekaard, J. A. (1993) De stad als merk: Een communicatie-kijk op city marketing, *City Marketing*, 6: 7–12.

Kumar, K. and Dissel, H. G. v. (1998) The Merchant of Prato – Revisited: Toward a Third Rationality of Information Systems, *MIS Quarterly*, 22(2): 199–226.

Kunkel, J. H. and Berry, L. L. (1968) A Behavioral Concept of Retail Image, *Journal of Marketing*, 32(4): 21–7.

Laesser, C. (2008) National PP Tourism Management: The Swiss Case, Paper presented at 17th International Leisure and Tourism Symposium, Barcelona, 21 May, ESADE.

Lebo, H. (2002) *Study by UCLA Internet Project Shows E-mail Transformed Personal Communication after Sept. 11 Attacks*, University of California, 6 February. Available at: www.uclanews.ucla.edu/Docs/3009.htm; accessed 23 June 2002.

Leemans, H. (1994) *The Multiform Book: Using Information in Purchasing Hedonic Products*, Delft: Eburon.

Lengkeek, J. (2001) Leisure Experience and Imagination: Rethinking Cohen's Modes of Tourist Experience, *International Sociology*, 16(2): 173–84.

Lindstrom, M. (2005) *Brand Sense: How to Build Powerful Brands Through Touch, Taste, Smell, Sight & Sound*, London: Kogan Page.

Long, N. (1997) Agency and Constraint, Perceptions and Practice. A Theoretical Position, in H. d. Haan and N. Long (eds) *Images and Realities of Rural Life*, Assen: Van Gorcum, pp. 1–20.

Loonstra, P. B. M., Wijk, G. v. and Go, F. M. (2004) Leveraging the Capacity of the Personal Digital Assistant in the Emerging Age of Ambient Intelligence: The Rent a Mobile Guide Case, in A. Frew (ed.), *Proceedings of the International Conference on Information and Communication Technologies in Tourism*, pp. 96–105, ENTER 2004, Cairo, January, Vienna/New York: Springer Verlag.

Lovelock, C. (2002) *Services Marketing: People, Technology, Strategy* (4th edn), New Jersey: Prentice Hall.

Lovelock, C. and Wright, L. (2002) *Principles of Services Marketing and Management* (2nd edn), New Jersey: Prentice Hall.

Maathuis, O. J. M. (1999) *Corporate Branding: The Value of the Corporate Brand to Customers and Managers*, Rotterdam: Erasmus University.

MacCannell, D. (1973) Staged Authenticity: Arrangements of Social Space in Tourist Settings, *American Journal of Sociology*, 79(3): 589–603.

MacCannell, D. (1999) *The Tourist: A New Theory of the Leisure Class*, (First California Paperback edn), Los Angeles: University of California Press.

MacInnes, D. J. and Price, L. L. (1987) The Role of Imagery in Information Processing: Review and Extensions, *Journal of Consumer Research*, 13(4) March: 473–91.

MacKay, K. J. and Couldwell, C. M. (2004) Using Visitor-Employed Photography to Investigate Destination Image, *Journal of Travel Research*, 42(4) May: 390–6.

MacKay, K. J. and Fesenmaier, D. R. (1997) Pictorial Element of Destination in Image Formation, *Annals of Tourism Research*, 24(3): 537–65.

MacKay, K. J. and Fesenmaier, D. R. (2000) An Exploration of Cross-Cultural Destination Image Assessment, *Journal of Travel Research*, 38(4) May: 417–23.

Magala, S. J. (2001) *Under Construction (Identities, Communities and Visual Overkill)*, ERIM Report Series: Research in Management, Rotterdam: Erasmus Research Institute of Management, October. Available at http://hdl.handle.net/ 1765/84.

Magala, S. J. (2002) *Elective Identities (Culture, Identization and Integration,)*, ERIM Report Series: Research in Management, Rotterdam: Erasmus Research Institute of Management, October. Available at: http://hdl.handle.net/1765/238.

Mansson, C. (2003) *Cultural Voyage Dubai: 11 Vignettes* [video], CNN International Creative Service.

Marcussen, C. (2008) *Trends in European Internet Distribution of Travel and Tourism Services*, Centre for Regional and Tourism Research, Denmark, 28 January. Available at: http://www.crt.dk/uk/staff/chm/trends/htm; accessed 3 June 2008.

Markwell, K. W. (1997) Dimensions of Photography in a Nature-Based Tour, *Annals of Tourism Research*, 24(1): 131–55.

Matrix, S. E. (2002) The Age of Access: Commodifying Cultural Experiences in the Infotech Society (Book Review), *The Journal of Literacy and Technology*, 2(1). Available at: http://www.literacyandtechnology.org/v2n1/matrix.html; accessed 1 December 2004.

McCabe, S. and Stokoe, E. H. (2004) Place and Identity in Tourists' Accounts, *Annals of Tourism Research*, 31(3): 601–22.

McCannell, D. (1973) Staged Authenticity: Arrangements of Social Space in Tourist Settings, *American Journal of Sociology*, 79(3): 589–603.

McDougall, G. H. G. and Fry, J. N. (1974) Combining Two Methods Of Image Measurement: Semantic Differential and Open-End Technique, *Journal of Retailing*, 50(4): 53–61.

McKenna, R. (2002) *Total Access*, Boston, Mass.: Harvard Business School Press.

McLean, F. and Cooke, S. (2003) Constructing the Identity of a Nation: The Tourist Gaze at the Museum of Scotland, *Tourism, Culture and Communication*, 4(3): 153–62.

Melissen, J. (2004) Publieksdiplomatie: Een goed tandem met branding, in H. H. Duijvestijn (ed.), *Branding NL: Nederland als merk*, The Hague: Stichting Maatschappij en Onderneming, pp. 39–50.

Milnam, A. and Pizam, A. (1995) The Role of Awareness and Familiarity with a Destination: The Central Florida Case, *Journal of Travel Research*, 33(3): 21–7.

Mittal, B. and Lassar, W. M. (1996) The Role of Personalization in Service Encounters, *Journal of Retailing*, 72(1): 95–109.

Molenaar, C. (1996) *Interactive Marketing*, Farnham: Ashgate.

Molenaar, C. (2002) *The Future of Marketing: Practical Strategies for Marketers in the Post-Internet Age*, London: Pearson Education.

Moore, S. (2001) Expressions of Support Surprise Muslims, *Los Angeles Times*, 26 September (Reproduced in Muqbil, Imtiaz. (2001) *Travel Impact Newswire* Online, edn 41, 27 September].)

Morgan, N. and Pritchard, A. (1998) *Tourism Promotion and Power: Creating Images, Creating Identities*, Chichester,: John Wiley.

Morgan, N. and Pritchard, A. (2004) Meeting the Destination Branding Challenge, in N. Morgan, A. Pritchard and R. Pride (eds) *Destination Branding: Creating the Unique Destination Proposition* (2nd edn) Oxford: Elsevier, pp. 59–78.

Morgan, N., Pritchard, A. and Pride, R. (2004) Introduction, in N. Morgan, A. Pritchard, and R. Pride (eds) *Destination Branding: Creating the Unique Destination Proposition* (2nd edn) Oxford: Elsevier, (pp. 3-16).

Morgan, R. (1999) A Novel, User-Based Rating System for Tourist Beaches, *Tourism Management*, 20(4): 393–410.

Mossberg, L. (2007) A Marketing Approach to the Tourist Experience, *Scandinavian Journal of Hospitality and Tourism,* 7(1): 59–74.

Muqbil, I. (2004a) Identity Is Not a Zero-Sum Game, *Travel Impact Newswire* (E-mail newsletter), 46, 18 July, Bangkok.

Muqbil, I. (2004b) To Drive Change, Change the Driver, *Travel Impact Newswire* (E-mail newsletter), 34, 25 May, Bangkok.

Nakheel (2008) *The Palm Jumeirah: Key Facts.* Available at: from http://www. nakheelmediacentre.com/document.php?fileid=299; accessed 2 July 2008.

Netcraft (2008) *August 2008 Web Server Survey,* 29 August. Available at: http://news.netcraft.com/archives/web_server_survey.html; accessed 16 September 2008.

Nielsen, C. (2001) *Tourism and the Media,* Melbourne: Hospitality Press.

Noordman, T. B. J. (2004) *Cultuur in de citymarketing* (*Culture in City Marketing*) (*in Dutch*) The Hague: Elsevier/Reed Business Publications.

Nooteboom, B. (2000) *Learning and Innovation in Organizations and Economies,* Oxford University Press.

Normann, R. and Ramírez, R. (1993) Designing Interactive Strategy: From Value Chain to Value Constellation, *Harvard Business Review,* 71(4): 65–77.

Norris, C. (2002) *Deconstruction: Theory and Practice* (3rd edn), London: Routledge.

O'Dell, T. and Billing, P. (2005) *Experiencescapes: Tourism, Culture and Economy,* Copenhagen Business School Press.

Ohmae, K. (1995) *The End of the Nation State: The Rise of Regional Economies,* London: HarperCollins.

Olins, W. (1999) *Trading Identities: Why Countries and Companies Are Taking On Each Other's Roles,* London: The Foreign Policy Centre.

Oliver, R. L. (1999) Whence Consumer Loyalty, *Journal of Marketing,* 63 (Special issue): 33–44.

Onians, D. (1998) The Real England, *RSA Journal (Royal Society for the Encouragement of Arts, Manufactures & Commerce),* 145(5484): 40–9.

Ooi, C. S. (2004) Brand Singapore: The Hub of 'New Asia', in N. Morgan, A. Pritchard, and R. Pride (eds), *Destination Branding: Creating the Unique Destination Proposition,* (2nd edn), Oxford: Elsevier, pp. 242–60).

Padgett, D. and Allen, D. (1997) Communicating Experiences: A Narrative Approach to Creating Service Brand Image, *Journal of Advertising,* 26(4) Winter: 49–62.

Page, S. J. (2003) *Tourism Management: Managing for Change,* Oxford: Butterworth-Heinemann.

Palfreyman, D. and Al Khalil, M. (2003) 'A Funky Language for Teenzz to Use': Representing Gulf Arabic in Instant Messaging, *Journal of Computer Mediated Communication,* 9(1) [Online]. Available at: http://jcmc,indiana,edu/vol9/ issue1/palfreyman.html; accessed 30 December 2008.

Pan, S. and Ryan, C. (2007) Analyzing Printed Media Travelogues: Means and Purposes with Reference to Framing Destination Image, *Tourism, Culture and Communication,* 7(2): 85–97.

Parasuraman, A., Zeithaml, V. and Berry, L. L. (1985) A Conceptual Model of Service Quality and Its Implications for Future Research, *Journal of Marketing,* 49(4): 41–50.

Paul, D. E. (2004) World Cities as Hegemonic Projects: The Politics of Global Imagineering in Montreal, *Political Geography,* 23(5): 571–96.

Piecowye, J. (2003) Habitus in Transition? CMC Use and Impacts Among Young Women in the United Arab Emirates, *Journal of Computer Mediated Communication,* 8(2): [Online].

Piët, S. (2004) *De emotiemarkt: De toekomst van de beleveniseconomie,* Amsterdam: Pearson Education Benelux.

Pike, S. (2002) Destination Image Analysis – a Review of 142 Papers from 1973 to 2000, *Tourism Management*, 23(5): 541–9.

Pike, S. (2005) Tourism Destination Branding Complexity, *Journal of Product and Brand Management*, 14(4): 258–9.

Pine II, B. J. (1993) *Mass-customisation: The New Frontier in Business Competition*, Boston, Mass.: Harvard Business School Press.

Pine II, B. J. and Gilmore, J. H. (1998a) Welcome to the Experience Economy, *Harvard Business Review*, 76(4): 97–105.

Pine II, B. J. and Gilmore, J. H. (1998b) Welcome to the Experience Economy (Comments and Rejoinders,) *Harvard Business Review*, 76(4): 173–6.

Pine II, B. J. and Gilmore, J. H. (1999) *The Experience Economy: Work is Theatre and Every Business a Stage*, Boston, Mass.: Harvard Business School Press.

Plapler, R. and Chan, R. (2007) *Gulf Real Estate Study*, Dubai: FutureBrand.

Poiesz, T. B. C. (1989) The Image Concept: Its Place in Consumer Psychology, *Journal of Economic Psychology*, 10(4): 457–72.

Polunin, I. (2002) *Destination Branding: Creating the Unique Destination Proposition* (2nd edn) (Book review), Moonshine Travel Marketing Eclipse (7), pp. 1–5. Available at: http://www. moonshine.es/ECLIPSE/E7.pdf; accessed 9 APril 2007.

Ponette, E. (2000) De identiteit waarin ik geloof (The Identity in Which I Believe,) in P. D. Roover and E. Ponette (eds), *Hoe Vlaams zijn de Vlamingen? Over identiteit (How Flemish Are The Flemish? About Identity*, Leuven: Davidsfonds, pp. 86–92.

Prahalad, C. K. and Ramaswamy, V. (2000) Co-opting Customer Competence, *Harvard Business Review*, 78(1): 79–87.

Prahalad, C. K. and Ramaswamy, V. (2004a) Co-creating Unique Value With Customers, *Strategy & Leadership*, 32(3): 4–9.

Prahalad, C. K. and Ramaswamy, V. (2004b) Co-creation Experiences: The Next Practice in Value Creation, *Journal of Interactive Marketing*, 18(3): 5–14.

Prahalad, C. K. and Ramaswamy, V. (2004c) *The Future of Competition : Co-Creating Unique Value With Customers*, Boston, Mass.: Harvard Business School Press.

Prahalad, C. K. and Ramaswamy, V. (2004d) The New Frontier of Experience Innovation, *MIT Sloan Management Review*, 44(4): 12–18.

Pride, R. (2004) A Challenger Brand: Wales, Golf As It Should Be. in N. Morgan, A. Pritchard and R. Pride (eds), *Destination Branding: Creating the Unique Destination Proposition* (2nd edn), Oxford: Elsevier, pp. 159–68.

Pritchard, A. and Morgan, N. J. (1998) 'Mood Marketing'. The New Destination Branding Strategy: A Case Study of 'Wales' The Brand, *Journal of Vacation Marketin,g* 4(3): 215–29.

Pritchard, A. and Morgan, N. J. (2001) Culture, Identity and Tourism Representation: Marketing Cymru or Wales?, *Tourism Management*, 22(2): 167–79.

Pruyn, A. T. H. (1999) Imago: een analytische benadering van het begrip en de implicaties daar-van voor onderzoek, in C. B. M. Van Riel (ed.), *Handboek Corporate Communication* (2nd edn), Alphen aan den Rijn: Samson, pp. 139–75.

Pruyn, A. T. H. (2002) *All Eyes Are on Kwatta: On the Dangers of a Myopic View on Marketing Communications*, Inaugural lecture, Enschede, University of Twente, 5 September.

Rahman, S. (2003) DCA Revises Growth Projection for Passenger Traffic, *Gulf News*. Available at: www.gulfnews.com, Dubai, 1 June.

Reilly, M. D. (1990) Free Elicitation of Descriptive Adjectives for Tourism Image Assessment, *Journal of Travel Research*, 28(4): 21–6.

Rein, I. and Shields, B. (2007) Place Branding Sports: Strategies for Differentiating Emerging, Transitional, Negatively Viewed and Newly Industrialised Nations, *Place Branding and Public Diplomacy*, 3(1): 73–85.

Reiser, D. (2003) Globalisation: An Old Phenomenon That Needs to Be Rediscovered for Tourism, *Tourism and Hospitality Research*, 4(4): 306–20.

Reuters (2001) *Net Traffic Soars in Wake of US Tragedy*, Reproduced by Nua Internet Surveys. Available at: www.nua.com/surveys; accessed 23 June 2002.

Reynolds, W. H. (1965) The Role of the Consumer in Image Building, *California Management Review*, 7(3): 69–76.

Richards, G. (2002) Gastronomy: An Essential Ingredient in Tourism Production and Consumption, in A. Hjalager and G. Richards (eds), *Tourism and Gastronomy*,, London/New York: Routledge, pp. 3–20.

Riedl, J., Konstan, J. and Vrooman, E. (2002) *Word of Mouse: The Marketing Power of Collaborative Filtering,* New York: Warner Books.

Riezebos, H. J. (1994) *Brand-added Value: Theory and Empirical Research About the Value of Brands to Consumers,* Delft: Eburon.

Rifkin, J. (2001a) Age of Access, *Resurgence* (207)Available at: http://resurgence.gn.apc.org/issues/rifkin207.htm; accessed 6 December 2004.

Rifkin, J. (2001b) *The Age of Access: The New Culture of Hypercapitalism, Where All of Life Is a Paid-For Experience,* New York: Penguin Putnam.

Ringle, K. (2003) Dazzling Dubai, *Smithsonian*, 34(7) October: 1–3, 46–8.

Ritchie, J. R. B. and Crouch, G. I. (2003) *The Competitive Destination: A Sustainable Tourism Perspective,* Wallingford: Cabi Publishing.

Ritchie, J. R. B. and Ritchie, R. J. B. (1998) The Branding of Tourism Destinations: Past Achievements and Future Challenges, in P. Keller (ed.), *Proceedings of the International AIEST Conference,* pp. 89–116, *Destination Marketing – Scopes and Limitations*, Marrakech, September, St-Gall,Switzerland: International Association of Scientific Experts in Tourism.

Ritzer, G. (1998) *The McDonaldization Thesis: Explorations and Extensions,* London: Sage.

Ritzer, G. (2003) Rethinking Globalisation: Glocalization/Grobalization and Something/Nothing, *Sociological Theory*, 12(3): 183–209.

Roberts, K. (2005) *Lovemarks: The Future Beyond Brands* (Revised edn), New York: powerHouse Books.

Rojek, C. (1993) *Ways of Escape: Modern Transformations in Leisure and Travel,* London: Macmillan.

Rutheiser, C. (1996) *Imagineering Atlanta: The Politics of Place in the City of Dreams,* New York: Verso.

Ryan, C. (2000) Tourist Experiences: Phenomenographic Analysis, Post-Positivism and Neural Network Software, *International Journal of Tourism Research*, 2(2): 119–31.

Ryan, J. R. (1994) Picturing pPlaces, *Journal of Historical Geography*, 30(3): 332–7.

Ryan, J. R. (2003) Who's Afraid of Visual Culture?, *Antipode*, 35(2): 232–7.

Said, E. (1978, 1991) *Orientalism: Western Constructions of the Orient,* Harmondsworth: Penguin.

Said, E. W. (1981) *Covering Islam: How the Media and the Experts Determine How We See the Rest of the World,* London: Routledge & Kegan Paul.

Saldanha, A. (2002) Music Tourism and Factions of Bodies in Goa, *Tourist Studies*, 2(1): 43.

Sampler, J. and Eigner, S. (2003) *Sand to Silicon: Achieving Rapid Growth Lessons from Dubai,* London: Profile Books.

Saranow, J. (2004) Travel Advice From a Stranger's Diary, *Wall Street Journal*, September 28. Available at: http://online.wsj.com/public/us; accessed 14 December 2004.

Schmidt, M. (2001) Using an ANN-approach for Analyzing Focus Groups, *Qualitative Market Research: An International Journal*, 4(2): 100–12.

Schmitt, B. (1999) *Experiential Marketing*, New York: Free Press.

Schmitt, B. (2003) *Customer Experience Management: A Revolutionary Approach to Connecting With Your Customers*, Hoboken, NJ: John Wiley.

Schoemaker, S. (1996) Scripts: Precursor of Customer Expectations, *Cornell Hotel and Restaurant Administration Quarterly*, 37(1): 42–53.

Schumpeter, J. A. (1975) *Capitalism, Socialism and Democracy*, New York: Harper(Original publication 1942).

Scoop (2004) *Sociaal rapport Zeeland 2004* (*Zeeland Social Report*)Middelburg: Scoop.

Shapiro, C. and Varian, H. R. (1999) *Information Rules: A Strategic Guide to the Network Economy*, Boston, Mass.: Harvard Business School Press.

Sheldon, P. J. (1997) *Tourism Information Technology*, New York: CAB International.

Shih, C.-F. (1998) Conceptualizing Consumer Experiences in Cyberspace, *European Journal of Marketing*, 32(7/8): 655–63.

Shopping Developments in Dubai (2003) *Arabian Business*, December, p. 40.

Sinaeve, A. (2005) *Vlaanderen in beeld en daarbuiten: een iconografie van het Vlaamse landschap aan de hand van fotografie van Lucas Jodogne, Jan Kempenaers en Niels Donckers*(*Flanders in Images and Beyond*)Unpublished Masters' Degree Thesis, University of Leuven.

Sirakaya, E. and Woodside, A. G. (2005) Building and Testing Theories of Decision Making by Travellers, *Tourism Management*, 26(6): 815–32.

Sirgy, M. J. and Su, C. (2000) Destination Image, Self Congruity, and Travel Behaviour: Toward an Integrative Model, *Journal of Travel Research*, 38(4) May: 340–52.

Sontag, S. (2002) *On Photography* (Reprint of 1977 original edn) Penguin Classics Series, London: Penguin.

Statistics Center of Dubai (2006) *Dubai Statistics*, Dubai Municipality. Available at: http://www.dm.gov.ae/DMEGOV/OSI/dm-osi-mainpage.jsp; accessed 10 October 2007.

Statistics Center of Dubai (2007) *Dubai in Figures 2007*, Dubai Municipality. Available at: http://www.dm.gov.ae/DMEGOV/OSI/webreports/-199282233DIF-2007.pdf; accessed 19 May 2008.

Stensgaard, A.-B. (2003a) Emirates Launches Major New Conservation Initiative, *AME-Info*, 8 March. Available at:http://www.ameinfo.com/news/Detailed/ 19412.html; accessed 25 June 2003.

Stensgaard, A.-B. (2003b) Emirates places biggest aircraft order in history, *AME-Info*, 16 June. Available at: http://www.ameinfo.com/news/Detailed/25152.html; accessed 25 June 2003.

Ster, W. v.d. and Wissen, P. v. (1987) *Marketing en Detailhandel* (4th edn), Groningen: Wolters-Noordhoff.

Sternberg, E. (1997) The Iconography of the Tourism Experience, *Annals of Tourism Research*, 24(4): 951–69.

Straus, T. (2000) Commodifying Human Experience: An Interview with Jeremy Rifkin, *AlterNet*, 1 April. Available at: http://www.alternet.org/story/79; accessed 11 December 2004.

Stringer, P. F. (1984) Studies in the Socio-Environmental Psychology of Tourism, *Annals of Tourism Research*, 11(1): 147–66.

Stringer, P. F. and Pearce, P. L. (1984) Toward a Symbiosis of Social Psychology and Tourism Studies, *Annals of Tourism Research*, 11(1): 5–17.

Sweet, D. (2005) Telling a Richer Story, *ClickZ Network*, 27 May.Available at: http://www.clickz.com/experts/ad/rich_media/article.php/3508096; accessed 30 May 2005.

Swibel, M. (2004) Arabian Knight, *Forbes*, 15 March. Available at: http://www.forbes. com/forbes/2004/0315/092.html; accessed 20 May 2008.

Tapachai, N. and Waryszak, R. (2000) An Examination of the Role of Beneficial Image in Tourist Destination Selection, *Journal of Travel Research*, 39(1) August: 37–44.

Tatweer (2008) *Global Village Brings to GCC for First Time 'Disney Live! Presents Mickey's Magic Show' in Dubai*, Press release. Available at: http://www.tatweerdubai.com/En/ NewsArticle.aspx?NewsID=46; accessed 2 July 2008.

Technorati (2008) *State of the Blogosphere/2008*. Available at: http://www.technorati.com/ blogging/state-of-the-blogosphere/; accessed 18 October 2008.

Thomke, S. and Von Hippel, E. (2002) Customers as Innovators: A New Way to Create Value, *Harvard Business Review*, 80(4): 74–81.

Toffler, A. (1980) *The Third Wave*, New York: Bantam Books.

Tourism Flanders (2008) *Brand Guidelines*, Brussels.

Tourtellot, J. B. (2004) Destination Scorecard: 115 Places Rated, *National Geographic Traveler* (March): 60–7.

UAE Ministry of Information and Culture (2004) *Unites Arab Emirates Yearbook 2004*, Abu Dhabi: Trident Press.

Um, S. and Crompton, J. L. (1990) Attitude Determinants in Tourism Destination Choice, *Annals of Tourism Research*, 17(3): 432–48.

Urbain, J.-D. (1989) The Tourist Adventure and His Images, *Annals of Tourism Research*, 16(1): 106–18.

Urry, J. (2002) *The Tourist Gaze* (2nd edn), London: Sage.

Urry, J. (2003) The Sociology of Tourism in C. Cooper (ed.), *Aspects of Tourism*, Classic Reviews in Tourism Series, Vol. 8, Clevedon: Channel View Publications, pp. 9–21.

Uzzell, D. (1984) An Alternative Structuralist Approach to the Psychology of Tourism Marketing, *Annals of Tourism Research*, 11(1): 79–99.

Valck, K. d. (2003) Internet Communities as Marketing Instrument: About their Origins, Myths and Harsh Reality, *Markeur*, 2: 4–6.

Van Bruggen, G. H. (2001) *Marketing, Informatie en Besluitvorming: Een inter-organisationeel perspectief*, Inaugural address, Rotterdam, Erasmus Research Institute of Management, Erasmus University.

Van der Heijden, J. G. M. (1995) *The Changing Value of Travel Agents in Tourism Networks: Towards a Network Design Perspective*, Management Report No. 234, Rotterdam: Erasmus Institute for Advanced Studies in Management, Erasmus University, November.

Van Fenema, P. C. (2002) *Coordination and Control of Globally Distributed Software Projects*, Rotterdam: Erasmus Research Institute of Management, Erasmus University.

Van Gelder, S. (2003) *Global Brand Strategy: Unlocking Brand Potential Across Countries, Cultures and Markets*, London: Kogan Page.

Van Gelder, S. (2008) *Place 2.0*, 2 June. Available at: www.placebrands.net; accessed 13 August 2008.

Van Gelder, S. and Allan, M. (2006) *City Branding: How Cities Compete in the 21st Century*, London/Amsterdam: Placebrands.

Van Ham, P. (2001) The Rise of the Brand State: The Postmodern Politics of Image and Reputation, *Foreign Affairs*, 80(5): 2–6.

Van Ham, P. (2004) Nederland-Lite en de Opkomst van de Merkstaat, in H. H. Duijvestijn (ed.), *Branding NL: Nederland als merk*, The Hague: Stichting Maatschappij en Onderneming, pp. 19–26.

Van Ham, P. (2008) Place Branding: The State of the Art, *The Annals of the American Academy of Political and Social Science*, 616(1): 126–49.

Van Keken, G. (2004) *Zeêland...om grôôs op te wezen en om van te 'ouwen': Een studie naar de positionering van de Zeeuwse identiteit (Zeeland ... to Be Proud of and Love: A Study of the Positioning of the Identity of Zeeland,* Middelburg, Netherlands: Zeeland Bureau for Tourism.

Van Keken, G. and Go, F. (2006) Close Encounters: The Role of Culinary Tourism and Festivals in Positioning a Region, in P. M. Burns and M. Novelli (eds), *Tourism and Social Identities: Global Frameworks and Local Realities,* Advances in Tourism Research Series, Elsevier Science & Technology, pp. 49–60.

Van Keken, G., Govers, R., and Go, F. M. (2005) Resident Perceptions of Local Identity: The Case of Zeeland (Netherlands), in J. Du *et al.* (eds) (pp. CD-ROM), *The Fourth CPTHL Symposium on Consumer Psychology of Tourism, Hospitality, and Leisure Research,* Montreal, Canada: 17–20 July.

Van Raaij, W. F. (1995) *Geïntegreerde communicatie: Een Ontvangersperspectief,* Management Report No. 229, Rotterdam: Erasmus University, September.

Van Raaij, W. F. and Crotts, J. C. (1994) Introduction: The Economic Psychology of Travel and Tourism, in J. C. Crotts and W. F. v. Raaij (eds), *Economic Psychology of Travel and Tourism,* New York: The Haworth Press, pp. 1–19.

Van Rekom, J. (1994a) Adding Psychological Value to Tourism Products, *Journal of Travel & Tourism Management,* 3(3): 21–36.

Van Rekom, J. (1994b) Adding Psychological Value to Tourism Products, in J. C. Crotts and C. F. v. Raaij (eds) *Economic Psychology of Travel and Tourism,* New York: The Haworth Press, pp. 21–36.

Van Rekom, J. and Go, F. M. (2003) Cultural Identities in a Globalizing World: Conditions for Sustainability of Intercultural Tourism, in P. Burns (ed.), *Conference Proceedings, Global Frameworks and Local Realities: Social and Cultural Identities in Making and Consuming Tourism* (CD-ROM), Eastbourne, 11–12 September, University of Brighton.

Van Riel, C. B. M. (1996) *Identiteit en Imago: Grondslagen van corporate communication (Identity and Image: Foundations of Corporate Communication,)* (2nd edn), Schoonhoven, Netherlands: Academic Service.

Vervoorn, L. (2000) Rembrandt Zelf Haalt Bijna 200.000 Bezoekers, *Mauritshuis* Press release. Available at: www.mauritshuis.nl/nieuws/nieuws8.html; accessed 22 June 2002

Viswanathan, M. and Childers, R. L. (1999) Understanding How Product Attributes Influence Product Categorisation: Development and Validation of Fuzzy Set-Based Measures of Gradedness in Product Categories, *Journal of Marketing Research,* 36(1): 75–94.

Viviano, F. (2003) Kingdom on Edge: Saudi Arabia, *National Geographic,* 204(4): 2–41.

Vogt, C. A. and Fesenmaier, D. R. (1998) Expanding the Functional Tourism Information Search Model: Incorporating Aesthetic, Hedonic, Innovation, and Sign Dimensions, *Annals of Tourism Research,* 25(3): 551–78.

Vos, L. (2002) Van Belgische naar Vlaamse identiteit: een overzicht (From Belgian to Flemish Identity: An Overview,) in P. Gillaerts, H. v. Belle and L. Ravier (eds), *Vlaamse identiteit: mythe en werkelijkheid (Flemish Identity: Myth and Reality,),* Leuven: Acco, pp. 11–21.

Wang, Y. and Fesenmaier, D. R. (2002) Measuring the Needs of Virtual Community Members: An Empirical Study of an Online Travel Community, in K. W. Wöber, A. Frew and M. Hitz (eds), *Proceedings of the International Conference on Information and Communication Technologies in Tourism,* pp. 105–14, ENTER 2002, Innsbruck, Vienna/New York: Springer Verlag.

Wang, Y. and Fesenmaier, D. R. (2003) Understanding the Motivation of Contribution in Online Communities: An Empirical Investigation of an Online Travel Community, (CD-ROM), *TTRA Annual Conference,* St Louis, Miss..

Wang, Y. and Fesenmaier, D. R. (2004a) Modeling Participation in an Online Travel Community, *Journal of Travel Research*, 42(3): 261–70.

Wang, Y. and Fesenmaier, D. R. (2004b) Towards Understanding Members' General Participation in and Active Contribution to an Online Travel Community, *Tourism Management*, 25: 709–22.

Wang, Y., Yu, Q. and Fesenmaier, D. R. (2002) Defining the Virtual Tourist Community: Implications for Tourism Marketing, *Tourism Management*, 23(4): 261–70.

Weaver, D. and Lawton, L. (2002) *Tourism Management*, Milton, Queensland: John Wiley Australia.

Weber, R. P. (1990) *Basic Content Analysis*, (2nd edn), Quantitative Applications in the Social Sciences Series, Vol. 49, (ed. M. S. Lewis-Beck) Newbury Park, Calif.: Sage Publications.

Webopedia (2008) Definitions in Webopedia. Available at: http://www.webopedia.com; accessed 13 August 2008.

Wedel, M. and Steenkamp, J.-B. E. M. (1991) A Clusterwise Regression Method for Simultaneous Fuzzy Market Structuring and Benefit Segmentation, *Journal of Marketing Research*, 28(4): 385–96.

Wenger, E. (1998) *Communities of Practice: Learning, Meaning, and Identity*, Cambridge University Press.

Wenger, E., McDermott, R. and Snyder, W. M. (2002) *Cultivating Communities of Practice*, Boston, Mass.: Harvard Business School Publishing.

Werthner, H. and Klein, S. (1999) *Information Technology and Tourism: A Challenging Relationship*, Vienna: SpringerVerlag.

Williamson, D. A. (2007) Social Network Marketing: Ad Spending and Usage, *eMarketer*, December. Available at: http://www.emarketer.com/Reports/All/ Emarketer_2000478 .aspx?src=report_head_info_reports; accessed 18 October 2008..

Williamson, D. A. (2008) UK Social Network Marketing: Ad Spending and Usage, *eMarketer*, May. Available at: http://www.emarketer.com/Reports/All/ Emarketer_2000491.aspx?src= report_head_info_reports; accessed 18 October 2008.

Woelfel, J. (1998) *CATPAC II: User's Guide*, New York: Rah Press.

Woelfel, J. and Stoyanoff, N. J. (1993) CATPAC: A Neural Network for Qualitative Analysis of Text, Paper presented at the annual meeting of the Australian Marketing Association, Melbourne, Australia, September.

Wolf, P. C. (2003) Powered by Brands, *Travel Weekly*, 22 July. Available at: www.phocuswright. com; accessed 5 August 2003.

Woodside, A. G. and Lysonski, S. (1989) A General Model of Traveler Destination Choice, *Journal of Travel Research*, 27(4): 8–14.

WTO (World Tourism Organization) (2000) *Basic References on Tourism Statistics*, Available at: http://www.world-tourism.org/statistics/tsa_project/ basic_references/index-en.htm; accessed 12 January 2005.

Yang, G. (2004) *Skills, Wages and Working Conditions in the Hotel Sector*, Sector Survey Series, Dubai: Centre for Labour Market Research and Information (CLMRI), Tanmia, June.

Yeoh, B. (2005) The Global Cultural City? Spatial Imagineering and Politics in the (Multi) Cultural Marketplaces of South-East Asia, *Urban Studies*, 42(5): 945–58.

Zaltman, G. (2002) Hidden Minds: When it Comes to Mining Customer's Views, We've Only Scratched the Surface, *Harvard Business Review*, 80(6): 26–7.

Zawya (2007) *Emirates Signs $34.9 bn Contracts for 120 Airbus and Boeing* Planes. Available at: http://www.zawya.com/printstory.cfm?storyid=WAM 20071111103017880 &l=060500071111; accessed 20 May 2008.

Zawya (2008) *Dubai Holding Profile,* 26 March. Available at: http://www. zawya.com/cm/ profile.cfm/cid1002706; accessed 20 May 2008.

Zeithaml, V. A. and Bitner, M. J. (1996) *Services Marketing,* New York: McGraw-Hill.

Zukin, S. (1991) *Landscapes of Power: From Detroit to Disney World,* Berkeley and Los Angeles, Calif.: University of California Press.

Züll, C. and Landmann, J. (2004) Computer-assisted Content Analysis without Dictionary?, *Sixth International Conference on Logic and Methodology (RC33) – Recent Developments and Applications in Social Research Methodology,* Amsterdam, 17–20 August.

NAME INDEX

Aaker, D. A., 12, 15, 16, 49
Abu Dhabi, 76, 77, 153
Agassi, Andre, 93
Al Bu Falah tribe, 76
Al Khalil, M., 83, 84
Al Maha Desert Resort, 94
Al Maktoum International Airport, 94, 95
Al Maktoum, H.H. Sheikh Hamdan bin
    Mohammed bin Rashid, 95
Al Maktoum, H.H. Sheikh Mohammed bin
    Rashid, 74, 81, 95, 99, 164
Al Maktoum, H.H. the late ruler
    Sheikh Hasher bin Maktoum, 77
Al Maktoum, H.H. the late ruler
    Sheikh Maktoum bin Buti, 76
Al Maktoum, H.H. the late ruler
    Sheikh Maktoum bin Hasher, 77
Al Maktoum, H.H. the late ruler
    Sheikh Maktoum bin Rashid, 74
Al Maktoum, H.H. the late ruler
    Sheikh Rashid bin Saeed, 77, 98
Al Maktoum, H.H. the late ruler
    Sheikh Saeed bin Buti, 77
Al Maktoum, H.H. the late ruler
    Sheikh Saeed bin Maktoum, 77, 104
Al Maktoum, H.H. Sheikh Ahmed bin Saeed, 95
Alabbar, Hohammed Ali, 96
Albers, P. C., 144, 146, 155
Alcantara, N., 143
Alhemoud, A. M., 6, 18
Allan, M., 260
Allen, D., 6, 8, 18, 63, 147, 180, 190, 191, 205,
    256
Almeida Santos, C., 52, 147, 258, 264
AME Info, 83
Anderson, B., 20, 51, 61, 64, 65
Anholt, S., 10, 14, 15, 16, 18, 49, 59, 62, 109,
    113, 241, 243, 260, 265
Ankomah, P. K., 185, 186, 187
Antwerp, 110, 117, 118, 123
Appadurai, A., 8, 34, 56, 57
Arabian Adventures, 87, 96
Archer, K., 140, 141
Armstrong, E. G., 6, 18
Arnould, E., 184, 185, 220
Ashworth, G. J., 52, 53, 54, 55, 260

Ateljevic, I., 9, 66, 79, 147
Atkinson, R. C., 28, 29, 33
Australia, 66, 102, 142, 210, 218, 220

Baloglu, S., 41, 184, 185
Bani Yas tribe, 76, 105
Bardin, F., 87
Bastaqya, 103, 104, 106
Bateson, J. E. G., 68, 69, 70, 140, 191
Bayle, Peter, 27, 43
Bedouin, 11, 76, 104, 105
Beerli, A., 60, 135, 136, 185, 187, 188, 190,
    196, 239
Beheydt, L. J., 122
Belgium, 45, 53, 59, 107, 110, 117–27, 130,
    208, 211, 212, 215, 220
Belhane, 91
Berkeley, George, 27, 43
Bernstein, D., 195, 197
Berry, L. L., 32, 184
Bigné, J. E., 18, 150, 183, 187, 191, 192
Billing, P., 139
Birkigt, K., 50, 51
Bitner, M. J., 69, 140
Blackshaw, P., 40
Blackwell, R. D., 185, 186
Blain, C., 13, 14
Bloch, M., 35
Boorstin, D. J., 1, 31, 54
Boulding, K. E., 31, 148, 177
Bowen, J., 18, 68, 140
Bowes, G., 143
Brabant, 118, 119, 121
Brentano, Franz, 28, 43
Brinberg, D., 184
Britton, R. A., 72, 79
Brotherton, B., 173
Bruges, 117, 118, 123
Brussels, 117, 118, 122, 123, 128
Budtz, C., 264
Buhalis, D., 210
Burdett, A. L. P., 77
Burj Al Arab, 93, 96, 100, 260
Butler, R. W., 54,
Butler, T., 102
Buttle, F., 184

Cai, L. A., 264
Canary Islands, 208, 215, 216, 218, 223–5, 230, 238, 241
Carman, J. M., 195
Carson, P., 123, 124
Cary, S. H., 138
Castells, M., 2, 3, 7, 8, 34, 52, 53, 57
CATPAC, 156–8, 162, 209, 229, 231
Chan, R., 85
Chang, T., 141
Childers, R. L., 230
Cho, Y., 63, 68, 183
Chon, K.-S., 135, 187, 191
Christensen, G. L., 256
CIA, 75, 82, 151
Claeys, U., 123, 124
Clawson, M., 32
CNN, 80, 90, 102, 103, 206
Cohen, E., 9, 54, 55, 60, 66, 105, 141, 144, 147
Cohen-Hattab, K., 54, 60, 66
Colliers International, 85
Cooke, S., 20, 64, 105
Cooper, C., 19, 67
Cooper, K. J., 102
Cooper, P. J., 103
Couldwell, C. M., 183, 231
Crompton, J. L., 6, 18, 135, 185, 186, 187
Crotts, J. C., 30
Crouch, G. I., 49
Csikszentmihalyi, M., 137, 138, 184

Daems, S., 123, 124
Dann, G. M. S., 151, 183, 184, 185
Davies, P., 38
De Meulemeester, K., 123
De Roover, P., 123, 124
Decrop, A., 6, 186
Dellaert, B. G. C., 62, 186, 190
Derrett, R., 168, 174
Descartes, René, 11, 25, 26, 43
Dhar, R., 146, 190
Dietvorst, A. G. J., 53, 54
Dinnie, K., 254
Dissel, H. G. v., 4, 10, 38, 39
Doorne, S., 9, 66, 79, 147
Dredge, D., 58
DTCM, 76, 82, 85–9, 97, 102, 104, 151, 153, 154, 236
Dubai, 4, 8, 11, 21, 45–7, 57–60, 66, 70, 73–107, 130–4, 141, 147–8, 151–66, 167, 176, 178, 183, 191, 205, 207, 208–40, 241–2, 243–4, 249, 250–3, 257–8, 260, 263, 265, 269

Dubai Chamber, 76, 85, 96
Dubai International Financial Centre, 90, 100
Dubai Internet City, 90, 151
Dubai Media City, 90, 232
Dubai Palm Developers LLC, 92
Dubai Ports World, 95
Dubai Sports City, 92
Dubai Tourism Development Company, 93
Dubai World, 92, 94, 95
Dubailand, 92, 93, 96, 100, 215
Dutch East India Company, 110

Echtner, C. M., 6, 18, 33, 135, 179, 180, 181, 183, 185, 187, 196, 197, 205, 206, 209, 223, 256
Economist Intelligence Unit, 85, 95
Eigner, S., 98
Ekinci, Y., 254
Emaar, 93, 96
Embacher, J., 184
Emirates Academy of Hospitality Management, 82
Emirates Group (incl. Airline), 87, 94, 95, 96, 100
e-tid, 189

Fairweather, J. R., 17, 136, 144, 155, 185, 191
Fakeye, P. C., 18, 135, 187
Featherstone, M., 7, 12, 55, 61, 62
Federer, Roger, 93
Feighey, W., 144, 155, 183, 231
Fesenmaier, D. R., 5, 9, 10, 13, 17, 40, 41, 63, 66, 68, 71, 136, 143, 144, 146, 147, 148, 151, 157, 165, 166, 183, 184, 186, 190, 192, 205, 210
Flanders, 45–6, 59, 107, 117–29, 130, 208, 212, 215, 224, 226, 230, 232, 233, 238, 241
Flemish Department of Foreign Affairs, 128
Fletcher, J., 19, 67
Florida, 11, 208, 212, 215, 216, 223, 224, 226, 230, 232, 233, 238, 239, 241, 252
Fog, K., 264
Fonda, D., 78, 101
Fridgen, J. D., 30, 31, 32
Fry, J. N., 184, 209
Fuchs, M., 210
Fukuda-Parr, S., 53, 56

Gabr, H. S., 98, 104, 105
Gallarza, M. G., 41, 155, 180, 182, 183, 184, 196, 198, 205, 206, 256

Garlick, S., 144, 146, 155, 166
Gartner, W. C., 41, 60, 135, 184, 187, 188, 189, 190, 210, 231
Gertner, D., 5, 12, 16
Ghent, 117, 118, 123
Gibson, O., 80
Gil Saura, I., 182, 198
Gilmore, F., 109
Gilmore, J. H., 35, 36, 41, 55, 141
Gnoth, J., 13, 49, 62, 110, 257, 258, 264, 266, 267
Go, F. M., 6, 7, 8, 9, 10, 12, 27, 35, 40, 53, 57, 58, 61, 69, 104, 105, 139, 151, 168, 189, 191, 194, 200, 237, 258
Government of Dubai, 85, 88, 96, 103, 104, 152, 153
Govers, R., 10, 93, 151, 191, 194, 200, 208, 237
Graham, R., 78
Great Britain, 142
Greenwood, D. J., 54
Gretzel, U., 71, 144, 157, 166, 210
Guntrum, K., 151

Haahti, A., 197
Haider, D. H., 258
Hall, M., 169
Hall, S., 7, 15, 18, 20, 57, 63, 64, 65, 162, 163, 181
Hallowell, E. M., 3, 38
Halman, L., 122
Hammer, M., 60
Hankinson, G., 260, 265
Harvey, D., 2, 5, 7, 9, 10, 11, 45, 56, 57, 58, 206
Hawaii, 143
Haywood, M., 8, 40, 69
Heard-Bey, F., 76, 78
Heidegger, Martin, 28, 43
Heijl, M., 123, 124
Henderson, J., 100
Hirschman, E. C., 6, 17, 36, 136, 143, 146, 166
Hjalager, A., 169
Hoffman, D. L., 70, 144, 145, 147, 154, 155, 167
Hoffman, K. D., 68, 69, 70, 140
Hofstede, G., 65, 66, 113, 114, 184, 220, 221
Holbrook, M. B., 6, 17, 36, 136, 143, 146, 166
Hong Kong, 8, 90, 220
Hosany, S., 254
HRG, 87
HSBC, 81
Huang, J., 3, 38, 71
Hubbert, A. R., 191
Hult, G. T. M., 51
Human, B., 25, 26, 53, 56, 82, 139, 144, 146

Hume, David, 26, 27, 28, 43
Hunt, J. D., 18, 135, 180, 187
Huntington, S. P., 11, 59, 75, 148
Husserl, Edmund, 28, 43

Imagineers, The, 141
Ind, N., 113, 265
Internet World Stats, 82, 151
Internet.com, 261, 262
iTravelnet.com, 218

Jafari, J., 210
James, W. R., 29, 144, 146, 155
Jansen-Verbeke, M., 54, 104
Jebel Ali, 77, 87, 90, 92, 95, 164, 211
Jenkins, C. L., 93, 96, 99
Jenkins, J., 58
Jenkins, O. H., 183, 231
Jeong, S., 52, 147, 258, 264
Joachimsthaler, E., 12, 15, 16
Johnson, G., 49
Jumeirah, 87, 90, 92, 93, 94, 96, 162, 163, 164

Kant, Immanuel, 27, 28, 29, 43
Kapferer, J.-N., 12, 16
Kavaratzis, M., 260
Keillor, B. D., 51
Kelly, K., 31, 39
Kemerling, G., 25, 26, 27, 28
Kerber, J., 54, 60, 66
Kierkegaard, Søren, 28, 43, 206
Kim, H., 59, 66
Kitchin, T., 55, 62, 192, 264
Klein, N., 2
Klein, S., 2, 3, 7, 34, 35, 39, 40, 61, 231, 239
KLM, Royal Dutch Airline, 211
Klooster, E. v. h., 142, 143, 258, 264, 266, 267
Knetsch, J. L., 32
Konstan, J., 190
Kossmann, E. H., 118
Kossmann-Putto, J. A., 118
Kotler, P., 5, 6, 12, 13, 16, 18, 68, 140, 258
Kriekaard, J. A., 13
Kuala Lumpur, 8
Kumar, K., 4, 10, 38, 39
Kunkel, J. H., 32, 184

Laesser, C., 259
Landmann, J., 156
Lash, S., 7, 12, 55, 61, 62
Lassar, W. M., 69, 140, 149
Lawton, L., 68, 70

Lebo, H., 206
Lee, R. M., 57, 61, 104, 105
Leemans, H., 17, 136, 146, 180, 184, 186, 205
Lengkeek, J., 141
Leopold, 119
Leuven, 123, 211
Levy, S. E., 14
Lim, S., 141
Lindstrom, M., 142
Locke, John, 11, 26, 43
Long, N., 148
Loonstra, P. B. M., 263
Lovelock, C., 68, 140
Lysonski, S., 185, 186

Maathuis, O. J. M., 267
MacCannell, D., 9, 54, 67, 147
MacInnes, D. J., 33, 191, 209
MacKay, K. J., 9, 10, 13, 41, 63, 66, 68, 143,
    144, 146, 147, 148, 151, 165, 183, 184,
    192, 205, 231
Magala, S. J., 6, 59, 62, 102, 188, 239, 250, 262
Mansson, C., 104
Marcussen, C., 152
Markwell, K. W., 144, 155, 183
Martín, J. D., 60, 135, 136, 185, 187, 188, 190,
    196, 239
Matrix, S. E., 27, 37
McCabe, S., 56, 191
McCannell, D., 105, 249
McCleary, K. W., 41, 184, 185
McDermott, R., 2, 265, 266, 267
McDougall, G. H. G., 184, 209
McKenna, R., 36
McLean, F., 20, 64, 105
MeetURplanet.com, 218
Melissen, J., 50
Middle East, 11, 73, 74, 75, 78, 79, 80, 90, 101,
    106, 148, 164, 230, 235
Milnam, A., 135
Mittal, B., 69, 140, 149
Molenaar, C., 2, 3, 5, 37, 40
Moore, S., 28, 29, 43, 79, 80, 81
Morgan, N. J., 9, 15, 17, 52, 78, 79, 110, 144,
    147, 148, 151, 216, 217, 238
Morgan, R., 183
Mossberg, L., 141, 142
Mowatt, J., 82
Muqbil, I., 53, 59

Nakheel, 92, 95, 102
National Geographic, 2, 80, 216, 222, 232, 239
Netcraft, 3

Netherlands, The, 11, 31, 45, 58, 107–10,
    117–19, 122, 130, 133, 168, 174, 176,
    178, 187, 194–7, 202–6, 211, 212, 215,
    216, 218, 220, 237, 241
New Zealand, 142, 143, 172–3, 218, 220,
    257
Nielsen, C., 189
Noordman, T. B. J., 18, 20, 50, 51
Nooteboom, B., 39
Normann, R., 35, 38
Norris, C., 10
Novak, T. P., 70, 144, 145, 147, 154, 155, 167

Ohmae, K., 7, 8, 73
Olins, W., 14, 36, 62, 243
Oliver, R. L., 62, 192
Olson, J. C., 256
Onians, D., 61, 105
Ooi, C. S., 216, 217, 238

Padgett, D., 6, 8, 18, 63, 146, 180, 190, 191,
    205, 256
Page, S. J., 19, 67
Palfreyman, D., 83, 84
Palm Islands (Palm Jumeirah, Palm Jebel Ali,
    Palm Deira), 87, 90, 92, 95, 100, 260
Pan, S., 59
Parasuraman, A., 41, 42
Paul, D. E., 50, 140
Pearce, P. L., 30
Piecowye, J., 83
Piët, S., 36, 41
Pike, S., 14, 41, 180
Pine (II), B. J., 35, 36, 41, 55, 141
Pine, R., 9, 58
Pizam, A., 135
Plapler, R., 85
Poiesz, T. B. C., 30, 31
Polunin, I., 9, 14, 216, 217, 238, 254, 264, 265
Ponette, E., 122, 123
Prahalad, C. K., 37, 38, 139, 149
Price, L., 33, 191, 197, 209
Pride, R., 217
Pritchard, A., 9, 15, 17, 52, 78, 79, 144, 147,
    148, 151, 216, 217, 238
Pruyn, A. T. H., 3, 4, 30, 38

Rahman, S., 94
Ramaswamy, V., 37, 38, 139, 149
Ramírez, R., 35, 38
Reilly, M. D., 208
Rein, I., 92
Reiser, D., 58

Reuters, 90, 206
Reynolds, W. H., 179
Richards, G., 169
Richardson, S. L., 59, 66
Riedl, J., 190
Riemens, Ruden, 115
Riezebos, H. J., 12, 13, 16
Rifkin, J., 3, 4, 36, 41
Ringle, K., 75, 84, 99
Ritchie, J. R. B., 6, 18, 33, 49, 135, 179, 180,
    181, 183, 185, 187, 196, 197, 205, 206,
    209, 216, 223, 256
Ritzer, G., 56
Roberts, K., 172
Rojek, C., 146
Rotterdam School of Management, 211
Russell, Bertrand, 29, 43
Rutheiser, C., 140
Ryan, C., 59, 157, 179, 206
Ryan, J. R., 144

Said, E., 11, 78, 79, 80, 106, 235, 251
Saldanha, A., 146
Sampler, J., 98
Saranow, J., 40
Sartre, Jean-Paul, 28
Schmidt, M., 113, 157
Schmitt, B., 141
Schoemaker, S., 191
Scholes, K., 49
Schumpeter, J. A., 10
Scoop, 111
Shapiro, C., 37, 41
Sheldon, P. J., 40, 61
Shields, B., 93
Shih, C.-F., 70, 144, 147, 155, 167
Silicon Valley, 8
Sinaeve, A., 127
Singapore, 8, 100, 208, 212, 215–17, 220,
    223–4, 227, 230, 233, 238, 241, 252
Sirakaya, E., 185, 186, 187, 190
Sirgy, M. J., 184, 205
Snelders, D., 6, 186
Sontag, S., 146, 148
Stadler, M. M., 50, 51
Statistics Center of Dubai, 81, 82, 85
Steenkamp, J.-B. E. M., 230
Stensgaard, A.-B., 94, 95
Ster, v. d., 195
Sternberg, E., 144, 146, 155, 166
Stokoe, E. H., 56, 179, 191
Stoyanoff, N. J., 157, 208
Straus, T., 37

Stringer, P. F., 30, 31
Su, C., 184, 205
Sulayem, Khalid, 95
Sulayem, Sultan Ahmen, 95
Swaffield, S. R., 17, 136, 144, 155, 185, 191
Sweet, D., 38, 40
Swibel, M., 96

Tapachai, N., 6, 18, 180, 183, 191, 194, 205,
    206, 256
Tatweer, 92, 96
Technorati, 40
Thailand, 142, 220
Thomke, S., 37, 38
Toffler, A., 23, 34, 35, 40, 42, 44, 263, 264
Tourism Flanders, 123, 128, 129
Tourtellot, J. B., 216, 222
Travellerspoint.com, 208, 218
Troy, 142

UAE, 74–8, 81–5, 92, 94, 95, 102, 103, 105,
    151, 152
UAE Ministry of Information and Culture, 78
Um, S., 185, 186
Urbain, J.-D., 155
Urry, J., 17, 54, 58, 136, 139, 140, 155
Uzzell, D., 151

Valck, K. d., 258, 261
Van Bruggen, G. H., 7, 34
Van der Heijden, J. G. M., 35, 39, 70
Van Fenema, P. C., 6, 7, 12, 27, 39, 53, 61, 139,
    189
Van Gelder, S., 12, 16, 246, 254, 260
Van Ham, P., 10, 16, 49
Van Keken, G., 108, 168
Van Raaij, W. F., 13, 30
Van Rekom, J., 51, 61, 105, 264
Van Riel, C. B. M., 30, 31, 50, 51, 183, 195
Varian, H. R., 37, 41
Vervoorn, L., 206
Viswanathan, M., 230
Viviano, F., 80
Vogt, C. A., 5, 17, 136, 146, 147, 186, 190
Von Hippel, E., 37, 38
Vos, L., 118

Wales, 52, 208, 212, 216–18, 223, 224, 226,
    230, 232–3, 238, 241
Wallonia, 117, 122
Wang, Y., 40, 190
Waryszak, R., 6, 18, 180, 183, 191, 194, 205,
    206, 257

Weaver, D., 68, 70
Weber, R. P., 208
Wedel, M., 230
Wenger, E., 2, 265, 266, 267
Wertenbroch, K., 146, 190
Werthner, H., 3, 7, 34, 35, 39, 40, 61, 231, 239
Williamson, D. A., 39, 40
Wissen, v., 195
Wittgenstein, Ludwig, 29, 43
Woelfel, J., 156, 157, 208
Wolf, P. C., 13
Woods, Tiger, 93, 116
Woodside, A. G., 185, 186, 187, 190
Wright, L., 68, 140
WTO (World Trade Organization), 20

Yang, G., 82
Yavas, U., 197
Yeoh, B., 140, 141

Zaltman, G., 37, 256
Zawya, 95, 96
Zayed, H.H. Sheikh, 77
Zeeland (The Netherlands), 45–6, 107,
    108–16, 130, 133, 168–74, 176, 256
Zeithaml, V., 140
Zukin, S., 133
Züll, C., 156

SUBJECT INDEX

access, 4, 36
action oriented/conative characteristics of
    experience, 137
    see also characteristics of experiences
affective/emotional characteristics of
    experience, 137
    see also characteristics of experiences
affective/emotional image component,
    184–5
    see also components of image (affective,
    cognitive, conative)
alternative phenomenographic
    methodology of place image research,
    208–15
    see also place image research
ambient intelligence, 263
    see also ICT
analysis/research, 250–3, 255–7
    see also under perceived identity research,
    place image research, projected place
    image research
antecedent of image (quality, satisfaction,
    consumer decision making,
    post-purchase behaviour), 18
attributes of place image, 6, 18, 31, 135,
    180, 181, 205–6, 223–4, 231, 237–8,
    268
    see also characteristics of place image
authenticity, 9, 32, 53–5, 76
    see also commoditization
autonomous image formation agents, 41, 60,
    62, 67, 143, 187–8, 232
    see also image formation
    agents/information sources
awareness, 15, 17
    see also brand/name awareness

behavioural psychology, 30
    see also psychology
blip culture, 264
bonds, 39
brands/branding
    brand architecture, 260
    brand assets, 15, 17
    brand equity, 12, 13, 15, 16

brand identity (brand values, vision, visuals,
    name, narratives, colours, fonts,
    tone-of-voice and logo and slogan),
    13, 108–11, 115–16, 217, 238,
    254, 259
brand image, see image
brand loyalty, 13, 15, 17
brand/name awareness, 15, 17
brand personality, 14, 254–5
communities, 264–7
definition, 12, 16
living the brand, 265
of experience, 169–73
on-brand, 15, 139, 245, 259–60
perceived quality, 15, 17
promise of value, 14, 16
reputation, 177, 179

cases included in place image research,
    215–18
chambers of commerce, see place
    marketers
characteristics of experiences, 6, 17, 136–7,
    141, 143
    affective/emotional, 137
    cognitive/image/fantasies, 137
    conative/action oriented, 137
    multisensory, 6, 26, 29, 116, 136–7
    passive/gazing/absorbing v.
        participating/immersing, 141
    social interactions/encounters, 38, 71, 137,
        140, 174
characteristics of place image, 18, 180
    attributes, 6, 18, 31, 135, 180, 181, 205–6,
        223–4, 231, 237–8, 268
    common image characteristics, 135, 180,
        181, 206, 223–4, 229–31, 237, 268
    functional image characteristics, 6, 18, 135,
        180, 181, 223
    holistic image characteristics, 31, 135, 180,
        181, 205–6, 223
    psychological image characteristics, 6, 18,
        135, 181, 223
    unique image characteristics, 18, 135, 180,
        205–6, 223, 229–31, 237–8, 268

315

characteristics of services and product
offering of place (inseparability,
intangibility, heterogeneity/variability and
perishability), 68–70, 131, 139, 190, 247
city-states, 73, 238, 269
clash of civilizations, 11
co-creation, 37, 55, 139
cognition, 29
   constructive (inferences, stereotypes and
   schemata), 29
   mental imagery processing v. discursive
   processing, 33, 137
cognitive image component, 184–5
   see also components of image (affective,
   cognitive, conative)
cognitive psychology, 29, 43
   see also psychology
cognitive/image/fantasy characteristics of
experience, 137
   see also characteristics of experiences
colonialism, 78–9, 246, 251, 252
colouring elements of place identity
(symbolism, behaviour and
communication), 51, 256
   see also constructive elements of place
   identity
commercial spaces, 2
   see also spaces
commoditization, 54, 56, 147, 166
common place image characteristics, 135,
180, 181, 206, 223–4, 229–31, 237,
268
   see also characteristics of place image
communication of the place brand, 59, 255,
261
   see also place brand implementation
communities of practice, 2, 9, 265–6
competition, 5, 14–16, 49–50
competitive advantage, 49
components of image (affective, cognitive,
conative), 184–5
conative image component, 184–5
   see also components of image (affective,
   cognitive, conative)
conative/action oriented characteristics of
experience, 137
   see also characteristics of experiences
construction of the place brand/product
development, 255, 260
   see also place brand implementation
constructive cognition (inferences,
stereotypes and schemata), 29
constructive elements of place identity, 256

colouring elements (symbolism, behaviour
and communication), 51, 256
semi-static elements (size, physical
appearance and inner
mentality/culture), 50, 256
signifiers (great events/heroes;
food/architecture/arts/literature/
popular culture;
language/traditions/rituals/folk), 51,
65–6, 103–5, 256
structural elements (location and history),
50, 256
constructivism, 27, 29, 43
   see also philosophy
consumer decision-making, 14, 186
   see also destination choice behaviour
consumer/visitor identity (cultural, social,
personal and psychological
characteristics), see visitor/consumer
identity
content analysis, 190, 208–9, 222
   of pictures/photographs, 155–6
   of text, 156–7
   see also projected place image research
contestation
   of place identity, 52
   of projected place image, 147–8
convention bureaus, see place marketers
co-operation, 255, 264
   see also place brand implementation
corporate identity, 50
covert induced image formation agents, 41,
60, 62, 66, 143, 188, 232, 268
   see also image formation agents
created meaning of place, 63–7
   see also signifiers of place identity
cultural background/differences and
visitor/consumer identity, 221, 233–4
cultural production, 4, 141
culture (cultural identity/values) and place
identity, 50–3, 65–6, 103–5, 113–14
   see also signifiers of place identity

deconstruction, 9–12, 206–7
definitions, 16–20
   brands/branding, 16
   place brands/branding, 16–17
   place experience, 17
   place identity, 17–18
   place image, 18
   place marketing, 19
   product offering of place, 19
   projected place image, 19–20

tourism, 20
demand, 6, 9, 70, 245, 248–9
  see also supply
de-massified media, 40, 264
destination choice processes, 185–7
destination management/marketing
    organization, see place marketers
differentiation, 10, 13, 59, 128, 168
digital divide, 3, 36
disintermediation, 35, 39
diversity/plurality/heterogeneity/variability
    of place identity, 53
    of place image, 181
dynamic packaging, 38

economic psychology (and
    microeconomics), 30
  see also psychology
elements of place identity, see constructive
    elements of place identity
emotional/affective characteristics of
    experience, 137
  see also characteristics of experiences
empiricism, 26
  see also under philosophy, experiences
environmental psychology, 30, 32
  see also psychology
ephemerality, 2, 57–8, 205–6, 224, 232,
    246–7
essence/expression of the place brand, 255,
    257–60
  see also under brand identity, value match,
    experience concept
existentialism, 28, 43
  see also philosophy
exotic, 1, 215, 238
experiences
  affective/emotional characteristics, 137;
    see also characteristics of experiences
  characteristics, 6, 17, 136–7, 141, 143;
    see also characteristics of experiences
  cognitive/image/fantasy characteristics,
    137, see also characteristics of
    experiences
  conative/action oriented characteristics,
    137; see also characteristics of
    experiences
  empiricism, 26
  experience branding, 169–73
  experience concept, 173, 255, 259; see
    also place brand essence
  experience economy, 35, 141, 260
  experience icons, 260–1

experience networks, 139
flow/optimal autotelic experience, 137–9,
    145
hedonic consumption experiences
    (experiential/hedonic products), 5–6,
    17, 36, 71, 136–9
multisensory characteristics, 6, 26, 29, 116,
    136–7; see also characteristics of
    experiences
parallelization of experiences, 6
passive/gazing/absorbing versus
    participating/immersing, 141
place (consumption) experiences, see
    place experiences
real experiences (in material space), 1,
    139
social interactions/encounters (in social
    space), 38, 71, 137, 140, 174; see also
    characteristics of experiences
travel experiences, 13; see also place
    consumption experiences
vicarious, see vicarious place experiences
virtual experiences (in information space),
    1, 145; see also under vicarious place
    experiences, virtual/online
    environments
export, trade and investment agencies, see
    place marketers
extravagant expectations, 1, 4, 11, 233, 246,
    251

factor cost benefits, 5, 19, 67
fantasy/cognitive/image characteristics of
    experience, 137
  see also characteristics of experiences
FDI (foreign direct investment), 85
festivals
  and (culinary) place experiences, 168,
    174, 261
  and place identity, 52, 258–9, 264
flexibilization, 35
flows, see under global flows, spaces
    functional place image characteristics, 6,
    18, 135, 180, 181, 223
  see also characteristics of place image

gender and visitor/consumer identity, 235
global flows (media-, ethno-, techno-,
    finance-scapes), 7, 8, 57, 73
global hubs, 4, 73–4, 260
globalization, 7, 55–9, 81–8
  and place identity, 7, 55–9

globalization (*continued*)
  and place image, 7
  glocalization, 55–6, 83–4, 130
  grobalization, 55
  McDonaldization/Disneyization, 55, 130,
    246
  versus localization, 8, 55–9, 243
glocalization, 55–6, 83–4, 130
  see also globalization
government/public sector, 8–9, 14, 49, 67–8,
    89, 95–8, 117–20, 128, 147–8, 154, 162,
    165, 246–8, 251, 268
  see also place marketers
grobalization, 55
  see also globalization
guests and hosts, 41, 49, 70, 135, 173–4, 245–9

heritage and place identity, 49–50, 75–6
heterogeneity/variability
  of experience
    environments/places/spaces, 139–40;
    see also spaces
  of place identity, 53
  of place image, 181
  of services, *see* service characteristics
historic (literature) analysis, 117–23, 124–5
  see also under perceived identity
    research/analysis
history and place identity, 49–50, 55, 76–81,
    110–11, 121, 256
holistic place image characteristics, 31, 135,
    180, 181, 205–6, 223
  see also characteristics of place image
hosts and guests, 41, 49, 70, 135, 173–4,
    245–9
hotel performance, 86–7
human moment, 38

iconic projects, 88, 95, 100, 106–7
icons of experience, 260–1
ICT (information and communication
    technology), 2, 34, 59–63, 82–3
  ambient intelligence, 263
  and product offering of place, 70–1
  and projected place image, 59–63
  internet (world wide web), 36–7, 62–3,
    82, 261
  RDF (Resource Description Framework),
    261
  RSS (Rich Site Summary), 262
  virtuality/online or information space,
    see virtual/online environments/spaces

  Web 2.0, 39, 62, 143, 190, 262
idealism, 27, 28, 43
  see also philosophy
ideas (Descartes theory of adventitious,
    factitious and innate ideas), 25
  see also philosophy
identity, 4, 13, 26
  see also under brand, corporate, place,
    visitor
illusion (perpetuating system of perceptual
    illusion), 26–7, 54
  see also philosophy
image, 6, 13, 26, 31–2, 44, 179–80
  antecedent of (quality, satisfaction,
    consumer decision-making,
    post-purchase behaviour), 18
  components (affective, cognitive,
    conative), 184–5
  mental imagery processing *v.* discursive
    processing, 33, 137; *see also* cognition
  primary (through experience) and
    secondary (information sources),
    135–6
  projected, 26
  psychology, 29, 180, 181
  reputation, 177, 179
  research, *see* place image research
  self-focus/self-congruity, 28, 184–5, 205,
    236
  see also place image
image formation agents/information sources,
    41, 60
  autonomous image formation agents, 41,
    60, 62, 67, 143, 187–8, 232
  induced image formation agents: overt: 41,
    60, 62, 66, 188, 232; covert, 41, 60, 62,
    66, 143, 188, 232, 268
  organic image formation agents (solicited
    or unsolicited), 41, 60, 188, 190, 232;
    see also under word-of-mouth,
    word-of-mouse
imagined communities, 61, 64
  see also narratives of the
    nation/nation-ness
imagineering, 140–1, 261
immaterialism, 27
  see also philosophy
implementation of the place brand, 255,
    260–7
  see also under brand communication,
    co-operation, construction
induced image formation agents
  covert, 41, 60, 62, 66, 143, 188, 232, 268

overt, 41, 60, 62, 66, 188, 232
see also image formation
agents/information sources
information society, 34
information sources of image, see image
formation agents
information/virtual spaces, 3, 7, 61
see also under virtual/online
environments/spaces
inseparability, see service characteristics
intangibility, see service characteristics
interactivity, 144, 145
see also virtual/online
environments/spaces
internet (world wide web), 36–7, 62–3, 82,
261
see also ICT
investment, trade and export agencies, see
place marketers
issues
of place brands/branding, 14
of place identity, 51

knowledge and place identity, 49–50

language, 26, 29, 43, 65, 121, 256
lifestyle, 6
living the brand, 265
local residents and place identity, 51
localization
and place identity, 55–9; see also
globalization
v. globalization, 8, 55–9, 243; see also
globalization
logo, see brand identity
loyalty, 13, 15, 17

majlis, 78, 106, 265
mass communication, 2–3, 5, 40
mass-individualization, 34
material/physical spaces, 3, 7, 53, 139
see also spaces
McDonaldization/Disneyization, 55, 130, 246
see also globalization
media, 59–62, 67, 188, 231–3, 262
and projected place image, 59
de-massification, 40, 264
mega-/iconic projects, 88, 95, 100, 106–7
memory/memories, 13, 29, 31–3, 184
methodology of research, see under
perceived identity research, place
image research, projected place
image research

ministries of foreign affairs, see place
marketers
movies and vicarious place experiences,
142–3
multisensory, 33
experiences, 6, 26, 29, 116, 136–7; see also
characteristics of experiences

name awareness, 15, 17
see also under brands
narratives
of the nation/nation-ness (top–down),
63–4
projected image (top–down), 19, 59,
146–7, 264
stories/story telling (bottom–up), 15,
146–7, 189–91
nation state, 7
network society, 3

on-brand, 15, 139, 245, 259–60
online/virtual environments/spaces, see
virtual/online environments/spaces
organic image formation agents (solicited or
unsolicited), 41, 60, 188, 190, 232
see also under image formation agents,
word-of-mouth, word-of-mouse
overt induced image formation agents, 41,
60, 62, 66, 188, 232
see also image formation agents

participating/immersing v.
passive/gazing/absorbing experiences,
141
see also characteristics of experiences
partnership (public private), 17, 68, 107
passive/gazing/absorbing v.
participating/immersing experiences,
141
see also characteristics of experiences
perceived brand quality, 15, 17
perceived identity research/analysis, 108–29,
255–7
historic (literature) analysis, 117–23,
124–5
photo/picture research, 11–12, 115
resident perception, 108–16, 123, 126–9
results, 112–15, 126–9
survey method, 111–12, 123
see also analysis/research
perceived image, see image
perceived place experiences, see place
experiences

perceived place image, see place image
perceived place image research/analysis, see
    place image research
perishability, see service characteristics
personalization (of service and product
    offering/experience), 70, 139–40, 149,
    247
phenomenographic methodology of place
    image research, 208–15
  see also place image research
phenomenography, 73, 208, 237–9
phenomenology, 28
  see also philosophy
philosophy
    constructivism, 27, 29, 43
    empiricism, 26
    existentialism, 28, 43
    idealism, 27, 28, 43
    illusion (perpetuating system of
        perceptual illusion), 26–7, 54
    immaterialism, 27
    phenomenology, 28
    realism, 26, 29, 43
    scepticism, 27, 43, 55
    subjectivity (of constructivism), 28
    theory of ideas (Descartes adventitious,
        factitious and innate ideas), 25
photographs/pictures
    and perceived identity research, 11–12,
        115; see also perceived identity
        research/analysis
    and projected place image, 59, 144, 155–6
    content analysis, 155–6; see also projected
        place image research
physical and virtual, 38
  see also under experiences, spaces
physical/material spaces, 3, 7, 53, 139
  see also spaces
pictures, see photographs/pictures
place brand performance, 133–4
place brand performance gap, 41, 133–4,
    148–50
place brand satisfaction, 177–8
  see also satisfaction
place brand satisfaction gap, 41, 177–8,
    191–3, 229
place brand strategy, 45–7, 73–107
place brand strategy gap, 41, 45–7, 71–2
place brands/branding
    analysis, 250–3, 255–7; see also under
        perceived identity research, place
        image research, projected place
        image research

architecture, 260
brand identity, 13, 108–11, 115–16, 217,
    238, 254, 259; see also place brand
    essence
communication, 59, 255, 261; see also
    under projected place image, place
    brand implementation
communities, 264–7
construction/product development, 255,
    260; see also place brand
    implementation
cooperation, 255, 264; see also place
    brand implementation
definition, 13–4, 16
essence/expression, 255, 257–60; see also
    under brand identity, value match,
    experiences concept
experience concept, 173, 255, 259; see
    also place brand essence
image, see place image
implementation, 255, 260–7; see also
    under brands, co-operation,
    construction
issues, 14
living the brand, 265
on-brand, 15, 139, 245, 259–60
personality, 14, 254–5
place brand equity, see under brands
positioning, 6, 255
reputation, 177, 179
3-gap place branding model, 41, 245–9
value match, 254–5, 259; see also place
    brand essence
see also brands/branding
place experiences, 7, 17, 41, 114–15, 135
    definition, 17
    festivals (incl. culinary), 168, 174, 261
    vicarious, see vicarious place experiences
    see also experiences
place identity, 17, 41, 49–59, 63
    and culture (cultural identity/values), 50–3,
        65–6, 103–5, 113–14; see also signifiers
        of place identity
    and festivals, 52, 258–9, 264
    and globalization, 7, 55–9; see also
        globalization
    and heritage, 49–50, 75–6
    and history, 49–50, 55, 76–81, 110–11,
        121, 256
    and local residents, 51
    and localization, 55–9; see also
        globalization
    and power struggles, 9, 52

as anchor, 41, 53

as sustainable competitive advantage, 49

colouring elements (symbolism, behaviour and communication), 51, 256; see also constructive elements of place identity

constructive elements, see constructive elements of place identity

contestation, 52

critique/issues, 51

definition, 17

elements, see constructive elements of place identity

knowledge, 49–50

plurality/diversity/heterogeneity/variability, 53

research, see perceived identity research

semi-static elements (size, physical appearance and inner mentality/culture), 50, 256; see also constructive elements of place identity

signifiers (great events/heroes; food/architecture/arts/literature/ popular culture; language/traditions/ rituals/folk), 51, 65–6, 103–5, 256; see also constructive elements of place identity

structural elements (location and history), 50, 256; see also constructive elements of place identity

place image, 18, 41, 179–84

and globalization, 7; see also globalization

and place brands/branding, 14, 177

antecedent of (quality, satisfaction, consumer decision-making, post-purchase behaviour), 18

attributes, 6, 18, 31, 135, 180, 181, 205–6, 223–4, 231, 237–8, 268; see also characteristics of place image

characteristics, 18, 180; see also characteristics of place image

common image characteristics, 135, 180, 181, 206, 223–4, 229–31, 237, 268; see also characteristics of place image

definition, 18

functional place image characteristics, 6, 18, 135, 180, 181, 223; see also characteristics of place image

heterogeneity/variability/plurality/diversity, 181

holistic image characteristics, 31, 135, 180, 181, 205–6, 223; see also characteristics of place image

image formation agents/information sources, 41, 60; see also under autonomous, induced and organic agents

projected, see projected place image

psychological image characteristics, 6, 18, 135, 181, 223; see also characteristics of place image

self-focus/self-congruity, 28, 184–5, 205, 236

unique image characteristics, 18, 135, 180, 205–6, 223, 229–31, 237–8, 268, see also characteristics of place image

see also image

place image research/analysis, 194–240, 255–7

alternative phenomenographic methodology, 208–15

cases, 215–18

projected, see projected place image research

results, 202–7, 222–40

survey method, 195–200, 208–15

traditional methodologies, 182–4

see also analysis/research

place marketers, 8, 19, 68, 259

place marketing

definition, 19, 59

see also projected place image

places

product offering, see product offering of place

spaces of places, 3, 57

plurality/diversity/heterogeneity/variability

of place identity, 53

of place image, 181

polyinclusiveness (multiple spaces) (information, social, material and mental space), 6, 7, 12, 27, 173, 266

see also spaces

power

and place identity, 9, 52

and projected place image, 147–8

primary (through experience) and secondary (information sources) image, 135–6

private sector, 49–50, 67–8, 96–100, 141, 147–8, 154, 162, 165–6, 248, 250–1, 268–9

see also public sector

product offering of place, 19, 41, 67–71, 88–95

and ICT, 70–1; see also ICT

product offering of place (*continued*)
  characteristics (inseparability, intangibility,
    heterogeneity/variability and
    perishability), 68–70, 131, 139, 190, 247
  definition, 19
  experience networks, 139; *see also*
    experiences
  factor cost benefits, 5, 19, 67
  heterogeneous spaces/experience
    environments, 139–40; *see also* spaces
  personalization, 70, 139–40, 149, 247
  see also place experiences
projected image, 26
projected place image, 19, 41, 59–67
  and ICT, 59–63; *see also* ICT
  and media, 59; *see also* media
  contestation, 147–8
  created meaning, 63–7; *see also* signifiers
    of place identity
  definition, 19
  narrative of the nation/nation-ness
    (top–down), 63–4
  narratives (top–down), 19, 59, 146–7, 264
  power, 147–8
  visuals/photographs/pictures, 59, 144,
    155–6
projected place image research/analysis,
    151–67, 255–7
  analysis, *see* content analysis
  data collection, 152–4
  results, 157–65
  see also analysis/research
promise of value, 14, 16
  see also brands/branding
prosumer, 35
psychological image characteristics, 6, 18,
    135, 181, 223
  see also characteristics of place image
psychology, 28, 43
  behavioural psychology, 30
  cognitive psychology, 29, 43
  economic psychology (and
    microeconomics), 30
  environmental psychology, 30, 32
  of image, 29, 180, 181
  social psychology, 30
public private partnership, 17, 68, 107
public sector/government, 8–9, 14, 49, 67–8,
    89, 95–8, 117–20, 128, 147–8, 154, 162,
    165, 246–8, 251, 268
  see also place marketers,
    private sector
public spaces, 2
  see also spaces

quality of service, 69, 140, 149–50

RDF (Resource Description Framework),
    261
  see also ICT
realism, 26, 29, 43
  see also philosophy
relationscape/social space, 7, 38, 139
  see also spaces
reputation, 177, 179
  see also brands/branding
research/analysis, 250–3, 255–7
  see also under perceived identity research,
    place image research, projected place
    image research
resident perception research, 108–16, 123,
    126–9
  see also perceived identity
    research/analysis
residents and place identity, 51
results of research, *see under* perceived
    identity research, place image research,
    projected place image research
RSS (Rich Site Summary), 262
  see also ICT

satisfaction (consumer/visitor satisfaction),
    13, 191–2
  see also place brand satisfaction
scepticism, 27, 43, 55
  see also philosophy
self-focus/self-congruity, 28, 184–5, 205, 236
semi-static elements of place identity (size,
    physical appearance and inner
    mentality/culture), 50, 256
  see also constructive elements of place
    identity
sense of place, 7, 74
senses and experience, 6, 26, 29, 116, 136–7
  see also characteristics of experiences
service characteristics (inseparability,
    intangibility, heterogeneity/variability
    and perishability), 68–70, 131, 139,
    190, 247
  personalization, 70, 140, 149, 247
service quality, 69, 140, 149–50
signifiers of place identity (great events/
    heroes; food/architecture/ arts/
    literature/popular culture; language/
    traditions/ rituals/folk), 51, 65–6, 103–5,
    256
  see also constructive elements of place
    identity

situational and temporal environmental influences, 41, 187–9, 224
  see also autonomous image formation agents
slogan, see under brand,
social interactions/encounter characteristics of experience, 38, 71, 137, 140, 174
  see also characteristics of experiences
social networking, 39
  see also Web 2.0
social psychology, 30
  see also psychology
social space/relationscape, 7, 38, 139
  see also spaces
sociology, 28
spaces
  commercial spaces, 2
  information/virtual spaces, 3, 7, 61; see also virtual/online environments
  physical/material spaces, 3, 7, 53, 139
  polyinclusiveness (multiple spaces) (information, social, material and mental space), 6, 7, 12, 27, 173, 266
  public spaces, 2
  social space/relationscape, 7, 38, 139
  spaces of flows, 3, 8, 57; see also global flows
  spaces of places, 3, 57
stories/story telling, see narratives
strategic marketing, 34, 50, 269
strategy, see place brand strategy
structural elements of place identity (location and history), 50, 256
  see also constructive elements of place identity
subjectivity (of constructivism), 28
  see also philosophy
supply, 7, 9, 70, 245, 248–9
  see also demand
survey methods, see under perceived identity research, place image research, projected place image research
sustainable competitive advantage, 49
symbols/symbolism/emblems, 15, 65, 256
  see also constructive elements of place identity

telepresence, 70–1, 144, 145
  see also virtual/online environments/spaces
temporal environmental and situational influences, 41, 187–9, 224
  see also autonomous image formation agents

theory of ideas (Descartes adventitious, factitious and innate ideas), 25
  see also philosophy
  3-gap place branding model, 41, 245–9
tourism
  definition, 5, 20
  performance, 85–7
  product, 67
  promotion boards, see place marketers
  usual environment, 20
tourists/visitors, 5, 85, 88–9
trade, export and investment agencies, see place marketers
traditional methodologies of place image research, 182–4
trust, 10, 39, 70, 267, 269

unique place image characteristics, 18, 135, 180, 205–6, 223, 229–31, 237–8, 268
  see also characteristics of place image
usual environment, 20

validity, 238
value constellation, 35, 38
value match of the place brand, 254–5, 259
  see also place brand essence
value promise, 14, 16
  see also brands/branding
vicarious place experiences, 41, 59, 66–7, 142–4
  and movies, 142–3
  online/virtual, see virtual/online environments
  see also under experiences, place experiences
virtual and physical, 38
  see also experiences, spaces
virtual communities, 40, 61–2, 71, 143, 171–2
virtual tours, 63, 144
virtual/online environments/spaces, 61–2, 70–1, 144, 145, 248, 250
  interactivity, 144, 145
  telepresence, 70–1, 144, 145
  vividness, 144, 145, 248, 250
visitor/consumer identity (cultural, social, personal and psychological characteristics), 41, 184
  cultural background/differences, 221, 233–4
  gender, 235
visitors/tourists, 5, 85, 88–9
visuals/photographs/pictures and projected image, 59, 144, 155–6

vividness, 144, 145, 248, 250
  see *also* virtual/online
    environments/spaces

Web 2.0, 39, 62, 143, 190, 262
  see *also* ICT
West/Western, 12, 78–80, 103, 235–6
word-of-mouse, 41, 190, 231–2, 267
  see *also* Web 2.0, organic image formation
  agents

word-of-mouth, 41, 190, 231–2, 267
  see *also* organic image formation agents
world wide web/internet, 36–7, 62–3, 82,
  261
  see *also* ICT